The Complete Idiot's Reference Card

Top Ten Rankings in The WWF and The WCW

The WWF's Top Ten
1. Shawn Michaels
2. Rocky Maivia
3. Owen Hart
4. The Undertaker
5. Steve Austin
6. Dude Love
7. Kane
8. Ken Shamrock
9. Hunter Hearst Helmsley
10. Taka Michinoku

The WCW's Top Ten
1. Sting
2. Diamond Dallas Page
3. Hollywood Hogan
4. Ultimo Dragon
5. Lex Luger
6. Booker T
7. Ric Flair
8. Curt Hennig
9. Bill Goldberg
10. Eddy Guerrero

Wrestling Federations

You can't tell the players without a program, sometimes—and that's doubly true when you're trying to keep all the wrestling federations and associations straight. Here's a handy list of the organizations you're likely to run into in this book, along with their acronyms.

Name	Acronym
American Wrestling Association	AWA
Catch Wrestling Association	CWA
Century Wrestling Association	CWA
Championship Wrestling Association	CWA
Continental Wrestling Association	CWA
Empresa Mexican de la Lucha Libre	EMLL
Extreme Championship Wrestling	ECW
Global Wrestling Alliance	GWA
International Championship Wrestling	ICW
International Wrestling Enterprise	IWE
International Wrestling League	IWL
Japan Wrestling Association	JWA
Ladies Professional Westling Association	LPWA
Mid Continental Wrestling Association	MWA
Mid States Championship Wrestling	MSCW
New England Wrestling Association	NEWA
New England Wrestling Federation	NEWF
National Wrestling Alliance	NWA
Professional Wrestling Federation	PWF
Renegade Wrestling Federation	RWF
Southwest Championship Wrestling	SCW
Tri-State Wrestling Association	TWA
United States Wrestling Association	USWA
Universal Independent Wrestling	UIW
West Coast Championship Wrestling	WCCW
West Coast Wrestling Alliance	WCWA
World Championship Wrestling	WCW
World Wide Wrestling Alliance	WWWA
World Wide Wrestling Federation	WWWF
World Wrestling Federation	WWF
World Wrestling Association	WWA
World Wrestling Council	WWC

alpha
books

Universally Recognized "World Champions" of Wrestling

Every federation has its own championship belt, and usually recognizes only the performers within its own ranks as the world champion. But until the 1930s, there was only one title, it's lineage dating back to Frank Gotch and ending with Bronco Nagurski. Here's a list of those greats:

Name	History
Frank Gotch	1908. The first, the finest. Gotch defeated George Hackenschmidt to gain universal recognition as world titleholder. Retired 1913
Charley Cutler	1914. Winner of the tournament held to select Gotch's successor.
Joe Stetcher	1915. Defeated Cutler.
Earl Caddock	1917. Won the title from Stetcher
Joe Stetcher	1920. Wouldn't rest until he won his title back.
Ed "Strangler" Lewis	1921. Defeated Stetcher for the title. But he didn't keep it long.
Stanislaus Zbyszko	1921. Took Lewis's newly won title away.
Ed "Strangler" Lewis	1922. Regained title from Zbyszko, and hung onto it a little longer this time.
Wayen "Big" Munn	1925. Defeated Lewis.
Stanislaus Zbyszko	1925. Defeated Munn to hold the title a second time.
Joe Stetcher	1925. You can't keep a good man down. This was his third title win.
Ed "Strangler" Lewis	1928. History repeated itself as Lewis once again took Stetcher's title away.
Gus Sonnenberg	1929. Defeated Lewis
Ed Don George	1931. Pinned Sonnenberg.
Ed "Strangler" Lewis	1931. Forth title and counting.
Henri DeGlane	1931. Won title on a DQ by Lewis.
Ed Don George	1931. Beat DeGlane.
Dick Shikat	1929. Defeated Jim Londos to claim the title. Claim disputed, and a return bout scheduled to determine titleholder.
Jim Londos	1930. Won the return bout for the title.
Ed "Strangler" Lewis	1932. Claimed title by beating Shikat.
Jim Browning	1933. Defeated Lewis and claimed title.
Jim Londos	1934. Elevated his title claim to official recognition by beating Browning.
Danno O'Mahoney	1935. Defeated Londos for the title.
Dick Shikat	1936. Won title outright for the first time by defeating O'Mahoney.
Ali Baba	1936. Defeated Shikat.
Dave Levin	1936. Won on a DQ over Ali Baba. New Jersey Athletic Commission reverses decision and both claim the title.
Dean Detton	1936. Defeated Levin and claimed his portion of the title.
Everett Marshall	1936. Defeated Baba.
Lou Thesz	1936. Defeated Marshall.
Steve "Crusher" Casey	1938. Defeated Thesz. Took the title home to Ireland, so NWA awarded title to Marshall.
Lou Thesz	1939. Again defeated Marshall, takes the NWA title.
Bronko Nagurski	1939. Defeated Thesz.

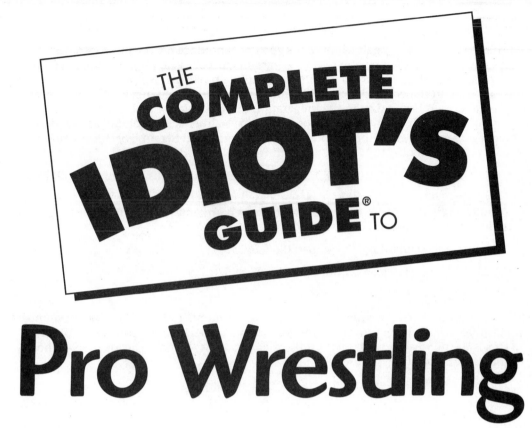

THE COMPLETE IDIOT'S GUIDE® TO

Pro Wrestling

by Captain Lou Albano, Bert Randolph Sugar, and Roger Woodson

alpha
books

A Division of Macmillan General Reference
A Simon & Schuster Macmillan Company
1633 Broadway, New York, NY 10019-6785

Macmillan Publishing books may be purchased for business or sales promotional use. For information please write: Special Markets Department, Macmillan Publishing USA, 1633 Broadway, New York, NY 10019.

International Standard Book Number: 0-02862395-9

Library of Congress Catalog Card Number: 98-89620

01 00 99   8 7 6 5 4 3 2 1

Interpretation of the printing code: the rightmost number of the first series of numbers is the year of the book's printing; the rightmost number of the second series of numbers is the number of the book's printing. For example, a printing code of 99-1 shows that the first printing occurred in 1999.

Printed in the United States of America

Alpha Development Team

Publisher
Kathy Nebenhaus

Editorial Director
Gary M. Krebs

Managing Editor
Bob Shuman

Marketing Brand Manager
Felice Primeau

Development Editors
Phil Kitchel
Amy Zavatto

Production Team

Development Editor
Nancy E. Gratton

Production Editor
Robyn Burnett

Cover Designer
Mike Freeland

Cartoonist
Jody P. Schaeffer

Illustrator
Bob Borgia

Cover Photo
Greg Farber

Designer
Nathan Clement

Indexer
Greg Pierson

Layout/Proofreading
Angela Calvert
John Bitter
Angel Perez

Contents at a Glance

Contents

11   Rowdy Rivalries of Revenge   149

19 Bone Crushers and Backbreakers: All the Right Moves   253

20 Masters of Illusion   269

21 Double Your Pleasure, Double Your Pain: Tag Teams   277

Foreword

As you undoubtedly know, I rarely speak out. But when I was approached to write the foreword to this book on professional wrestling, I thought it would be an honor to add my voice to it. An honor to attach my name to a book that is a must for all wrestling fans, one that takes you behind the scenes, behind the glitz and the glamour, and tells you about the great people, the great talent, and the great athletes in the world of pro wrestling.

I know there is a stereotypical picture of the professional wrestler. Most people think we're a lot of fake people, non-athletic, and all show. But we're totally different from what you've been led to believe. For even though we're outrageous and outlandish in the ring, we're different outside. Outside, we're real people: well-rounded, very approachable good guys doing what we're doing to earn a living.

Sure, I take it personally when someone says professional wrestling is "fake." After all, like all wrestlers, I have my pride. You've got to have great self-pride to face millions of people every week dressed in nothing but your underwear. But we know what we do is real—real in terms of our athleticism, real in terms of our ability to entertain, and real in terms of our being able to capture the imagination of people everywhere.

By people everywhere, I don't just mean kids. For even though our primary audience today is kids who are enthralled with the world of professional wrestling, we've been able to transform everybody into a kid—at least at heart. We have been able to reach the masses because professional wrestling is, bottom line, fun.

To give you an example of how we've transferred the fanatacism of kids to their parents, earlier this season I had the chance to visit Mark McGuire in the St. Louis Cardinals locker room. I thought it was funny when he asked me for an autograph for his son, who was a wrestling fan and had made his father into one.

I'm the luckiest wrestler in the world to be in the position I'm in. Through wrestling I've had a chance to reach out to the masses—not those typical masses you think follow wrestling, but to football players, baseball players, even cabinet members who like wrestling because it's entertaining and fun. And to reach out because of the exposure we've gotten on the Turner Broadcasting System, which televises us five hours a week, creating the opportunity to make new friends and fans for pro wrestling.

So, to my fans, to Turner Broadcasting, to the WCW and, not incidentally, to Lou and Bert for asking me to write the foreword to the book that every fan needs, I want to speak my piece and say, "Thank you for making professional wrestling what it is today... FUN!"

—GOLDBERG, WCW Champion

BILL GOLDBERG defeated legend Hollywood (formerly "Hulk") Hogan for the WCW World Heavyweight Championship title on July 6, 1998. A former star nose guard with the Georgia Bulldogs and NFL player with the Atlanta Falcons and Los Angeles Rams, Goldberg switched to pro wrestling when he suffered an injury. The 6'4" 285lb power-house is known for his crushing jackhammer and for inspiring "Gold-berg!" chants in arenas throughout the country.

Introduction

The year was 1949, the place was Washington, D.C., and like every young man who had not yet found girls, I found sports. Or what passed for sports in that time and that place—I found that wonderful world where picturesque names like Gorgeous George, Antonino Rocca, and Primo Carnera dotted the landscape...professional wrestling.

The defining moment for this then-young man and the world of wrestling was maybe when, as a 13 year old, I somehow found myself first to get through on a radio phone line with the now long-forgotten answer to an equally long-forgotten sports trivia question and won two free tickets to an upcoming "rasslin'" bout between Gorgeous George and Primo Carnera.

It was ecstasy. It was joy. And it was terror. For how on earth was a 13-year-old boy going to get away with attending a late-night wrestling bout held across town—and on a school night to boot!?

But that problem was soon solved. My mother, who was normally so a-sportive that she thought Sugar Ray Robinson was my Dad's first cousin on his father's side, assumed that because one of the names on the card was Primo Carnera, I'd won tickets to a boxing match. Boxing was far more "presentable" than wrestling, and since it was a free show (after all, I'd won *two* tickets), she decided she'd escort me to it.

Imagine her surprise when she found herself seated smack dab in the middle of a crowd of people, all looking like they were a few beans short of a three-bean salad. Many of her fellow female match-goers, women who were then known as "Hatpin Mary's," were running around the arena trying to stab a wrestler or two. Suffice it to say, the whole thing did not live up to her expectations.

But that made no never mind to her son.

I was immediately caught up in the moment—and *what* a moment! There was excitement going on everywhere around me.

That first wrestling bout I ever attended, however, was something of an anticlimax. Gorgeous George, he of the thick red neck and flabby white hide which made a marked contrast with his golden coiffure, tried a couple of underhanded moves on Carnera. All he got for his efforts was a disdainful sneer from his "Da Preem," as Carnera was often called. Then, grabbing one fish-belly-white leg out from under his adversary, Carnera lifted Gorgeous George aloft and slammed him back down on the mat, stepping down hard on the now prostrate George's abdomen.

The referee got down on all fours to pound the canvas three times. In two bats of an eye, the main event was over!

No matter. That was the beginning of a lifelong love affair with the sport-hyphen-entertainment of wrestling, and it hardly mattered that my appalled mother didn't speak to me for the next two months—my punishment for having dragged her to the event in the first place.

To be sure, the intensity of that first wild infatuation with wrestling dropped off rather precipitously once I discovered girls. However, this book gives me the opportunity to revisit that once-intense love that dates back to those more innocent days—more innocent for yours truly, *and* for wrestling itself. Professional wrestling since then has changed greatly, but then again, so have I. And so has society.

Back then, when men were men and women were glad of it, wrestling was a clear cut case of black-and-white: good guys were always good, bad guys were horrid. And there was nothing ambiguous in between. Now, in the days of laser light shows and tortured wrestling characters, things aren't so clear. But it's all still the greatest entertainment extravaganza there is.

So, while this book pays tribute to some of the wonderful legends of wrestling's early years, I've also tried to make it a no-holds-barred look at the whole, wacky, over-the-top world of wrestling. A world that would have made P. T. Barnum proud.

In this book you'll find:

➤ A history of wrestling, from its earliest days to the modern era of pay-per-view and multi-media events.

➤ Biographies of some of the major wrestling personalities, from the stars to the managers to the promoters, who contributed to making wrestling the greatest sport/ entertainment available today.

➤ Insider information on the rules, the moves, and the magic of professional wrestling.

➤ Advice on where to go and what you'll find when you get there if you're interested in a career in professional wrestling for yourself.

➤ Tips on how to keep up with your favorite stars, cash in on collecting, or meet up with fellow fans on the Internet.

Here's a rundown on what's in the pages to come:

Part 1, "This Crazy World Called Pro Wrestling," clues you in on the broad appeal of wrestling, and a brief overview of how the sport developed. You'll get your first introduction to the federations that run the sport, and the major figures behind the evolution of wrestling from its early "scientific" Greco-Roman days to today.

Part 2, "The Founding Fathers: Wrestling's Colorful History," provides you with the biographies of the greatest wrestlers of all time—yesterday, today, and maybe even tomorrow. Anecdotes of famous figures from wrestling's past and present are accompanied with photographs of some of the most memorable men—and women—you could ever hope to meet. And there's a chapter "Rowdy Rivalries of Revenge," that gives you all the inside scoop on the famous feuds that power wrestling's storylines.

Part 3, "Modern Madness: Wrestling Today," tells the story of how wrestling came from its carnival origins and was transformed into today's form—by focusing on the people who participated in that transformation. You'll learn about the managers and the promoters, and their long histories of hyping and developing their stars and their sport. And you'll learn about some of the specific ways wrestling was brought out of its

Depression-era doldrums and into modern times: the introduction of women's wrestling and novelty acts, the explosion of wrestling into television, and the world of arena wrestling—still the best way to see it, feel it, have it all.

Part 4, "All the Right Moves: Inner (and Outer) Workings of the Ring," moves off into a whole 'nother direction: Here you'll learn about where the wrestlers go to develop their skills, and where you can go yourself if you want a career in the sport. And it pulls back the curtain on how the classic and modern moves are done, as well as on how the tricks of the trade are pulled off. Plus, there's a quick peek inside the wrestling locker-room—the *real* insider's look at the wrestler's world.

Part 5, "Beyond the Squared Circle: Wrestling Extras," is included for you, the fan—it's everything you need to know if you want to keep track of your favorite wrestlers, managers, federations, or events. In it you'll learn where to go for information, collectibles, and even how to connect up with fellow fans on the Internet.

Extras

In addition to all this, there are sidebars scattered throughout the text. These will give you definitions of wrestling's colorful terms, insider's comments, a few warnings, and reminiscences and anecdotes from sportswriters and wrestlers. Here's what to look for:

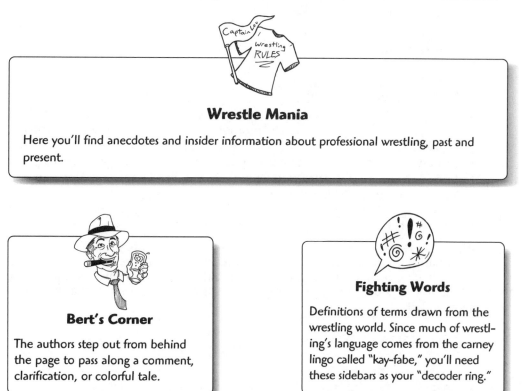

Wrestle Mania

Here you'll find anecdotes and insider information about professional wrestling, past and present.

Bert's Corner

The authors step out from behind the page to pass along a comment, clarification, or colorful tale.

Fighting Words

Definitions of terms drawn from the wrestling world. Since much of wrestling's language comes from the carney lingo called "kay-fabe," you'll need these sidebars as your "decoder ring."

Captain Lou's Corner

The authors step out from behind the page to pass along a comment, clarification, or colorful tale.

Body Slam

Warnings! There are things that you, as a fan, should know—so read 'em and heed 'em.

In Your Face

Short, sometimes scabrous quotes or observations about this wacky world and the people in it.

Acknowledgements

Without them, we'd have nothing to say—so here's our thanks to all the wrestling pros out there, from the performers to the promoters. And thanks to the federations, particularly the WWF, for their assistance on the project. A special thanks to Norman Kietzer and to Vince McMahon for giving us access to the photographes that enliven this book's pages. Finally, thanks to Gary Krebs and Bob Shuman at Alpha Books, and to Nancy Gratton for editing.

Trademarks

All terms mentioned in this book that are known to be or are suspected of being trademarks or service marks have been appropriately capitalized. Alpha Books and Macmillan General Reference cannot attest to the accuracy of this information. Use of a term in this book should not be regarded as affecting the validity of any trademark or service mark.

Part 1

This Crazy World Called Pro Wrestling

How many people do you know that can wear almost anything they want to work?

Does anyone you know show up to work in a mask? Unless you are an M.D. or are into robbing banks for a living, probably not. But in pro wrestling, the work force wears masks, makeup, capes, tights, bandannas, sunglasses, and all kinds of gadgets and plumage. And, like plumbers who bring wrenches to work, or lawyers who carry briefcases to their offices, the workers in pro wrestling bring their own tools. But in wrestling, those tools include baseball bats, metal chairs, chainsaws, ropes, and a whole host of other lethal-looking gadgets.

As Butch said to Sundance, "Who are these guys?" They are the players of pro wrestling.

Today's wrestlers get it on in style and with plenty of showmanship. In this part, they'll show you how it's done.

Muscle Mania and Mayhem

Wrestling—regular wrestling—can lay claim to being the oldest sport in the world. But that's not what we're talking about here. Although modern pro wrestling has its earliest roots in the classical form of the sport, what we're interested in right now is that body-slamming, head-locking, chair-throwing combination of sports spectacular and entertainment extravaganza. *That* is pro wrestling, and it appeals to millions and millions of fans throughout the world.

Today's pro wrestling has universal appeal, drawing its fans from all walks of life and all age groups—regardless of gender or nationality. And some surprising names turn up in the annals of its fans. In this chapter you'll learn about wrestling's broad appeal, and why the fans love it so.

Fans, Fans, from Everywhere

Arturo Toscanini, the dignified orchestra maestro of yesteryear, was a wrestling fan. He'd watch televised matches and get caught up in the action: "Keel heem! Keel heem!" he'd scream when one of his favorite fighters took a particularly nasty blow from an opponent.

Body Slam

Don't sneer at wrestling fans: You might be surprised at some of the celebrities that have turned out for the *Wrestlemania* events. Mary Tyler Moore, Robin Leach, Vanna White, Gladys Knight, Liberace, and Alex Trebec have all been in attendance at one event or another.

Bert's Corner

The two major organizations in wrestling today, responsible for most of the cable wrestling programming, are Vince McMahon Jr.'s *World Wrestling Federation* (WWF) in Stamford, Connecticut, and Ted Turner's *World Championship Wrestling* (WCW) in Atlanta, Georgia.

And how about former first lady Bess Truman? When asked what she'd miss most about leaving the White House at the end of her husband's term of office, she answered without hesitation: "Wrestling on Thursday nights."

Maestro Toscanini and Mrs. Truman are but two of pro wrestling's many illustrious fans. Other self-confessed admirers have included Douglas Fairbanks Sr., Will Rogers, Peter Ustinov, and Sean Connery. What attracts these notables, and every other fan, is wrestling's *drama*, its spectacle, its sheer energy and excitement. And for all those doubting-Thomas types out there who say that it's not for real—well, so what? It's there to enjoy, not to analyze.

Boob-Tube Brawls

Televised pro wrestling rules the airwaves today. The dueling TV broadcasts are *RAW is WAR/Warzone* and *Monday Nitro,* which run head-to-head on the USA and TNT networks. These shows are produced by the two major wrestling organizations—WWF (World Wrestling Federation) and WCW (World Championship Wrestling) who together "own" Monday late-nights. Their shows generate higher ratings than any other shows on cable TV—and out rate most broadcast network shows as well—while at the same time marketing their product, developing new major players, and building future generations of fans.

Before its recent explosion onto TV, wrestling's big-name performers could go for their entire careers without garnering a lifetime audience as big as the one that tunes in for a single Monday night broadcast. All of a sudden, these athletes went from not being a household name even in their *own* households to stars that are recognized on sight around the world! And there is more wrestling on TV today than ever before, thanks to cable. It's not just the matches themselves—now there are wrestling talk shows and interviews all over the tube. And then there are the pay-per-view major bouts. Wrestling's big, and as you'll soon see, it's big business too. But savvy marketing is not the whole secret to pro wrestling's success—fans get caught up in the whole show, and in the ongoing storylines of long-standing feuds between fighters and grudge matches between flamboyant characters. Wrestling's like a soap opera that way— fans develop strong attachments to their favorites. In fact, it's been said that wrestling has *replaced* the soap opera as the most popular fare on TV today.

Wrestle Mania

The WWF and WCW each have about one pay-per-view (PPV) broadcast each month. Leading into the PPV broadcasts, the regular Monday night shows spend time developing storylines that culminate in the PPV face-offs. Since the PPV shows are always broadcast on Sunday nights, the Monday after is always dedicated to handling the big fight's results, and then to begin setting up the storyline for the next PPV bout scheduled for the following month.

There are strong similarities between pro wrestling and soap operas, at least in the way that fans get hooked on them. Wrestling viewers watch each show, week after week, getting drawn into the storylines of feuds and personalities, just like soap-opera fans. And viewers come to believe in the flamboyant characters as if they were real people—forgetting the performer behind the character. When a wrestler becomes ill or gets injured in the course of a match, hundreds upon hundreds of fans will send get-well cards. The plot twists and cliff-hangers of soap operas are common devices in the wrestling shows, too—they are a way to ensure that fans will keep tuning in to see how things turn out.

The worlds of soap opera and wrestling merge for real: Hulk Hogan with Lisa Peluso of NBC's Search For Tomorrow, *on which Hogan made a guest appearance in June 1985. (Source: Associated Press)*

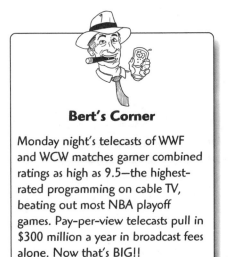

Bert's Corner

Monday night's telecasts of WWF and WCW matches garner combined ratings as high as 9.5—the highest-rated programming on cable TV, beating out most NBA playoff games. Pay-per-view telecasts pull in $300 million a year in broadcast fees alone. Now that's BIG!!

But even more, the characters and their motivations in pro wrestling are similar in to those in soap operas. Lines are clearly drawn—the good guy against the bad guy (though sometimes the good guy can be a "diamond in the rough," and the bad guy is one that you love to hate). If you follow "Stone Cold" Steve Austin, for instance, you know him as a beer-drinking, butt-kicking truth sayer who "raises some hell." And you're not going to miss a single one of his matches. But even if you don't like Austin, you'll *still* watch—in hopes that his arch rival, "evil" WWF owner Vince McMahon will surface to mercilessly do him in with his trademark props of red tape and heinous henchmen.

And then there's Shawn Michaels—one of pro wrestling's most popular figures for more than a decade. And beautiful, blond Sunny—one of the top-drawing female wrestlers of today. They all have fans—and foes—among their viewers, and all of them bring in the big audiences whenever they appear. With characters like these, and wrestling promoters who know all too well how to turn each match into an episode of high drama, it's no wonder that 36 million fans worldwide tune in faithfully to watch, week after week after week.

Beyond the Small Screen

Pro wrestling's popularity goes way beyond TV telecasts. Just drop in at your local newsstand and you'll see just how big it is—there are racks and racks of magazines devoted to the subject, with new ones springing up every day. And next time you're surfing the Web, try a quick search on pro wrestling—you'll be amazed at the number of sites you'll turn up, on everything from the major shows and organizations to homepages dedicated to individual fighters.

So what's the secret of pro wrestling's popularity? Simple—larger-than-life personalities, compelling storylines, exciting matches, and show-biz savvy. But the biggest part of pro wrestling's success is its legions of fans—every one of whom is proud to stand up and be counted as a loyal follower of the action.

Sure, sure—pro wrestling has many detractors. You know the type—the ones who turn up their noses at the hype and the hoopla, who sniff dismissively that "it's not a *real* sport." Well, you just can't please everybody—and some people may never be able to let themselves go and just *enjoy* the show. Too bad, 'cuz they're missing one heck of a *great* show. Real wrestling fans know that it isn't about scoring points, or even winning and losing—the show itself is the whole point. That's not so hard to understand, and 36 million people get the point, worldwide!

Wrestle Mania

Internet Web sites featuring wrestling are everywhere! And most have links to even *more* sites, so you can spend days digging up insider info, interviews, match results, trivia, photos, and sound clips, and much more! Official sites include **www.wwf.com** (the WWF homepage), **www.wcwwrestling.com** (for WCW info), and **www.ecwwrestling.com** (homepage for the Extreme Championship Wrestling organization).

The Greatest Show on Earth

So alright, you've got a compelling cast of characters and storylines complete with cliff-hangers and plot twists. You've got the fan magazines and Web sites, not to mention all the peripheral products—T-shirts and hats and the like. You've got show-biz savvy in the staging of events, too. Take one of pro wrestling's most popular shows, *Monday Nitro*. Each week's episode is filmed in a different city, but there are certain things that stay constant, week after week—especially the Nitro Girls who, like cheer-leaders in mainstream sporting events, fill in lulls in the action with dance routines to keep the viewers awake and attentive.

And don't forget the live events—talk about your nonstop, knock-down, total theater experiences— nothing can beat attending a real-live pro wrestling match. For the price of admission you become part of the action. There, along with every Tom, Dick, and Harriet, you can be ringside—booing the villain's every violation of the rules of fair play, and cheering your hero's every move. It's great catharsis for anyone who's ever had to put up with an overbearing boss or rude store clerk. When Steve Austin decks his evil boss, Vince McMahon, there's not a working stiff in the audience that doesn't feel just a little bit of vicarious vindication! With this kind of theater, who cares that it's not 100 percent "real."

Captain Lou's Corner

Everybody knows that sex sells—and wrestling's no exception. Sexy valets and the skimpily clad Nitro Girls keep the male fans tuning in or turning out to the arenas. It's all part of the show.

The Whole World's Watching

The people who do research at Turner Network, which telecasts *Monday Nitro*, are proud of the fact that their wrestling series beats out 62 percent of all broadcast programs in primetime among men between the ages of 18 and 34—the key wrestling demographic group. But that's only part of the picture—one of wrestling's largest and fastest growing groups of fans consists of women.

Bert's Corner

According to Hollywood Hogan, once wrestling's insiders went public that the bouts are choreographed (never, but *never* call them fake), the fan base exploded. Now it's not just the 18-to-34-year-old male demographic: Whole families buy tickets to the events.

Now I know there are some who still claim that wrestling is a man's entertainment and that if God meant for women to be part of the "squared circle" he'd have left in the curves. But that attitude is not only politically incorrect, it is *way* out of touch with today's reality. The women are indeed watching—and they're every bit as loyal as the men.

What's the attraction? Maybe it's the "hunk factor," as one 18-year-old fan called it in an interview for *USA Today*. Her favorite wrestler is Bill Goldberg, "Because he's beautiful," she says. But there's more to female fandom than an appreciation of Chippendale bodies in mid ring. For some, it's the pure energy and charisma of the wrestlers. For others, it's the show and storylines. But whatever their reason for watching, women are openly embracing wrestling, and wrestling welcomes them with open arms.

Wrestle Mania

Before the late 1930s, wrestling was almost exclusively a men's night out. Mildred Burke, former women's wrestling champion, was the first of her gender to enter the ring. She tells of the first match she ever attended back in 1937 in Kansas City: "...in a crowd of 3,000 or 4,000, you'd see maybe six or seven women at the most—they were probably the wives of the wrestlers...." Women didn't really start coming out to wrestling matches in large numbers until women began participating as wrestlers.

Along with the traditional male fans and, now, the female contingent, wrestling is also a huge draw with the kids. That's not so hard to understand—kids have always had their heroes. Whether those heroes come from real life, like Magic Johnson or Michael Jordan, or from the world of fantasy, like Superman, Flash Gordon, or *Star Trek*'s Captain Kirk, kids are always looking for somebody to look up to. And wrestling has always provided its fair share of heroes—larger-than-life figures whose tremendous size and exciting exploits make them real-life cartoon characters any kid can idolize and try to emulate.

And as society has changed, wrestling's heroic characters have changed to reflect the times. Gone are the days of easy answers, black and white, good and evil oppositions. The moral ambiguity of today's world shows up in the characters of today's popular fighters—even some of the essentially "good guy" characters have their moments of cynicism, even the "bad guys" have some rationale for their "badness."

Body Slam

As more and more younger viewers have gotten hooked on wrestling, it has come up for some heavy criticism. The foul language, the nonstop violence, and the sexual innuendo have all been cited as bad examples for the kids. Still, as Bonnie Hammer, senior Vice President of the USA network says, "my husband grew up watching it, and he wound up in Harvard Divinity School."

Wrestling's stars quickly became mainstream celebrities: Hulk Hogan and Mr. T hosting NBC's Saturday Night Live. (Source: Associated Press)

And the whole marketing aspect of pro wrestling has changed to reflect the changing times and its changing audience. It borrows from the energy of MTV videos and rock concerts with laser light shows and steam streams. It's total entertainment now, and the younger fans have responded by the millions. Wrestling has never been for the easily offended, or for the faint of heart—but it has now become an entertainment that has something to offer to everyone in the family, youth included.

I Can't Look...Wait, Let Me See!

Let's be honest—we're all fascinated with disasters. If there's an accident on the highway, you can be sure that all the passing cars will slow down to rubberneck even if that means tying up traffic for miles. And movie theaters make big box-office money on blockbuster violent movies. If it's gory, ghoulish, bloody, or just plain bad, we're interested.

The same is true for sports. Racing fans watch, partly, in hopes of seeing one of those speeding cars careen out of control. And football fans delight in multi-body pileups. Not to mention hockey, which is so well-known for its on-ice fights that Rodney Dangerfield cracked the joke: "I went to a fight the other night and a hockey game broke out." Violence is big box office in all aspects of American society.

Wrestle Mania

Wrestling hit new heights of popularity when WWF owner and promoter Vince McMahon staged the first *Wrestlemania* in front of 23,000 screaming fans at Madison Square Garden and broadcast the bout live on pay-per-view. The first broadcast featured Hulk Hogan, Rowdy Roddy Piper, Paul Orndorff, Cowboy Bob Orton, Jimmy "Superfly" Snuka, Barry Windham, Mike Rotundo, Nikolai Volkoff, The Iron Sheik, King Kong Bundy, and Andre the Giant. A star-studded cast included Mr. T, Liberace, Muhammad Ali, Billy Martin, and Cyndi Lauper.

Maybe that's why wrestling appeals to so many—it plays to these baser instincts of ours. After all, it surely delivers on the promise of violence—with it's repertoire of headlocks, dropkicks, and body slams. Nothing else comes as close to satisfying our fascination for the grisly and the gruesome—not even a Bruce Willis movie.

Wrestlers bash each other over the head with chairs, toss each other off 16-foot-high cages, and whip their rivals with barbed wire, baseball bats, or whatever else comes to hand. They slam their opponents' heads into turnbuckles, caskets, dumpsters, or anything else that's nearby. Whatever works, you can bet it's been tried. But it's all in fun.

Granted, wrestling has come under fire in recent years for all its bone-crushing violence, its physical and verbal abuse. But it's all about *performance!* You need to come to a match with as much suspended disbelief as you would to any movie. But that doesn't mean it's all fake. It's like what retailing giant John Wannamaker said when he was asked if he was wasting his money on advertising: "Half of it is wasted, half not. The problem is, I don't know which half." The same is true for wrestling—some of it's real, some not, and it's up to you, the knowledgeable fan, to figure out which is which.

In Your Face

Is everybody pleased with wrestling's admission that some of the show is staged? Not at all. "If you print that kind of stuff, it ruins it.... People like to forget it's pretend," says Eric Bischoff, former wrestling announcer, sometime wrestler, and current president of the WCW.

It's a given—wrestling is a great game of illusions. And it's fun for the fans to try to figure out how much is just a trick. But there's one thing that's *very* real—the injuries. I know, because I've had almost every bone in my body broken, one time or another. My nose has been broken 14 times—and I've always hoped that whoever broke it last would put it back where it belonged. And my experience is not unique. Yukon Eric lost his ear in a bout with Killer Kowalski, as did Cactus Jack—he caught his ears in the ropes while battling Vader. Steve Austin was momentarily paralyzed by an Owen Hart piledriver, Bruno Sammartino had his neck broken during a bout against Stan Hansen, and the Fabulous Moolah has given up keeping track of her broken bones. "The body gets beaten up," says Macho Man Savage. And several wrestlers, such as Ray Gunkel and Gino Garibaldi, have died in the ring.

Death in the Ring: Wrestlers who have died during a match

Eddie Baker	Jack Lewis
Jim Browning	Gordon McKinley
Dennis Clary	Buddy O'Brien
Mike DiBiase	Mike Romano
Eli Fisher	Joe Shimkus
Gino Garibaldi	Tex Wright
Ray Gunkel	Steve Znoski
George Kinney	

Seeing Is Believing? Or Not...

So what's real and what's not? Well, first of all, the athletes themselves are real. Pro wrestlers are among the finest athletes in the world. Thanks to their training, they're able to perform almost superhuman moves each and every night and withstand an enormous amount of sheer physical punishment. They're in good enough shape to be able to do all the right moves with near-perfect timing. They have agility, ability, and amazing energy. They take their injuries in stride, preferring to keep on performing while injured rather than watch from the sidelines. And they do it all under the watchful glare of the TV camera.

So, clearly, the athletes are real—and so is their athleticism. But the moves—that's often another story entirely. Did Hulk (now "Hollywood") Hogan *really* lift Andre the Giant up over his head, or did he get a little collaborative help from Andre? Are those real punches, or is there a little showmanship borrowed from movie-style staged fighting. That's for you to figure out!

But while you can call it entertainment and you can call it performance, don't even *think* about calling pro wrestling "fake." Those are real athletes, performing real moves, choreographed or not. To call them fake is to insult the level of training and dedication these athletes bring to their line of work. And that could be, as it says on cigarette packages, "hazardous to your health."

Just ask comedian Richard Belzer, who challenged Hulk Hogan to put a headlock on him. Hogan complied with a side headlock, which cut off Belzer's blood supply. When the Hulk let go, Belzer was out cold and dropped to the floor. Or go talk to *20/20*'s John Stossel. On the TV show, he challenged Dr. D. (David Schultz) and got his ears boxed.

Wrestlers are understandably touchy about being called fakes. One of today's top wrestlers, Goldberg, has an outstanding challenge: He welcomes anyone to try to stand up to his famous "spear-ram" (which involves him charging his opponent from about 10 feet away)—he says that if they can get up after the charge "they can call it a fake," but not before.

Bert's Corner

In many states, professional wrestling is labeled "entertainment," not sport. Vince McMahon of the WWF was largely responsible for this distinction, removing wrestling from the jurisdiction of state athletic commissions which were established to oversee the sport of boxing, not wrestling.

In Your Face

Wrestlers have personas, and storylines are tailored around them. Says Stone Cold Steve Austin: "My character is a blue-collar-type thing. I gotta go out there and be unimpressed by authority. They tell me I can't do something, I go ahead and do it.... It's kinda like a soap opera."

As the legendary TV personality and one-time wrestling commentator Steve Allen once said, "wrestling is only as fake as your imagination is fake, as your daydreams are fake." The illusions are created through *real* athleticism, *real* showmanship, *real* hard work, and *real* training. As a result, the fans get *real* enjoyment. That's good enough for me!

Bigger Isn't Necessarily Better

Most wrestlers are widebodies, and some are more so than others. Gorilla Monsoon weighed in at 400 pounds. I'm over 300. Andre the Giant, at 500-plus, defied any and all categories. I remember one especially huge wrestler, Haystack Calhoun, who weighed in at over 600 pounds (when a scale big enough to handle him could be found). Haystack's battle cry was "There are going to be a lot of human pancakes around here before I get finished."

But while there are some wrestlers who look like poster children for "Save the Whales," pro wrestling also has its bodies beautiful. These wrestlers clearly have spent more time raising barbells than beer bottles. In tights, with well-oiled bodies, these athletes are appreciated by both men and women as ideal specimens of manliness. And let's not forget the female wrestlers. They bring a whole new dimension to the concept of "feminine pulchritude."

Shawn Michaels is one wrestler whose physical attributes can be appreciated by male and female fans alike. His thick, muscular body tapers to his remarkably trim waist and washboard stomach—his overall physical presence is awe inspiring. And Michaels knows how to use that presence to good effect—he's quick to pose down, treating the crowd to a series of body-building postures that make men envious and women—well, you know. Shawn has been called the "Heartbreak Kid" and it's easy to see why.

Captain Lou's Corner

The heat pro wrestling takes for being fake is really unfair. Pulitzer Prize–winning sportswriter Red Smith once attended a "real" boxing match in the company of Lou Thesz (one of wrestling's all-time greats), and rumor had it that the fight was fixed. No one believed it until the KO came on a flimsy backhand. Smith said to Thesz: "Lou, I'll never write an unkind word about wrestling again. At least you guys make it look like a contest."

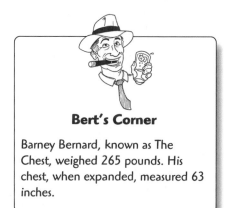

Bert's Corner

Barney Bernard, known as The Chest, weighed 265 pounds. His chest, when expanded, measured 63 inches.

Keeping the Tradition Alive

Only baseball rivals professional wrestling in its ability to keep its history alive, with generation after generation of fans and players passing along its heritage and its lore.

Younger fans learn from their fathers (or mothers, for that matter) that Gorgeous George was yesterday's version of Hulk Hogan. Bill Goldberg is today's version of Bruno Sammartino. And so the comparisons across the years go on.

Long-time fans still treasure their memories of watching a Dusty Rhodes or a Bobo Brazil in action. Real old-timers will talk of Antonino Rocco or Ricky Starr, Lou Thesz or Strangler Lewis. These were the great performers of pro wrestling's past and their exploits are still remembered by knowledgeable fans and passed along to the younger generation. And when the Austins and Undertakers and Goldbergs of today are gone, their names will also be writ large in the memories of today's afficionados, to be passed along to the next generation of fans. Tradition plays a major role in professional wrestling's popularity and mystique. So now let's look at some of that history—because to understand wrestling's past is to have a greater appreciation for its current appeal.

The Least You Need to Know

➤ Millions of people from all walks of life follow pro wrestling on a regular basis.

➤ Wrestling combines compelling characters and storylines of the soap opera with the variety and excitement of a three-ring circus.

➤ Although wrestling is not considered a sport in the true sense of the word, its performers are real athletes—some of the best in the world. They perform real moves, suffer real injuries, and provide real entertainment.

➤ There are as many different types of wrestlers as there are types of fans— everyone can find a favorite to cheer for, or somebody they can love to hate.

➤ Wrestling's rich history and tradition have been passed down from generation to generation of fans.

Chapter 2

A Brief History of Wrestling

> ### In This Chapter
>
> ➤ Wrestling comes to America: Greco-Roman and catch-as-catch-can styles
>
> ➤ Promoters and pretense: The carney contribution
>
> ➤ Wrestling becomes rasslin'
>
> ➤ The first showman

Once upon a time wrestlers wrestled—I mean really wrestled. Some historians have traced its ancestry to the ancient Egyptians, then on to the Greeks and the Romans. I mean, wrestling seems to go all the way back to before the time of the Great Flood.

But that's not the type of wrestling we're talking about here. We're talking about the body-slamming, head-bashing entertainment that has come to be known as professional wrestling—a form of entertainment that is as American as baseball, basketball, and apple pie. And *that* wrestling has a history all it's own, as you'll see in this chapter.

From the Old World to the New

Old World wrestling was of the Greco-Roman variety, which had certain rules—no holds were allowed below the waist, and when one of the combatants hit the ground it constituted a *fall*. In contrast to this "long-hair" variety was the more commercial form of wrestling, like the matches that used to be held in old German beer gardens. Although *scientific* in nature, the main idea of these wrestling exhibitions was to sell beer.

The longer an exhibition match lasted, the more beer the beer garden sold. And so, the two wrestlers would lock each other in their arms and stay in one position for 30, 40 minutes, or more. Then one would straighten his arm slowly, flexing his muscles ever so slightly. The customers would go wild and celebrate this "victory" by ordering more beer. Finally, when the wrestlers got thirsty, one would be thrown to the ground with a mighty thud and they would rest and drink for 30 minutes or so. And so on through the long, wet night, lasting five or six hours.

Fighting Words

Old World wrestling is called **scientific**—meaning it was based upon specific holds, moves, rules, and skills—to distinguish it from the choreographed, entertainment-oriented style that developed into modern pro wrestling.

The Carney Connection

When wrestling was brought to American shores by German and Irish immigrants, it was given a New World twist. Beginning in the post-Civil War period, wrestling bouts were staged at country fairs or touring carnivals in "At Shows" (short for Athletic Shows), where wrestlers with colorful costumes, equally colorful nicknames, and fictionalized biographies would wrestle each other or accept challenges from all local comers.

Wrestle Mania

According to wrestling writer Joe Jares, "Vermont was, in the early 1700s, America's first hotbed of wrestling. Most popular was the Irish 'collar and elbow style,' in which each wrestler would start by placing one hand on his opponent's shoulder on or near the collar line and the other hand on the arm just above the elbow. 'Just step down and finger me collar, I doubledang dare ye,' was a typical challenge."

The carney At Shows featured wrestlers engaging in exhibition matches or challenging all comers from the audience in time-limit contests for money—say $25. The challenger could win in one of two ways: by pinning the star or by managing to stay in the ring with him for 15 minutes. For the star, evading the pin was easy—all he had to do was remain on the defensive for the entire time limit. But staying the limit raised a real risk that the carnival operator could lose money if the local favorite—or "local yokel," as he was called—managed to go the distance.

Hookers and Hoaxes

The carneys, who lived by their wits, employed all sorts of tricks to avoid paying money to the local heroes: They paid an operative to hide behind a curtain at the back of the ring, ready with a baseball bat to take out the challenger; or they employed *hookers* or *hooks*, wrestlers who, using crippling holds unknown or illegal in competitive matches, put an end to the challenge before the local could *sting* the carnival. If the local was good enough to stay with the carney wrestler, the hooker would maneuver him into a backdrop, where he would be whacked on the head with a 2 × 4 by a confederate, ending his daredeviltry and preserving the carnival's money.

Barnstorming Brouhahas

At approximately the same time that carnivals traveled the highways and byways of nineteenth-century America, wrestling barnstormers were traveling the back roads, working by hook and crook to shake money out of the rubes. They promoted money matches for themselves against the local strongmen wherever and whenever they could find them, making side bets with the townsfolk on the outcome. There was a lot of connivance, sometimes with the willing assistance of the local hero, to make sure the underdog always won—and, if done convincingly, the two could stage a rematch and sting the marks all over again. The barnstormers' bottom line was money, not victories, the beginnings of wrestling as a performance sport.

Bert's Corner

In the old days there were three classes of wrestlers: the *hooker* was the most proficient, an able wrestler with wrestling knowledge, ability and strength, and with a bag full of old carnival *hooks* in his repertoire; the *shooter* was a scientific and competitive wrestler; and the *journeymen*, the largest group, performers who could wrestle just a little.

Captain Lou's Corner

Besides Washington, Lincoln, and Teddy Roosevelt, other presidents who wrestled included Zachary Taylor, William Howard Taft, and Calvin Coolidge.

Homesteading: Wrestling Comes Home to Roost

Both the carnivals and the barnstormers had a stimulating effect on early America, not only reminding those who had left the tradition of wrestling in the Old World of its existence in the New, but also bringing this new form of entertainment to the yet-unexposed masses.

It was but a short hop, skip, and pin to the next stage in wrestling's development: matches held in small halls and saloons, much like the old German beer garden experience. Advance men hung up posters announcing the coming of the matches and stayed in town to *homestead*, that is, to promote wrestling. With both the traveling carnivals and the barnstormers spreading the popularity of wrestling and carrying it to the masses—particularly the European immigrants who had long been interested in the sport in all its forms—wrestling was on the threshold of becoming Americanized.

Presidential Power

Three of the four faces on Mount Rushmore were wrestlers: George Washington was the champion of the colony of Virginia and Teddy Roosevelt wrestled at Harvard. However, the most famous of all was Abraham Lincoln, a giant of a man who, at 6 feet, 4 inches, was taller by far than most of the men of his day and age.

Early in life Lincoln had developed great wrestling skills and soon earned a reputation around his native Springfield, Illinois after defeating a local street fighter named Jack Armstrong. No, not *that* Jack Armstrong—the "All American Boy" from Hudson High in the 1940s—but the one from Springfield circa the 1840s. The bout had been arranged by a local saloonkeeper who had offered Lincoln $10 if he could throw Armstrong.

The curious were drawn from miles around to New Salem, where Lincoln was then employed as a clerk, to see the match. The betting action among the sports was brisk, most of it being placed on the shorter but more powerfully built Armstrong. But once the match started, it was no contest. "Lincoln lifted him by the throat," wrote Carl Sandburg, "shook him like a rag and then slammed him to a hard fall." Armstrong merely shook his head and said, "He's the best feller that ever broke into the settlement."

Stories and storytellers have it that Lincoln was engaged in a wrestling match when couriers came to tell him in 1860 of his nomination for the presidency by the Republican convention.

Wrestle Mania

By the 1880s, Greco-Roman wrestling was all the rage. It was a style developed in Europe in the 1860s and in America a decade or so later. But, truth to tell, the Greco-Roman style of this period had little similarity to the classic style of the early Greeks and Romans. To score a fall in Greco-Roman wrestling, a wrestler had to throw his opponent so that his two shoulders touched the mat simultaneously. Neither tripping nor holds below the waist were allowed. This form of wrestling, called "long-hair" wrestling by some of the older wrestlers like Lou Thesz, persists today in a modified form as an Olympic sport.

Wrestling's early days were marked by interminable bouts, including one in 1881 between William Muldoon, who claimed to be "the champion," and Clarence Whistler, "The Wonder of the West" at New York's Terrace Garden Theater.

For nearly seven hours, the two huffed and puffed as first one and then the other got down on the carpet and attempted to turn the other over on his back or locked hands behind heads in a Greco-Roman match marked by constant cries of "I want my dollar back!" and "Get up and do something!"

Finally, at about four o'clock in the morning, with most of the spectators at the theater bar in the outer lobby, the proprietor ordered the lights turned off and the crowd, which had foregathered at nine the previous night, trudged out of the theater, "swearing and growling," according to *The New York Times*.

Captain Lou's Corner

The earliest recorded wrestling match in the new world was in 1871: A match for "the championship of the United States and Canada and $2,000" was staged at Titusville, Pennsylvania. Major J. H. McLaughlin threw one Nathan Dorrance. McLaughlin proclaimed himself champion and issued challenges to other wrestlers to wrestle him for the title.

Professional Wrestling's Roots

Wrestling's roots were so solidly embedded in the European culture that most of the first wave of great American wrestlers was made up of first-generation Americans of European descent, most from small-town America, and European immigrants—wrestlers such as Martin "Farmer" Burns, William Muldoon, Theor. Bauer, Ernest Roeber, and Evan "Strangler" Lewis. They combined Greco-Roman and catch-as-catch-can wrestling, with one match, between Lewis and Roeber in 1893, alternating for five falls between the two disciplines. This last type of wrestling (catch-as-catch-can) was initially popularized by Frank Gotch and Tom Jenkins at the turn of the century. It allowed wrestlers to grasp any part of their opponent's body, and falls were scored whenever both shoulders of a wrestler touched the floor at the same time. One of the quaint rules covering the style read: "The referee shall slap on back or shoulder the wrestler securing the fall, so that the under man will not be strained by being held too long in a possibly painful position."

The immigrant experience continued with the second wave of American wrestlers, most coming from mid America, with wrestlers like Frank Gotch, Tom Jenkins, and Dan McLeod, joined by "The Russian Lion" (George Hackenschmidt), who had won international tournaments in Europe and came to the United States to defend his title. Gotch and Hackenschmidt would put on two of the most celebrated bouts in wrestling history, and two of the most controversial.

Gotch Gets the Lion

The first bout, for the supremacy of the wrestling world, was held at Chicago's Dexter Park Pavilion in 1908. It was generally believed that Hackenschmidt's bear hug and inside trip would be more than enough to make Gotch submit. However, "Hack" was unable to get Gotch in his grasp all evening—and was later to complain that Gotch had slathered himself in oil to make him all but impossible to grab. His inability to grab Gotch, coupled with Gotch's continual roughhousing and fouling, finally drove Hackenschmidt to quit after two hours and three minutes. The referee had no alternative but to disqualify Hackenschmidt and award the decision and the title to Gotch.

For the next three years Hackenschmidt campaigned for a rematch, finally getting one in 1911 at Chicago's new Comiskey Park in what was billed as The Match of the Century. Once again, foul tactics reared their ugly head. Only this time it wasn't during the match itself, but beforehand.

Seems that Gotch and his entourage had planted a hooker, Ad Santell, in Hackenschmidt's training camp. Three weeks before the match, Santell purposely injured Hackenschmidt's knee, but made the injury look like an accident.

With but one leg and public prejudice running in favor of two, Hackenschmidt tried to call off the bout. But the promoters, who had already spent the advance ticket money, pleaded with him to keep his injury a secret and go ahead with the bout. "The Russian Lion" agreed, but only if Gotch agreed to let him win one of the three falls and carry him to a face-saving end. Gotch double-crossed him and pinned the helpless Hackenschmidt in two straight falls.

Wrestle Mania

In what may have been the biggest upset in wrestling history, "The Peerless" Frank Gotch, thought to be unbeatable, was defeated by Fred Beell when he won the third of three falls after throwing Gotch out of the ring, Gotch striking his head on the floor. When the woozy Gotch finally re-entered the ring, Beell pinned him to take the American Heavyweight Championship on December 1, 1906, in New Orleans.

The End of the First Golden Age

The press got wind of Gotch's duplicity and not only turned their backs on the match, but also on the sport itself. That, and Gotch's retirement two years later to tour with the Sells-Floto Circus giving wrestling exhibitions, spelled the end of wrestling's first golden era. It would also mark the end of scientific bouts that took forever and a day— and sometimes a night as well.

Some time in the mid 1920s a promoter named Toots Mondt, taking his cue from vaudeville, decided enough was enough—sometimes too much—and installed a time limit in all matches. Then he introduced several innovations, such as the flying dropkick, to make wrestling more interesting and exciting for the fans. But the sport's resurgence in popularity can be tied, like that of any form of entertainment, to its superstars. And by the 1920s wrestling had one: Ed "Strangler" Lewis.

Wrestling's First Superstar

Paul Gallico, the famed sportswriter, labeled the 1920s "The Golden Age of Sports," and placed five superheroes in the decade's pantheon of greats: Babe Ruth of baseball, Red Grange of football, Jack Dempsey of boxing, Bill Tilden of tennis, and Bobby Jones of golf. Had he but added a sixth it would have been Ed "Strangler" Lewis of wrestling. In fact, Lewis even looked like Ruth—fat and balding with a big chest and small, toothpick-thin legs. But nobody, but *nobody*, was ever better than Lewis in the long history of professional wrestling.

Strangler Lewis puts a headlock on Hans Kampher. (Source: Norman Kietzer)

After winning bout after bout with a monotonous regularity—usually ending the match with his signature strangulation hold from which no opponent could escape— and creating an undercurrent of displeasure among the fans, Lewis and his brain

21

Captain Lou's Corner

Born Robert Fredrich, Ed "Strangler" Lewis derived his ring name from the earlier wrestler, Evan "Strangler" Lewis, as well as from his signature hold, the strangulation submission. He perfected this hold by pressing a wooden dummy between his arms and crushing it until it broke.

trust—manager Billy Sandow and promoter Toots Mondt, who, along with Lewis, were known as "The Gold Trio"—decided it was necessary to "do business" (agree to lose once in awhile) to keep wrestling fans interested. But even though he was to "lose" the title four times—in a career of over 6,200 matches in his long career he was to "lose" only 33 times—The Strangler would win it back an equal number of times, most in straight "shooting" matches (that is, he won without tricks or pre-agreements, solely on his skills as a wrestler).

One of The Strangler's greatest matches took place in Madison Square Garden in 1933, when Lewis, by then so long in the tooth he almost stepped on his overbite, defended his title against Ray Steele. On this night of nights, the crowds were lined up around the block to see Lewis finally "get his" from the challenger, Steele.

The bout began with the two circling each other—Lewis, by now fat, fifty, and balding; Steele, the body beautiful and weighing a trim 220. But almost from the start, it was no contest. Steele could do nothing with The Strangler. The fans, yawning at the lack of action in this scientific bout, began to stamp their feet. Realizing he was hopelessly outclassed, Steele finally resorted to punching Lewis and the referee disqualified him 20 minutes into the match.

Bert's Corner

Despite his enormity, Lewis was extremely agile—it was well-nigh impossible to get behind him as he continually circled, bearlike, to prevent his opponents from getting the drop on him. He was able to impose his will on everyone he faced. When he wanted to.

Wrestling Becomes Rasslin'

By the time Lewis' career had wound down, the feverish '20s had been replaced by the troubled '30s. And the American Dream had become a nightmare as breadlines took the place of the boom and bust atmosphere of the previous decade.

Depression-Era Depression

Like all other forms of entertainment, wrestling struggled for its very existence—people without enough money to fill their bellies with food had very little extra to spend on frills and extravagances like entertainment.

Still the sport labored on, with wrestlers like Dick Shikat, Jim Londos, Jim Browning, and Gus Sonnenberg passing the title around like a parcel nobody wanted. But then again, wrestling was a sport nobody wanted either. Especially in its interminable, never-ending matches which produced thousand-yard stares in its fans.

Wrestle Mania

Despite the Depression, Jim Londos became a big draw, pulling in gates of $70,000 in Yankee Stadium versus Ray Steele in 1931; $60,000 in Fenway Park versus Ed Don George in 1934; and $86,000 versus "Strangler" Lewis in Wrigley Field in 1934—the largest gate since Gotch and Hackenschmidt in 1911.

Wrestling Goes to College

And so the promoters tried several innovations to lure the fans, including putting a time limit on the matches of 10 to 15 minutes, in an effort to liven up the sport, much as baseball introduced the "lively ball" in 1930 to increase that sport's offense. Promoters also started scheduling novelty bouts—women's wrestling, tag teams, and even mud wrestling.

Captain Lou Remembers

Herman Hickman, one of the greatest linesmen in the history of college football, went to the same school I did—the University of Tennessee. He once told me how he got into professional wrestling: "In 1932 money was a scarce item, and there weren't many jobs floating around even if you did weigh 230 pounds, had made the All-American football team, and could recite a conglomerate of verse. So, when Rudy Dusek, the oldest and the mastermind of the wrestling Dusek Brothers, undertook to sell me on the idea of becoming a professional wrestler, he did not find it difficult. He mentioned something about the possibility of making $1,000 a week and becoming champion of the world. He could have got me for less than half of that, and he did."

But the biggest innovation was to recruit a new breed of wrestler—former collegiate football stars—in an attempt to capitalize on their names and popularity. The first of this new breed was Wayne "Big" Munn, a lineman from the University of Nebraska back in 1920. By the 1930s, Gus Sonnenberg of Dartmouth and the University of Detroit, "Jumping" Joe Savoldi of Notre Dame, Herman Hickman of Tennessee, and Bronko Nagurski of the University of Minnesota and the Chicago Bears all left the gridiron for the wrestling arena.

Football Players Who Became Wrestlers

Player's Name	Ring Name	University or Pro Team
Jack Adkisson	Fritz von Erich	Southern Methodist University
Richard Afflis	Dick the Bruiser	University of Nevada
Ellis Bashara	n/a	Oklahoma State
Kay Bell	n/a	Washington State
Sam Cordovano	n/a	Columbia
Mike DiBiase	n/a	University of Nebraska
Ed Fischer	n/a	Rutgers
Dory Funk Jr.	n/a	West Texas State
Terry Funk	n/a	West Texas State
Verne Gagne	n/a	University of Minnesota
Bob Geigel	n/a	University of Iowa
Bill Goldberg	n/a	University of Georgia
Kevin Greene	n/a	Auburn
Herman Hickman	n/a	University of Tennessee
Curtis Iaukea	King Curtis	California
Walter Johnson	n/a	Los Angeles State
Alex Karras	n/a	University of Iowa
Charles Kemmerer	Babe Sharkey	Temple
Gene Kiniski	n/a	University of Arizona
Bill Kusisto	n/a	University of Minnesota
Ernie Ladd	n/a	Grambling
Butch Levy	n/a	University of Minnesota
Albert Lolotai	Alo Leilani	Weber Jr. College
Len Macaluso	Legs	Colgate
Mayes McClain	n/a	University of Iowa
Ed McDaniel	Wahoo	University of Oklahoma
Jim McMillen	n/a	University of Illinois
(Dr.) Bill Miller	n/a	Ohio State
Angelo Moson	n/a	Notre Dame
Wayne Munn	Big Wayne Munn	University of Nebraska
Leo Nomellini	n/a	University of Minnesota
Jack Pasek	n/a	University of Nebraska
Jack Riley	n/a	Northwestern
Joe Savoldi	Jumping Joe	Notre Dame
Gus Sonnenberg	n/a	Dartmouth and University of Detroit
Wilbur Snyder	n/a	Utah
Donald Stansauk	Hard Boiled Haggerty	Denver
Woody Strode	n/a	UCLA
Arthur White	Tarzan	University of Alabama

But the addition of Nagurski, Hickman, and the rest of the collegiate greats was not enough to turn wrestling's fortunes around. As the hand of the Great Depression closed her all-enveloping fingers around the nation's wallet, wrestling, like all other forms of entertainment, continued to suffer.

Wrestling's fortunes didn't improve throughout World War II. Those who wanted wrestling in the proverbial "worst way," got just what they asked for: Promoters combed the country signing babes in swaddling clothes and throwing nets over anybody this side of the undertaker to fill its depleted ranks. But wrestling was on the cusp of a monumental breakthrough, courtesy of a new-fangled household appliance called television.

Wrestling's First Showman

Television and professional wrestling were made for each other. Professional wrestling offered an almost made-for-television format, tailored to the dimensions of the TV tube. And, in a symbiotic relationship, television offered wrestling an entirely new group of fans and fans-to-be. Soon wrestling was being offered up from arena and studio alike almost every day of the week—and served on Fridays more times than fish. But the wrestling boom of the late 1940s and early 1950s wouldn't have been possible had it not been for one man: Gorgeous George.

With Lana Turner bleached-blond hair and a bag full of gimmicks—including marching into the arena to the strains of "Pomp and Circumstance"— Gorgeous George always put on a show: having his formally attired valet spray the ring with an atomizer filled with perfume-scented disinfectant called, appropriately enough, "George No. 4"; wearing his fur-trimmed robe; and giving away "Georgie Pins" to the crowd. Gorgeous George became wrestling's biggest-ever draw. The man introduced as "The Human Orchid, The Toast of the Coast" became wrestling's poster boy. And, not incidentally, became wrestling's first pure "performer," setting the stage, for wrestling's all-new direction: showbiz.

Captain Lou's Corner

Nagurski had not only led the Bears to four championships, but had been all-pro four seasons. However, finding that the owner of the Bears, George Halas, "threw nickels around like manhole covers," and that his efforts weren't being adequately rewarded, he opted instead for a wrestling career and became one of the biggest attractions of the 1930s.

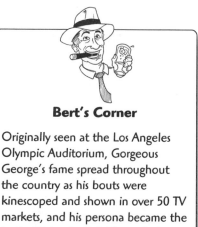

Bert's Corner

Originally seen at the Los Angeles Olympic Auditorium, Gorgeous George's fame spread throughout the country as his bouts were kinescoped and shown in over 50 TV markets, and his persona became the butt of jokes by Bob Hope, Jack Benny, Red Skelton, and others. He even made an appearance on *Queen for a Day*.

From that point on, wrestling became "rasslin" as hordes of masked men, high-stepping Germans, monocled lords, Indian chiefs, Arab chieftains, and all other manner of gimmicked-up "rasslers" followed in Gorgeous George's wake. The second golden age of wrestling had begun.

Soon, however, television, which had used wrestling as mere filler, found other programming. Wrestling sank back into oblivion until the 1980s, when promoter Vince McMahon found a way to use the media to his own advantage, and wrestling roared into its third golden age—one that it is still enjoying.

The Least You Need To Know

➤ While wrestling is one of the oldest sports in the world, it became Americanized through carnivals and barnstormers after the Civil War.

➤ Wrestling's high point as a sport came with the two Frank Gotch–George Hackenschmidt matches.

➤ Ed "Strangler" Lewis became wrestling's first superstar and is still arguably the greatest wrestler in history.

➤ Abe Lincoln and George Washington, along with four other presidents, were wrestlers.

➤ Gorgeous George was wrestling's first showman, and changed wrestling forever.

Chapter 3

The Glue That Holds It All Together: Organizations and Federations

While the wrestlers are the stars of the show—the players, if you will—the organizations and federations that stage the matches are the basis of wrestling, its very fabric. And have been since the beginning of wrestling.

The organizations and federations of today are a natural outgrowth of the old-time promoters who turned the sport of wrestling into a form of mass entertainment. They are the ones who are responsible for promoting wrestling, publicizing it, and plotting its course.

Today there are two major organizations on the professional wrestling landscape—the World Wrestling Federation (WWF) and the World Championship Wrestling (WCW)—and several smaller ones survive and thrive, and more appearing every week, or so it seems. Only the most hard-core fan can keep track of who is who and who belongs to which. You can't tell the players without a scorecard—and you have to update it all the time.

This chapter will give you an overview of promoters and their world—how they came into being, how they grew, and what stars they feature—and try to sort it out for you.

In the Beginning

Back about the time Father Adam first heard the stampede of the apple sellers, there were no organizations nor federations. There were only barnstormers, carnival operators, and just plain ol' hustlers who homesteaded areas, staking out the territory and holding wrestling bouts there. These early-day Barnums of wrestling were con men, most of whom had shaken hands with the process server more than once.

And they were the forerunners of the wrestling promoter, the freelance entrepreneurs who roamed the landscape in the early 20th century. They had no more legal right to control a territory than a claim jumper, but they agreed among themselves to respect their territorial boundaries. Soon the countryside took on the look of a patchwork shed put together by drunken carpenters, as each territory abutted and sometimes even overran an already-established one.

Their ranks were filled with boxing promoters such as Jack Curley and Jesse McMahon, ex-wrestlers such as Toots Mondt and Ed "Strangler" Lewis, and promoters such as Jack Pfefer, who came straight into wrestling with no previous career stops along the way.

By the 1930s the wrestling landscape was as depressed as the rest of the country. The champions had the life spans of mayflies, while matches were interminable, going on until the wee hours of the morning. Promoters were double-crossing what few attractions they still had, not to mention each other. Accordingly, crowds, with the notable exception of those who came out in droves to watch Jim Londos (wrestling's *only* consistent drawing card during this period), had fallen off disastrously. Something had to be done, and fast. The promoters were barely earning enough to survive on.

Body Slam

A word of warning to wrestling fans: Once you master the basics of the game, pick one of the two major organizations (the WWF or the WCW) to keep track of. Trying to follow all the many organizations out there will only give you Excedrin Headache #38—there are just too many of them to keep straight.

Promoter Toots Mondt understood that wrestling fans would no longer stand for even the biggest name wrestler holding a headlock on an opponent for five minutes or more. He borrowed an idea from vaudeville—the blackouts, where acts lasted but a few minutes—and gave wrestling fans more entertainment bang for their buck by imposing time limits of 10 or 15 minutes. Other innovations of the era included the introduction of "character" wrestlers, good-guy/bad-guy oppositions, and novelty acts like midget wrestling and women wrestlers.

More promoters got into the game as it became more viable. Rudy Dusek in Nebraska, Ed White in Chicago, Pinkie George in Iowa, Tony Stetcher in Minnesota, Ray Fabiani in California, Paul Jones in Atlanta, LeRoy McGuirk in Tulsa, Nick Gulas and Roy Welch in Nashville, Sam Muchnick in St. Louis, Morris Sigel in Houston, and Paul Bowser in Boston.

They weathered the tough times of the Depression and emerged into the sunshine of the eagerly awaited post-war boom. That's when wrestling suddenly found itself in a boom of its own—this one courtesy of television. All of a sudden, the new golden age of wrestling had arrived and the promoters were going to make sure they made the most of it.

Most of the promoters formed an organization in 1948 called the National Wrestling Alliance (NWA), which covered the entire West Coast from Seattle to San Diego, and included Texas, Oklahoma, Kansas, Missouri, and almost the entire South, plus Mexico, Australia, and parts of Japan and Canada. But the NWA was an organization in name only. It was really a loosely knit confederation of promoters, most of whom were, in the words of Lou Thesz, "hypocrites and lowlifes who'd stage a dogfight if they thought it would draw money."

In his on-line book *Hooker: An Authentic Wrestler's Adventures Inside the Bizarre World of Pro Wrestling* (at www.twe-online.com, go to the Official Lou Thesz Web page), Thesz recounts one NWA annual meeting where the membership had listened to a report from "some self-important judge from Texas who'd been brought in to mediate an internal dispute between two Texas promoters. The judge had obviously resolved the matter in a way to fatten his own pockets and, at the end of his report, one promoter stood up and said, 'Well, this guy looks like the type who'd steal a hot stove and come back the next day for the lid, so I suppose he'll fit right in with us.' A lot of people laughed at the remark, but some members got indignant, as always happens when someone hits too close to the truth."

Bert's Corner

In the 1930s, both baseball and football found it necessary to add action to the games if they wanted to keep the crowds coming in. Baseball "juiced up" the ball, and in 1935 pro football legalized the forward pass from anywhere behind the line of scrimmage. In those days, it seemed *everything* had to speed up the action if they wanted to keep the fans coming.

In Your Face

Along with Mondt's innovations, several other ways to draw in the crowds were devised during the depressed 1930s: tag team matches, women's wrestling, novelty acts, gimmicks, and not unimportantly, the introduction of "character" rasslers— the opposition of good guys versus bad guys. All these were enough to allow wrestling to survive, but prosperity would have to wait awhile.

The typical NWA convention had all the back slapping found at a Shriner's convention and all the back stabbing found at a reunion of the Borgia family, as each promoter tried to get the better of fellow alliance members. Vince McMahon Sr., was the only major promoter not to join the NWA. He controlled the Washington, D.C. territory, which ran from Richmond, Virginia up to Lewiston, Maine.

McWrestling: The McMahons and the WWF

Even though wrestling's cast of characters always seems to be changing, there has been one constant throughout the years—the McMahon family. The patriarch of the McMahon clan was Jess McMahon, a boxing promoter who turned to wrestling. A debonair, handsome gentleman of indeterminate age, Jess had co-promoted the heavyweight championship boxing match between Jess Willard and Jack Johnson in 1915, and then joined Tex Rickard in bringing big-time boxing to Madison Square Garden. From there it was an easy transition into promoting wrestling bouts, first in the Garden and then throughout the East Coast.

Unto the Second Generation

His son, Vince McMahon Sr., became the second member of wrestling's First Family to enter the game on the promotional side. Originally Vince Sr. ran something called Capital Wrestling out of Washington, D.C.—a territory which covered the eastern seaboard from Virginia all the way up to Maine and as far west as the Alleghenies, about the same region covered by America's first coaxial (television) cable. The near approximation of McMahon's territory and the area covered by the coaxial cable gave McMahon a huge advantage in selling his local wrestling bouts to the fledgling TV medium, which was desperately searching for programming to fill its screens.

Vince Sr. teamed up with the old promoter, Toots Mondt, who controlled the talent just as Vince controlled the TV access. Together they became the most successful wrestling promoters of the late 1940s and early 1950s.

Capital Wrestling's territory was so large and its operation so successful and lucrative, that they didn't need the National Wrestling Alliance. And so they went on their merry way, stronger as a single entity than the NWA was as a coalition.

Capital Wrestling's Rise to the Top

One of Capital's first great attractions was Antonino Rocca, the Argentine acrobat whom they imported in the late 1940s. Then they brought in Gorgeous George from the West Coast, and he caused an instant sensation—he was, after all, a made-for-television celebrity. McMahon and Mondt carried on a "Cold War" with the NWA throughout the 1950s, but in 1961 the war heated up over a new wrestler on the scene, "Nature Boy" Buddy Rogers.

Former champion "Nature Boy" Buddy Rogers, retired from the ring but still involved with wrestling, with Jimmy Snuka. (Source: Norman Kietzer)

Rogers, the biggest draw since Rocca and Gorgeous George, had won the NWA World Heavyweight Championship belt from Pat O'Connor at Chicago's Comiskey Park in 1961. But soon thereafter the NWA found that "their" champion had gone over to Toots Mondt, who had taken over Rogers' bookings and was using him exclusively in the McMahon-Mondt eastern circuit. Only on rare occasions would a magnanimous Mondt consent for Rogers to wrestle for NWA promoters, allowing barely a handful of dates each month.

Things got so bad that Sam Muchnick, then head of the NWA, was heard to mumble aloud to anyone who would listen: "Toots controls Rogers now and he's seeing to it we can't even use our own champion." Muchnick persuaded the venerable Lou Thesz, who had first held the world championship back in 1937 and five times thereafter, to take on

Captain Lou's Corner

I've associated with Vince Sr. since 1952, when I first started wrestling. And I would drop in at the Franklin Park Hotel in Washington to visit all the time—and to receive my bookings. Well, one time during a drop-in visit, I met this little kid who was then about 11 years old. The kid kicked me in the leg. That handful would one day grow up to be Vince Jr.—and he remains a handful to this day.

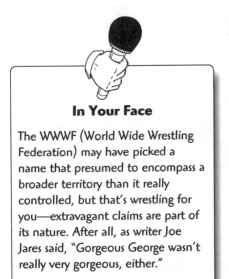

In Your Face

The WWWF (World Wide Wrestling Federation) may have picked a name that presumed to encompass a broader territory than it really controlled, but that's wrestling for you—extravagant claims are part of its nature. After all, as writer Joe Jares said, "Gorgeous George wasn't really very gorgeous, either."

Rogers and bring the belt back home. But even though Thesz was to beat Rogers in one fall in January of 1963, the east coast circuit continued to recognize Rogers as "champion."

Four months later, in May of 1963, McMahon and Mondt formed the World Wide Wrestling Federation (WWWF). And while not precisely "world wide"—it covered only the eastern seaboard—it was an impressive territory with an impressive sounding name. Soon one of the Ws was dropped and it became the WWF.

Shortly thereafter, the McMahon-Mondt tandem came to an end. Mondt, who had been on the scene since God knows when—and even God wasn't sure of the when—decided to pack it in and sold his interest in the WWF back to Vince McMahon, Sr. then resold that interest to Gorilla Monsoon, Phil Zacko, and Arnold Skaaland, keeping a majority interest in the new entity for himself.

A New McMahon Twist

In 1983, Vince sold his interest in the WWF to his son, Vince Jr. What followed was a nationwide wrestling blitzkrieg—a take-no-prisoners war of expansion that would radically change the world of professional wrestling.

Vince Jr. was able to voyage, Columbus-like, into the territories of other promoters because of the dawning of cable TV and the production values made possible by another innovation, videotape. His theory was, what worked in the Northeast could be exported and made to work nationally—and internationally. So he declared war on the other promoters and invaded or bought up their territories.

Wrestle Mania

"My dad would never have sold me his end of that company, nor for that matter would the other stockholders have followed if they knew what I was going to do," Vince McMahon Jr. said. "He just thought I was going to continue to operate in the Northeast and respect the other promoters and their territories.... He said, 'Oh, my God, now you've just angered half the promoters in the business.'" But Vince Jr. had his own plans, so after he bought out his dad's partners he began syndicating his television programming into Los Angeles, then St. Louis, then throughout the country.

While he was carrying out this "scorched-earth policy," Vince Jr. was vulnerable: "We did it all with mirrors, it was all cash flow. Had those promoters known that I didn't have any money, they could have killed us."

But the point is, they *didn't* know. And even if they had, it's doubtful that the disorganized organization known as the NWA could have held Vince Jr. off. Rather than banding together to repel his invasion, they bickered among themselves and kept their heads firmly planted in the sand while Vince Jr. planted his WWF flag across the country, changing the face of professional wrestling forever. Of the 20 regional promoters operating throughout the country in 1984, fewer than five remained by 1989.

Wrestlemania

If there was any one moment that defined the success of the WWF, cementing its position at the top of the wrestling ladder, it was *Wrestlemania*. Truth to tell, Vince Jr. had actually been thinking about it for a long time as a new way to put the WWF on the map. The idea had its roots in McMahon's perception of wrestling: He knew that the WWF was in the entertainment business, much like Broadway and Hollywood were. And so, borrowing from their example, he began planning attractive main events and bringing in celebrities who were, in his word, "hip"—who could add to the event and help make it into an entertainment.

Captain Lou's Corner

The idea came to McMahon, he said, while he was on vacation with his wife Linda. According to McMahon, he turned to her and said "We're going to do a big promotion and we're going to close-circuit it all over the country [there was no pay-per-view back then] and we're going to call it *Wrestlemania*."

Soon Vince Jr. began pulling together all the elements for *Wrestlemania I*, bringing in the likes of Hulk Hogan, Sergeant Slaughter, the Iron Sheik, and celebrities such as Muhammad Ali, Liberace, and Billy Martin. But Vince Jr. has always been open to new ideas—he encourages his staff to give him creative input. It was in that atmosphere that I went to Vince with an idea: Wendi Richter versus the Fabulous Moolah. Though in reality it became me, Captain Lou, versus Cyndi Lauper.

Girls Just Want to Have Fun

Maybe I should explain how that came about. It started a few years before, on a plane from Puerto Rico. There I was, just sitting there, when a young lady came over. "Cripes," I said—or something that sounded like it—"it's Cyndi Lauper." She introduced herself and said she'd been a wrestling fan all her life, then asked if I would like to be in a video she was making of her big hit "Girls Just Want to Have Fun."

Captain Lou's Corner

There's no truth to the rumor that Cyndi Lauper is my daughter. Yes, I played her father in all those videos—"She Bop," "Girls Just Want to Have Fun," "Time After Time," and "Goonies"—and her real mother played the mom. But I was just acting—you know, artistic license, or something like that.

While we were filming the videos—a sort of merging of the worlds of wrestling and rock—Rowdy Roddy Piper saw an opportunity to create some mischief. He asked me to appear on his TV show, *Piper's Pit*, for what I thought was going to be a straight interview. He started egging me on about male supremacy and, being a bit chauvinistic anyway, I took the bait and made some rather rash remarks, like "Women are garbage and only good for having babies and cleaning the house."

Well, that tore it. To make it worse, one night down at Madison Square Garden I ran into Cyndi and we started in. Again, I said some intemperate things, like "You were just a dirty little broad before you met me...." and so on. Cyndi wasn't going to take that, so she fired back: "Tell you what, fat man—I'm going to put a woman wrestler up against one of your choice. And if my woman wins, you're going to have to apologize and admit women are at least as good as men, maybe even better!"

The Battle Between the Sexes

Cyndi picked Wendi Richter to carry her banner—a young lady out of Texas who was then rising in the WWF ranks. My choice was a natural: The Fabulous Moolah, the women's champion.

Bert's Corner

The formal challenge of Moolah versus Richter was issued on Roddy Piper's show, since he had stirred up the trouble to begin with. And while Lou was somewhat worried about the Fabulous One having to face Wendi, he had to accept the challenge to save face.

Once I persuaded Vince to include the Moolah-Richter match on the first *Wrestlemania,* I had to go out and publicize it to make it pay off. I went on the Letterman show, and wouldn't you know it—a whole bunch of women's libbers started picketing me and booing in the audience. I told Letterman that they were really calling out "Lou, Lou...," and added, "I have the body women love and men envy." Needless to say, it went over like stale pizza.

To top it all off, Wendi Richter won, and I had to eat my words. But all in all, it was a successful promotion, and it added to the success of *Wrestlemania I.* So although Vince Jr. was the man behind the promotion, I feel I had a large part in turning it into the major promotion that it became. *Wrestlemania* became the standard for wrestling—its Super Bowl—and made the World Wrestling Federation number one in the world of wrestling.

Mr. T versus Rowdy Roddy Piper in the first Wrestlemania, *held at Madison Square Garden. (Source: Associated Press)*

The WCW: Wrestling Takes a Turn for the Better (Ratings)

Wrestlemania made the WWF. Not just with the publicity—which McMahon played for all it was worth—but because its coverage established the WWF as truly worldwide.

Now McMahon was able to continue his onslaught against the other promoters, using television as his primary weapon. This time, unlike what happened in wrestling's earlier golden age back in the 1950s, *McMahon* used the medium instead of the other way around. The new cable channels were scrambling for programming that McMahon was able to provide, even if he had to buy up the air time to shut out the competition.

Bert's Corner

Wrestlers switch from one organization to another, almost overnight. I'll never forget the time Ravishing Rick Rude appeared on an ECW telecast one Friday, only to turn up on the WWF the next Saturday. If you're tracking a wrestler and can't find him, make a quick check on the Internet to see if he's changed organizations.

As more and more promoters folded up their tents and faded into the sunset, the WWF filled the void with its shows, which were now telecast on every newly minted cable channel. The notable exception was ESPN, which carried wrestling from Jim Crockett's NWA circuit.

Crockett was the only promoter left to carry the banner against the WWF—all the others had gotten out. Also gone were Verne Gagne's once powerful AWA in the Midwest and Fritz Von Erich's WCCW in Texas. Crockett's North Carolina-based organization became, by default, the NWA. His stars were equal to those in the WWF—Dusty Rhodes, Ric Flair, and others of equal stature—but the trouble was that nobody outside of Charlotte knew them. The WWF's monopolization of cable kept them off the tube. Crockett soldiered on anyway, losing money hand over handstand.

Wrestle Mania

It's hard enough to follow who belongs to which organization or federation, and now there are subgroups to make the picture even more confusing. In the WCW there is the New World Order (nWo); in the WWF, there's D-Generation X (D-X). These are not true organizations, but instead are groups of wrestlers that form part of a story line within the federations. Interfederation feuds between the WWF and WCW can't be staged since the two federations do not do jointly promoted shows, intrafederation feuds are promoted instead.

Turner Tries to Take Charge

It looked like McMahon held all the cards and could dictate terms to television networks, most of which were so eager to keep their wrestling programming that they rolled over on his command. All except for Ted Turner, of the Turner Broadcasting System (TBS).

Rumor has it that Turner was upset with Vince Jr.'s demands for time slots. Or that he was pissed with McMahon for buying up some of Crockett's talent, which was now showing on TBS. Whatever the reason, Turner decided to declare war on McMahon and bought up Crockett's promotional territory. According to McMahon, Turner called to gloat about his new acquisition, announcing that he was now in the rasslin' business. "Good," said McMahon, "*we're* in the entertainment business." And McMahon hung up.

WWF Lineup

Animal (now of Legion of Doom 2000, formerly of Road Warriors)

Stone Cold Steve Austin

Paul Bearer

Bradshaw (a.k.a. Justin Bradshaw, Blackjack Bradshaw)

Cactus Jack (a.k.a. Mick Foley)

Chyna (of D-Generation X)

D-Lo Brown (of Nation of Domination)

Dude Love (a.k.a. Mick Foley)

Bad Ass Billy Gunn (of D-Generation X and New Age Outlaws)

Owen Hart

Hawk (now of Legion of Doom 2000, formerly of Road Warriors)

Hunter Hearst Helmsley (of D-Generation X)

Jesse "Road Dog" James (a.k.a. The Roadie, now of D-Generation X and New Age Outlaws)

Jeff Jarrett (a.k.a. Double J)

Kane

Mankind (a.k.a. Mick Foley)

Marvelous Marc Mero

Vince McMahon Jr.

Rocky Melvin (a.k.a. The Rock)

Shawn "The Heartbreak Kid" Michaels

Savio Vega (a.k.a. Kwang)

Ken Shamrock

Too-Cold Scorpio (a.k.a. Flash Funk)

Undertaker (a.k.a. The Dead Guy)

Vader (a.k.a. Big Van Vader)

X-Pac (was Syxx in WCW, the 1-2-3 Kid in WWF)

While Turner had bought Crockett's business, he hadn't bought the NWA designation—at least, according to what remained of the loose alliance of regional promoters from the territory. They sued Turner for his use of the NWA initials. That made no nevermind to Turner—he just changed the initials to WCW, as in World Championship Wrestling. It was, after all, already the name of his number-one TV show on Saturday nights.

It turned into all-out war between the two moguls, now. And although Turner lost money for the first eight years, this man never blinked. Having accomplished his primary purpose, preventing McMahon and the WWF from monopolizing cable-TV wrestling, Turner was also creating his own programming for TBS, a superstation that beamed its signals all across the country.

With Turner's WCW, McMahon was faced for the first time with the WWF not being the top wrestling dog—and with the defections of some of his top stars from the ranks. And it seemed as if the standard wrestling good-guy versus bad-guy scenario had run out of steam, too: After four decades it suffered from thematic exhaustion. So he hit upon a new plan to pump up interest and work a twist on the old routine—he cast *himself* as a baddie and started a feud with Stone Cold Steve Austin. This struck a responsive chord among the fans and shot the WWF, and its new *RAW is WAR* show, back to the top.

Today the war between wrestling's promoter titans pits Turner's money against Vince's ingenuity. And although Turner can always outspend Vince, Vince can always fight back with new ideas, newfangled plot lines, and outrageous gimmicks. McMahon cut deals right and left to keep Turner out of the top arenas. Turner's response was to start his own pay-per-view shows, cluttering the already crowded PPV schedule and diluting the impact of *Wrestlemania*.

WCW Lineup

Booker T (of Harlem Heat)

Diamond Dallas Page

Flyboy Rocco Rock (of Public Enemy)

The Giant

Bill Goldberg

Johnny Grunge (of Public Enemy)

Juventud Guererra

Chavo Guerrero

Eddie Guerrero

Scott Hall (a.k.a. Razor Ramon)

Hollywood Hogan (a.k.a. Hulk Hogan)

Chris Jericho

Chris Kenyon

Lido (of Raven's Flock)

Lex Luger (a.k.a. The Total Package)

Dean Malenko (a.k.a. The Man of 1,000 Holds)

Kevin "The Big Sexy" Nash (a.k.a. Diesel)

Psycosis

Scott Putski (a.k.a. The Polish Prince)

Raven

Stevie Ray (of Harlem Heat)

Scotty Riggs (of Raven's Flock)

Sting

Ultimo Dragon (a.k.a. Last Dragon)

Alex Wright (a.k.a. Das Wunderkind)

The two soon began a game of "anything you can do I can do better." Take the WWF's *Monday Night Raw* program, for instance. It had always been a huge success—a showcase of sorts for the WWF and a major promo venue for the PPV events. Turner countered by moving his own show to Monday nights, calling it *Monday Nitro*. Then Turner did what every promoter has done from time immemorial—he started raiding the WWF's roster for stars.

First to come over was Hulk Hogan, who had to change his name to Hollywood Hogan in the face of a lawsuit by the WWF when it claimed rights to the original name. Turner changed Hogan's persona as well—turning him into a baddie. WCW's ratings went through the roof, and *Monday Nitro* passed *RAW is WAR* in the ratings for the first time.

"Hulk" Hogan had to go "Hollywood" upon leaving the WWF for Turner's WCW: The WWF owned his old ring name. (Source: World Wrestling Federation)

The ECW and the Rest of the Federations

You'd think that with the WWF and the WCW so dominant, there'd be no room left over for any other organizations. But you'd think wrong. Today it seems that everyone and their kid brother has set up a wrestling territory.

As the two major organizations changed their storylines from a focus on blood and simulated maimings to more convoluted plots and juvenile raunchiness, more busty valets and managers and more human action-figure acrobatics, they left a void. Hardcore wrestling—the way it used to be, with lots of blood, weapons, and over-the-top violence—was left behind. But not for long.

The organization that best exploited the void left by the WWF and WCW was Eastern Championship Wrestling—the ECW. The ECW presented alternatives to the fare offered by the WWF and WCW: harder story lines, lots of blood, plenty of weapons, and violence.

The ECW began its life in a bingo hall in South Philly in the early 1990s, the creation of Tod Gordon and the wrestler Eddie Gilbert. When Gilbert left, he was succeeded by wrestling visionary Paul Heyman. In an earlier, WCW life, Heyman had been known as Paul E. Dangerously. Heyman changed the "E" in the ECW from "Eastern" to "Extreme," bought infomercials on major TV stations in major markets in the wee, wee hours of the morning, and brought the newly named Extreme Championship Wrestling organization to the attention of millions of fans who were hungry for the old-time violence.

While the roster of the ECW carries several names familiar to wrestling fans—Terry Funk, Bam Bam Bigelow, Rick Rude, among others—it's the hard-edged characters like The Sandman and Sabu, and strippers working as ring valets, that brought it a big following. Big enough for the ECW, which began in a bingo hall, to graduate to pay-per-view.

King Kong Bundy of the Century Wrestling Alliance (CWA) (Source: Norman Kietzer)

ECW Lineup

Bam Bam Bigelow	Sabu
Chris Candido	The Sandman
Shane Douglas	Al Snow
Tommy Dreamer	Rob Van Dam
Spike Dudley	Taz
Balls Mahoney	

The ECW has become a semi-major organization, though not quite in the league of the WWF and the WCW. And it has proven that there is room for others. Now the number of wrestling affiliations has begun to mushroom, including the Century Wrestling Alliance (CWA), the International Wrestling League, the United States Wrestling Association (USWA) and even vestigial remnants of the old NWA.

CWA Lineup

Abdullah the Butcher	The Metal Maniac
Tony Atlas	Curtis Slamdawgg
King Kong Bundy	Vic Steamboat
Lumberjack Rick Fuller	Kevin Sullivan
El Mascarado	Superfly Snuka

USWA Lineup

Brickhouse Brown	Dutch Mantel
Brian Christopher	Akeem Muhammid
Bill Dundee	Karem Olojuwan
J.C. Ice	Sir Mo
Jerry Lawler	Wolfie D.
Mabel	

The Least You Need to Know

➤ Wrestling promoters are lineal descendants of the old-time carney promoters.

➤ The NWA was wrestling's first major organization.

➤ The McMahon's—Jess, Vince Sr., and Vince Jr.—are wrestling's First Family of promoters.

➤ Vince McMahon Jr., through cable TV and *Wrestlemania,* made the WWF the premier wrestling organization in the world

➤ Ted Turner used his superstation, TBS, and the WCW to challenge the WWF in an all-out, head-to-head war for promotional supremacy.

➤ Besides the two major wrestling organizations, there are dozens of other affiliations on the wrestling landscape today.

Chapter 4

Smoke and Mirrors

In This Chapter

➤ Creating reality in the wrestling ring

➤ Tricks of the trade

➤ Staging the sound effects

➤ The very real reality of pain

Remember that wonderful line Jack Nicholson, as the Joker, uttered in the movie *Batman* as he marveled at his antagonist: "How does he *do* those things?" Well, that line could be applied to wrestling as well.

How do wrestlers do those things? Like flying off the top rope and landing on an opponent's chest or throat without smashing him into smaller, tidier pieces? Like hitting an opponent with an iron folding chair without rendering the hittee senseless? Like smiting the opponent with a jarring punch that sounds like it should have felled six or seven bystanders? Like a smaller man lifting his mammoth opponent high above his head and smashing him to the mat with the greatest of ease? In this chapter, you'll find out.

Reality Is in the Eye of the Beholder

Now, I don't think I'm telling tales out of school or giving away any trade secrets when I tell you that what you see in professional wrestling is not always what you get. I know, I know—it *looks* real. But there's a secret, one I will let you in on.

Professional wrestling creates the illusion of violence. And what the wrestlers do in the ring looks real. But it isn't. After all, a real hammerlock could break a guy's arm; a real step-over toehold, could destroy his ankle.

And after all, what is "real" these days, anyway? The fights on the Jerry Springer show? No, but they call that television. The sham news report on CNN about nerve gas? No, but they call that news reporting. The moves and falls in professional wrestling? No, but the critics call those fake. See the difference? Neither do I.

Years ago, Arlo Guthrie and Country Joe McDonald taught us that the world was absurd, not what it was supposed to be. Theater, television, movies, wrestling—it's all about suspended disbelief, making what is not real into what appears to be real. And the moves, maneuvers, and manipulations in a wrestling ring are as real as it gets, sort of like those of movie stuntmen who are portraying their on-camera antics as *real-real*.

Fighting Words

Real-real means the real deal, the genuine article, the honest fact. Lots of moves, leaps, and holds are choreographed in pro wrestling, but there's still a lot of real-real going on in the ring, too. It's up to the fan to spot which is which.

Fighting Words

Professional Wrestling's roots are so intertwined with old carnival operators—or "carneys"—that the language of wrestlers today is called **kay-fabe**, a derivation of the carnival dialect where the con men could discuss the con right in front of the mark without the mark knowing it.

I know there are those out there who think it's sacrilegious to consider any alternative to their belief that wrestling is not real-real. Others believe it's all make believe. Or, as Hulk Hogan has said, "For those who believe, you don't need an explanation; for those who don't believe, no amount of explaining will do."

I straddle the middle ground—admitting that some of it ain't quite what it seems and some is. So let me try to explain how, in many cases, only the ring is square.

To understand professional wrestling and how it got to where it is, you must first understand its background, its ancestry. Professional wrestling, as we know it today, is an outgrowth of carnival "At Shows," run by men who, if you had but shaken their hands, would have you counting not only your rings but also your fingers afterward. And in a world where a scam a day kept the creditors away, carney operators always had enough scams to stay one step ahead of them. The carneys, as they were called, even invented a language of their own so they could talk to each other about cheating someone right in front of his face. Today, the wrestling world has its own version of that invented language called *kay-fabe*.

When the carneys teamed up with pure old-fashioned hustlers and barnstormers, it's no wonder that wrestling lost its resemblance to the scientific style of the old days and became more a performance sport. These men traveled from town to town, touting "champions" with phony biographies who offered to take on anyone in the audience. Or each other. All in the name of money. And if these early promoters were in danger of losing money they would stop at very little—even hitting a local yokel over the head with a bat—to avert a payoff of any kind.

Any wonder that wrestling, based in such chicanery, should develop into the form of entertainment we have today? Alright, now that we've established professional wrestling's somewhat less than noble ancestry, we now know that we can take many of the things that happen in the ring with the proverbial grain of salt. And others with an entire barrel full.

Spikeless Punches and Other Sleights of Hand

How, you may ask, can a person take repetitive blows to the head from a huge, strong opponent and keep coming back for more? The answer can be found in some basic laws of physics and in an audience's ability to suspend disbelief. Put the two together, and you have spectacular theater in the squared circle.

The most well-known law of physics, almost the first rule in Physics 101, involves the collision of parallel flat surfaces—this "disperses the force of impact across the plain of contact." Every time a wrestler whacks another with a folded chair, they hit something flat, like the back, with the flat part of the chair. And guys leaping off the top strand of ropes always aim at a man either standing up (so that he can be caught) or lying completely prone, so that they can collide chest to chest—flat body part to flat body part.

Flat to flat is the first rule then. Which might explain why moves like the clothesline and the forearm smash are so popular among wrestlers—they're dramatic and they follow rule #1.

Second rule: Attackers will never put their full weight behind a blow. Rather, a wrestler will soften it by going off to the side, when possible, so that rather than frescoing his opponent, he is merely lacing him gingerly. Whenever possible, wrestlers take care of each other, help one another, work together. And while nothing is staged to 100 percent guarantee that one will not hurt another, wrestlers do take precautions not to. Pain is no problem for these gifted athletes—but missing the next show—now *that's* a problem.

So while the fans may *see* contact, *hear* contact, and *believe* there was contact, what contact there was, in the main, was incidental—and the effect illusory. Because although a punch actually lands, it has very little impact and is rarely as forceful or as lethal as it looks and sounds. It is not delivered with the fist—at least not a closed fist—as much as

Bert's Corner

Oh, sure, some wrestlers new to the business or in mom-and-pop circuits are so bad that you can see their moves, which might appear almost burlesque-y. These are wrestlers who are not very good at the art of performing and it can almost be instructive to watch them. Then you'll know just how good "good" can be.

with the forearm. The fist, after all, is bony and hard, while the forearm softens the blow for both wrestlers while, at the same time, it makes a loud, slapping sound. And even on those rare occasions when the closed fist is employed, the punch is "pulled"— although contact is made, there is very little power behind it.

Jerry Lawler leaps onto an opponent with a punch at the ready—he'll land "flat to flat" and pull that punch for great dramatic effect but little real damage (Source: Norman Kietzer)

Then there are the slaps, as opposed to the closed-fist hits. An open-handed slap makes lots of noise and stings only a little, reddening the recipient's skin just a bit. Little damage is done, but the reverberating sound carries throughout the arena and adds to the illusion of reality, visually as well as audibly.

"Chops," those punches in which the arm comes down in an axe-like move, work in a similar manner. Keep your eye fixed on a wrestler throwing a chop, or a chopping punch, and you may see the edge of his hand being turned at the very last second— turning it into a slap instead of a hard chop.

Only the Ring Is Square

Anyone looking at the enclosure called the "ring" can see that it's not a ring at all, but instead a square area. If the very name of the area where wrestling takes place is not what it's called, then it's no surprise that what happens inside it isn't quite what it seems to be either.

But whatever you call the ring (it's sometimes called the "squared circle"), its ropes, turnbuckles, and aprons offer great opportunities for moves and maneuvers.

First there are the turnbuckles. Those are the four corner posts that hold the ropes and sometimes carry advertising for hotels or beer or some such. The padding on the turnbuckles is very thick and is one of the softest, most flexible places in the ring. It not only cushions blows extremely well, it is as safe a place as a wrestler can find— outside of the dressing room, that is. And it has its uses as a gimmick, too—George "The Animal" Steele often bit the turnbuckles and ripped them apart with his teeth as part of his shtick. However, on those rare occasions when the padding slips and the metal part of the turnbuckle shows through, it can be extremely dangerous.

Then there are the ropes themselves. There was a time when they were meant for the sole purpose of defining the sphere of action, for keeping wrestlers inside the ring. Now, however, they have become part and parcel of most wrestlers' repertoires, either as a platform from which to jump or as a cantilever from which to propel themselves. And wrestlers with derring-do have used ropes for gravity-defying aerial gymnastics worthy of Douglas Fairbanks Sr.— who, not incidentally, used to attend wrestling bouts in the old days to pick up pointers for his stuntman antics in silent movies.

Jimmy "Superfly" Snuka was arguably the best at flying off the ropes. This human cannonball could manage almost three complete rotations of his balled-up body between the time he left the top rope and the time he landed atop his opponent— the guy lying flat on the canvas at the time. But how can men jump from somewhere up in the stratosphere and land on another without crushing him into a virtual pancake? Sorta the same way porcupines make love, that's how—very carefully.

One way to do it is the near miss. This is a jump executed to look like a direct hit when, in fact, the flying wrestler has landed close to—but not on— his opponent. Another is to make the landings flesh-to-flesh—knees, elbows, and other hard, bony parts are kept out of the way and don't make the impact. Instead, the wrestlers go belly-to-belly. In this maneuver, most of the power of the jump is absorbed by the jumping wrestler's hands and knees when they hit the canvas—which also gives a good loud impact.

Bert's Corner

The term "ring" was first used in boxing's bare-knuckle days, when spectators would form a circle around the combatants and throw any fighter who had entered their midst back into the "ring" to continue fighting."

Captain Lou's Corner

The ring's turnbuckles are well padded. When you hit one, or are thrown against one, you're not going to be hurt—unless the padding has slipped. It has other uses as well. George "The Animal" Steele, whom I once managed, would bite the turnbuckles and rip them apart with his teeth as part of his shtick.

But a flying maneuver like this can be injurious to your health if you are not very accurate. If you get it wrong there's a strong chance that someone will be hurt and a great stunt will have gone bad.

Then there's the mat itself. Mats in the old days were toted around from place to place, from smoky beer halls to church basements. Dirty and bacteria-laden, they were dangerous to the wrestlers, especially to their eyes, in those pre-penicillin days. After years of getting his face rubbed into the canvas, Strangler Lewis went partially blind. Things are better today—the mats are clean and antiseptic. And they're used in two types of rings: the boxing ring, which is hard, and the wrestling ring, which usually has springs built under the mat.

Sgt. Slaughter slamming his opponent to the mat for a resounding thud (Source: Norman Kietzer)

The wrestling ring, with its springs, makes the moves and falls look more acrobatic and even more devastating. Seeing a wrestler bounce off the canvas almost doubles the effect of the blow—and provides some of the mock violence our society seemingly enjoys. But when a bout is held in a (springless) boxing ring, the great bounces just don't happen. The moves and falls don't look as impressive, and the chance of injury to the wrestlers is greater.

Slamming and Jamming

There's a whole lot of slamming and jamming going on in a professional wrestling bout. Wrestlers are often abused in ways that would cripple or maim lesser mortals. If all the moves you see in a wrestling bout were real-real, the wrestlers would soon be ground into powder, their bodies unable to bear up under the wear and tear of constantly being driven into the mat.

If you've watched many televised wrestling events, you've seen wrestlers lift other, often heavier, wrestlers over their heads and then, as the laws of gravity would dictate, slam them into the mats. What you may not see is that the wrestler being lifted is assisting in what seems to be his own destruction. He's helping the lifter—either by pushing off the mat or by holding onto his opponent's trunks or some other handy spot to help both of them keep their balance.

And, when slammed to the surface, the trained professional knows how to tuck his chin, roll his shoulders, and prepare his body for as soft a landing as possible. Don't think the fall doesn't sting—but don't buy into all the pain and suffering either. Learning how to fall and how to roll with a punch is essential for successful pro wrestlers, many of whom turn the moves into an artform.

Body Slam

If a 300 pound wrestler, like yours truly, lands on another wrestler's stomach or arm with an extended knee, the effect could be devastating. Still, it's a frequently used move—the key to executing it properly is to manage a near miss like those used for a closed-fist punch.

Pulling Your Leg—and Other Holds

Legs have meant different things to different people. I always thought that without two pretty good ones, you couldn't get to first base. And neither could your sister. In the world of wrestling, legs mean two things: They are good weapons and they are good targets. Of all the action in the ring, legwork is most likely to be the closest to the real McCoy—the most real-real.

When legs are used as weapons, there is room for some magic. For example, a wrestler who does a leg drop has options as to how the contact will be made. After all, the human thigh has a lot of meat surrounding the bone. This makes the thigh a good contact point for the leg drop, the flesh acting as padding that protects both wrestlers. Or a wrestler might choose to make an impressive leg drop without inflicting much damage by landing with the back of his knee on a contact spot. The knee can be bent split seconds before impact to lessen the effect of the blow.

Then there is the knee drop. This uses the extended knee as a striking force. If not executed properly, this move could be very painful, for both the wrestler being attacked and the wrestler making the drop.

The leg also makes an especially inviting—and extremely vulnerable—target. Many submission holds involve an attack on a wrestler's leg or legs. And like I said, most times, action involving leg holds, twists, and the like are real. When you see a wrestler with his leg or legs bent backwards, you can assume it's no act.

And while we're dealing with the lower half of the anatomy, let's not forget kicks. Some wrestlers in modern pro wrestling get their "kicks" out of kicks, although purists and defenders of old-time scientific wrestling believe that they have no place in wrestling.

49

Everyone can surely agree that a full-powered kick can be, as they say, detrimental to one's health. But a truly professional wrestler can control it, ending the move with a near miss, which is all but impossible to see in a live bout, but plain to see in televised matches.

Another way of minimizing the damage done by a powerful-looking kick is to use the inside or arch portion of the boot, not the toe of the foot. This reduces the risk and the inevitable pain. Kicking with the inside of the foot takes the power out of the kick at the last second (remember the flat to flat rule). It looks real because it *is* real—except the sound of the impact is exaggerated.

Experienced wrestlers know where to accurately place their kicks to avoid real damage to the opponent. For example, kicking someone in the kneecap could easily result in a painful and crippling career-ending injury. But kicking the knee from the side won't do much damage when the kicker and his opponent are working together. There's plenty of "give" in a kick to the side of the knee, which is not the case with a frontal attack on the knee. And remember, wrestlers work together to prevent career-ending injuries. After all, they're in the same profession—the same union, so to speak.

Finally, well-placed kicks are always to fleshy parts of the body, like the thigh, which is well padded. Kicks to other parts of the anatomy vary in safety: Properly placed kicks to the gut, shoulder, or biceps are acceptable—and they're not likely to hurt too much.

Ric Flair versus Ricky Steamboat: athleticism and grace in the ring. (Source: Norman Kietzer)

As long as the wrestlers are well-trained, experienced, and working in tandem, there is no reason for the one being kicked to "kick." However, one missed flying kick to the throat could spell disaster to the wrestler on the receiving end.

The Best Stuntmen in Modern Wrestling History

Terry Funk: Still wrestling at almost 50, he still does what's called a "Moonsault"— a backward somersault off the top turnbuckle for the pinfall. Youngsters today know him as "Chainsaw Charlie."

Ray Misterio Jr.: A *mascarada*—a masked wrestler from Mexico—he invents new acrobatic maneuvers every match and often appears to defy gravity.

Shawn "The Heartbreak Kid" Michaels: His athleticism is first class: In big matches—cage matches, ladder matches, and so on—he always delivers.

Superfly Jimmy Snuka: The father of modern wrestling in many ways. He dived off things (ropes, turnbuckles, and so on) in Madison Square Garden in the 1970s and upped the athleticism ante for everybody.

Rowdy Roddy Piper and Ric Flair: Neither are outrageously athletic nor acrobatic, but both, have a tremendous understanding of the psychology of a match and perform with style and impeccable timing.

Gimmicks and Fakery

Rope-walking (or -dancing) is not the only trick of the wrestling trade. There are literally bags full of gimmicks and misdirections—all of these are part of wrestling magic.

Let me tell you about the first time I became aware of gimmickry in wrestling—and it wasn't in a "real" wrestling bout. Back in 1952 as a young Captain Lou, I had just started out in wrestling. Seems that one of Jackie Gleason's advisors had called Vince McMahon Sr. in search of four wrestlers to put on a skit for "The Great One's" variety show (this even predated the *Honeymooners*).

Vince Sr. called me up to the old WWF office and said "The pay is $750" (that was for all four of us—after the office took a third of the fee there was $500 for us to divvy up). Vince laid out the plot: We were going to wrestle Jackie Gleason—or, more exactly, Jackie's character, Reginald van Gleason. And so the four of us—me, Tony Altimore, Skull Murphy, and Arnold Skaaland—showed up at the Ed Sullivan Theater in Manhattan to do the skit. And all Gleason told us was, "Gentlemen, if I get hurt, the skit's off." So we made up our minds then and there to make sure nothing happened to him.

The skit called for Skull and me to face Arnold and Jackie, with Tony acting as the referee. After the introductions, which had me as "The Monk" and Jackie as "The legendary wrestler, Reginald van Gleason the Third," Gleason came onstage in a Turkish sedan chair carried by four beautiful girls and surrounded by midgets, with him waving to his fans like a potentate.

After the sedan chair had been put down ringside by his four carriers, Gleason got off and stood there for a second, clothed in a leopard loincloth. Truth to tell, although he was dressed like Tarzan, he looked more like Jane to me.

Now the bout started. Gleason pulls out a can opener that he had stashed in his trunks and uses it to unscrew the turnbuckle—out of which he pulls a bottle of vodka. He takes a swig, then walks over and hits me. Following the script, I fly out of the ring. He then takes a shot at my partner, who also flies out of the ring. He looks at his partner, Arnold, who goes over to shake hands with him for a job well done. BOOM! He hits Arnold too, sending *him* flying out of the ring. And when I say we flew, I mean it: We were all attached to harnesses that had us flying around like Peter Pan.

Hidden Gimmicks

An exhaustive list of gimmicks used in wrestling is impossible. Here's just a sample of the kinds of things you'll see appearing in the ring:

Wrestler	Gimmick
Terry Funk	Branding Iron (The Double Cross)
New Jack	Fork
Ivan Koloff	Big chain
Jerry Lawler	Knuckle chain
Ric Flair (when a baddie)	Brass Knux
Hacksaw Jim Duggan	2×4
Axl Rotten	Barbed-wire covered baseball bat
Honky Tonk Man	Guitar
Sandman	Caning stick (a Hong Kong punishment tool)
The Sheik	Fire Ball
The Great Muta	Green mist (blown from the mouth)
Lex Luger	Metal plate surgically inserted in forearm
Hans Schmidt	Riding crop
Sting	Baseball bat
Dusty Rhodes	Cowbell
Colonel Mustafa	Iraqi flag
Big Boss Man	Night Stick

Managers	Gimmick
Jim Cornette	Tennis racket
Jimmy Hart	Megaphone
Freddie Blassie	Cane
Johnny Polo	Polo mallet
Paul E. Dangerously	Cell phone

And these days, *everybody* uses chairs and crashes through tables.

Now I don't mean to say that in regular wrestling bouts we use harnesses, but we've used just about everything else, especially hidden gimmicks. In the four decades I've been in wrestling, I've seen hundreds of them.

Gimmicks Galore

Dr. X used to hide a piece of metal in his mask to make his head butts all the more effective. Harry Finkelstein brought a piece of soap into the ring for rubbing into his opponent's eyes. Chief Chewchki secreted sheets of sandpaper studded with carpet tacks in his trunks, and Count Dracula carried a hidden bottle labeled chloroform. Killer Tim Brooks wore heavy objects in his elbow pad, and Professor Toru Tanaka snuck salt into the ring. Fidel Castillo brought in fish hooks, and Mario Galento managed to sneak rolls of pennies past the referee's inspection. The list can go on forever—it's truly amazing how much storage space you can find in a pair of wrestling trunks.

And sometimes the gimmicks are more obvious. Johnny Kace and Nicoli Volkoff would enter the ring with a large, leather-padded log to use on their opponents. Brother Johnathan brought in a large snake. I personally favored using a 2×4 to inflict punishment on my opponents. Each of these gimmicks brought the fans into the act, inciting them to shout to the referee where the foreign object was hidden. Of course, if I was ever caught, I would just tell the ref that it wasn't a "foreign" object at all, but bought right here in the good ol' U.S. of A. And the gimmicks never, ever maimed or crippled an opponent. That was part of the magic!

Gimmicks Gone Wrong

Sometimes, however, things could go wrong. Like the time Mario Galento was wrestling Billy Hines. Galento had grabbed Hines in a headlock and pulled his roll of pennies out of their hiding place to use in the mugging. The penny roll cut Hines above the eye, requiring at least 15 stitches to close the bloody wound.

Speaking of blood—over the years many fans have asked if we use blood capsules, like you see in movies. Maybe it used to be—in the old days there was even a practice called *blading*—a small sliver of a razor would be hidden in the wrestler's trunks or bandages and used to slice open his forehead. But while today's wrestling is not entirely innocent of the charge of bloodletting, it is not—I repeat *NOT*—a blood sport. Not anymore, at any rate—especially in these days of diseases that can be transmitted through blood. Not like boxing.

Fighting Words

Blading means using a piece of razor to open a cut and get the blood flowing—wrestlers often did this to themselves during a match in the early days of wrestling. The usual place to cut was the forehead, since it leaves almost no scar and the blood flows freely.

Blading is a thing of the past, so when blood flows in the ring, it's the real deal (Source: Norman Kietzer)

Wrestling got its bloody reputation on the basis of a single well-publicized match fought back in the 1970s: the bout between Fred Blassie and Rikidozan in Japan. During the course of the match, Rikidozan ran into the ropes and was cut—badly. Blassie, always on the lookout for a gimmick, warmed to the scent of blood and made like Count Dracula, making as if he was sucking Rikidozan dry. This made Blassie a sensation in Japan. He pretended to sharpen his teeth into pointed fangs. He'd walk down the streets of Tokyo and suddenly turn around to the mobs following him to give them a fearsome grimace, exposing his fangs. It is said that three or four of those frightened fans following him suffered heart attacks on the spot.

The attack on Rikidozan in the ring, and the heart attacks suffered by his Japanese fans not only furthered Blassie's reputation as a bloodsucker, it also began giving wrestling a bloody reputation. All of a sudden wrestling magazines were blaring headlines like "Where there's Blood there's Blassie," "Bloodbath of the Year," "Bloody War," "A Saga Written in Blood," and so on.

But that was two decades ago. Today wrestling has so many other things going for it, it doesn't need to excite the bloodlust of its fans to prove that the action is spontaneous. You want to see blood today, go to a hockey game.

The Sounds of Pain

Wrestlers, their managers, and especially promoters are well aware of the importance that sound effects have in a match. Wrestling has a language all its own, one that dates back to ancient times, when the participants would grunt, yell, or scream as they made their moves or took their hits.

I'm not talking here about the verbal abuse heaped on villains and nonfavorites by the fans. I'm talking about the sounds made by the wrestlers to "hype" or excite the audience. The more a hit sounds like it hurts, the more the fans believe it *must* have hurt. Since wrestling is entertainment, sound effects enhance its entertainment value. So wrestlers have learned to make the sound effects as much a part of the performance as the holds and gimmicks themselves.

Remember the ring: The springs underneath create a hollow cavity, so that when big men bounce off the mat, the sound of impact reverberates throughout the auditorium. It's especially effective when the wide back of a big wrestler hits the mat: You get the visual effect of the bounce, and the audio effect of the echoing BOOM of impact.

Slapping, too, generates lots of noise. And then there are things like the flat, metal folding chairs. The sound of one of those hitting the flat of an opponent's back is impressive.

Captain Lou's Corner

All of my bleeding has come from steel cage matches, where almost every time you ran your face into the fence surrounding the ring, you'd cut yourself on it's sharp edges. I mean, anyone who's seen my face knows that I'm no raving beauty—but I'm not likely to purposely cut my face with a razor or anything else and become even less of a beauty.

Wrestle Mania

Gestures are another way the wrestler communicates with the audience. Nothing subtle, mind you—the wrestlers are playing to the whole crowd, not just the front rows. One of the best at using gesture is Hulk Hogan: He can command the entire arena with a *single* movement. Hogan nudges the audience with his gestures, connecting with the crowd with an extended arm, a pumped fist, or a toss of his golden mane, until the noise of the fans reaches a decibel level that could bring down the Walls of Jericho. Other virtuosos of gesture are Shawn Michaels and The Undertaker.

Grunting is also part and parcel of every wrestler's repertoire. It not only adds to the overall effect of the impact, it underscores it for the audience. And the screaming and hollering of mock pain adds to the overall effect of theater.

Fighting Words

A **cauliflower ear** is a condition common to wrestlers and boxers—anyone who takes a lot of hits to the ear. When the ear has been damaged enough to bleed internally it calcifies, like bone. Yukon Eric's ear was pretty much *all* cauliflower by the time he wrestled Kowalski.

Injuries and Accidents

No matter how choreographed, no matter how practiced, sometimes things go wrong. And when they do, when a near miss becomes a non-miss, when a safe fall falls short, you get injuries—and sometimes death.

I have had almost every bone in my body broken, and most wrestlers can't get through a career without a serious injury. The most famous one happened in Montreal during the early 1950s, when Walter "Killer" Kowalski took on Yukon Eric. On a missed attempt at a knee drop near Yukon Eric's head, Killer caught and knocked off Eric's *cauliflower ear!*

Stone Cold Steve Austin's Epic Injury

One of the scariest injuries of recent times happened in front of millions of fans on pay-per-view. It was a championship match between Stone Cold Steve Austin and Owen Hart, one which Austin was scripted to win—but not before Hart planted Austin smack-dab on his head, causing Austin to fall heavily and hurt his neck. Austin lay there, unable to feel anything from the neck down, and Hart, sensing Austin's inability to move, had to think fast. Handling the unmoving Austin ever so gingerly, Hart began maneuvering, as much to stall for time as to try to set up a satisfactory ending to the match.

Finally, after what seemed an eternity, Hart managed to wrestle the almost inert Austin so that he was actually on top. The ref quickly counted Hart out and a couple of WWF officials jumped into the ring to help Austin to his feet, drape the intercontinental belt across his shoulder, and lift his limp arm in victory. Austin was then taken to a hospital, still complaining that he couldn't feel anything.

In the end, the diagnosis was not as frightening as it could have been—the damage was a pinched nerve (called a "stinger"). It was serious enough, however, for the doctors to tell him to take it easy in the ring from then on.

More recently, Mickey Foley (also known as Cactus Jack, Mankind, and Dude Love) lost part of his right ear when, during a match in Germany a few years back, his head got caught between the ropes. So make no mistake about it: Not all you see is just smoke and mirrors. Some of it, unfortunately, is all too real.

The Least You Need to Know

➤ Closed-fist punches are difficult to stage, so forearms are often used instead.

➤ The bounce of wrestlers in the ring is due, in part, to springs under the canvas.

➤ Leg holds are usually the most realistic moves in wrestling.

➤ Sound effects are extremely important, because they involve the fan and bring excitement to a professional wrestling match.

➤ Wrestlers learn to take hits and falls similar to how movie stuntmen work.

➤ No matter how practiced and rehearsed a match, the chance of injury is still great.

Chapter 5

Rules?! What Rules?

In This Chapter

➤ The concept of rules

➤ Referee rules

➤ Group rules

➤ On the spot rules

There's the Golden Rule, rules of thumb, and wrestling rules. And all three are honored more in the breach than in the observance. So, as you can probably guess, this chapter on the rules of pro wrestling is going to be a short one.

Textbook rules for sports are supposed to be the very mortar that holds a contest together, controls its action, and determines the winner and loser. Wrestling's rules, however, are like quicksand—they shift constantly to satisfy the demands of the moment. The plain truth of the matter is that few of the rules in wrestling today are observed. But there are still a few—a very few, and on these pages you'll learn what they are.

Rules Are Made to Be Broken

In fact, the extremes of the moment seem to call for their own rules. Take the case of George Zaharias, for example. George was a member of the infamous Zaharias Brothers, major wrestlers of the 1930s. When asked about his conversion from a *babyface* to a *villain*, George explained it this way: "One night in Memphis in 1930, I said to this promoter, 'Look at my eyes, they're all cut. Nobody wrestles by the rules.' And this old promoter told me, 'Hit him first!' So I became a villain and saw to it that there were always fireworks when I wrestled."

Back in the days when there was a clear distinction between babyfaces and baddies, only the bad guys would be the rule breakers. Now, however, the line between good guys and bad guys has become increasingly blurred. It seems that anybody worthy of a jockstrap could give less than two snaps of their fingers about the rules.

Fighting Words

Babyface (or, often, just *face*)—a good-guy wrestler who fans usually cheer for. *Villain*—the bad-guy wrestler who tries to bring down the face in a match.

Most fans have a strong belief in right and wrong and in the idea that rules are rules. But in a society that has adopted an attitude that is more and more "in your face" and "stick it in your ear," the fans will support their heroes even if they test the elasticity of the rules and revert to a code that concerns itself more with convenience than with honor.

But there were rules for wrestling, once upon a time, just as there are for any other sport. The New York State Athletic Commission's first set of rules covering wrestling read, in part, as follows:

"Matches to be decided by falls, two out of three or three out of five, as may be agreed upon in making the match. All matches shall be limited in time to two hours. Should there be only one fall in the two hours, the winner of that fall will be declared the winner of the contest....

"The referee will be instructed by the Commission to disqualify any wrestler who indulges in the following unfair and foul methods: striking, scratching, gouging, any display of bad temper, strangle-holds, so-called head-holds, toe-locks, and scissors holds, which are held specially for the purpose of punishing an opponent, are declared to be foul methods and, if indulged in, the offender will be at once disqualified and the match given to the opponent. He will further be punished by having his license revoked."

It all sounds so quaint, doesn't it?

Once wrestling was categorized as an entertainment rather than a sport, the control of the state athletic commissions was gone, but even as late as 1954, the New York State Athletic Commission was still attempting to impose strict rules. It was fighting a losing battle, however, and today there is no controlling body outside the federations themselves to impose or enforce rules in pro wrestling.

Ways to Win a Match

Of course, there have to be *some* rules—after all, without any there'd be no way of telling when a match was over. There are five traditional ways to win a wrestling bout, according to the rules. Sometimes they're honored, sometimes not:

1. *The Pinfall:* Pin your opponent's shoulders to the mat for a three count.

2. *Submission:* Similar to making an opponent say "uncle"—making him (or her) "tap out." Once a wrestler has submitted, he is supposed to be released from the hold that brought him down—but that doesn't always happen. Many's the time you'll find other wrestlers breaking into the ring to free their trapped colleagues. And referees are supposed to break the hold when one wrestler has submitted—but most referees are no match for the big bruisers in the ring, so the submission hold is often held long after the wrestler has cried "uncle."

3. *Disqualification:* When an opponent breaks the rules, (or stipulations of the match—whatever they may be at the time) or his allies interfere with the match in progress, the offending wrestler is disqualified. Punching with a closed fist is supposed to be grounds for disqualification, but no one's been DQ'd for it since time immemorial. The same is true about foreign objects—they're not allowed in the ring, but they turn up all the time.

Body Slam

Submission rules are needed to keep wrestlers from being injured too badly. Some holds, like the sleeper holds, can do a great deal of damage if applied and held for too long. A wrestler, therefore, must be given the option of extricating himself from a dangerous hold by way of submission.

4. *Count Out:* When a wrestler has been out of the ring for 20 seconds while his opponent waits in a neutral corner; or if the fallen wrestler does not make it back into the ring in the allotted time, the bout is awarded to the wrestler in the corner. But should that wrestler leave the neutral corner the count begins again from the start (unlike in boxing, where the count is just suspended until the boxer returns to his corner). You'd be surprised at the number of wrestlers who do not know, or ignore, this rule—so that the referee never gets to 20.

5. *Render your opponent unable to continue:* The sleeper hold, for example, can earn a victory for the wrestler applying it, even if his opponent never submits and is never pinned.

The Ring-Rope Rule

If a wrestler has a hold on his opponent and the opponent manages to get part of his body under—or on—the ring ropes, the hold must be broken before the count of ten. This rule also applies for illegal holds, like choke holds.

But there are ways around this. If the hold is broken and then reapplied, the count starts all over again—a loophole in the rules that allows a villain to choke his opponent for somewhat more than the union scale—provided that he never chokes his opponent for more than ten consecutive seconds (that is, in a single application of the hold).

The ring-rope rule has been exploited by smart wrestlers—they grab the ring ropes when in trouble. And if they can't do that, they will lay an ankle on the ropes, which is all that's required for the referee to break the hold. This is one of the few rules that is religiously observed.

True veterans of the wrestling wars have been known to use the ring ropes for leverage to help them attain a pin, since they know that the referee will be paying close attention to their opponent's shoulders and not take notice of the infraction.

Don't Touch That Man in the Middle

Outside of a bank guard in Alaska, who has to distinguish between regular customers wearing ski masks and the bank robbers wearing the same thing, the wrestling referee has one of the most arduous jobs in the world. Not only must he be fast enough to get out of the way of projectiles weighing upwards of 300 pounds flying around the ring at warp speed, he must also stay out of their way when they rumble in his direction. And he's got to avoid getting rolled upon when the two behemoths are on the mat and he's down there beside them trying to tick away three seconds by pounding the canvas to signify a fall.

Bert's Corner

One of the earliest rules in wrestling was "Thou Shalt Not Touch the Referee." One wrestler who did was Everett Marshall, who was suspended by the Pennsylvania State Athletic Commission in 1934 after attacking referee Ben Paul in a December match against Jim Londos.

The wrestlers each know, or should know, what the other is going to do, and where each will wind up after every move—the referee often does not. And a referee who is not fleet of foot, or unable to intuit what's going to happen next is in real danger of getting severely injured.

Many's the time we've witnessed something like what happened during *Wrestlemania XIV*. If you were watching, you saw Shawn Michaels, "The Heartbreak Kid," get a figure-four on Stone Cold Steve Austin. Once Austin broke that hold, Michaels followed up with a sleeper hold. Meanwhile, referee Mike Kiona was driven into a corner—"bumped," if you will. But "ref bumps" seem to happen all the time.

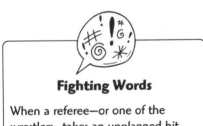

Fighting Words

When a referee—or one of the wrestlers—takes an unplanned hit, that's a **bump**. While most of the action in the ring is choreographed, sometimes accidents do happen.

Michaels now made as if he was going to give his famous "foot to the chin" kick—but he missed his move and Austin stunned him instead.

With the ref out of the action, guest referee Mike Tyson had to step into the ring. He was *supposed* to be in league with Michaels, but he counted his purported cohort out with the obligatory 1-2-3. Austin took the

WWF heavyweight title that night, and when Michaels confronted Tyson for his duplicity, he got clocked for his efforts with a well-aimed punch. A referee is also charged with keeping control of the riot that is going on all around him. But even armed with a rulebook—and even when he's even playing a role in the storyline of the bout—the man in the bow tie is often overmatched when faced with a pair of huge wrestlers who are determined to make mincemeat of the rules. But one thing is for real-real—they can't make mincemeat of the referee. Any wrestler who does so, does so at his peril: The penalty for such shenanigans is usually a stiff fine and a suspension, especially in those states where there is still a state-run athletic commission overseeing the bouts. You just don't mess with the ref.

Captain Lou's Corner

Guest referees are used sometimes, like when Vince McMahon was in a recent bout between Stone Cold Steve Austin and Dude Love. Most of the time the wrestlers respect the referees enough not to hurt them, at least on purpose. But such is often not the case when "Vinny Mac" is acting as guest referee.

Referees have to stay close to call violations, so if the action gets out of hand, they're in harm's way. (Source: Norman Kietzer)

Tag-Team Rules

It's double your pleasure, double your fun—and double trouble for the referee when tag teams get together on the card. The rules themselves are simple: Two wrestlers go up against two others, but *only* two wrestlers (one for each side, of course) are supposed to be in the ring at any one time. The match starts with one man—called the *legal* man—from each team in the ring. In order for a wrestler to get his partner into the act, the legal man must touch, or *tag* his partner's hand: thus the name, *tag team*. Once the tag has been made, the new man becomes the "legal" man, and the first wrestler—the one who made the tag—has ten seconds to vacate the premises.

Those are the rules. In most tag-team matches, however, time is often too short for a course in etiquette, and the wrestlers seem to have misplaced the rule book. We've seen wrestlers play the tag-team hokey-pokey—you know, "you put your left foot in, you pull your left foot out"— to get closer to the tag. We've seen double-teaming during the 10-second changeover interval. And we've even seen teammates dress alike so the referee, having trouble figuring out which wrestler is which, illegally scores pinfalls without realizing it.

As is true of most wrestling rules, tag-team rules were obeyed far more often in the past than they are today. Now it's quite common to have all four wrestlers surge into the ring at once, while the referee is reduced to clinging to the back of one of them like a shell on a turtle, futilely trying to restore order.

Refs still make at least some attempt to enforce tag-team rules. But their problems are compounded because, while they're trying to keep track of four wrestlers, they're also trying to deal with the wrestlers' managers or valets. Just about everybody usually ends up attempting to insinuate themselves into the fray—either by actively joining in the melee or by causing distractions so their wrestler can gain the upper hand. As a manager I have resorted to jumping up and down, shouting, and screaming. I've done just about anything I could think of to exhort my wrestlers and distract the referee or the opposing team. I've even taken to shouting "three…three…" when the referee seems to forget how to count that high before one of the opposing team jumps up off the canvas. And manager Freddie Blassie will do anything to stave off the inevitable, legal or not. He'll even use his cane to yank one of the opposing tag-team member's legs if it looks like he's going to manage to get to one of Freddie's wrestlers.

Bobby Heenan, The Grand Wizard, and Mr. Fuji, as well as other managers of *my* day—not to mention today's current crop of managers like Jimmy Hart, Sensational Sherri, and Ted DiBiase—we all have a job to do. That's to ensure that our wrestler wins—by hook or by crook.

Bert's Corner

It's bad enough that refs have to worry about all four of the tag-team wrestlers ending up in the ring at once. Even worse when the managers and valets get into the act, too. But when visiting wrestlers—or other wrestlers appearing later on the bill—join in the fun, well…you might say things can get a little out of hand.

Mr. Fuji did it by throwing salt, Jimmy Hart does it with a megaphone. And none of us has ever been above jumping into the ring to lend vital assistance to our fallen charges if the moment was right.

So. Rules for tag-team matches? As they say in New York—fuhgeddaboudit!

By the Seat of Their Trunks

Some rules are written in stone. Others are made up to suit the moment. Those on-the-spot rules can vary greatly, and are known as "stipulations." If both wrestlers agree ahead of time to wrestle under certain conditions that differ from the usual conventions, those conditions—or stipulations—become the rules. For example, a "Falls Count Anywhere" match obviously breaks the rule that the wrestling is supposed to happen only in the ring. In such a match, the action can spill out onto the arena floor. It can be carried into the crowd and can even spread to the concession stand. Or a match can have a weapons stipulation, as in a Brass Knux Match which allows—actually, requires—that the wrestlers use brass knuckles. And there are Cage Matches, fought in an enclosed ring, where the rules are very different from a regular ring match.

Dress Code? What Dress Code?

It has been said that men wear clothes for warmth, women for spite, and children 'cause they have to. But in wrestling, none of this counts. Wrestlers can wear trunks, tights, blue jeans—even stretch pants. Me, I always dressed as if the Goodwill box just threw up on me. And most of the women wrestlers wear something they just threw on and damned near missed!

If there's anything like a dress code restriction, it has to do with the show itself. For instance, if the wrestler is dressed in full cowboy regalia—with hat, boots, the whole magilla—that's alright. But if there are heels on those boots, they're there for one reason only—to smash the opponent's face in. That is definitely *not* alright. Unless, of course, the heels are there as a gimmick. Other than that, anything goes. After all, this is *wrestling!*

The Least You Need to Know

➤ What rules there are in wrestling are made to be broken.

➤ Foreign objects aren't allowed in the ring—unless stipulated before the bout.

➤ The referee has one of the hardest jobs in the world.

➤ Tag-team partners are supposed to tag each other before entering the ring.

Part 2

The Founding Fathers: Wrestling's Colorful History

What makes fans love to watch two people grapple in the squared ring? Maybe more interesting, why would anyone want to get beaten up, held under a sweaty armpit, or hit over the head with a metal chair?

Crazy as it might seem, professional wrestling is extremely popular with both fans and wrestlers alike. Wrestling is a multi-million dollar industry with hundreds of thousands of fans.

How did basic wrestling grow into professional wrestling? The vision of a few founding fathers started the movement. As momentum grew, pro wrestling took on more power than almost anyone could imagine. In this part of the book, we introduce you to the legends of the ring.

Bert Sugar

Chapter 6

Wrestling's Warriors Extraordinaire

In This Chapter

➤ Gotch and Hackenschmidt

➤ The Strangler—greatest wrestler of all time

➤ Lou Thesz claims the crown

➤ How Jim Londos got his name

➤ The Glorious Gorgeous George

Only a few graybeards who have not collapsed under the weight of their collective memories may remember the Founding Fathers of wrestling, but these are the colossi who bestrode the ranks of wrestling in times past. Their legends date all the way back to the early days, and so they are part and parcel of professional wrestling's early glory days. In this chapter you'll learn about some of the titans who were truly the legends of the ring.

The Peerless One

Frank Gotch's thumbnail bio in *Who's Who in American Sports* (National Biographical Society, 1938) reads: "b. April 27, 1878, Humboldt, Iowa; d. ?. At 5'11" and 210 pounds, Gotch was an exceptionally strong, clever wrestler. He was one of the early catch-as-catch-can wrestlers, after Tom Jenkins had popularized the style. He won the title from Jenkins in 1905, and except for one brief period held it until his retirement in 1913, winning 154 of 160 official matches. He lost the title in 1906 to Freddie Beall when, after Gotch was knocked out by banging his head against a ring post, Beall pinned him, but he beat Beall easily in a rematch."

What this entry doesn't say about the man called The Peerless One is that Gotch was to professional wrestling what John L. Sullivan was to boxing: its first universally recognized major attraction, and the founding member of the long line of professional wrestling champions that extends to this day.

Early Career

From the time of his debut in Humboldt against Marshall Green, in 1899, until his retirement almost 14 years later in 1913, Gotch was professional wrestling's most popular attraction. He first won the championship in Bellingham, Washington, in 1904, beating Tom Jenkins to win the heavyweight title, then lost it back to Jenkins the following year in Madison Square Garden. He lost to Jenkins again two months later at the Garden. The first fall of that match went to Jenkins in an hour and 27 minutes; the second went to Gotch in 36 minutes; and the third and deciding fall went to Jenkins again, this time in just 11 minutes.

Gotch would finally win back the title in 1906, only to lose it later in the year when challenger Fred Beall won the third and deciding fall by throwing Gotch out of the ring, rendering Gotch *hors de combat* when he struck his head on the cement floor. But 16 days later, Gotch would reverse that loss in two one-sided falls to become the American heavyweight champion for the third time.

World Class

But Gotch earned everlasting fame in his two matches against George "The Russian Lion" Hackenschmidt, the European champion. Their first match, to decide the world's heavyweight championship, was three years in the making—it finally took place on April 3, 1908, at Chicago's Dexter Park Pavilion.

The bout was highly controversial. *The New York Times* reported that Gotch "side-stepped, roughed his man's features with his knuckles, butted him under the chin, and generally worsted Hackenschmidt until the foreigner was at a loss how to proceed." Hackenschmidt continually complained to the referee about such infractions, but the ref turned the proverbial deaf ear to his plaints. Finally, after two hours and three minutes, The Russian Lion threw up his hands in resignation and quit the match. The referee promptly awarded the match, and the championship, to Gotch.

Hackenschmidt would later charge that Gotch "dug his nails into my face, tried to pull my ear off, and poked his thumb into my eye." Moreover, the Russian claimed that Gotch's body was "literally soaked in oil," making the American all but impossible to grasp.

In Your Face

In his on-line book *Hooker*, wrestling great Lou Thesz wrote, "The picture that emerged of Gotch was that of a man who succeeded primarily because he was, for lack of a kinder description, a dirty wrestler. Gotch would gouge, pull hair, and even break a bone to get an advantage in a contest, and he was always careful to have the referee in his pocket too, if you follow my meaning."

Gotch was famous for his toe hold, demonstrated here (Source: Norman Kietzer)

The controversy that arose after the match dictated a return bout, which took another three years to arrange. This time, determined to get what Thesz has described as "an illegal edge," Gotch employed Ad Santel, a known hooker—someone willing to hurt, even cripple, an opponent—to insinuate himself into Hackenschmidt's training camp as a training partner, where he would purposely injure The Russian Lion. The hooker, who was paid $5,000 for the mugging, did so—all but ruining Hackenschmidt's knee.

Now Hackenschmidt, unable to participate fully in the big return match, pleaded with the promoters to postpone it. But the promoters, who had spent most, if not all, of the advance money (some $87,000 in Taft dollars), declined and the bout went on as scheduled, in front of an estimated 35,000 at Chicago's spanking-new Comiskey Park. The bout itself was anticlimactic, with Gotch prevailing over the injured Hackenschmidt in two straight—and quick—falls.

The press, having caught wind of Gotch's dirty deed, became disillusioned with the sport of wrestling, which up to that time had been front-page sports news. Now, wrestling coverage found itself buried under the shipping notices in the back of most newspapers. This was the beginning of the end for wrestling's first glory years—a tailspin hastened by Gotch's retirement the following year to tour with the Sells-Floto Circus as a wrestling "act."

Gotch injured his leg in an exhibition match at a Sells-Floto performance in Kenosha, Wisconsin, in 1916, and would never wrestle again. Within a year he was dead—according to Thesz, of either syphilis or uremic poisoning.

Captain Lou's Corner

All claimants to world championship honors trace their lineage back to Frank Gotch, the first universally recognized catch-as-catch-can champion who made his mark in the first decade of the 20th century.

The Strangler

The greatest name in the long and storied history of professional wrestling wasn't even the real name of the man who carried it. Ed "Strangler" Lewis, who would replace Gotch in the affections of professional wrestling fans, performed epic feats for over three decades and, in the process, entered his professional name in the pages of wrestling as its greatest wrestler of all time. His record, in a time when record keeping was only a sometime thing, was estimated at over 6,000 bouts with only 33 losses.

Born Robert Friedrich in Madison, Wisconsin, in 1890, young Friedrich adopted the name Ed Lewis at the age of 14 to keep his parents from discovering his activities. The "Strangler" nickname would come later, as much a tribute to his deadly use of the headlock as to the original holder of the name, Evan "Strangler" Lewis, who had wrestled back in the 1880s.

Young Friedrich-Lewis was working his way through college in Lexington, Kentucky as the school's athletic director when he was discovered by manager Billy Sandow. At that time he looked nothing like a wrestler—he weighed all of 175 pounds and had what might delicately be called a spavined back. But he showed potential, having already met such outstanding wrestlers as Charley Cutler, Fred Beall, and Americus, so Sandow took him under his wing.

The Birth of the Strangler's Trademark Hold

Sandow and Lewis studied and practiced day after day, perfecting the hold that would become Lewis's signature—the headlock. Finally, after months of intensive training, Sandow decided that his charge was ready for competition. He entered Lewis in the International Wrestling Tournament, held at the Metropolitan Opera House in New York. The tournament, a three-month competition (November 1915 through January 1916) featured more than 50 of the world's best wrestlers, with big-name wrestlers such as Alex Aberg, Waldek Zbyszko, Charles Cutler, and B. F. Roller. In the end, it was Lewis and his headlock who was to emerge victorious.

Lewis's headlock had by now become so famous—and so deadly—that it was all but impossible to get wrestlers to train with him. And so, with no human targets willing to accept his embrace, Sandow devised a substitute—a wooden dummy with several sets of springs inside to provide high resistance. Lewis was to practice with that dummy day in and day out, squeezing the two halves together until he had all but squeezed the sawdust out of it—perfecting the deadly hold in the process.

In addition to his unbeatable, unbreakable headlock, Lewis also possessed enormous defensive skills. With the extra weight he'd gained under Sandow's watchful eye, Lewis looked like a dancing bear as he maneuvered around the ring.

Championship Material

This defensive maneuvering nearly derailed Lewis's career before it really got off the ground. Challenging heavyweight champion Joe Stecher in a bout in Omaha in 1916,

Lewis put on his offensive nonoffensive tactics for the entirety of the bout. The fans, disgruntled with Lewis and frustrated with his refusal to go on the offense, showed their displeasure by constant jeering, even going so far as to shower the ring with seat cushions. Finally, after five hours, the bout was declared a draw. Four years later, Lewis beat Stecher in a bout lasting one hour and 41 minutes.

In all, Lewis would win and lose—and win back—the heavyweight title five times over the next 12 years, as if the championship belt was on a long rubber band that he held in his hands. He lost it to Stanislaus Zybszko in 1922 only to win it back again later that year. He lost it again to Wayne "Big" Munn in 1925, after which the belt circulated among Munn, Zbyszko, and Stecher—only to come back to Lewis when he beat Stecher in 1928. He lost it again to Jumping Joe Savoldi in 1929, then beat the man who beat Savoldi—Ed Don George—in 1931. He lost it after that to Henri DeGlane in 1931, but in 1932 he got it back by beating then title-holder Dick Shikat.

With Lewis laying waste to the entire wrestling landscape, wrestling had come to a standstill. The fans were more than bored with Lewis, who was winning bout after bout with startling frequency and alarming monotony. But Lewis and Sandow knew that wrestling was, bottom line, a business, and that although owning the heavyweight title was like owning the keys to the bank, the monotony of Lewis always winning meant that the bank was rapidly running dry of funds. Something had to be done—the belt was going to have to be put on loan.

In the fall of 1924, Sandow attended a University of Nebraska football game and came away with the idea that he could make a wrestling attraction out of one of the Cornhuskers' stars, a 6'6" giant of a player named Wayne "Big" Munn. Persuading Munn to try his hand—and the rest of his anatomy—at wrestling, Sandow took him under his wing just as he had done for Lewis years before—training him and getting him matches with wrestlers he could control.

Munn captivated sports fans throughout the Midwest and, on January 8, 1925, captured the heavyweight title by "beating" Strangler Lewis. It was pure performance, and the first time that a performer—a nonwrestler—would wear the champion belt. The match with Munn was significant, primarily because it heralded the beginning of wrestling as performance art rather than as a sport.

Lewis's last competitive match was against Lee Wycoff at Madison Square Garden in 1938, but throughout this Indian summer of his career he was all but invincible. Those few times he lost, he lost for the sake of the show. And he was rewarded handsomely: Over his long career he earned an estimated $4 million. He was, simply stated, the greatest there ever was.

Bert's Corner

Joe Stecher, U.S. titleholder during the 1920s, looked like a tuberculosis patient from the waist up. But from the waist down he was one of the most powerful wrestlers ever. Stecher was famous for his training regimen, which consisted of placing sacks of grain between his knees and popping them by applying leg pressure.

Wrestle Mania

Strangler Lewis suffered from a malady common among early wrestlers—trachoma, a contagious viral disease of the inner membrane of the eye that causes inflammation and can lead to blindness. In those days before penicillin, the treatment was a stone that was scraped against the surface of the eye. Trachoma was caused by tiny organisms that collected on the dirty canvases, then common in wrestling, especially in smaller towns. It spread from wrestler to wrestler on towels or even through contact with sweat. Lewis eventually went blind from his untreated trachoma. Others who suffered with the disease included Lou Thesz and Gus Sonnenberg.

On retiring, Lewis set up a training camp in New Jersey and crowds would come to watch him train at $1.00 a head. A lot of the town residents would challenge him, feeling that if they beat—or even looked good—against the World's Champion they'd gain instant immortality. Lewis declined each and every offer, saying: "You want to wrestle me? Before you do, there's a little guy over there. Beat him and you can wrestle me."

That little guy was Frank Jensen, one of the great "shooters" of his day. Jensen would, of course, proceed to hand the challenger his head on a silver platter, leaving the local fellow scratching his head in wonder: "If *he* did that to me, imaging what The Strangler would do."

Jim Londos, The Golden Greek

Jim Londos, known in the wrestling world as "The Golden Greek," was the most popular wrestler of the 1930s. However, he was born Christopher Theophelos, and used that name throughout his early years in the sport. How he came by his ring name is a story that can only happen in Hollywood—where a Frances Gumm becomes a Judy Garland—or in wrestling.

One day, the story goes, he walked into his promoter's office, to find Ed White (the promoter) preoccupied. "CHRIS THEOPHELOS!" White shouted in his best imitation of a ring announcer, unaware of the presence of the young man whose name he was intoning in stentorian tones. Catching sight of his visitor, White asked "How does that sound to you?" Chris was forced to admit, "nobody would remember it, even if I won." Right, said White, and hurried on to say, "So let's change it."

Well, Theophelos's favorite writer was Jack London, author of *Call of the Wild*, so White went back into his ring announcer act: "In this corner, Chris London...no, no—with your accent it has to be a Greek name.... London, London,... Londos. That's it! Chris Londos? No. What about Jim Londos, Champion of the World!!!" It sounded great to both, and the newly-named warrior ultimately went on to become a great champion.

Jim Londos is credited with executing wrestling's first "sleeper hold" in the main event of a card at New York's Yankee Stadium in June of 1931. The controversial hold, which enabled Londos to defeat Ray Steele in one hour and nine minutes, was, in the wrestler's own words, "simply a new hold I've perfected which shuts off the jugular vein."

Lou Thesz

An athlete's greatness is measured by many things: consistent performance, accomplishments transcending time, overall excellence, and dominance. No wrestler, with the exception of Ed "Strangler" Lewis, ever accomplished so much over so long a period of time and dominated the sport more than the great Lou Thesz.

Lou Thesz is on his way to the mat, caught in a body scissors by Gene Kiniski. (Source: Norman Kietzer)

Thesz was introduced to wrestling at the age of eight by his father, once a Greco-Roman wrestler in his native Hungary. The city of St. Louis—where Thesz's family now

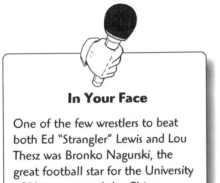

In Your Face

One of the few wrestlers to beat both Ed "Strangler" Lewis and Lou Thesz was Bronko Nagurski, the great football star for the University of Minnesota and the Chicago Bears. Nagurski won the NWA heavyweight title from Thesz in 1939.

lived and after which Lou was named—was a hotbed of wrestling. Each and every ethnic neighborhood in the southern part of the city sported an amateur club where children were taught the sport and competitions were staged as entertainment.

With support from his father, the young Thesz soon became extremely adept at Greco-Roman wrestling, winning many of the citywide club competitions. And on seeing his first professional wrestling match, the young Thesz fell in love with the sport in *all* its forms.

Under his father's tutelage, young Lou practiced for hours, weaving and swerving, straining and shoving in the Greco-Roman style that had by now gone the way of the horse and buggy. He became so good at his craft that George Tragos, a former Olympic champion from Greece then living in St. Louis, came to see him. After one look, Tragos was moved to say, "This is a future champion."

Tragos Takes Over

With that, Tragos took over Lou's training. As legend has it, one day after a particularly heavy workout in the gym, Tragos told his protege, "Lou, take a rest for a few days. I'm setting up an appointment for you to wrestle a friend of mine. He's pretty good so I want you to be in top shape." The youngster, confident of his abilities, answered, "Sure. Who d'ya want me to wrestle? Strangler Lewis?" Trago eyed the youngster, now a strapping 210-pound, six-foot tall athlete, and answered slowly: "That's exactly who you're going to wrestle."

Strangler Lewis recalls the meeting this way: "I could see right away that if he had nothing else, this Thesz squirt had the *look* of a real wrestler. I had a feeling I was about to have my hands full, unless he fainted first. Poor Lou kept staring at me as though I was a god or something. And for a few minutes after we squared off it looked as though I'd have to stick a hot coal in his pants to get him moving. Then we started to wrestle, and this 17-year-old hunky pinned me in 22 seconds with a combination arm-bar and half-nelson."

Lewis decided then and there that Thesz was to be the next champion, his successor to the unofficial title of "greatest wrestler in the world." And he promptly took control of Thesz's training and management.

Lewis's judgment wasn't far off—Thesz *did* become world champion, though it took four years to get there. Everett Marshall, a powerful wrestler out of Colorado, had beaten Thesz to the crown, having beaten Ali Baba, who had beaten the last of the long string of wrestlers who had held the title after Lewis.

Meeting With Marshall

To get a shot at Marshall, Thesz first had to learn the ropes, literally—he took on all comers as part of his apprenticeship. One of those early opponents was former amateur champion Ray Steele who, in Thesz's words, "was even tougher than his name sounds." Steele knocked Thesz on his keister in the opening seconds of the bout, but Thesz escaped from a combination toe hold and hammerlock to turn the tables, gaining a win over Steele and, in the process, earning a crack at Marshall's title.

The match against Marshall, held in St. Louis at Kiel auditorium on the night of December 29, 1937, was one of the toughest matches in Thesz's career—maybe the toughest in the annals of pro wrestling. It lasted three full hours, with Thesz winning the last two falls. Both men were exhausted after the bout—Marshall had to take three months to recuperate. But when the bout ended, Marshall took the time to shake Thesz's hand and tell the new champ, "Congratulations. Now your troubles are just beginning."

And so they were. Now every shooter in the business was out gunning for the 21-year-old champion, looking to take the title from him. Like Lewis before him, Thesz would lose and win back the title five more times, facing such greats as Bronko Nagurski, Steve Casey, Whipper Billy Watson, Dick Hutton, Baron Michele Leone, and Gene Kiniski in epic battles.

After World War II, Thesz cemented his claim to the championship by taking on, and beating, anyone who deserved a shot at the title. The newly formed National Wrestling Alliance recognized him as their champion in 1949. From that point on, he defended the title not only for himself, but also for the NWA as he battled against wrestlers from other organizations who challenged his supremacy. Two such bouts were against Gorgeous George and Baron Michele Leone, two West Coast claimants to the title.

Thesz would retire and make more comebacks than Frank Sinatra, only making his final exit from the ring in 1973, when he was in his 70s. Even then, the still perfectly proportioned Thesz said "I feel like I'm 22 years old." And for many who watched him take his leave, not only did Thesz still *look* young, his memories as heavyweight champion for 18 years kept every one of his fans feeling young at heart.

Captain Lou's Corner

Lou Thesz was such a tough man to handle in the ring that at a recent roast honoring this wrestling legend, one roaster, Gene LeBell, elicited guffaws when he suddenly leaped up and stood behind Thesz. "There!" LeBell shouted, "I finally got behind you!"

The Gorgeous One

Many people think that modern professional wrestling began with Gorgeous George. And, in a way, they're right.

The wrestler who became known as "The Human Orchid" began life as plain ol' George Wagner, born in Seard, Nebraska, and raised in Houston, Texas. As a wrestler he was more than adequate—he was even, in the estimation of no less an authority than the immortal Lou Thesz, "a good wrestler." But it was not his wrestling that would ultimately make him a legend—it was his showmanship.

*The Human Orchid,
Gorgeous George (Wagner)
in a publicity pose.
(Source: Norman Kietzer)*

The Metamorphosis Begins

The development of the character who would become known the world over as "Gorgeous George" was a slow process involving several steps. One of the first was his 1939 wedding, performed mid ring in Eugene, Oregon, to a local cashier. The wedding drew so many fans that George and his new bride, Betty Hanson, took the act on tour, repeating it in several arenas around the country.

The next step in the metamorphosis from George Wagner to Gorgeous George happened soon after, when Betty made her new bridegroom a special robe, which he took to ostentatiously folding and carefully placing in his corner before each bout. The audience took to riding him for his fastidiousness until, finally, Betty got into a shouting match with some ringside fans and ended up slapping one. That brought double the crowd to the next match—and quadruple the noise of the fans as they booed George mercilessly while he went through the robe-folding routine. In retaliation, George took even *more* care with the offending garment, and one of the greatest drawing cards of wrestling in the Pacific Northwest came into being. And George became an unequivocal "baddie." From there, the next stop was L.A.

In Los Angeles, the evolution of Gorgeous George continued. By the mid 1940s, his once brown hair had become auburn and he was wearing it longer and wavier. Concerned about it, George went to see two hair stylists, Frank and Joseph of Hollywood, who recommended that he let it grow long and dye it blond—if, that is, he "had the guts." Of course, he did.

Then George heard from an old wrestling friend of his, Sterling Davis, who had traveled down Mexico way and made a name for himself by throwing gardenias to the crowd. Now known as Gardenia Davis, Sterling was making a real name for himself. Taking a page from Davis's book, George decided to make something of his new coiffure—he wouldn't throw out flowers, he'd throw bobby pins. And not just any old bobby pins—these would be golden "Georgie" pins, costing $85 per half pound.

The Glorious Gorgeous One Goes Big-Time

By now George was calling himself "Gorgeous George," and his fame was spreading courtesy of the national radio broadcasts of the top comedians of the era: Bob Hope, Jack Benny, and Red Skelton. They'd work his name and act into their routines and jokes: "George wants to join the Navy and have the world see *him*." Or "Gorgeous George always walks into a room voice first." And "[Gorgeous George] would go broke if he had to pay taxes on what he *thinks* he's worth."

With the advent of television, George's name and fame spread ever further. Postwar America was hungry for celebrities who mirrored their new, carefree attitude, and Gorgeous George fit the bill, appearing on TV so often that he was called "Mr. Television."

Constantly working on his act, George introduced nuances into almost every move, every arched eyebrow, every word. His extravagant entrance was worthy of a Roman emperor. First he would send his valet down the aisle carrying a little silver tray and other accessories. The valet entered the ring, placed the tray in a corner, and spritzed the area with a perfume-scented disinfectant that George called, alternatively, "Chanel No. 10—why be half safe?" or "George No. 4."

Next came George's triumphal entrance. To the scratchy strains of "Pomp and Circumstance," he would walk slowly down the aisle, stopping every now and then to tell a fan that he was "beneath

Bert's Corner

Gorgeous George not only changed the face of wrestling, he changed its casting as well—he was the first to switch to using female valets in 1958, changing the look of wrestling forever.

contempt." Then he would haughtily enter the ring, the valet holding the ropes just far enough apart so George wouldn't have to bend too far, and he'd wipe his dainty white shoes on the red carpet that the valet had respectfully laid out for him in the corner. After the valet had removed the spun-gold hairnet which held his locks in place, George would walk around so that the crowd could appreciate his looks, which of course brought on a round of booing. Next he removed his fur-trimmed robe—one worthy of Liberace—and handed it over to the valet for the ostentatious folding ritual, inspiring further antagonism from the crowd. After a few more spritzes of disinfectant by the valet, George would finally, reluctantly, submit to the referee's obligatory hands-on inspection for gimmicks or grease, but he would pull back midway through the inspection, shouting "Take your filthy hands off me!" at which point the valet would rush forward and spray disinfectant on the referee's hands.

The ring announcer's introduction came next: "The Human Orchid, the Toast of the Coast, Gorgeous George!" And then the bell sounded, sending Gorgeous George into his bout mode: a gouging, biting, kidney-punching villain. His favorite hold was the "flying side headlock," in which he would grab his opponent in a traditional headlock and then fall back to the mat, flipping his opponent. He had become a phenomenon: part celebrity and part wrestling's version of "the man you love to hate." With kinescopes of his bouts at L.A.'s Olympic Auditorium being televised across America, requests for his services were pouring in. Gorgeous George was in such demand that he was able to dictate terms to the promoters: a guaranteed $100,000 or a third of the gate. And, finally, he came east to strut his primping and preening act in Madison Square Garden.

A Star Is Born

Red Smith, writing in the 1940s for the *New York Herald-Tribune*, tells of the first time he ever saw Gorgeous George, at Marye Ward Hair Stylists on East 57th Street in Manhattan. "The back room of this ladies' barber shop was pretty well jammed when Gorgeous George arrived wearing long blond curls and somewhat formal afternoon attire—black coat with mother-of-pearl buttons on the sleeve, soft white shirt with nine-inch points on the collar, striped trousers hung on braces. Ahead of him came a valet spraying the joint with an atomizer," Smith wrote. "After a long while they took the dryer off Gorgeous George's skull, brushed him up, and he arose, his head a mass of lovely, soft curls. 'Now I feel more relaxed with my hair done,' he said. 'I allus feel such a mess before.'"

Smith, who attended the bout that night between George and Ernie Dusek, one of the notorious Dusek brothers out of Omaha, wrote afterwards: "It is difficult to do justice to Gorgeous George's act, this side o' the libel laws. Groucho Marx is prettier than he, Sonny Tufts a more gifted actor, Connie Mack a better rassler, Happy Chandler funnier, and the Princeton Triangle Club has far superior female impersonators."

Whatever the media thought, Gorgeous George was all the rage for awhile, and he brought the cult of personality into the wrestling game, having become a cult unto himself. He was one of a kind at the time, but soon others would follow where he led as wrestling turned from the competitive sport of its early days to the showmanship of the 1950s.

The Least You Need To Know

➤ Frank Gotch was living proof that, in wrestling, nice guys finished last.

➤ Ed "Strangler" Lewis was probably the greatest wrestler of all time.

➤ Lou Thesz held the championship title for 18 years.

➤ Gorgeous George brought wrestling all the way into the world of showbiz and showmanship.

Chapter 7

Post-War Wrestlers and the New Pro Wrestling

It can't be ignored: when George Wagner finally finished his metamorphosis into Gorgeous George, pro wrestling as we know it today was born. And waiting in the wings were athletes from all over the world, ready to take the sport all the way back to bright lights and screaming fans. With the post-war crop of wrestlers, whole new dimensions of excitement and action were explored. These, then, are the men who brought wrestling into the television age and this chapter will tell you all about them.

Antonino Rocca

Wrestlers are given to exaggerations: Everything is "the best," "the biggest," or "the worst." But no one—no one—ever engaged in exaggerations like Antonino Rocco, the self-described "greatest wrestler in the world."

And if wrestling is a world of make-believe, it's only fitting that it has someone like Antonino Rocca, who was himself unbelievable. Take the time he told an interviewer, with a straight face, that he had once wrestled 17 Chavante Indians, giving each a broken arm with his fearsome wrist lock. Any ethnologist could tell you that no more than one or two of these natives of the Amazonian rainforest have ever been close enough to civilization to see a Coca-Cola bottle, but this was Rocca's story and he stuck to it.

Beginnings: Far from Amazonia

What few facts can be pieced together about Rocca indicate that he was born in Treviso, Italy some time around 1923, was christened Antonino Biasetton, and emigrated with his parents to Buenos Aires when he was about 15, in 1938. What happened between then and 1947 we can only guess at, but to hear Rocca tell it, he was, by turns, a track star, a fencing great, a master rugby player—you name it, he claimed to have done it. In 1947, while wrestling in Buenos Aires, he was spotted by a tourist named Nick Elitch—himself an ex-wrestler—who knew he had stumbled onto something potentially big. Elitch called Dr. Karl Sarpolis, a wrestling promoter in Texas and described Rocca's barefooted antics: leaps, flying moves, dropkicks. After listening to 10 minutes of ravings, Sarpolis told Elitch to put Rocca on a plane, pronto.

Wrestle Mania

The dropkick has been around since the 1930s, when it was first introduced by Gus Sonnenberg. And Rocca renewed its popularity with a whole new generation of fans. But even Rocca couldn't equal the feats of a wrestler named Marvin Mercer. Mercer could deliver his own variation, called "The Atomic Dropkick," and land back on his feet like a circus acrobat.

Rocco planted his size 13 feet on American soil in June of 1947 with a thump that would be heard around the wrestling world. For the next 13-plus years, he would remake the sport.

Rocca's Aerial Athleticism

All of Rocca's moves were soon on display: his mid-air splits, his leaps from the top rope onto the shoulders of his opponents (he'd ride them around like a jockey at the local racetrack), and his Argentine backbreaker. He actually made two debuts. The first was in Houston, against Lord Blears. The second came after he listened to the blandishments of New York promoter Toots Mondt, who brought him to Brooklyn's Ridgewood Grove in 1948 to face Benito Gardini.

An up-in-the-air Rocca brought a whole new dimension to wrestling (Source: Norman Kietzer)

Antonino Rocca

Gardini recalled the experience this way: "When he started flying at me out of nowhere, I was shocked. First thing I knew he's running toward me—then he disappears and wham! I got those big bare feet in my face. Then, when I get up, he gets me in the chest, wham! It's like running into a battering ram." As if that weren't bad enough, Gardini suffered another indignity: "He jumps onto the ring post. I think he's running away, but no—he comes sailing toward me like a big bird and the next thing I know I'm carrying him around the ring on my shoulders, with his legs locked around my head so I can hardly breathe."

Single-footedly, Rocca became wrestling's greatest gate attraction during its golden age. His gravity-defying acrobatics and his challenge that no human could get out of his "Argentine backbreaker" stirred the imagination of wrestling fans everywhere and brought them out in record numbers, revitalizing the once-moribund New York wrestling scene—especially energizing the city's large Latino population.

Bert's Corner

The 247 pound, well-proportioned Rocca would wow the crowds with his pre-bout antics, sometimes going into the ring, dropping to the mat, and doing 200-300 push-ups before the bout started.

Promoter Mondt crowed, "Rocca has done more for legs than Betty Grable," and Rocca's mere presence insured a packed house. His matches against Gene Stanlee at Madison Square Garden in 1949 and 1950 drew the biggest gates of the era. In 1950 he was picked by the East Coast wrestling brain trust as the man to beat Primo Carnera after the latter had won 321 consecutive bouts and became the biggest drawing card in wrestling.

Despite Rocca's popularity, some scoffed at his style. One of those, Lou Thesz, called Rocca's wrestling, "just slapping with feet." Thesz beat Rocco at least three times, though Rocco would always claim he'd never been beaten.

Detractors or no, Rocca went on his merry way. He loved the spotlight and the adulation of the fans. And even though Mondt was probably helping himself to two-thirds of Rocca's purses, Rocca was satisfied with his adoring fans, an attendant to open doors for him, and a limo for the ride back to his hotel.

Captain Lou's Corner

Another acrobatic star of the 1950s was Ricki Starr, who had studied ballet and put his training to use in the wrestling ring. He danced around on ballet slippers and delivered shots with a Bolshoi Ballet maneuver. His combination of skills in both dance and wrestling made him a very colorful attraction.

I can still remember seeing him as he waltzed into the offices of Mondt and Vince McMahon Sr., a camelhair coat thrown over his large shoulders, a big cigar in his hand and an ear-to-ear smile on his face. He was fully prepared to be oohed and aahed over. And when his star began to wane, he teamed up with another Latino favorite, Puerto Rican star Miguel Perez to form a popular, and lucrative, tag-team partnership. He said, "there are more than a half million Puerto Ricans in New York. These people needed a hero, a symbol to look up to and cheer. By teaming with Perez, I became that symbol."

Rocca always had an overblown view of himself. Whether he was telling anyone within earshot, "I just made a million in oil back in Argentina," or "I'm worth four million," or claiming to have conquered more women than Wilt Chamberlain, he was pure Antonino Rocca. And while everything he said could be taken with a whole shaker full of salt, the one thing that was no exaggeration was his impact on wrestling in the 1950s.

Killer Kowalski

If only one legend could represent professional wrestling, it might be Wldadek "Killer" Kowalski. No other wrestler has ever been more intimidating than The Killer. He was feared, reviled, and despised. Adjectives used to describe him include vicious, tough, mean, ruthless, rough, and destructive.

Tall, almost Lincoln-esque compared to the huge wrestlers of his day, the homicidal-looking Kowalski more than made up for his lack of wrestling heft by using whatever methods were at hand—or foot—to win, regardless of the rules. His arsenal included biting, kicking, gouging, and clawing—in short, anything it took to disable an opponent. His most famous maneuver was his notorious "throat stomp," delivered by landing on an opponent's Adam's apple (one foot landed on the throat, the other simultaneously thumped onto the floor with equal force to heighten the effect but lessen the impact).

Killer Kowalski crashes down on opponent Ed Carpentier (Source: Norman Kietzer)

Even acknowledging the special effects the impact of the move was horrific. Ask Verne Gagne, who explained what it felt like: "I was on the floor and he just jumped up in the air and landed feet-first on my windpipe," Gagne tried to explain to author Joe Jares in a strained voice. "It knocked the breath out of me. It's a pretty rough hold if his aim isn't just right." And one night it wasn't—which is where the legend of Killer Kowalski began. That was the night in Montreal, in 1954, when the Killer ripped off Yukon Eric's ear in a bout at the Forum.

Kowalski's Cauliflower Incident

Yukon Eric's ear wasn't just any ear—it was a cauliflower ear so large and calcified by the many blows it had received that it was barely attached to Eric's head. It was an inviting target for Kowalski as he mounted the top rope and leaped on his prostrate opponent for his famous throat stomp. He missed his landing, his heel grazed Eric's head, and he pinned the ear to the mat. Eric tried to twist free, but by twisting he merely severed his calcified ear in the process.

Kowalski fought his way back to the dressing room through a hostile crowd, their chorus of boos blending with the wail of an ambulance siren outside. Of the ear, Kowalski merely said: "It was so cauliflowered, it would have fallen off by itself if it had had a chance to." But the fans wouldn't have any of Kowalski's rationalizations, and when he returned to the Forum the next week, a record crowd of 14, 657 incensed fans greeted him with jeers, chanting "Le Killer."

The Toughest Man of All

His name soon became legendary, and he was in demand throughout the world. Everyone wanted to see the man who, decked out in his unique purple tights with lightning bolts on both sides and his glittering gold boots, had severed a man's ear from his head. Ask any wrestler of the era who his toughest opponent was and they'll all come back with the same answer: Killer Kowalski. Bruno Sammartino, who wrestled them all, said, "I've wrestled many tough men in my career, but no one was as vicious, as rough, or as tough as Killer."

What motivated this man? His philosophy of wrestling, was: "I would use anything in my power to knock my opponent into submission. Only winners make the big bucks, and I was determined to be a winner." In life outside the wrestling ring, Killer Kowalski was a winner too. He was a soft man who read, painted, took photographs, and went on religious retreats. Outside, he could be a perfect gentleman, but inside the ring, Killer Kowalski was anything but.

Verne Gagne

Just when it seemed that all wrestling's technicians had disappeared entirely, chased out by the showmen, a wrestler with the striking features of a Viking god and going by the name of Verne Gagne came onto the scene to evoke comparisons with the great wrestlers of yore.

Gagne knew the intricacies and subtleties of wrestling, having been the four-time Big Ten wrestling champion, twice the NCAA champion, and a member of the 1948 Olympic squad. Added to this were his impressive credentials as a football player at the University of Minnesota, where he starred as a halfback and played in the 1949 College All-Star game, and you had the makings of a helluva athlete—and wrestler.

From College to the Canvas Mat

Gagne considered a career in pro football first, saying that the world of professional wrestling was "too rough and show-offish for me. I was the typical college type then...you know, fast and purely scientific. All the extra frills and gaudiness of pro wrestling gave me the wrong impression at first." But he turned his back on a promising career in football to become a pro wrestler. There were those who didn't think he'd make it, at first. One was Minneapolis promoter Tony Stecher, brother of the great Joe Stecher. Tony wasn't impressed, thinking the then 195 pound Gagne "too light for a good wrestler." Still, he put Gagne in against Abe Kashey in April 1949, for his pro wrestling debut.

Verne Gagne with an arm bar hold on Nick Bockwinkel (Source: Norman Kietzer)

Gagne won the match but failed to win over Stecher, who still harbored doubts about the ability of this great college wrestler to make it in the professional ranks. So Gagne headed out for Texas where he struck the proverbial oil, selling out every arena in the area. As Gagne recalled it: "Promoters all over heard of my success in Texas. It was the turning point." By the time he returned to his home base of Minneapolis, Gagne had "discovered the meaning of showmanship," adding, "and I realized that to be a good showman was a lot more difficult than to be a good wrestler."

The combination of good wrestling and showmanship made him a crowd favorite—and a winning one at that. He took the NWA junior heavyweight title just a year and a half after his debut against Kashey. This was just the beginning for the appealing wrestler with the well-chiseled good looks and equally well-chiseled moves.

Gagne moved up to the heavyweight ranks and by the end of 1951 he was wrestling the top names in the field, including the legendary Lou Thesz. Their

Bert's Corner

The very few scientific wrestlers in recent years all learned their trade as college wrestlers, and can be counted on the fingers of one hand. The very short list includes Verne Gagne, Danny Hodge, Dr. Bill Miller, Bob Backlund, and Ric Flair.

bout on October 27, 1951, in Milwaukee for the NWA title was what old-timers would call "a wrestler's wrestling match." Many called it the greatest bout of modern times, one which reminded many who saw it of the famous Jim Londos-Strangler Lewis match back in Madison Square Garden in 1932.

The Gagne-Thesz match was science versus science as each got a quick start out of the blocks. Both took one fall in the best-two-out-of-three championship match. Both pulled out all the stops in the third and deciding fall. Gagne was trying to work Thesz into his special sleeper hold, and Thesz tried mightily to execute his own pet move, the reverse body slam. Neither succeeded—each knew exactly what the other had in mind—so the match ended in one of those rarities of modern wrestling, a draw.

The Quest for the Title

Gagne would eventually win the U.S. heavyweight title in September of 1953 and keep it for 31 months, until he was toppled by Wilbur Snyder in April of 1956. He would win the title for a second time in April of 1958 by beating Dick the Bruiser in Chicago. But it was the world title that Gagne thirsted for. This was the title that Lou Thesz seemed to be constantly winning, and losing, in alternate bouts.

In 1959 Gagne finally beat Edouard Carpentier, who had himself beaten Thesz to gain the NWA title. However, several members of the NWA chose to ignore Carpentier's, and therefore Gagne's, claim to the title, instead continuing to recognize only Thesz. Fed up, Gagne tucked his title belt under his arm and walked—forming the American Wrestling Alliance (AWA) in 1960. As Gagne himself explains his defection from the NWA: "I won the belt from Eduoard Carpentier. He won over Lou Thesz, the NWA champion. Many promoters felt that Thesz was getting himself disqualified too often so that he could hold onto his title." (The belt doesn't change hands in a disqualification.) "A group of them got together and said if he got disqualified against Carpentier in their match, Carpentier would be awarded the title. That's exactly what happened."

Whatever the reason, Gagne now owned the belt, which traced its ancestry all the way back to Frank Gotch. And now a new wrestling circuit, the AWA, was formed, covering a territory which extended from Indianapolis on the east through Chicago, Milwaukee, and Minneapolis, all the way to Omaha and Denver in the west. For the next two decades the American Wrestling Alliance would ride on Verne Gagne's broad back and on the title belt he held.

By the time he retired in the early 1980s, Gagne had built a legacy. He'd also brought in a group of new wrestlers and taught them the ropes, including Bob Backlund, Ric Flair, Ken Patera, and Ricky Steamboat, among countless others.

A Living Legend—Bruno Sammartino

It has long been something of a bar argument over who was the "greatest" in wrestling history. Some graybeards will inevitably bring up the names of Gotch or Hackenschmidt, while others will pull out yellowing newspaper clippings to invoke the names of Strangler Lewis, Jim Londos, or Lou Thesz. But for the wrestling fan of the 1960s there is only one name, Bruno Sammartino, who was called by promoter Vince McMahon Sr. "The greatest athlete as well as the greatest wrestler of all time."

Bruno Sammartino takes down Stan Stasiak (Source: Norman Kietzer)

However noble his standing in the minds of wrestling fans, the legend of Bruno Sammartino was anything but noble in its beginnings. Born and raised in the Abruzzi and Molise regions of Northern Italy, up in the Apennine mountains, young Bruno and his family endured the hardships of World War II and the Nazi occupation of the area. His father had gone to America before the war and communication there was nonexistent, other members of the family were killed, and the rest subsisted on whatever they could find—foraging for grass under deep snows and once living off the carcass of a dead horse for two months.

Coming to America

After the war, Bruno's father was finally able to make contact with the family back in Italy. He had settled in Pittsburgh, and wrote "You're coming to America, the land of opportunity." Bruno, then age 13, packed up and headed for America with the rest of his family.

They boarded a cargo ship in Naples and were locked in the hull of the boat. When they arrived in New York, they were quarantined with the rest of the passengers for TB. Finally released, they traveled to Pittsburgh to join Sammartino Sr. Bruno took one look at his father's cold-water flat and said, incredulously, *"This* is the land of opportunity?"

But the 13-year-old Sammartino would soon find that indeed it was. For shortly after his arrival, the 67-pound youngster was introduced to weight training. By the time he was 18 he weighed 257 pounds, could bench-press 565 pounds 38 times consecutively, and had won the title of Mr. Pennsylvania.

The first time I laid eyes on Bruno, at a gym right off Eighth Avenue in New York where wrestlers go, I was impressed by his brute strength as he lifted weights. And by his size, his brawny arms, his massive chest, and his shoulders, which always looked like you could serve them to a sit-down dinner for six. The source of his then 6-foot, 270-pound body was his exercise regimen, his diet, and his refusal to take any sort of drugs—especially steroids.

He caught the eye of Vince McMahon Sr., too. McMahon was then planning to establish his own wrestling circuit, independent of the then-dominant NWA. He decided that Bruno would be the perfect man to head the new organization's assault on both the NWA and the East Coast establishment.

Moving on up With the McMahon Machine

By 1963, Bruno was headlining in New York, the fans rejoicing in his strength and brawling, and Bruno, The Tower of Power, rewarding their support with win after win. Then McMahon decided to make his move on the NWA. When Lou Thesz beat NWA World Champion Buddy Rogers in one fall in January of 1963, McMahon broke away from the NWA to form the WWF, continuing to recognize Rogers as the champion. But Rogers' title was only temporary. On May 17 of that year, Sammartino pinned an injured Rogers in less than a minute in a bout at Madison Square Garden.

Bruno's reign as champion was to last for eight long years, during which time he defended the title successfully against the likes of Gene Kiniski, Killer Kowalski, Lou Thesz, Ray Stevens, John Tolas, Johnny Valentine, Freddie Blassie, Dr. Bill Miller, Professor Tanaka, and Waldo von Erich. Finally, on January 18, 1971, Bruno lost his title to Ivan Koloff—The Russian Bear—in a controversial match, and afterward went into semiretirement. After 10 months out of the ring, he was back, and he retook the title from Stan Stasiak by the end of the year.

Honor and Integrity: The Sammartino Hallmark

During his second go-round as champion, Bruno suffered a serious injury—a broken neck—in a title bout against Big Stan Hansen. Many feared that Bruno was permanently damaged, but the man who had always gone from strength to strength overcame his injury. In a rematch against Hanson—a wild brawl-filled bout at Shea Stadium—he evened the score by thoroughly thrashing this man that, he believed, had intentionally injured him.

Bruno would lose the crown a second time, in a controversial bout with Superstar Billy Graham at Baltimore's Civic Center in 1977. And although many in the audience and watching the bout on TV at home thought that Graham stole the title, Bruno never once complained about the outcome.

That was the hallmark of Bruno Sammartino—he was a man who carried himself without insolence and without boasting. His words and actions were steel-true and blade-straight. Bruno was never afraid to say what he believed, and many's the time that his relations with the WWF were somewhat less than cordial because he always said what he thought. Maybe this is why he captured the hearts and minds of so many wrestling fans during the 1960s.

The von Erich Saga

The biography of Fritz von Erich in the Fall 1959 issue of *Wrestling Revue* began: "Nazi Germany was on its last legs. Before long, Russian and American flags would fly over Berlin and a guy named Hitler would make an ash of himself. Meanwhile, however, discipline for both soldiers and civilians was hard. One day, between air raids, a battalion of infantry passed an almost deserted playground. Several boys were lifting weights, oblivious to the carnage going on about them. One of the lads caught the Prussian officer's eye. He halted his unit. 'You—the big one—come here!' he shouted. The big one walked over slowly. The officer sneered. 'Here I have to put up with rabble like this...,' he pointed to his men, 'while specimens like you are wandering around. You're big enough to be in the army. Why aren't you?' But the tall blond boy never flinched. 'I am only 14 years old,' he said."

The bio would go on to recount how the Prussian officer took a swipe at the boy with his swagger stick and how the 14-year-old tore the stick away and threw the officer to the ground. It would tell of how one observer, a corporal, looked up the youngster after the war and pleaded with him "to recapture our physical prestige" by becoming a wrestler. To this the boy is said to have answered: "I am going to America to wrestle. I am going to cripple every *schwienhunt* of an American wrestler I meet. Single-handed, I will continue the war against the Yankees!"

And Now, for the Real Story

There's only one problem with this story: Fritz von Erich was, in reality, Jack Adkisson, a tough 6'4", 260 pounder who had played football for Southern Methodist University back in 1948 and 1949 and had probably never been closer to Germany than Paris, Texas.

But in the immediately post-World War II era, being a German was visual shorthand for being a villain, and Adkisson entered the wrestling arena as the quintessential villain. His long-time partner, Cowboy Bill Watts, said "The German gimmick was a natural. With that scowl of his, he was an easy guy to hate." Equally easy was his selection of a German moniker: He borrowed the name Fritz from a member of his family, and Erich was his mother's maiden name.

As he traveled the state of Texas and beyond, he developed yet another gimmick, his deadly "Iron Claw" grip. And Adkisson/von Erich soon converted his Iron Claw into an iron grip on wrestling in and around Dallas, developing World Class Championship Wrestling (WCW), which soon became a family enterprise as he brought in five of his six sons to become part of a family show.

Fritz von Erich may have invented the "Iron Claw," but he shared it with his sons. Kerry von Erich uses it to good effect on Ric Flair (Source: Norman Kietzer)

The von Erichs—David, Kerry, Kevin, Mike, and Chris—soon became the hottest thing to hit Texas since salsa, and the WCW caught fire along with them. They played to full houses at the Sportatorium, with occasional superstar extravaganzas at the Cotton Bowl and Texas Stadium. The weekly WCW TV shows were syndicated in 66 U.S. television markets, Japan, Argentina, and the Middle East.

Tragedy in the Second Generation

But in the 1980s, the von Erich success story suddenly turned tragic. David, probably the best wrestler of the bunch, died during a 1984 tour of Japan. The rumored cause was a drug overdose, but the official word was that he'd suffered an intestinal hemorrhage. In his honor, a gigantic David von Erich Memorial Show was staged at Texas Stadium.

A couple of years later, a second von Erich brother, Mike, had a close brush with death involving drugs, but Fritz told anyone who would listen that Mike suffered from toxic shock syndrome. It was impossible to mask his condition, and the von Erichs had to resort to having him score one-punch or single dropkick wins to cover up his inability to perform for long in the ring. In 1987, Mike committed suicide, and again a memorial show was staged, this time honoring both David and Mike at the Texas Stadium. And, as with the earlier memorial show, the stadium was jammed with fans.

With Mike's death, it fell to Kerry to carry the von Erich banner. By this time, ESPN had begun broadcasting Texas wrestling, and Kerry quickly became a favorite on the show. Kerry battled Ric Flair winning, and then losing, the WCW and NWA championships. But tragedy stalked Kerry, too: Soon after losing the title to Flair, Kerry was involved in a motorcycle accident in which he severely dislocated his right ankle.

Recovery and Return to Glory

Nobody wanted to see Kevin and Chris wrestle: The fans wanted Kerry, of the Greek-godlike features and flowing blond hair. Without a wrestling son to pump up attendance, promoter Fritz von Erich had to resort to trickery to punch up his weekly TV show ratings—including a faked heart attack, with ambulance and all.

Meanwhile, Kerry's rehabilitation had to be rushed. It consisted of putting a walking cast on the ankle and shooting his leg full of novocaine. All it took was one match: Kerry was in agony as soon as the painkiller wore off, and he ripped up his ankle during that bout. In the end, the injured foot had to be amputated.

Recovery took another year, this time, but Kerry came back sporting an artificial foot. The TV announcers, unaware that he had lost a limb, said "Kerry hasn't lost a step." And to most observers, he hadn't. Having become so adept at wrestling on one foot, and having learned to spend as much time as possible hanging onto the ropes, Kerry made it all but impossible for the fans to detect any difference in his post-accident prowess.

Rumors circulated that something was wrong—very wrong—with his foot, fueled in part by his refusal to remove his wrestling boots in public. But Kerry was so adroit at hiding his injury that Vince McMahon hired him away from the WCW and introduced him into the WWF as The Texas Tornado. With his departure from the WCW, there were no remaining big attractions and the crowds at the Sportatorium began to dry up. With that, ESPN dropped its weekly WCW show.

Death, Drugs, and Disaster

Tragedy continued to stalk the von Erich clan. In 1991, 21 year old Chris committed suicide. Then Kerry ran afoul of the law and was caught forging prescriptions for drugs to ease his constant pain. Facing jail time, Kerry followed his brothers Mike and Chris, taking his own life in 1993. Finally, the patriarch of the family, Fritz, succumbed to brain cancer in August of 1998. The first family of professional wrestling, was all gone but for Kevin.

Recently, a wrestling writer traveled down to Dallas to visit the one-time shrine of the von Erich family, the Dallas Sportatorium, where the WCW once held its weekly wrestling shows. He found the once-proud arena under new management with some hint of a porno operation going on just outside and down the road. All traces of the von Erichs were gone. All that remains are the fans' memories—of Jack Adkisson as Fritz von Erich and the sun-god good looks of Kerry when he was in his prime as the pride of the southwest.

The Least You Need To Know

➤ Antonino Rocca's spectacular leaps in the ring added an airborne element to wrestling's magic.

➤ Killer Kowalski brought new meaning to the term "baddie" when he snapped off Yukon Eric's cauliflower ear.

➤ Verne Gagne was a pure athlete, but his showmanship was second to none.

➤ Bruno Sammartino returned class, style, and substance to pro wrestling.

➤ The von Erichs were, and remain, wrestling's first family of wrestlers.

Today's Stars

The immediate post-war years saw wrestling growing in popularity and gaining in showmanship. All the ingredients were in place for the rock 'em, sock 'em story-driven bouts of the 1980s and 1990s. All it took was character development and some savvy manipulation of the media best suited for the spectacle that pro wrestling had become. And as fast as the modern variation on the wrestling theme developed, new wrestlers with new personas and new gimmicks were ready to show the world just what the sport was all about. Here are a few of the biggest and best on the current wrestling scene. If you don't see one of your favorites here, don't despair—there's lots more in Chapter 9.

Stone Cold Steve Austin, Workingman's Hero

Originally from Victoria Texas, Steve Austin personifies that state's claim to doing everything larger than life. At 6 foot, 2 inches and 252 pounds, Austin is a powerful figure and an impressive force in the wrestling ring. Always a fan favorite, he's at the height of his popularity today, with his T-shirt sales far outselling even Hulk Hogan at *his* peak.

Austin began wrestling in 1989 in the NWA but quickly moved into the WCW as "Stunning Steve," paired with Brian Pillman as the tag team called The Hollywood Blondes. The team was highly successful, winning all the tag team titles until the WCW management chose to break up the team, having Austin concentrate on singles bouts. Austin was decidedly *not* pleased to see his successful tag-team action ended by management, and never managed to get a chance at Hulk Hogan's world title.

WCW's Eric Bischoff fired Austin from the federation over the telephone, and Austin went off to the ECW for a short while, using this time to perfect his Stone Cold persona—originally a violent, anti-everything character.

Austin joined the WWF in 1996, performing as The Ringmaster, managed by Ted DiBiase. Soon, however, he started using his Stone Cold character, and even though his persona had the attitude of a serial killer, he soon became the WWF's most popular wrestler, and he feuded with Owen Hart, former tag-team partner Brian Pillman, Rocky Maivia, and Bret Hart. After taking the championship title in March 1998 (at *Wrestlemania XIV*) from Shawn Michaels, his character has had an attitude adjustment, and Austin has become a non-conforming, working-man's hero. These days his major feuds are with Vince McMahon, Mankind/Dude Love, and Kane and the Undertaker.

Tattoo Artists' Wrestler of Choice: Bam Bam Bigelow

When Momma Bigelow first laid eyes on her baby boy Scott, on September 1, 1961, she had no idea that he'd turn into the 6-foot, 3-inch, 368-pound behemoth we know today as Bam Bam. Bigelow began his wrestling career as Crusher Yircov in 1985, but the Bam Bam moniker came soon after—specifically, Bam Bam Bigelow, the Beast from the East.

Bam Bam Bigelow

Bigelow's most famous match was the main event at *Wrestlemania XI* in 1995, where he went up against New York Giants linebacker (and wrestling neophyte) Lawrence Taylor—Bam Bam lost. His response to fans who chided him for losing? "You should see the check I got!"

Today Bigelow wrestles in the ECW, where he conspires with that promotion's primo villain, Shane Douglas, and Chris Candido. Oh, and his most striking physical feature? The tattooed flames that cover his bald head.

Cactus Jack

Born Mick Foley on June 7, 1965, in Bloomington, Indiana, and raised on Long Island, in New York, Cactus's persona always claimed to be from Truth or Consequences, New Mexico (the only town in the United States that agreed to change its name when bribed by a game show).

The 6'4", 277-pound Foley has more wrestling personas than your average cat has fleas. He wrestles as Dude Love, a hippie ladies' man, and Mankind, a self-mutilating creep. Trained by the legendary Dominic DeNucci, Cactus Jack made his pro debut in June of 1983 in Clarksburg, Texas, as Cactus Jack Manson. He gained fame during the late 1980's working for World Class Championship Wrestling in Texas as part of General Skandor Akbar's organization.

Cactus Jack moved to NWA/WCW in 1989 and his matches became increasingly violent. A feud with Vader in 1984 ended in a brutal bout that caused Cactus Jack hundreds of stitches. The feud came to a head when Jack faced Vader in Munich, Germany, and lost his right ear when his head got caught between the ropes.

After a memorable stint in ECW from 1995 to 1996, Cactus Jack moved to the WWF where, wrestling as any one of his other three personas, he has become a superstar. His 1998 cage match against the Undertaker was as wild as wrestling gets—during the match he was tossed from the top of the cage straight through a ringside table, dislocating his jaw and knocking out three teeth. That bout hits the record books as one of the most memorable in WWF history. No wonder—after all that damage, he still insisted on finishing the match.

In Your Face

Sometimes you really can't tell the players without a program—wrestlers switch federations or change persona with increasing frequency. If you want to follow one or more current wrestlers, track them on the internet—most of the big ones have their own web pages, not to mention the ones maintained by their fans.

Terry Funk

Terry Funk was born on June 30, 1944, in Amarillo Texas. His father, Dory, and his older brother, Dory Jr., were both champion wrestlers before he got into the act. A side note: Dory Jr. and Terry are the only brothers to have each won the NWA World Heavyweight Championship.

Terry Funk in full regalia

Like his brother and his dad, Terry was a respected scientific wrestler early in his career. The 6'1", 247-pound Terry soon developed into a hardcore pro wrestling legend, featured in some of the most violent matches of all time, both in Japan and the United States. His trademark finishing move is the spinning toe hold.

Funk amazed his critics in 1997 when, at the age of 53, he won the ECW championship on the *Barely Legal* pay-per-view event. He put on an astonishing performance that included a moonsault—a backward somersault off the top turnbuckle to land with a thud onto his prone opponent in the ring.

In addition to wrestling, Terry has appeared in several movies, such as *Over the Top*, and has made several guest appearances on such television shows as *Thunder in Paradise*.

A Life Lived in the Ring: Eddie Gilbert

Born in Lexington, Tennessee, on August 14, 1961, Eddie Gilbert's promising career began when he paired up with his dad, Tommy Gilbert, in tag-team matches when he was only 16. It ended 17 years later when he was struck down with a heart attack at the age of 34. Though his career was cut short, this Lexington, Tennessee, wrestler made a name for himself in the top promotions as a good wrestler. He was seen as a natural "baddie," but at 5 feet, 10 inches, and 222 pounds, he just didn't have the size to make it to the number-one villain spot.

Gilbert worked for just about every promotion there was, leaving them almost as fast as he entered them. Not for lack of supporters, however. He was particularly well-known for his creative booking. He was also assistant to Dusty Rhodes for Jim Crockett's Georgia Championship Wrestling circuit.

He joined the WWF in 1982, but before he could establish himself there he was seriously injured in a car accident, breaking his neck. Several months later, after he'd recovered a bit, he returned to the WWF as Bob Backlund's protege, only to have his neck rebroken by the Masked Superstar. In 1984 he took on the name Hot Stuff and began managing a group of bad guys who wrestled under the aegis of Hot Stuff, Inc. Gilbert held titles in the USWA, the UWF, and the WWC, and partnered with Tommy Rich, Brian Christopher, and Jerry Lawler.

Eddie Gilbert throws Ron McFarlane

Gilbert's heart could truly be said to belong to the ring: he married twice to wrestling women—first to Missy Hiatt, a valet, and then to Madusa Micela, a wrestler in her own right. And Gilbert's tradition lives on in The Dark Patriot, the persona of Eddie's brother, Doug Gilbert.

Scott Hall

Scott Hall was born in Miami, Florida, on October 20, 1959. His early athletic involvement was as a basketball player for St. Mary's University in Maryland. The 6'8", 287-pound Hall only began to wrestle professionally in 1984 and didn't become a big star until eight years later.

Hall wrestled as Starship Coyote and as the Diamond Studd during his early years. In May 1992, after stints in the AWA and NWA, Hall joined the WWF and became famous as Razor Ramon, a "Cuban" wrestler who chewed a toothpick and tossed it into the face of his enemies. Razor Ramon's finishing move was called the the "Razor's Edge."

During the early 1990s, Hall took part in what has been called the greatest match (you may have noticed by now that there were lots of "greatest matches"—that's wrestling for you) in the WWF's history: the "Ladder Match" where he fought versus Shawn Michaels for *Wrestlemania XI*. Hall won that match handily, even though he will long be remembered for the fall he took from the top of the ladder to the ring. Scott left the WWF in the spring of 1996 in order to join the WCW and has returned to working under his real name. He's one of the founders of the "outlaw" group, New World Order, and still wrestles as a member of that outfit.

Hulk/Hollywood Hogan

Probably the best-known figure to come out of pro wrestling, the Hulkster was born Terry Bollea on August 11, 1953, in Venice Beach, California. He's 6 foot, 8 inches tall and weighs in at 275 pounds. His early career was a little slow to take off. He began in 1978, under the management of Jimmy Hart, and in 1979 moved to the WWF as a baddie with Freddie Blassie for his manager. He couldn't manage to defeat the then-champion, Bob Backlund, so he moved on to spend several years in the now-defunct AWA where he began to develop the great fan following that he's had ever since.

Hogan took a brief detour from wrestling to appear in the third installment of the Rocky films, playing a wrestler named Thunderlips. That role catapulted him to the status of household name.

In 1983, Hogan returned to the WWF, this time playing a good guy defending all things American against the Iron Sheik. He defeated the Sheik for the WWF title on January 23, 1984, and the fan phenomenon known as "Hulk-A-Mania" was born.

The first Wrestlemania's were largely Hulk Hogan affairs: He was featured in the main event matches in all but one of those years. Perhaps the most famous one was his battle with Andre the Giant, in *Wrestlemania III*—he pinned the til-then all but invincible Andre to the roar of thousands of cheering fans. He lost the belt back to Andre in 1988, but got it back in short order.

Hulk Hogan's most famous WWF feud was with Andre the Giant, against whom he had some of his most memorable matches.

At *Wrestlemania VI* he lost the belt again—this time to the Ultimate Warrior in a "straight" match (no cheating, no interfering), which was a rare occasion indeed—Hogan almost always won his matches in the WWF.

Ted Turner lured Hogan over to the WCW in 1994, taking on Ric Flair and winning the title in his first match. He couldn't use the name "Hulk"—the WWF owned the rights to the name—so he was rechristened "Hollywood" Hogan, a reference to both his movie career and his Hollywood lifestyle.

In the WCW, Hogan's good guy character was not going over well—fans were booing him no matter what he did. So he took a little time off to make a film and returned as a baddie and an outlaw member of the New World Order (nWo) with Scott Hall and Kevin Nash. As leader of the group, Hogan scored personal success—and helped bring the WCW a hugely successful few years, from 1996 through 1998.

As a bad guy, Hogan loses as often as he wins, but that doesn't matter much to the fans—he's still one of the biggest attractions and best-known names in all of pro wrestling.

Lex Luger

Born Lawrence Pfohl on June 2, 1958, in Chicago, Illinois, Luger played a stint in the Canadian Football League. He moved on to play for the Orlando Bulls of the United States Football League in 1985. He began wrestling in local Florida promotions soon thereafter.

With his 6'5", 265-pound bodybuilder's physique, Luger quickly moved up to join the NWA/WCW, where he became known as The Total Package. Luger left the NWA/WCW in 1992 to join Vince McMahon's short-lived World Bodybuilding Federation. In June 1992, Luger was injured in a motorcycle accident in Atlanta and had to have a metal plate inserted in his arm. He's still got that plate—which he's been known to use to great effect as a weapon when he's working as a villain.

Lex Luger, overpowering an opponent

Luger wrestled as The Narcissist in the WWF until 1995, after which he took on the persona Lex "Made in the USA" Luger. He was at one time the WWF's number-one hero, feuding with then-WWF champ Yokozuna.

From 1995 to the present, Luger has worked for WCW where he remains one of wrestling's top stars. Luger's favorite finishing move is the "Torture Rack," which involves draping his opponent across the back of his neck and pulling down on both halves of the body with his arms.

Gorilla Monsoon

On June 5, 1939, in Rochester, New York, the Marella household was blessed with the birth of little Gino—who could have guessed that he'd grow up to stand 6 feet, 7 inches and weigh 401 pounds. With that kind of size, it seemed only natural not only that he'd become a wrestler, but that he'd take on the world as a vicious villain. Wild Red Berry managed Marella, by this time renamed Gorilla Monsoon, and the 1960s saw him rise to the top of the WWWF Tag-Team championship with Killer Kowalski. By the early 1970s he had become a favorite of the fans.

While his wrestling career was always successful, he attained worldwide notoriety in 1976 when Muhammad Ali climbed into the ring with him. Monsoon circled Ali for a few moments, then put the boxing champ into his trademark airplane spin. Ali, perhaps concerned about avoiding injury before his scheduled bout with Antonio Inoki that was just weeks away, scampered away at the first opportunity.

Gorilla Monsoon Mauls El Mongol

After Monsoon retired from active wrestling, he stayed on with the WWF as announcer. He paired up with former manager Bobby Heenan to become one of wrestling's great TV announcing teams. He is known for his long-winded wordiness, particularly when describing the body parts of the wrestlers in the ring. He is currently (1998) serving as the WWF president.

Kevin Nash

Kevin Nash was born on July 9, 1960, in Las Vegas, Nevada, and raised in Southgate, Michigan. At 7' and 356 pounds, he played basketball for the University of Tennessee. After college he worked as a nightclub bouncer for a time before beginning his wrestling career with WCW.

With little experience but lots of size going for him, Nash originally experimented with a few gimmicks, but they were mostly unsuccessful. Using the name Steel, he started out as one half of the tag team The Master Blasters, in which he was partnered by Blade. Then, as a solo wrestler, he took the persona of Oz—he wore a mask and a green cape in the ring. After that he became Vinnie Vegas, an oversized lounge lizard.

Nash's career finally took off, however, when he moved to the WWF in 1993 as Diesel, Shawn Michael's bodyguard. In this persona he went on to become the WWF World Heavyweight Champion by defeating Bob Backlund on November 26, 1994. The title match lasted only six seconds—but sometimes that's all it takes. Nash returned to WCW in 1996 where, teaming up with Scott Hall, he remains a top star as a founding member of the New World Order.

Captain Lou's Corner

Sometimes a gimmick or partnership is all it takes to blast a wrestler's career into the stratosphere. It's all a matter of finding what works for you, and get's the fans attention at the same time.

Rowdy Roddy Piper

Roderick Toombs was born on April 17, 1951, in Glasgow, Scotland, and grew up to become one of the biggest stars of the early *Wrestlemania* era: Rowdy Roddy Piper.

Piper wrestled with the NWA during the late 1970s, but his real rise to fame came only after he began starring in *Piper's Pit,* an interview and commentary segment of the WWF television shows of the early 1980s. This was no ordinary talk show: Piper's interviews with wrestling's heroes and villains during these segments inevitably ended in a fight.

Piper's trademark finishing move has always been "The Sleeper." Being from Scotland, Piper wore a kilt much of the time (except for when he was actually wrestling) and occasionally played the bagpipe. He teamed with Paul Orndorff to face Hulk Hogan and Mr. T at the first *Wrestlemania*. His most famous feud was against Superfly Jimmy Snuka. The feud began when Piper hit the beloved son of the Fiji Islands with a coconut.

In 1996, he served as interim president of the WWF, filling in for Gorilla Monsoon during a time when Monsoon was too ill to fulfill his duties. Piper still wrestles occasionally for WCW, where he is featured in a long-standing feud with the evil Hollywood Hogan. That's only to be expected: Hollywood's fame in movies is great, but Piper is wrestling's premier movie star, having played the lead in many action films and made-for-TV movies.

Rowdy Roddy Piper: Even the trunks are Scottish tartan

Ravishing Rick Rude

Born Richard Rood in the mid 1950s on December 7, in Robbinsdale, Minnesota, the 6'4", 246-pound Rude began his professional wrestling career in the mid South region in 1984. Back then he was managed by Jim "The Anvil" Neidhart and accompanied by his beautiful valet, Angel.

From his successes in the mid South he moved on to wrestle for World Class Championship Wrestling in Texas, where he was managed by Percival Pringle (the manager and wrestler now known as Paul Bearer). He moved on to NWA/WCW in 1986, but then made the switch to the WWF during the spring of the following year.

Rude returned to WCW in 1991, where he remained until a 1994 back injury forced him to retire from active wrestling. Since the beginning, Rude's gimmick has never

Bert's Corner

Although the old-time wrestling circuits and territories are no longer valid, it's still appropriate to refer to regions when you're talking about wrestlers who are not (or not yet, anyway) affiliated with the two cable-based Federations—the WWF and the WCW. Thus, early in his career Rick Rude worked the mid South region, until he was ready to sign on with one of the major federations.

changed. He comes on as God's gift to women. When he kisses them, they faint. When he wiggles his hips, they squeal. And he can't wrestle without addressing the crowd over the public address system: "Stop the music! Why don't you fat, stupid people from [insert your town here] shut up and let your women see what a real man looks like!"

Rude's favorite finishing move is called the "Rude Awakening." Rude won the NWA World Championship in 1994, defeating Ric Flair, and held that belt for six months before losing it in Japan to Hiroshi Hase. Rude remains active in the wrestling world these days as a three-piece-suit-wearing bodyguard for the New World Order.

Sabu

Michigan-born Terry Brunk (born December 12, 1964) is the nephew of Ed Farhat, better known to early wrestling fans as the original Sheik. But in the world of creative wrestling reality, Brunk is a mute from Bombay, India, named Sabu. He's worn this persona since his earliest days in wrestling, beginning in the early 1990s as Sabu the Elephant Boy working the Mid-South region. Sabu is known for his recklessly masochistic maneuvers in the ring—behavior that has left him seriously injured on more than one occasion.

Sabu's risk taking is all too real—those long thick scars that crisscross his chest, stomach, back, and arms are the souvenirs of his many barbed-wire matches in Japan while he was making his reputation as a hardcore wrestler. He popularized the use of wild dives and flips out of the ring. He even broke his neck once, when he took a fall.

Randy "Macho Man" Savage

Born Randy Poffo on November 15, 1952, Randy spent 5 years in the St. Louis Cardinals, Cincinnati Reds, and Chicago White Sox minor league systems before becoming a wrestler. He started out wrestling as a masked man, "The Spider." He joined the WWF in the 1970s for a few years, moved on, then returned to the McMahon fold in 1984 along with his manager and wife, Miss Elizabeth. (The marriage of their wrestling personas outlasted their real-life union—they divorced in the early 1990s.)

In 1994, Savage moved over to the WCW and began his long-running feud with Hollywood Hogan. He's been in and out of the nWo since the group's beginning. He is one of only four men to win both the WWF and WCW world championship titles during the course of his career.

Ken Shamrock

Born in 1962, Ken Shamrock is considered to be one of the best "shooters" in the wrestling profession today. He started wrestling in the late 1980s, and gained fame wrestling in straight matches in Japan. He currently wrestles for WWF, where he's highly popular. Shamrock is known to "snap" when he loses a match, attacking anybody in his path, including referees.

Faarooq (Ron Simmons)

This Warner Robins, Georgia, native son was born on May 15, 1962, and grew to be a strapping 6-foot, 2-inch, 260-pound Florida State football star. After his spectacular collegiate career in the late 1970s, for which he received serious consideration for the Heisman Trophy, he eventually migrated into a solo professional wrestling career in Florida. From his beginnings in 1986 he built a solid reputation, but achieved national fame only in 1990 after he teamed up with Butch Reid as the tag team "Doom" in the WCW. Doom, managed by the notorious Woman, started out as masked wrestlers but quickly lost their face coverings when they defeated the Steiner Brothers on May 19. This victory earned them the WCW World Tag Team title, which they held onto until February 1991, when the Freebirds defeated them.

In 1992, Simmons was once again working solo, and in that year he became the first African-American wrestler to win a world championship, which he won for the WCW. Since the mid 1990s, Simmons has wrestled for the WWF as Faarooq, leader of a racially mixed gang known as the Nation of Domination.

Jimmy Snuka

Born James Reiher in the Fiji Islands on May 18, 1943, Snuka began wrestling professionally in 1969 in Hawaii. During his earliest years as a pro wrestler he wrestled as Jimmy Kealoha.

After five years of featuring in wrestling matches in the Pacific northwest, Snuka moved to Texas where he became the WCCW champion in 1977. He finished out the decade of the '70s working for the NWA, where he was managed by Buddy Rogers and was frequently teamed with Paul Orndorff and Ray Stevens.

Snuka became a superstar in the 1980s with the WWF where he waged a long and furious feud against Rowdy Roddy Piper. He was one of the earliest of the high-flying wrestlers, and because of his expertise in these moves he became one of the most influential wrestlers in history.

It was his airborne antics that earned him his nickname of Superfly. Snuka was certainly the first wrestler of his size (6', 250 pounds) to sail through the air the way he did. He is most famous for being the first wrestler ever to jump off the top of a cage during a cage match. Snuka disappeared from the scene for a time, but re-emerged in the ECW where he won their version of the World Championship in 1992.

The Ultimate Warrior

One of the most wildly popular yet mysterious figures in wrestling history, the Ultimate Warrior is known for his face paint and incredible bulging muscles. He was one of wrestling's top stars until one day he vanished without a trace. No one in the last 20 years has had more false death rumors circulated about him than the Warrior.

The 6'5", 275-pound wrestler was born June 16, 1957, in Queens, New York, as Jim Hellwig. Since the WWF owns rights to the wrestling name Ultimate Warrior, Hellwig recently had his own personal name legally changed to The Warrior. He began his wrestling career in the early 1980s as Rock, and formed, with the wrestler Flash, the tag team Blade Runners. (Flash went on to become Sting.)

Warrior first gained national recognition as the Dingo Warrior, working for Fritz von Erich's World Class Championship Wrestling in Texas during the late 1980s. The highlight of his career came during *Wrestlemania VI* in Toronto, when he pinned the previously invincible Hulk Hogan to win the WWF World Heavyweight Championship. Today, the Warrior stars in his own comic book and has recently returned to active wrestling, once again doing all he can to make life miserable for his old foe, Hulk (now Hollywood) Hogan.

Wrestle Mania

One phenomenon of the modern pro wrestling industry is the way that top stars can diversify their careers beyond the ring. Hulk (now Hollywood) Hogan and Roddy Piper have had successful movie careers, Ultimate Warrior has a comic book hero modeled after him, and I (Captain Lou) did my Cyndi Lauper videos. And now we've got Jesse "The Boy" Ventura—governor of Minnesota!

The Least You Need To Know

➤ Mike Foley, a.k.a. Cactus Jack and a half dozen other characters, is the ace quick-change artist when it comes to persona.

➤ The Funk family has given wrestling fans two generations of fine wrestlers, from Dory Sr. to Terry and Dory Jr.

➤ Wrestlers often come to the business from other athletic pursuits: Scott Hall and Kevin Nash come from the basketball courts, Lex Luger from body-building.

➤ Perhaps the best-known figure to come out of wrestling is Hulk (now Hollywood) Hogan.

➤ Lots of today's wrestlers have real appeal for the female fans: Ravishing Rick Rude is just one of the beefcake stars.

➤ Jimmy Snuka's airborne antics are reminiscent of Antonino Rocca's memorable moves, but Snuka's skills are undeniably all his own.

Chapter 9

Feisty, Flashy, Colorful Charac-
ters of Notoriety

In This Chapter

➤ Movie serials, vaudeville, and the birth of the wrestling villain

➤ Being bad's a blast

➤ The changing faces of wrestling's evil ones

As you learned in Chapter 2, things got so bad for wrestling during the Depression years of the 1930s that a penny for your thoughts was considered a good deal. Scientific bouts of yore, lasting one and two hours, were passé; their lack-of-action induced yawns and thousand-yard stares in fans who responded by coming dressed as empty seats. Something—anything—had to be done to inject excitement into the sport before it, too, became passé.

Some time during this crucial life-and-death period for professional wrestling, one of those penny thoughts sprang from some promoter's fertile and fervid imagination, an idea borrowed from the old movie serials. He would create odious characters who could threaten the well-being of the hero—much like the villain Ming the Merciless in the old Flash Gordon serials. And the hero could then escape from the edge of one disaster only to find himself facing another, and another, and another—until he finally crushed the villain under the humdrum heel of Good.

On the pages that follow we'll take you through the largest Rogue's Gallery this side of Dick Tracy's roster of villains—a veritable wrestling version of "Boo's Who."

Enter Villain, Stage Left

Many of the evil characters created for these scenarios were mere cardboard caricatures of what bad guys should look and act like. But they all possessed one common trait: Their evil was omnipresent and unremitting, a dangerous threat to be countered at all costs by the mighty avengers who fought on the side of Right. Originally just marginally objectionable, the evil characters soon went all the way to violent, amoral, even immoral. And they slashed, fought, and menaced their way to despicableness until they achieved the aim striven for by dramatists since Aristophanes—audience empathy.

How well did this new storytelling style of pro wrestling work? George Lenihan, a heel's heel, told author Joe Jares "It's hard for customers to work up a fever week after week cheering for some nice guy. But the world never seems to run short of boos."

Wrestle Mania

Wrestling's colorful characters have changed over time to reflect changing attitudes in society. From the earliest bad guys—mostly supercilious lords and masked marauders—through a long cowboy and Indian era, through the McCarthy era fixation with evil commies, all the way up to the ambiguously-played, but essentially good guy, Stone Cold Steve Austin, the workingman's hero and his nemesis, the evil manager Vince McMahon. Wrestling's storylines have always suited the temper of the times.

And what began as just a few villains soon became an entire army of loathsome, sadistic, evil, grinning baddies. Now fans were treated to the spectacle of their favorite "baby faces" getting the bejabbers beaten out of them by the baddie and then barely escaping from their foes' fearsome clutches in the nick of time—just like Flash Gordon and Dale managing to escape in their rocket ship seconds before Ming the Merciless could catch them and feed them to the Lizard Men.

It was great theater, and fans began flocking back to the arenas week after week to cheer for a real-live enactment of the cliff-hanger action popularized by the movie serials of the day. And with real-life action heroes, there was always the question: Will he, or won't he, survive *this* time?

However, the baddies were still just stereotypes—cardboard cutouts all developed according to a single pattern by the promoters. The wrestler who was to flesh out the concept of the villain and turn it into a fully formed character, at least as far as wrestling fans were concerned, was none other than that prototype of modern-day baddies, Gorgeous George.

A Peerage of Uppity Lords

Name	Description
Lord Alfred Hayes	British-born champion in the 1950s. Manager and announcer in the U.S. in the late 1980s and early 1990s.
Sir Oliver Humperdink	Really from Florida. A "heel" manager during the 1980s.
Lord Athol Layton	Canadian-born wrestler of the 1950s.
Lord Littlebrook	Midget wrestler.
Lord Steven Regal	Current British-born star who has worked both the WCW and WWF.

The Original Ultimate Evil One

The Gorgeous One did not so much change the nature of the baddie—described by one anonymous writer of the time as "disloyal, untrustworthy, unkind, and irreverent, not to mention sadistic and cruel"—so much as he changed the *degree* of villainy. Along with his plentiful evil vibrations and bag full of dirty tricks, all borrowed from the old school of stage and screen villainy, Gorgeous George added his own elements, all calculated to heat the blood of the crowd. But it wasn't just his haughtiness, his evil vibes, or even his underhanded tricks that made him into the arch villain of all villains. It was his vanity—especially his long, bleached-blond hair that became a visual shorthand for identifying villains. Soon the rings were filled with the likes of Freddie Blassie, Johnny Valentine, Eddie and Jerry Graham, John L. Sullivan, Rip Hawk, Ripper Collins, the Fargo Brothers, and hundreds of others, all peroxided, posturing purveyors of perniciousness.

Captain Lou's Corner

Gorgeous George doesn't fit into any regular baddie category. And he never did. He got to be a heel just by being the most utterly obnoxiously, overbearingly irritating character in wrestling. All he had to do was turn up in his fancy robe with that spritzing valet of his and the fans were ready to settle in for a night of hissing and booing.

Calling Central Casting...

Following hard on the heels of these red-blooded, blond-haired heels came an invasion of characters right out of central casting, as promoters soon began adding new flavors of foulness to the genre. The smorgasbord of baddies ranged from goose-stepping Nazis to deceitful Orientals to turbaned Turks to Russian commie rats to Iranian do-badders—to any stereotype the promoters could think up to mirror our society's ever-present but ever-changing fear and distrust of foreigners.

115

Remember Harvey Korman's character in *Blazing Saddles*, Hedley Lamarr, ordering Slim Pickens to "get me an army of the worst dregs ever to soil the face of the West…I want rustlers, cutthroats, murderers, desperadoes, mugs, pugs, thugs, nitwits, half-wits, dimwits, vipers, snipers, muggers, buggerers, bushwhackers, hornswogglers, horse thieves, train robbers, bank robbers…,"and on and on? Korman could have saved himself the trouble and instead just looked for his recruits in the wrestling rings of the 1940s and 1950s. They were all there.

It was almost as if the promoters believed that without villains, there could be no heroes. So they rounded up a bunch of the usual suspects—or reasonable facsimiles thereof—to give the heroes some menace or other to triumph over.

Baddie Is as Baddie Does

Who among us hasn't wanted to play the bad boy, the mischievous kid who never grew up? For generations we've watched as Charlie Chaplin, Lou Costello and Jerry Lewis of yesteryear, and more recently Jim Carrey of today have played the bad little kids locked up inside all of us. Not that we're going around ripping the wings off flies, mind you—we're just having fun thumbing our nose at society and its strict rules that are supposed to regulate our behavior but seem to have been written by someone who doesn't want us to have any fun.

Well, that's how it was for me, anyway. I wanted to have fun in my chosen profession—wrestling—and decided that the best way to have it was being a baddie. Like Lou Costello always said, "I'm a baaaaaaaaad boy."

Now I know what you're probably going to say: That I became a baddie to compensate for a lack of wrestling ability. But that's not so. I had the ability. But being a baddie is just a lot more fun. And, between us, what else was a guy with a mug and build like mine going to be? A hero? Get real!

So I took on the trappings of a bad guy, including my cockamamie gimmick of a safety pin in my cheek, which I sorta borrowed from a wino I once saw down in the Bowery down in lower Manhattan. It gave me character, if not dignity, and a uniqueness that I could market as a legitimate baddie.

And I had other gimmicks to reinforce my image as a heel. Like my can opener—all wrapped in white tape, natch, so the crowd could see it when I pulled it out of its hiding place in my oversized trunks. I'd pull it out and prepare to hit my opponent with it, and the can opener would fall out of my hand so the opponent could pick it up and come after me. Then he'd hit me with my

Bert's Corner

Captain Lou's bark has always been a lot worse than his bite. He always talked a tough game, but he was most famous for his fleetness of foot. Not his fancy footwork in the ring, mind you, but his tendency to scamper on up the exit aisle whenever it looked likely that he was going to take his lumps from his opponent.

own weapon—imagine that!—and BOOM I'd be on the floor, writhing in pain. And as he'd go up to his corner for his big finish, I'd roll under the ropes and flee like a flash to the dressing room.

That's called "selling the gimmick." By that point I'd have the fans into the act, yelling and screaming, "You gutless fat so-and-so! Stay and fight!" (Only they'd use worse words than "so-and-so.")

A Herd of Heavyweight Heavies

Some bad guys were cast as bad just because they were too darned *big* to be good. Here's a few wide-bodies and their weight stats:

Name	Weight
Benny McGuire	727 lbs.*
Billy McGuire (Benny's twin)	727 lbs.*
Happy Humphrey	620 lbs.
Haystacks Calhoun (William Calhoun)	601 lbs.
Curly Moe	555 lbs.
Yokozuna	550 lbs.
Haystacks Calhoun Jr. (John Brody)	526 lbs.
Andre the Giant	520 lbs.
Loch Ness (Giant Haystacks in the U.K.)	505 lbs.
Mabel (forget what the name implies, he's a guy)	503 lbs.
Earthquake (John Tenta)	503 lbs.

* Claimed weight, never verified.

But using my Houdini-esque escape move means I was never beaten. One time Vince McMahon Sr. asked me why I did that and I told him, "Vince, once you beat me the people are going to be happy, but my *shtick* is over." I mean, if I stood and fought, I'd have about as much chance as a luckless pyromaniac who sneezes on his last match. I was no match for some of the characters I wrestled, and instead of standing my ground I pulled the he-who-runs-away-lives-to-battle-another-day routine. That's how I managed to wrestle the great Bruno Sammartino 13 times, filling the arena—whether it was Madison Square Garden or Buffalo's War Memorial—to capacity and all heated up, and still leave them excited enough to come back and see me wrestle Bruno again.

Same thing with Andre the Giant. Heck, he could have beaten me with one hand tied behind his back—maybe even both. But he never actually beat me, because I just fled the ring. That was part of my bad guy thing. Break the rules or break my neck? I'd break the rules every time.

Gimmick's Galore

There are other bad guy gimmicks. Take Dick the Bruiser. On a TV show, some time back in the early 1960s, the announcer told the audience that a big birthday cake at ringside was for Cowboy Bob Ellis, a real good guy. According to the announcer, some homeless kids had saved up their last pennies to buy the cake for their hero. So what did the Bruiser do to prove he was a baddie? He came out and stomped on the cake, right on camera, that's what! Another time his opponent got a cake presented to him by a little girl all dressed up in her Sunday best and the Bruiser came bursting into the ring, pushed the little girl aside, and smashed the cake right into the babyface's face.

It's like Mae West's old song says: "It's not what you do, it's the way that you do it." You play to the fans, you heat them up, you insult their hero, and you generally play at being the baaaaadest dude ever seen. That's all, brother, that's all.

Managerial Metamorphosis

After some action-filled years in the ring, when the fire in my belly became just an ache in my legs, I took my bad guy act up to the next level. I decided to become a manager—a baddie manager.

Let me tell you how I worked that one out. One of my wrestlers was Jimmy "Superfly" Snuka…he of the acrobatic moves off the ropes. Well, at the time, Snuka was also a bad guy. It was a perfect match up—made in wrestling heaven, you might say—between a baddie wrestler and an equally baddie manager.

In Your Face

Managers and bad guys are a staple in modern wrestling—even when the manager is a promoter. Vince McMahon Jr.'s evil managerial-class character is scripted to give every working-stiff wrestling fan a foe to boo drawn straight from the frustration of his (or her) work-a-day life. When you can't yell at your boss, he makes a perfect replacement.

So there we were, down in Atlantic City, walking the beach, when some of the people sitting on their towels began screaming at us: "You fat b*****d, leave Snuka alone. He's a good guy…*you're* the one who makes him what he is!"

One of those little light bulbs that cartoonists draw appeared over my head and I went to Vince Sr. with a great idea: "Know what, Vince?" I said, "Let's switch Jimmy to a babyface." So we go on the air and I'm doing an interview with Vince Jr. and I say, "Jimmy Snuka's from Samoa, Fiji, somewhere like that—they're all the same, those Polynesians. They got brains like BB's. Put their brains in a pigeon or a parakeet and they fly backwards…." Then, as an afterthought, I add, "Now, look, nothing against the Samoan people…everyone should have one for a pet."

With that, McMahon looks at me and says, "Captain Lou…" but before he could get anything more out, motormouth me threw in yet another insult: "Look, I get the guy $200 a week. I bought him a 1960 Chevy and other things…" And McMahon says, "But Captain Lou, the man's making five to six hundred thousand a year." "So what?" I snapped, "I'm investing his money for him." Vince Jr. asked, "What happened to it?" "It was a total loss," I laughed.

Jimmy's just standing there, open-mouthed and fuming, when suddenly Ray Stevens rushes in from off camera and together we slam-dunk Snuka to the ground. So now Jimmy wants to wrestle me. "Sure," I tell him. "I'll get you in the ring and take out my cockamamie gimmick and nail you with it." Anyway, that's how I stayed in character as a bad guy, and how I turned Snuka into a babyface.

From Good to Evil, From Evil to Good

Switches aren't that infrequent, whether from heel to babyface, like Snuka, or vice versa. Some wrestlers have recycled their careers on a local level—like Freddie Blassie did in Los Angeles and Ray Stevens did in San Francisco, all the while keeping their bad-guy union cards when appearing elsewhere. But usually this kind of change is done on an across-the-board basis, like when Gorilla Monsoon went from bad to good, or when Hulk Hogan, Black Jack Lanza, and Johnny Valentine went the other way.

Body Slam

While characters switch from good to bad pretty often, you've got to be careful how you do it. After all, credibility, at least to some tiny degree, needs to be maintained or the fans can lose interest.

Most of the time the changeover from good to bad (or the opposite) is because of the fans—just as it happened in Jimmy's case. As Shawn Michaels put it: "The fans decide who is good or bad."

One of the great old-time wrestlers, Jack Armstrong, agrees. He said, "The crowd really dictates it. The crowds seemed to hate me, so why not follow up on it?" Armstrong also added one more element to the equation of why wrestlers change over. "I play it for all I can. The more people I can put in the seats, the more I make." And that's the name of the game in wrestling as it is in any other field—making more money.

Bert's Corner

Masked men are a mainstay of wrestling and always have been. And in the U.S. it usually means "baddie." But in Mexico, everybody wears masks—good, bad, and everybody in between.

The changeover usually occurs faster than Kato's. You remember him, the Green Hornet's trusty sidekick? On the nationally syndicated radio show, he changed his nationality overnight on Friday, December 5, 1941, from Japanese to Filipino the day after Pearl Harbor.

Usually, though, there's a good reason for the change. And that reason is usually spelled m-o-n-e-y. Why not? After all, that's why we're in this game in the first place. And second place, too.

How the W(r)est(ling) Was Won

America has played cowboys and Indians since the mid 19th century. At least since 1883, when Buffalo Bill opened his Wild West Show featuring his Congress of Rough Riders and Sitting Bull—with his band of warriors who had slaughtered the troops of General Custer seven years earlier.

A Round-Up of Straight Shooting Cowboys

While every wrestler who ever worked in Texas has used the cowboy gimmick at one time or another, there are a few who were cowboys no matter where they worked. Here's a sampling:

Name	Description
Cowboy Pat Fraley	West Coast wrestler from the 1930s through the early 1950s. Sometimes he took off his cowboy hat and wrestled as the Green Panther.
Cowboy Bob Ellis	Started in the late 1950s in Texas and wrestled all over the country.
Clarence "Cowboy" Luttrell	Wrestler in the 1950s and 1960s who turned promoter in Florida in the 1970s.
The Cowboy Connection	A wild west tag team made up of Bobby Jaggers and R. T. Tyler. They wrestled in the late 1980s.
Texas Cowgirls	Joyce Grable and Wendi Richter, a tag team of the 1980s.

Buffalo Bill's Wild West Show ran for two decades, making the West and the opposition of cowboys and Indians a part of Americana. It was a theme picked up by the newly minted movie industry, starting with the very first movie plot line, in 1903: *The Great Train Robbery,* starring Bronco Billy Anderson.

That the whole Wild West saga was a fiction made no difference to the generations who fell in love with the concept. The Buffalo Bill that they idolized was a pulp-fiction hero made up by writer Ned Buntline, who fictionalized and romanticized the deeds of a grubby, besotted buffalo hunter he found asleep under a Conestoga wagon. Nor did it make any difference to the audiences of moviegoers that Bronco Billy Anderson was really Max Aronson of Little Rock, Arkansas. The Wild West was America's singular claim to fame, and the people bought into it, hook, line, and sinker.

The Good Guys Wear White Hats

What's all this got to do with wrestling? Well, it was only natural that wrestling promoters would exploit this ready-made legend. By the 1930s they were presenting their own version of the Wild West Show, with their *own* cowboys and Indians. Most of those who were cowboys were from Texas or Oklahoma, or wrestled there. But some just took on the persona. And in the main they were babyfaces—straight shooters patterned after movie personalities like Tom Mix. An occasional cowboy, like Black Jack Lanza, would go astray, but even those would return to the good-guy fold.

Circle the Wagons, Boys!

On the other hand, many of those who were presented as Indians were as corny as Indian corn. Lou Thesz remembers one—Chief Chewchki—who wrestled back in the 1930s. He was, in Thesz's words, "the strangest character I ever met in professional wrestling." Thesz told of one of the Chief's gimmicks: When he arrived in a new town, Chewchki would promptly pitch a teepee on the City Hall lawn. When the cops arrived to oust him, the Chief would "have to have his fun first," telling the police, "White man! Chichi Indian!" in a B-movie accent. "This land Indian land. Me stay here!" Well, the cops would finally run him off, but not before the newspapers had shown up. So Chewchki got a bundle of free publicity, which helped tremendously at the gate." But then Thesz added the kicker: "My father said to me 'he's no more an Indian than I am. He's actually a Serbian gypsy and he'll steal you blind if he gets the chance.' Pop had seen a lot of gypsies in Europe when he was a boy, and he'd recognized Chewchki's accent."

Another Indian who had strayed far from the range was a friend of mine who wrestled under the name of Chief Jay Strongbow back in the 1950s. In reality, Chief Jay Strongbow was Joe Scarpa, and I always had fun calling him a member of the "Woppaho" Tribe.

Captain Lou's Corner

Indian characters were there at the start of professional wrestling and they're still going strong today. And it's one of the few character categories where you're just as likely to find a character playing a persona that's really his own.

A Tribe of Indians on the Warpath—Part 1

Here are some of the early Indian wrestlers who made the persona popular, roughly in order of their appearance in the ring:

Name	Description
Chief Thunderbird	First "Indian" wrestler to enter the ring in full headdress. Started in 1933. Popular in both the U.S. and Europe. Real name: Baptiste Thomas.
Joseph War Hawk	True Canadian Mohawk. He wrestled in Canada and on the East Coast during the 1930s. Father of Chief Don Eagle, who followed his dad's footsteps into the wrestling ring.
Chief Little Wolf	Started in the carnivals in 1934 and worked until the late 1950s.

continues

continued

Name	Description
Chief Osley Saunooke	A true Cherokee. Played football in the 1920s, then wrestled from 1936 through the late 1950s.
Chief Jay Strongbow	Real name, Joe Scarpa. Started wrestling in the late 1940s. Still a major act in the 1970s, when he became a star for the WWF. When Gorgeous George ran for president in 1952 (yes, he really did), Strongbow served as his campaign manager.
Chief Sunni War Cloud	A legitimate Wassek Indian. Wrestled from the late 1940s to 1971.

Imaginative promoters created Indians out of whole cloth—not to mention hand-woven blankets. There was Chief Little Wolf (who went by the name Benny Tenario on his driver's license), Chief Sunni War Cloud (known to his neighbors as Sonny Chorre), Chief Thunderbird (a Canadian whose visa read Baptiste Pauli), and other so-called chiefs from every tribe imaginable. There was even an African-American out on the coast who wrestled under the name Tiger Nelson, who had the chutzpah (an Indian word) to bill himself as a member of the Blackfoot tribe. It was as if wrestling was marching to the song from *Annie Get Your Gun*: "Choctaws, Chickasaws, Chippewas…. We are Indians, too."

With all these Indian chiefs circling the wrestling rings throughout the 1940s and 1950s, you had to wonder who was left to handle tribal affairs.

Wrestling, Indian Style

But even while these sham Indians were performing in the ring with all the credibility of Boris Karloff (who once played an Indian chief in a movie), there were plenty of "Honest Injuns" around. There was Chief Osley Saunooke, a 300-plus pound Cherokee. And there was Chief Don Eagle—in actuality only the son of a chief, but what the heck. And many, many other legitimate native American wrestlers.

A Tribe of Indians on the Warpath—Part 2

The Indian persona has a lot of staying power. Here's another helping of headdress-wearing wrestlers from the 1950s onward:

Name	Description
Chief Don Eagle	Son of Joseph War Hawk. Legitimate Mohawk. Wrestled in the midwest in the early 1950s—even held the 1950 AWA world title, for three days before losing it to Gorgeous George. Committed suicide in 1966 at the age of 41.

Name	Description
Chief Big Heart	Southern-born star of the NWA in the late 1950s.
Little Eagle	Worked with Chief Big Heart in Texas in 1959.
Billy Two Rivers	A true Mohawk Indian. Wrestled throughout the South during the 1950s and 1960s.
Chief Lone Eagle	Worked the Mid-South circuit in the 1950s and 1960s. Accompanied to the ring by his wife, Bonita.
Princess Tona Tomah	A Chippewa Indian from Minnesota. Wrestled during the 1950s and 1960s.
Billy Red Cloud	Legitimate Chippewa. Worked the Minnesota circuit in the 1960s.
Danny Little Bear	Teamed with Chief Thundercloud in the 1960s. Little Bear had a wrestling sister named Princess Little Cloud.
Don Running Bear and Billy Two Eagles	Tag team on the Northwest circuit in the 1960s.
Chief Kit Fox	Sometimes teamed with Chief Big Heart. Career ended in a serious car crash in the early 1970s.
Steve Little Bear	Canadian wrestler of the 1970s.
Chief Wahoo McDaniel	Played football in the NFL for the Oilers, Broncos, Jets, and Dolphins as Ed McDaniel. Was a big NWA star from 1966 through 1989.
Jules Strongbow	No relation to Chief Jay Strongbow. Real name, Frank Hill. Wrestled in the 1980s.
Tanaka	Real name: Chris Chavis. Wrestled in the WWF in the early 1990s.

All the Indians, real or faux, had the same shtick: They would enter the ring wearing a war bonnet, moccasins, and war beads. They'd go through some tribal dance—a war dance, rain dance, any kind of dance—and then let out a long, loud, war whoop. And there were gimmicks, like the one employed by Little Beaver—a midget wrestler who slugged his opponents with his moccasins.

But all of them—whether real or ring wannabees—worked on the side of Good, just like Tonto with his pardner, the Lone Ranger. They rode in to avenge ring wrongs.

Foreign Invaders

As the Great Depression took hold and wrestling began to lose its grip, promoters turned more and more to gimmickry to draw in the fans. One way was to ring changes on the good versus evil theme by expanding the field of baddies.

Wrestle Mania

Wrestling's reliance on foreigners to provide its stock characters in the ring goes back a long way. And it was based on the idea that pitting any "All American Boy" against some evil outsider would bring in the fans. Well, it sure succeeded in that goal. Especially in the classic battles between Hulk Hogan and the evil Iron Sheik. That one kept the fans coming back in droves for match after match.

Wrestling has always had its share of Terrible Turks and other foreign bad guys, but now it began to add to its repertoire of wrongdoers: Indians, hillbillies, British Blue Bloods, and so on. But the really big influx of baddie characters was to wait until the end of World War II. Then, wrestling began borrowing from the plot lines of comic books, which had used the war as a backdrop for its heroes to battle against the forces of evil. Heroes like Captain America, taking on his archenemy, the evil Nazi Red Skull. And like the Torch, who fought against Gestapo agents with names like Python and Rabbit. Wrestling began to sponsor what might best be described as its own GI Bill for enemy agents.

A Gaggle of Goose-Stepping Germans

Name	Description
Hans Hermann	German-born, but fought for the U.S. during World War II. Teamed with Fritz von Erich for a time. Retired in the late 1950s.
Fritz and Waldo von Erich	Not related to one another. A team of goose-stepping Nazis until Fritz left the ring to become a promoter and start his dynasty of wrestling sons.
Killer Karl Krupp and Kurt von Steiger	A Nazi tag team. They worked through the 1970s.
Hans Schmidt	Worked Ohio and the upstate New York circuit in the early 1960s.
Fritz and Hans Schnabel	Actual brothers from Bristol, Connecticut. They wrestled from the late 1940s to the mid 1950s.
Karl and Kurt von Brauner	Wrestled from about 1960 through 1976.
Skull von Crush	Tennessee wrestler of the 1990s.

Name	Description
Kurt von Himmler and Kurt von Poppenheim	Tag team in the Northwest in the 1950s.
Frederick von Schacht	"Milwaukee's Murder Master" who wrestled during the postwar years through 1950.
Kurt and Skull von Stroheim	Performers on the Southern circuit in the 1960s.
Baron von Raschke	Last of the Nazi characters to use the claw hold made famous by Fritz von Erich. Started in 1966 and stayed active into the 1990s.

Evil Doers From Evil Empires

With international political correctness their least concern, promoters introduced a number of grim reapers of violence who generally fell into one of two enemy camps: goose-stepping, swastika-laden, jackbooted Nazi brutes, or sly, cunning, devious Japanese snakes in the grass.

The thinly disguised Germans all sported Third Reich-sounding names: Karl von Hess, Fritz von Goering, Otto von Krupp, Hans Schmidt, Karl von Sholt, Killer Karl Krupp, Count von Zuppie, Kurt and Karl von Brauner, Karl von Stronheim, Fritz von Erich, and any other variation on the German theme you could think of. And to a man they were all swinish, arrogant, and thoroughly Teutonic, refusing to stand for the Star Spangled Banner, turning their backs on the American flag, and declaring their intention to grind the hero under the heel of their jackboots, win the championship for the Master Race, and take the belt back to the fatherland for safekeeping.

A Sushi Selection of Evil Orientals

Name	Description
The Great Togo	Real name: Tio Taylor. The prototype of the evil Japanese wrestler. Carried out a long feud with Antonino Rocca in the early 1950s. Wrestled into the early 1970s.
Tokyo Joe	Sometime tag-team partner of The Great Togo during the later stages of Togo's career.
Kenji Shibuya	NWA villain from 1956 until the early 1980s.
Professor Toru Tanaka	WWF wrestler from 1960s to the 1980s. Also known for his role as Odd Job in the James Bond film *Goldfinger*.
Dr. Hiro Ota	Sometime tag team partner of Professor Toru Tanaka during the mid 1970s.
The Great Moto	Real name: Charles Iwamoto. Bearded giant. NWA villain of the 1950s and 1960s.

continues

continued

Name	Description
Tor Kamata	A.k.a. Dr. Moto. AWA villain in the 1960s, WWF heel in the 1970s.
Mr. Pogo	NWA villain of the 1970s and early 1980s.
Masa Saito	Real name: Masanori Saito. NWA wrestler of the 1970s. WWF wrestler of the 1980s. Teamed in the WWF with Mr. Fuji.
Mr. Fuji	Real name: Harry Fujiwara. WWF wrestler of the 1970s and manager in the 1980s and 1990s.
Fujihiro Niikura and Hiroshi Hase	Team that wrestled in the 1980s in Canada as the Viet Cong Express
The Great Kabuki	Real name: Akihisa Mera. NWA wrestler of the 1980s, known for long hair covering his face and "blowing the mist," a green spray that he exhaled into the eyes of his opponents.
The Great Muta	Real name: Keiji Muto. Recreated Kabuki's act during the early 1990s in the WCW, mist and all. Still guest stars on WCW as a member of the Japanese wing of the nWo. He's a big movie star in Japan under his real name.
Bull Nakano	Evil woman wrestler. Feuded with the blond and beautiful Alundra Blaise in the WWF during the mid 1990s.
Yokozuna	Really one of the Wild Samoans tag team wrestling in the persona of an evil Japanese Sumo wrestler. WWF champion in 1994.
Sonny Oono	Evil WCW manager who currently works with Japanese wrestlers when they make guest appearances on *Monday Nitro*.

The Japanese, or Oriental, wrestlers were all cast as cunning. Their treachery consisted of such devious tricks as throwing salt in their opponents' eyes or resorting to illegal karate chops and sleeper holds. They wore thin beards and mustaches and crewcuts, wooden clogs, and ceremonial robes. Their names bespoke their treachery: Mr. Moto, Professor Toro Tanaka, Mr. Fugi, Hiro Matsuda, and the like.

Homegrown Foreigners

Whatever they called themselves, most of these wrestlers' laundry name tags didn't match their ring monikers. Hans Schmidt was a French Canadian from Montreal named Guy Larose. Fritz von Erich was really Jack Adkisson of Texas. Most of the "Japanese" hailed from Hawaii or Samoa. No matter. The fans ate this stuff up.

Cold Warriors

As memories of World War II began to dim in our rearview mirror, the promoters continued to mirror the temper of the times. They found a whole new foreign menace to offer up to the fans in the form of villains: Russian heels from the reddest part of Communist Russia. With shaven heads and handlebar mustaches, wearing Cossack tunics and lamb's-wool Astrakhan hats, these baddies played their parts with varying degrees of convincingness. The Russian invasion included Ivan Bulba, Ivan Poddubny, Mastros Kirilenko, Ivan Koloff, Professor Boris Malenko, and Ivan Rasputin—and a whole Party Congress of no-goodniks from central casting who carried on with the Cold War in the ring.

Bert's Corner

Not surprisingly, the vogue for evil Commies suffered a serious blow with the fall of the Berlin Wall. Once the Cold War ended, it became a little tough to take mad Russian bombers and commie rats seriously.

Redskis, Russkis, and Commie Creeps

Name	Description
Comrade Soldat and Tovarich Maxim Gorky	Bearded "brother" tag team. Wrestled in Canada and on the West Coast during the 1950s.
Ivan Kalmikoff	NWA villain of the 1950s and 1960s. Was a manager for a time during the 1970s.
Ivan Kameroff	"The Russian Strongman," a bodybuilder who became an NWA star in the 1950s and 1960s
Ivan Koloff	Began wrestling in 1961. Managed by Captain Lou in the WWWF during the 1970s. Moved to the NWA during the 1980s and was still active on the independent circuit during the early 1990s.
Nikita Koloff	Real name: Scott Simpson. "Nephew" of Ivan Koloff. Wrestled in the NWA and WWF from 1985 to 1991.
The Russian Brute	AWA heart puncher of 1988.
The Russian Assasin	Pacific Coast wrestler of the 1990s.
Soldat Ustinov	1980s tag team partner of Boris Zukhov.
Igor Volkoff	Canadian wrestler of the 1980s.
Nikolai Volkoff	Began pro career as Bepo Mongol. As Volkoff, wrestled mainly for the WWF from early 1970s to 1995. Still active.
Nikolai Zolotoff	Character portrayed by Butcher Vachon during the late 1950s in Texas.
Boris Zukhov	Real name: Jim Darrell. Wrestled from 1982 to the early 1990s in the AWA and WWF.

Like their German and Japanese counterparts of earlier decades, these wrestlers had their origins a little closer to home: Ivan Rasputin, the Mad Russian, was really Hyman Fishman from Boston. But rather than brooding about the legitimacy of the wrestlers' claims to Russian nationality, fans once again flocked to the arenas to see their heroes tie patriotic red-white-and-blue cans to the baddies' red Commie tails.

Middle Eastern Madmen

From Commies, it was but a short hop, skip, and oil strike to the next wave of baddies, the Arabs—who hit their peak of popularity during the oil crisis of the early 1970s. These fiendish villains came attired in burnooses, usually with a camel imprint, and turbans. They'd enter the ring carrying their nation's or emirate's flag and a Muslim prayer rug, which they would roll out and bow down on, to the assorted hisses and boos of the assembled crowd. Then the Sheik or some other variation thereof—they all had names that sounded like Abou ben Adem—would try to apply his signature hold like the "Camel Clutch" or the "Arabian Airplane Spin" to the hero, who would strike back in the name of America—and in the name of every fan who ever waited on line for hours to get gas.

An Emirate of Oily Sheiks

Name	Description
The Sheik	The original. Wrestled fron 1952 until the early 1990s.
Sheik Abdullah Ali Hassan	Real name: Jack Kruger. Southern wrestler in the early 1980s.
Sheik Adnan El-Kaissey	Wrestled from 1959 through 1977, a heel manager after that, working out of the Dallas Sportatorium through the early 1990s.
The Iron Sheik	Probably the best known, thanks to his feud with Hulk Hogan. One-time WWF champion. Real name: Jose Azzerri. Really from Iran. When U.S. enmity changed from Iran to Iraq he switched his claimed nationality to Iraqi and called himself Colonel Mustafa.

It was great theater, great fun, and great gate too. Especially for the juvenile fans who now saw real-life comic-book villains come to life in the ring and get the bejesus beaten out of them by their heroes—all-American heroes at that.

Wrestlers From Another Dimension

The promoters, having exhausted the possibility of inhumane humans, now began to explore inhuman humanoids—outer-worldly creatures whose depravity stood out in stark contrast to the simple unscrupulousness of worldly heels like the Germans, Russians, Japanese, and Arabs.

The Twilight Zone Contingent

Name	Description
Leatherface	Star of the 1990s. Wrestles in Japan and the Mid South circuit. Bases his character on a psycho killer in *The Texas Chainsaw Massacre*. Claims his mask is made out of the faces of vanquished foes.
The Mummy	Real name: Beji Remirez. Wrestled in Texas in the 1960s.
Raven	Real name: Scott Levy. Also wrestled as "Scotty the Blood," and as Johnny Polo. ECW and WCW favorite in the 1990s. Bases his character on the Edgar Allen Poe poem. Ends every interview with the exclamation: "Nevermore!"
The Shadow	Real name: Marv Westenberg. Also wrestled as the Masked Black Spider. Wrestled for the AWA in the 1930s.
Soultaker	Real name: Charles Wright. Uses voodoo to incapacitate opponents. Wrestled for the WWF in the 1990s. Also known as Papa Shango, Kama Mutafa, and the Godfather.
Kevin Sullivan	NWA/WCW wrestler from 1970 to the present. A devil worshipper back in the days before it was fashionable.
Undertaker	Real name: Mark Calloway. WWF wrestler of the 1990s. Comes from "the Dark Side"—but refuses to rest in peace.
Vampiro Americano	Real name: Justin Bradshaw, who played the character briefly during the 1980s.
Vampiro Canadiense	A Canadian bloodsucker who terrorized Mexico City in the 1990s.

Wrestling's always had more men in masks than you could find in Nome, Alaska, on a frigid day. Even in the early days, bad guys wore masks: red masks, black masks, white, green, and purple masks. And their names gave a hint of the unspeakable horror they were likely to wreak on the hero: There were Phantoms, Invaders, Terrors, Avengers, Flashes, Doctor X's, and just plain ol' "The Masked Man."

Usually there was some gimmick that went with the mask, the most common being that, if beaten, they'd unmask in the ring. Several did lose to the good guy, but when they'd rip off the hood, they'd reveal a second mask underneath. (Author Joe Jares remembers one fan hollering "It's not a sport anymore, it's a striptease.")

Captain Lou's Corner

One of those I managed who came close to being one of the outer-worldlies was George "The Animal" Steele. George was really a very nice man, formerly a high school teacher out of Detroit. But you'd never know it to look at him. The Animal was a slack-jawed, drooling creature. His body was so be-furred he looked like he was wearing a mohair sweater. He spent the entire bout chewing up the turnbuckles in the corners.

But in the 1940s a whole new subspecies of masked baddies was born. Now they added skulls and crossbones or other fiendishly clever satanic markings to their masks. Some started to wear head-to-toe fluorescent skeleton outfits, or took on names like The Black Demon, or The Gorilla (who was wheeled up to ringside in a cage), or Joe "Jungle Boy" Vettucci, or The Clawman, or The Mummy. Evil truly seemed to lurk in the heart of wrestling-dom.

It always seemed that the heavies of the ring were also the real-life heavyweights: their beer bellies were in sharp contrast to the muscular development of the hero's form. But these hounds of hell served their purpose, and served it well. Their job was to menace the hero. And all were the creations of the sorcerers and mad scientists known as wrestling promoters—who'd created them to underscore the battle between Right and Wrong, Good and Evil, and between wrestling's version of the minions of Ming and the goodly Flash Gordon. They gave the heroes the pretext for saving the world from destruction, at least on wrestling night.

The Least You Need to Know

➤ The Good-Guy/Bad-Guy storyline was invented by promoters to bring fans into the arenas during the Great Depression era.

➤ Wrestling's plot lines were enhanced by borrowing from the movie serial cliff-hangers and from comic book characters.

➤ The cowboy and Indians legends of 19th century Americana gave wrestling some of its first truly colorful characters.

➤ World War II saw the start of the foreign invader baddie explosion.

➤ As America shifted focus from enemies of the World War II era to the Cold War and the Oil embargo, wrestling's cast of baddies expanded to include more and more lethal "foreign" enemies.

Chapter 10

More Flashy Characters: The Who's Who and What's That of Today's Pro Wrestling

In This Chapter

➤ More of wrestling's great heroes, villains, beasts, and beauties

➤ Further background and bios on the stars of today

➤ Stars of tomorrow: The new faces in today's pro wrestling

Many of today's new wrestling fans have only a passing recognition of some of the greatest performers, past and present, who've stood out larger than life, like the carvings on Mount Rushmore. Wrestling's recent explosive growth, however, was built on these stars, body slam by body slam, toe hold by hammer lock, over the past two decades.

And even when fans *do* know some of the great competitors by name, they have little awareness of their many accomplishments. In this book we've tried to remedy that situation, and in this chapter we'll just keep at the job. Learn here about wrestling's good guys and bad guys, the beauties and the beasts—in short, learn the hitherto unknown stories of wrestling's storied modern legends and its legends-in-the-making. And while you're reading, cheer them on—because the cheering of the fans is what wrestling's all about!

Bob Backlund: Clean Cut but Clearly Tough

The 6-foot, 1-inch, 234-pound Bob Backlund was much, much smaller when he was born in Princeton, Minnesota, on August 14, 1950. Red-headed and freckled, his open-faced charm has led to comparisons with Andy Griffith's boy, Opie and (less flatteringly) Howdy Doody. He started out in amateur wrestling, winning the championship, but it wasn't long before he was knocking on pro wrestling's door. He joined Verne Gagne's AWA lineup in 1974, where he built a reputation for a gimmick-free, purely scientific style. During the next couple of years he wrestled for the NWA, and then joined the WWWF in 1977, where he was to finally confront his destiny as a star.

Bob Backlund takes his punishment from Jimmy Snuka (Source: Norman Kietzer)

Early in his WWWF career, Backlund showed great promise, which came to fruition on February 20, 1978: That's when he bested Superstar Billy Graham and took the championship belt. The belt stayed in his possession for nearly six years: He lost it at last to the Iron Sheik at Madison Square Garden in December of 1983.

After losing the belt, Backlund wasn't seen much for the rest of the 1980s—he had a few matches here and there but no real visibility. In 1992, however, he was back in action for the WWF with a vengeance. He'd made the transformation from a clean-cut, clean wrestler to a bow-tied heel, basing his character on everybody's worst memory of the high-school teacher from hell. The fan's loved the new Backlund, and he was on his way to stardom.

Gone Before His Time: Bruiser Brody

Controversial throughout his wrestling career, Bruiser Brody remained so in his untimely death, by stabbing, at the age of 42. Born Frank Donald Goodish on July 14, 1946, in Albuquerque, New Mexico, Brody joined the pro-wrestling world in 1973. A tremendously popular, hardcore brawler, the Bruiser stood 6-foot, 4-inches and weighed in at 284 pounds.

Bruiser's main claim to fame was his willingness to give the crowds what they wanted in the blood and gore line—he bled so much that by the end of his career his forehead was so scarred it looked like tripe. For 16 years, Brody wrestled—first as one of the WWWF's monsters, where he tried and failed to take the title from Bruno Sammartino; and second in World Class, where he began in the late 1970s in the persona of a nemesis to Fritz von Erich. A decade later he finished as a tag-team partner for Kerry von Erich's sons.

Bruiser Brody gives Gino Hernandez a headache (Source: Norman Kietzer)

The Bruiser's running feuds were against the Spoiler, Ox Baker, and Dick the Bruiser. He was hugely popular with the fans and would probably still be wrestling today had he not had a run-in with a Bayomon, Puerto Rico, local promoter and wrestler by the name of Jose Gonzalez. In circumstances that remain unclear, Gonzalez fatally stabbed Brody, but claimed the injury was inflicted in self-defense. Gonzales was tried for murder and acquitted. Showing perhaps the worst taste in the history of a sport never known for tastefulness, Gonzales parlayed his notoriety from the stabbing into becoming the number-one heel of his wrestling organization.

King Kong Bundy

Little Chris Palies of Atlantic City, New Jersey, born on November 7, 1957, grew up to be the huge, 6–foot, 4-inch, 446-pound wrestling monster we all know as King Kong Bundy. He got his start in the wrestling business in 1976, working under the name Chris Canyon. It was only after he began working for Fritz von Erich in Texas that he first started to make waves in the wrestling world as King Kong Bundy. His leap into superstar status occurred when he was featured in the main event at *Wrestlemania II*: a cage match against Hulk Hogan.

Bundy left wrestling behind for awhile in the late 1980s, when he got bitten by the acting bug. He appeared in Richard Pryor's movie *Moving* and turned up on an episode of *Married...With Children*. His face became famous well beyond the realm of wrestling fandom when he appeared in a computer commercial. The spot showed him in a wrestling ring, sitting at a desk and trying in vain to figure out how to use a competitor's computer.

King Kong Bundy versus Mr. Wrestling II (Source: Norman Kietzer)

In 1994 Bundy returned to wrestling, for a brief time wrestling in the WWF under the management of Ted "The Million Dollar Man" DiBiase. Since then, however, Bundy has been working the independent circuit, where he often goes up against the equally huge Bam Bam Bigelow.

Star of Stage, Screen, and the Squared Circle: El Santo (The Saint)

Rudolfo Guzman Huerta, later to become famous in wrestling circles as El Santo (The Saint), was born in Mexico in 1919. Also called The Man in the Silver Mask, Huerta became Mexico's number one, most popular wrestler of all time. El Santo wasn't just the country's premiere *lucha libre* (wrestling) star for the decades from the 1940s to the 1960s, he was also the number-one movie box-office champ of Mexico. He made more than 60 movies in the 1960s and 1970s, playing superhero El Santo—often accompanied by his fellow masked wrestlers, Blue Demon and Mil Mascaras. In the movies, he had all the proper James Bond moves: fast car and sexy babes. But instead of fighting spies, he kept the world safe from such otherworldly villains as Dracula, Frankenstein, the Wolfman, and the Mummy. Perhaps most memorably, in one movie he even went straight to Hell to take on Satan himself in the ring.

Off-screen, El Santo gained fame as one of the first wrestlers to dive over the top rope to human torpedo his opponent on the arena floor. His matches were always high-octane excitement, and the fans loved him.

After the 1970s and with the end of his film career, El Santos "went Vegas" Mexico-style: He put together an action nightclub act to perform in the clubs of Mexico City. He died on February 5, 1984, after one such performance. Legend has it that he was buried with his mask on. Today, his legend lives on in the career of his son, El Hijo del Santo, el Mascarada de Plata.

Ric Flair

Ric Flair was born in Minnesota on February 25, 1949. A big man (6-foot 1-inch, 245 pounds), it's not surprising that he played offensive guard on the football team at his college, the University of Minnesota. But once he came into the wrestling fold, it was clear that he belonged.

Flair is called "The Nature Boy"—a nickname originally belonging to '50's wrestler Buddy Rogers, and he enters the ring with the strut that the original Nature Boy perfected. Flair is known to be cocky and arrogant—but then, he's a 13-time NWA/WCW world champion and 2-time WWF champ, so he's got something to be cocky about. He's held a world title every year from 1981 to 1997.

Captain Lou's Corner

Among his many contributions to modern pro wrestling, Flair formed one of the very first of the "outlaw" groups that have become so popular. His group was The Four Horsemen, with Arn Anderson, Ole Anderson, Tully Blanchard, and Flair, managed by J. J. Dillon. After a popular run, the group broke up in 1997.

*Ric Flair in one of his
many battles with the
legendary Dusty Rhodes
(Source: Norman Kietzer)*

Flair's feuds have been long and memorable, including long-running battles with
Dusty Rhodes, Ricky Steamboat, Kerry Von Erich, Vader, and Hulk Hogan. Perhaps his
most famous fan is former president George Bush.

Sometimes Biggest Is Best: The Giant

The 7-foot, 4-inch, 450-pound Giant was born Paul Wight, a native of South Carolina.
His physical resemblance to Andre the Giant is so strong that when he first came to the
WCW in 1995 it was said that he was from France and was Andre's son. That early bit
of legend-inventing hasn't been mentioned in a few years now, however, so it can be
assumed that it's been dropped from the big guy's bio.

Resemblances notwithstanding, The Giant is in many ways a physically unprecedented
wrestler: He is every bit as big and tall as Andre, but he's about 20 times more agile.
The Giant has even been known to climb to the top of the ropes so that he could dive
down onto his opponent. He's the heaviest man in wrestling history to deliver a flying
drop kick.

The Giant has drifted in and out of the nWo and its various factions, never keeping
with one alliance for very long. For a little while, part of his shtick was to enter the

ring smoking a cigarette, while the announcers frantically warned the kids in the audience not to smoke because it would stunt their growth. He's media friendly, too, just in case he decides to contemplate a show biz career after his wrestling days are over. He recently appeared as a game show celebrity panelist on the Nickelodeon program *Figure It Out*.

Superstar Billy Graham

The original blond, bald, muscular WWF champion, Graham is the prototype from which Hulk Hogan was ultimately to be built. Born September 10, 1943 in Paradise Valley, Arizona, Graham was a teenaged body-building phenomenon. The physique that ultimately won him the Mr. Teenage America contest was, by his own admission, created with steroids.

Graham entered the world of professional wrestling in 1969, first for a variety of NWA promotions as a tag-team partner for such stars as Dr. Jerry Graham (billed as his brother), Pat Patterson, and Ox Baker. But it was when he made the move to the WWF in the 1970s that he really broke into superstar status.

Superstar Billy Graham chokes opponent Billy Robinson (Source: Norman Kietzer)

After he lost the belt to Bob Backlund in 1978, Graham left the WWF to work the independent circuits, but physical problems—particularly arthritis—severely cut his schedule short. Graham later learned that his physical problems were the result of his early abuse of steroids.

Graham attempted a comeback in the WWF in 1987, but that was cut short. He carried on with his schedule of public appearances into the 1990s, but his active wrestling days were by now definitively over. He has since dropped from public view. Since leaving wrestling, Graham has had several operations on his damaged joints, and enjoys painting at home.

Bret Hart

Bret Hart was born on July 2, 1957, in Calgary, Canada. He's no shrinking violet—his favorite self-description is "The best there ever was, the best there is, and the best there ever will be."

Hart joined the WWF roster in 1985 and stayed with the federation until 1997. His first manager was Jimmy Hart, who teamed him with Jim "The Anvil" Neidhart as the original Hart Foundation—one of the most successful tag teams of the 1980s.

The 1990s saw Hart having great success as a singles wrestler. Over the first seven years of the decade he carried on memorable feuds with Shawn Michaels, Yokozuna, Jerry Lawler, Steve Austin, and his own brother, Owen. A contract dispute brought an end to his WWF affiliation in 1997, and he went over to the WCW to join Hollywood Hogan's New World Order.

Hunter Hearst Helmsley

This Greenwich, Connecticut-born wrestler has one very impressive item in his pedigree: he originally trained under the legendary Killer Kowalski. He did a brief stint wrestling for the WCW as "Jean Paul Levesque," but has mostly worked for the WWF. His first character with the McMahon organization was a something of an elite snob, but he's modified his persona somewhat and is now a highly charismatic character.

Helmsley is probably best known for having taken over from an injured Shawn Michaels as leader of D-Generation X, where he has the popular Chyna (a women's body-building champ). His outlaw group is usually pitted against Rocky Maivia's Nation of Domination.

Junkyard Dog

Born Sylvester Ritter in Charlotte, North Carolina, JYD was one of the most popular wrestlers of the early 1980s, peaking during the Hulk-A-Mania years of the WWF.

Before that, this 6–foot, 3-inch, 305-pound wrestler proved wildly popular in the Mid-South Wrestling Alliance, where he carried on a running feud with the Freebirds. One fan even pulled a gun on the Freebirds when JYD was blinded in the ring. He was one of the first wrestlers to use theme music when coming into the ring, and he originated the chant "Who dat, who dat think he can beat this Dog?" (The chant has since been taken over by the New Orleans Saint.)

Junkyard Dog hams it up for the camera (Source: Norman Kietzer)

In the WWF he became synonymous with Queens' song "Another One Bites the Dust." His finishing move was the Big Thump—a body slam. Junkyard Dog was a featured wrestler in the early *Wrestlemanias* and on the WWF's first pay-per-view, *The Wrestling Classic*.

JYD wrestled in the independents in the early 1990s when personal problems kept him out of the WCW and the WWF. He died in 1998 in an automobile accident.

Kane

It's not uncommon for a wrestler to work under different names during his professional wrestling career, but this fellow has had more names than Elizabeth Taylor. He was born Glen Jacobs in Knoxville, Tennessee, and he grew up to be one of the biggest men in the business today. He stands 6-feet, 7-inches, and weighs in at 345 pounds.

Kane began his career in the late 1980s as Jim Powers. He then moved to the Mid-South territory in the early 1990s, where he wrestled for Jerry Lawler as Doomsday. He made his first WWF appearance in 1993 as the Black Knight, a one-time-only character who battled on Lawler's behalf in that year's *Survivor* series pay-per-view event.

He then did a stint on Jim Cornette's short-lived Smoky Mountain Wrestling promotion in 1995, under the name of Unabom. Later that same year he returned to the WWF, this time in the recurring role of Isaac Yankem, Jerry Lawler's Evil Dentist (who had rotten teeth). But in 1996 Jacobs took on his most successful and most famous role. That's the year that he made his first appearance as Kane—the masked and theoretically horribly disfigured brother of The Undertaker.

Ernie "The Big Cat" Ladd

One of the all-time great wrestling villains, Ladd used a black version of Killer Kowalski's in-ring persona. He came into wrestling at the end of a pro football career in the 1960s that featured stops with the San Diego Chargers, the Houston Oilers, and the Kansas City Chiefs.

Born in Rayville, Louisiana, on November 28, 1938, Ladd was a big fellow even as a youth. At 6-feet, 9-inches, and 315 pounds, he was a natural for football, as he was for wrestling, when he got around to it. He never spent any time wrestling in preliminary bouts—he became a main-eventer right away. When he punched and stomped in the WWWF, where he engaged in a feud with Andre the Giant, he was managed by the most evil of all evil managers, The Grand Wizard.

Ernie Ladd versus Killer Kahn (Source: Norman Kietzer)

During a stint with the Cleveland-based National Wrestling Federation in the early 1970s, Ladd proved his willingness to use ethnicity to pump up interest in a feud: He repeatedly referred to crowd-favorite, Dominic De Nucci, as "that spaghetti bendah"!

Ladd's promising career was limited from the start by leg problems, and he was forced into a premature retirement by his football-ravaged knees in the early 1980s. But The Big Cat continues to appear at Old-Timer events.

Jerry "The King" Lawler

Born November 12, 1949, in Memphis, Tennessee, the 6-foot, 234-pound Lawler began his wrestling career in West Memphis, Arkansas, in 1970 and worked the Gulf Coast circuit until the mid 1970s. Then he moved to the Mid-South region to stay. Lawler became champion there about 100 times over the next 20 years, and won the 1988 World Class title by defeating Kery von Erich. He picked up the AWA title by pinning Curt Hennig in that same year.

Lawler is best known as the obnoxious, fast-talking announcer on WWF broadcasts these days. But he still shares his time between his WWF duties and his weekly Memphis shows. Many times Lawler works as a heel in the WWF and as a babyface in Tennessee, which doesn't confuse the Memphis fans at all.

Lawler is best known for his mainstream feud with comedian and inter-gender wrestling champion Andy Kaufman in 1981. He's also a talented cartoonist who enjoys drawing his colleagues during his spare time.

Rocky Maivia

Rocky Maivia is probably the man the WWF fans most love to hate. He's a third generation wrestler: both his grandfather, Peter Maivia, and his father, Rocky Johnson, were men of the squared circle in their days. He started out in 1996 as a face, but the fans weren't buying that persona. They booed him no mater what he did, so he went with the flow and became a ruthless and arrogant baddie.

Before entering wrestling, Rocky was an All-American football star for the University of Miami. He's now the "ruler" of his outlaw group, Maivia's Nation of Domination, an African-American group that has included Faarooq, D-Lo Brown, Kama, and Ahmed Johnson.

Shawn Michaels

Another son of Texas, Shawn Michaels hails from San Antonio. He's been a leading attraction for the WWF since the early 1980s. He started out in a tag team with Marty Jannety—they called themselves The Rockers. He's since gone on to become one of the most popular wrestlers among female fans.

Michaels is known for highly athletic, risky moves in his matches, and for his ability to absorb incredible amounts of punishment. His most famous bouts are also probably the most famous WWF events ever held: *Wrestlemania X's* "Ladder Match" against Razor Ramon (the winner had to grab the Intercontinental title belt from the top of a ladder), and 1997's "Hell in a Cell" bout against the Undertaker. In that same year he formed the popular outlaw group, D-Generation X, which he later handed off to Hunter Hearst Helmsley after suffering injuries in the ring.

Pedro Morales

Vince McMahon Jr. has long had the business philosophy that, when promoting a show in New York City, you've got to have a Latino wrestler on the card. There's a huge following for pro wrestling in the Latino community, and an ethnic wrestler will bring out the fans in droves. As a general rule, an ethnic wrestler would work mid card, but Morales was a special case—he rode that opportunity straight to the top.

Born on November 3, 1942, in Culebra, Puerto Rico, the 6-foot, 240-pound Morales wrestled in California during the late 1950s and throughout the 1960s. By the time he defeated Ivan Koloff in Madison Square Garden on February 8, 1971, to win the world title, he'd worked many of the regional circuits. Morales held on to his title until December 1, 1973, when he lost it in Philadelphia to Stan Stasiak.

Pedro Morales versus Bulldog Brower (Source: Norman Kietzer)

Morales spent the remainder of the 1970s wrestling in the NWA and did another brief stint in the WWF in the early 1980s. He finished his career in Puerto Rico, retiring in 1984.

Diamond Dallas Page

Page Falkenberg was born in Tampa, Florida. Although at 6-feet, 5-inches, and 260 pounds, he was a physical natural as a wrestler, Page began his pro wrestling career as a manager in Verne Gagne's AWA during the 1980s. He represented the Freebirds and Badd Company, entering the ring as a wrestler himself in 1991 with the WCW.

Wrestle Mania

Outlaw groups aren't really independent of the federations that sponsor their matches—that's just part of the story line that justifies their existence. They're supposed to be breaking away from their federation's rules, and for that reason they go after the "loyal" wrestlers who stay with management. The Four Horsemen, D-Generation X, and Maivia's Nation are all currently very popular outlaw groups. The nWo (New World Order) is the WCW's top outlaw group.

Because of his size, Page was originally teamed with Vinnie Vegas (who later became Diesel, then Kevin Nash) as the Vegas Connection. In real life, Page is married to Kimberly Falkenberg, known to wrestling fans as The Booty Man's valet, The Booty Babe; and as the Diamond Doll, valet to Johnnie B. Badd. She then moved on to become a member of the Nitro Girls.

Page remains one of the few WCW wrestlers who has never abandoned his original affiliation to join the nWo or any of its factions. (Only Goldberg comes to mind as similarly loyal.) This has led to repeated beatings at the hands of the outlaw groups, which has meant working with injuries for most of the late 1990s.

Flyin' Brian Pillman

Born on May 22, 1962, Brian Pillman died far too young, at the age of 35, of heart failure. He had overcome a childhood plagued with health problems to play pro football for the Cincinnati Bengals in the early 1980s, then moved into professional wrestling in 1986.

In 1990, Pillman burst into the national view when he joined up with the WCW. Two years later he was paired with Steve Austin as a tag team called the Hollywood Blonds. But his real fame came later, when he wrestled solo as The Loose Cannon.

Just prior to this time, Pillman had been in a terrible car accident, having rolled his off-road vehicle and broken his ankle. Unable to wrestle, he came up with a gimmick so crazy that no promotion would take him on: Theoretically out of work, he made appearances at both ECW and WWF cards, looking like a drug-crazed lunatic. He'd sit in the audience but keep trying to get into the act, only to be ejected by security.

Pillman did manage to come back to active wrestling, but it was clear that the old ankle injury was still bothering him, and it was rumored that he was consuming huge quantities of painkillers. (His story is so similar to that of Kerry von Erich that it's creepy—except Pillman still had his foot attached.)

His final gimmick was a storyline that had him "winning" Marlena from Golddust in a match, then sending Golddust videotapes of Marlena in her skimpy leather outfits in motel rooms. The plot had just been played out to allow Golddust his revenge—he'd just defeated Pillman in a loser-wears-a-dress match—when the end came. In 1998 Pillman went to his hotel room after a match and died of heart failure. As a man who could make the fans suspend their disbelief, Pillman had no peer.

Harley Race

One of the NWA's greatest wrestlers of all time, Harley is a seven-time holder of the NWA world heavyweight championship. His winning streak set a record that was broken only after the explosive arrival of Ric Flair on the wrestling scene.

Born on April 11, 1943, in Kansas City, Missouri, the 6-foot, 1-inch, 268-pound Race was burly even in his youth. He became the personal protege of wrestling promoter Gus Karras, who trained Race in the ways of pro wrestling in St. Jose, Missouri. When Race finished up at school, Race was ready to become one of the sport's true superstars.

Race began his wrestling career in 1959 in the AWA, a Midwest promotion. His move to superstar-dom came in 1965, when he teamed up with Larry "The Ax" Hennig. Together they defeated Crusher and Dick the Bruiser to win the AWA tag-team titles. As a solo, Race was the NWA World Heavyweight Champ throughout the 1970s, surrendering the title in 1983 when Ric Flair became the promotion's top man. In the mid 1980s, Race worked in the WWF and won the "King of the Ring" tournament in 1986.

Forced by injuries into retirement from active wrestling in 1988, Race worked in the WCW as a manager. On January 25, 1995, he was seriously injured in a car accident, which cut short his managerial career.

Harley Race shows off his championship belt (Source: Norman Kietzer)

Golddust (Dusty Rhodes)

The son of the legendary Dusty "The American Dream" Rhodes, Dustin Runnels was born on April 11, 1966, in Austin, Texas. It was inevitable that the son of a wrestling great like Rhodes would grow up to follow in his daddy's footsteps, especially when that son turned out to stand 6-feet, 5-inches and weigh 254 pounds.

Dustin began his wrestling career in Florida in 1988 as The Natural, and then moved to the WCW as the tag-team partner of Ricky "The Dragon" Steamboat with great success. With Steamboat he briefly held the world tag-team title—a feat he would later duplicate with Barry Windham.

In October of 1995, his career took a bizarre twist, when he began appearing for the WWF as Golddust, an effeminate man from Hollywood who wore a gold costume, a long blond wig, and full makeup. His manager was the cigar-smoking Marlena, a Hollywood director type (played by Rhodes's real life wife, Alexandra York). At first, Golddust's character was openly gay, even going so far as to try to put the moves on Roddy Piper, but he was eventually explained away as merely being outrageous.

The Golddust character was dropped in 1998, and Rhodes began wrestling under his real name, with the persona of a born-again Christian who preaches against the naughtier goings on at the WWF.

Jake "The Snake" Roberts

Born Aurlian Smith, Jr, Jake Roberts spent his childhood growing up on Stone Mountain, in Georgia. He began his pro career in 1974 in Baton Rouge, Louisiana. Jake has wrestled for all the major promotions, but when he joined the WWF he really exploded with the fans.

The 6-foot, 5-inch, 246-pounder was always known as a capable wrestler, but he really caught the public's eye when he started arriving in the ring with his pet snake, Damian. After successfully knocking out his opponents with his finishing move (the DDT), he took to placing Damian on their prone forms, so that when his hapless foes awoke they'd find themselves face to face with serpentine terror. Jake used this particular gimmick to great effect on Andre the Giant, scaring the big man half to death.

Jake Roberts subdues The Grappler (Source: Norman Kietzer)

Roberts retired in 1994 but returned to the WWF briefly two years later, posing as a Bible-quoting wrestler. His return was noteworthy for his loss to Stone Cold Steve Austin in the 1996 Royal Rumble—a loss that began Austin's meteoric rise to superstardom. Jake still wrestles occasionally on the independent circuit.

Sergeant Slaughter

Born with a chin and jaw that resembled Dudley Doright's, Robert Remus was never going to win beauty contests. This son of Paris Island, South Carolina, joined the pro wrestling business in 1977 in the Pacific Northwest. At 6-feet, 3-inches, and 310 pounds, and with a face only his mother could love (maybe), he started out as the facetiously named Beautiful Bobby Remus. That was fated never to last, however, and he soon became Sergeant Slaughter for good.

Slaughter was an NWA wrestler until the mid 1980s, when he switched to Vince McMahon's WWF. There he not only became a wrestling superstar, but was also immortalized in a best-selling action-figure as well.

Sgt. Slaughter takes flight with the help of his opponent, Bob Backlund (Source: Norman Kietzer)

Slaughter left the WWF for a time to wrestle on the independent circuit, but returned to McMahon's fold in 1990 as a villain on the side of the Iraqis during the Gulf War. That year he battled the (then good guy) heroic Hulk Hogan in the main event of *Wrestlemania*. He briefly held the WWF World Heavyweight Championship title in 1991, defeating the Ultimate Warrior for the belt but ultimately losing it to Hulk Hogan, two months later.

Slaughter is now retired from active wrestling, but he still can be seen working in the WWF as Commissioner Slaughter. In this new persona he is an ineffectual keeper-of-order, trying to stop the bad boys of D-Generation X from wreaking havoc. All he usually gets for his pains is mockery of his chin size.

Davey Boy "The British Bulldog" Smith

David Smith was born in Leeds, England, on November 27, 1962. This 5–foot, 9-inch wrestler started out in 1978 as a light heavyweight, and soon took his career to the Pacific Northwest, where he wrestled with Bret and Owen Hart. He kept it all in the family, you might say—marrying one of the Hart sisters. He came to the WWF with the Dynamite Kid as The British Bulldogs, a tag-team duo managed by yours truly, Captain Lou. The pair won the WWF tag-team belts at *Wrestlemania II* by defeating Greg Valentine and Brutus "The Barber" Beefcake on April 7, 1986. They promptly lost them again to the Hart Foundation (Bret Hart and Jim "The Anvil" Neidhart) on January 26, 1987.

Smith was injured in a car accident in July of 1989, and disappeared from the wrestling scene for a year to recuperate. He must have spent a good part of that time in the weight room, because when he returned to the WWF in 1990 as The British Bulldog (now a solo act) he had reconfigured himself as a 245-pound muscle monster.

Ever loyal to the in-laws, when Bret Hart made his controversial move from the WWF to the WCW in 1998, Smith followed along. Gotta keep peace in the family!

The Undertaker

Mark Calloway was born on March 24, 1962, in Dallas, Texas, and it's doubtful that anyone would have predicted he'd grow up to be the bizarre, ghoulish Undertaker of WWF fame. He started out in the late 1980s wrestling for the NWA as Mean Mark Callous, but became an instant superstar when he joined the WWF. There he grew his hair long and donned the garb of a gravedigger. Taking the name The Undertaker, he was first managed by Brother Love, then by Paul Bearer (who later deserted him to manage his long-lost "brother" Kane). The Undertaker rarely spoke, except to say "I will NOT rest in peace." His most famous matches have been stipulated as casket matches—the winner has to push the loser into a coffin and slam the lid shut. He's won the WWF world heavyweight championship in 1991 and in 1997.

> ### The Least You Need to Know
>
> ➤ Today's pro wrestling stars carry on the traditions of athleticism and showmanship established by their forebears.
>
> ➤ The trend to outlaw groups has given birth to such memorable gangs as nWo, D-Generation X, and Rocky Maivia's Nation of Domination.
>
> ➤ The storylines for pro wrestling's performers have become more involved and bizarre, as in the case of Kane and The Undertaker.

Chapter 11

Rowdy Rivalries of Revenge

In This Chapter

➤ Kerry von Erich and Rick Flair's battle royal for the championship belt

➤ Dusty Rhodes' quest for The American Dream

➤ The living legend tackles the superstar

➤ Black Jack the Giant Killer—not!

➤ Rick Flair and Harley Race: Caged warriors

There have been some famous go-togethers throughout history, as well paired as salt and pepper. These twosomes have sprung up in every field imaginable: in the Bible there's Cain and Abel; in mythology there's Romulus and Remus; in music, think of Gilbert and Sullivan; in finance there's Dow and Jones; in comedy, there's Martin and Lewis; and in politics, there's Franklin and Delano.

Wrestling's no different. It's twosomes are called rivalries, and the pages of wrestling's long history book are filled to repletion with them, going all the way back to the Gotch-Hackenschmidt rivalry in the first decade of the 20th century.

Some are more memorable than others. What makes one special? Certainly it's the build-up preceding a match, but there's usually something much, much more, as well. The participants, the stakes they're wrestling for, and how it ends. In this chapter you'll read about some of the classic match-ups that excited wrestling fans over the years—many of them real grudge matches in which the grunts and groans of pain were sometimes very, very real.

Kerry von Erich Versus Ric Flair

It was the quest for "10 pounds of gold," (what Ric Flair called his championship belt) that made for a memorable set of matches between Flair and Kerry von Erich.

Von Erich first challenged Flair for that belt in April of 1982. A few minutes prior to the match, the Great Kabuki had attacked von Erich, damaging Kerry's knee and almost rendering him *hors de combat*. Almost, but not quite. Von Erich, in the best tradition of "the show must go on," insisted on wrestling Flair even with his injury. The bout ended unsatisfactorily, with Flair being disqualified—and since a belt cannot change waists on a DQ, Flair retained the belt and the title.

Ric Flair in one of his epic battles with Kerry von Erich (Source: Norman Kietzer)

Von Erich and Flair were to battle three more times that year. The last time was a cage match, which ended in what might best be described as chaos once Freebird Michael Hayes, the referee, became involved. Hayes got caught up in the action and decided to take on Flair himself, proceeding to punch him out. Then, looking down at the inert form of the champion, Hayes called for von Erich to fall atop him for the pin. Kerry, however, declined the offer. A disgusted Hayes started to leave the cage with Kerry in pursuit, earnestly trying to explain himself, when Flair revived and fetched von Erich a kick in the back for his good sportsmanship. In the melee that followed, von Erich bled so profusely that officials at ringside had to stop the proceedings, leaving Flair still in possession of his "10 pounds of gold."

In the year and a half that followed, Flair first lost, then regained the belt in bouts with Harley Race. During that same time span, tragedy struck the von Erich family as Kerry's brother David died during his tour of Japan. Now Kerry had a new incentive—to win the belt for his fallen brother.

It happened on May 6, 1984, in front of 44,000 screaming fans at the Texas Stadium. In 22 action-packed minutes, Kerry defeated Flair. Finally the "10 pounds of gold" belonged to him. And to the memory of his brother, to whom Kerry dedicated the belt in an emotional post-fight oration, shouting out: "I gave my all—for David!"

Dusty Rhodes Versus Kevin Sullivan

Dusty Rhodes was wrestling's own embodiment of the American Dream. A colorful wrestler who was beloved by all fans, Rhodes had an opponent who was everything Dusty wasn't: Kevin Sullivan. Sullivan was the quintessential villain who claimed to be a follower of Satan and who said he dealt with the dark underside of the occult. Whatever the truth, he came off as an evil, satanic force and proved to be the perfect foil for Rhodes in one of wrestling's greatest rivalries.

Kevin Sullivan humiliates Dusty Rhodes (Source: Norman Kietzer)

Both Rhodes and Sullivan were wrestling under the NWA banner in Florida and that state just wasn't big enough for the both of them. And so it was that on Christmas night, 1983, Rhodes and Sullivan battled it out in a "Loser Leaves Florida" cage match (the loser would be barred from competing in the state for 60 days). Before the confrontation, the fans and press alike ballyhooed the grudge match, believing themselves prepared for Sullivan's well-advertised dirty tactics. But they could never have expected what transpired in the ring that night.

On that holiest of nights, someone in a Santa Claus get-up visited Sullivan and presented him with a Christmas present. Those close enough could see through the disguise and recognize Jake "The Snake" Roberts, Sullivan's cohort. The gift turned out to be a weapon, which Sullivan used to pound Rhodes with from the proverbial pillar to post, turning him into a bloody mess and forcing him to leave the state.

The Midnight Rider Makes the Scene

Within days, however, a mysterious masked wrestler known only as the Midnight Rider appeared in Florida arenas. It became an open secret that the Midnight Rider was none other than Rhodes. And it became even more clear when, after the 60 days of banishment from Florida was lifted and Dusty Rhodes could then re-emerge in the local arenas, the Midnight Rider rode off into the sunset, never to be seen again.

While Rhodes was waiting out his 60-day exile, Sullivan, the man who had sworn allegiance to the Dark Forces, created a new sidekick, known as the Purple Haze. Dusty was introduced to him first-hand during an appearance on the TV show *Championship Wrestling* from Florida, when the two mugged him, beating him up on camera. Leaving Rhodes in a dusty pile wasn't enough for the pair, as they tried to set fire to his eyes. Then Sullivan hissed into the cameras: "Never fool with the powers of the occult. That slob Rhodes did, and look what happened to him...he's a beaten man."

Sullivan's next attack was not long in coming. While Rhodes was a guest at a 10-year anniversary celebration with friends, well wishers, and family—and not incidentally in front of hundreds of thousands of TV viewers—Sullivan gate-crashed and hurled a bottle of ink in Rhodes's direction. The missile missed its intended target, striking Rhodes's younger sister, Connie, in the eye instead. Enough was enough for Rhodes, and he vowed to "pay back Sullivan for all his dirty deeds."

Rhodes Returns

Now it was Rhodes's turn to use ink as a weapon—signing a contract to avenge the dastardly deeds of Sullivan. The grudge match to end all grudge matches was set for the Lakeland (Florida) Civic Center. On the night of the bout, the arena was filled to overflowing with Dusty Rhodes fans, with 2,000 more turned away at the door. As Rhodes entered to the strains of the Allman Brothers "Midnight Rider," every man, woman, and child roared in support. In seconds, the cheers turned to jeers as the diabolic Sullivan entered the ring screaming "The American Dream will die!"

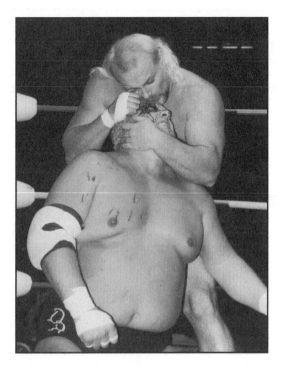

Sullivan ignores the rules against biting—no dirty trick is beneath him (Source: Norman Kietzer)

From the moment the bell sounded, and before its echo had been stilled, Rhodes was on the attack. His pent-up anger erupted with a fury that had Sullivan on the defensive. Even Sullivan's usual bag of dirty tricks were ineffective in the face of the torrential attack.

Then, just when it seemed that victory was his, Rhodes was surprised by the entry of a new player—a masked man that was, or appeared to be, the Midnight Rider. This, however, wasn't the Midnight Rider the fans remembered from Rhodes time in exile—it was an imposter who now leaped into the ring to come to the aid of the fallen Sullivan.

The masked invader set upon the American Dream with a nightmarish fury, driving him into the canvas like a proverbial tenpenny nail and then continuing to pound until Rhodes was senseless. Satisfied that the American Dream would not awaken, the ersatz Midnight Rider gathered up the remains of Sullivan and hauled him off to the dressing room.

It would later be revealed that the masked intruder had been Sullivan's newest protege, Kaima—proof positive that Sullivan would use any trick, however dastardly, to beat the great American Dream and deny him his revenge. Judgment Day would have to wait.

Bruno Sammartino Versus Superstar Billy Graham

The ultimate measure of Bruno Sammartino's greatness was his strength. Time and again, in matches against some of the greats of his time, despite having absorbed terrific punishment, The Living Legend would be able to call upon his reserves of strength to turn the event, and his opponent, over on their backs. The tougher the competition, the better he liked it. As one of his admirers cooed, "Bruno threw all his challengers against a brick wall and those who got up he let wrestle him for the championship."

The Superstar Challenges the Legend

One of those who upped and challenged Bruno was rough, tough Superstar Billy Graham, of the golden locks and bulging muscles. On April 30, 1977, at Baltimore's Civic Center, Graham stepped into the ring to succeed where so many before him had failed.

On that night of nights, Graham entered the ring first and for a full three minutes he used the ring as his stage—strutting, posing, and preening. But the uproarious reception that greeted the emergence of The Living Legend from his dressing room put an end to all that. Graham merely pulled in his feathers and retreated to his corner, there to watch Bruno bathe in the fans' adulation.

As the house lights dimmed, the audience fell into a quiet, almost church-like hush, anticipating another great Bruno comeback and victory. Then the bell rang and the two warriors came to mid ring, circling each other warily and each seeking an opening.

The Battle Is Engaged

Within seconds the two had joined, like bull moose in heat—their arms intertwined and their muscles straining against one another, both looking for the advantage, the edge. Then Graham got in a well-timed kick to the champion's legs and the action was under way.

For the next 10 minutes the two warriors fought furiously, but neither was able to break through the other's defenses any more than you could open a Maryland clam with your bare hands. No one could get an upper hand—or upper leg, for that matter. Bruno, now frustrated in his efforts to get to Graham, grabbed the blond Superstar by his tresses and began banging his head into the turnbuckle. Graham fell to the floor, his face a bloody mess.

Having tasted his own blood, Graham now fought back with a fury, assaulting the champion and catching him up in his dread Superstar Bear Hug. As Sammartino flopped around in Grahams arms like a big fish out of water, it looked as if Graham's famous submission hold might carry the day—and carry off the championship belt.

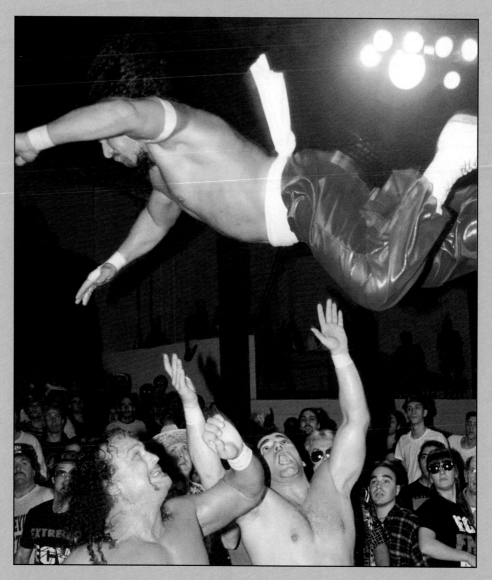

Sabu dives onto Doug Furnas and Phil Lafon.
(Source: Timothy A. Walker)

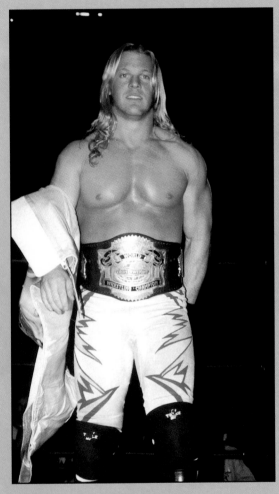

Chris Jericho wears the championship belt.
(Source: Timothy A. Walker)

Hollywood Hogan (WCW): Caged!
(Source: Timothy A. Walker)

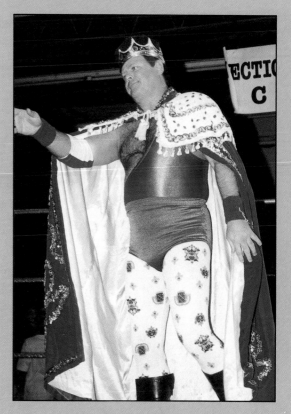

Jerry "The King" Lawler (WWF) in full regalia.
(Source: Timothy A. Walker)

Goldust (WWF), now wrestling as Dustin Runnells (WCW), is the son of legendary Dusty Rhodes.
(Source: Timothy A. Walker)

Wrestling's big on cheesecake: the ECW's beautiful Francine.
(Source: Timothy A. Walker)

Wrestling has its beefcake too: Edge.
(Source: Timothy A. Walker)

Battling Bruisers: King Kong Bundy vs.
Demolition Ax.
(Source: Timothy A. Walker)

Monster Maulers: Frenchy Rivera vs.
Nick Dinsmore.
(Source: Timothy A. Walker)

Super Nova and Johnny Handsome (ECW)
take flight.
(Source: Timothy A. Walker)

WCW's Ric Flair, poised for action.
(Source: Timothy A. Walker)

Bloodied but unbowed: Doug Gilbert.
(Source: Timothy A. Walker)

An early Hulkster nemesis: the Iron Sheik.
(Source: Timothy A. Walker)

Terry Gordy vs. Perry Saturn: heading for a fall.
(Source: Timothy A. Walker)

But even though he applied every ounce of pressure at his command, Graham could not break the strength nor the spirit of the Living Legend, and Sammartino managed somehow, someway, to break free.

Both now began showing the strain of the last 15 minutes of pitched battle. But now Sammartino, famed for his feats of arms, began some feats of feet as well. He backed Graham up into his own corner and drove him to his knees with a series of kicks. Suddenly there was Graham begging for mercy. But Sammartino would have none of that, and punctuated each and every one of Graham's pleas with yet another kick.

A Title Lost—and Won

Then, just as it seemed that Sammartino had the bout in his grasp, the man called "The People's Champion" turned to those whose opinion he prized the most, his fans, to ask them for their support in continuing his attack. Bruno's posturing was a tactical error—one that ranks right up there with Jack Dempsey's failure to retreat to a neutral corner after flooring Gene Tunney. And Sammartino's error would cost him the title, much as Dempsey's momentary lapse cost *him*.

For as soon as Graham saw Sammartino turn away to the audience he reached out and grabbed Bruno's leg, dragging him down to the mat where he pinned the soon-to-be ex-champion's shoulders to the canvas. Referee Jack Davis, unaware that Graham was using the ropes for leverage to hold Sammartino down, began the count. "One... Two...Three..." It was all over. Unbelievably, the Living Legend had been defeated.

Official protests were lodged by Bruno's camp, but the Maryland State Athletic Commission, ignoring Graham's obvious use of the ropes to secure the final pin, ruled that once a decision had been rendered it could not be overruled. Graham, hearing of the controversy caused by his victory now said "It's finally over. You can talk all you want about controversy, foot on the ropes, blood on my brow, the state athletic commission, or anything you want. But no matter what you say, I am still the champion. I don't have anything else to say...this here belt says it all."

Andre the Giant Versus Black Jack Mulligan

It's no wonder Andre the Giant was called "The Eighth Wonder of the World." He was so big at 495 pounds that you could print Goodyear on his back and float him over arenas. And so big that few would dare to challenge him. One who did was Black Jack Mulligan, and therein lies the tale of one of wrestling's biggest grudge matches of all time.

Black Jack Mulligan was a man among men himself, standing some 6'9" tall and weighing more than 300 pounds, with cowboy boots and his infamous "Claw" to use when the going got tough. In addition to being huge, Black Jack was also a skilled practitioner, able to use his strength and speed to bedazzle his opponents and impose his psychological and physical will on them.

Andre the Giant versus
Black Jack Mulligan
(Source: Norman Kietzer)

Mulligan had only recently joined the WWF with the stated purpose of wrestling the belt from its then-champion, Bob Backound. Frustrated in his attempts, he announced to all that he would become a giant killer instead, and take on the man who looked like the guy Jack met at the top of the beanstalk—Andre the Giant.

Like the cat that ate cheese and sat in front of the mouse hole with baited breath, Mulligan tried to bait the trap for Andre, calling him "the freak" and even once jumping into the ring to lend his aid to two men battling Andre, battering the Giant into submission.

But the sleeping Giant stirred. He wanted revenge, in the worst way, and was determined to get it. A match between the two behemoths was quickly arranged.

It was a BIG match, in more ways than one. The second the bell sounded for the classic confrontation, Andre and Black Jack attacked one another, trying mightily to vent their anger on each other. It was less a wrestling bout than a dogfight. It was attack, attack, attack, as first one, then the other took a turn. Soon even the ring proved too small to contain the fury of the combatants and the action spilled over onto the floor outside the ropes.

Mulligan somehow managed to maneuver the Giant into his deadly "Claw" hold and held it until he had brought blood from Andre's face. But once he released it, fear gave wings to his feet—Mulligan soon looked like an Olympic 100-meter gold medallist as he fled the premises for the dressing room, leaving a furious Andre far behind.

The official decision read "Double DQ" with both counted out. And while the title of the true "giant" of the wrestling world had gone undecided, one thing was certain—this had been the "biggest" grudge match in wrestling history.

Ric Flair Versus Harley Race

While the rest of America was sitting down to Thanksgiving dinner on the last Thursday of November, 1983, the eyes of the wrestling world were focused on a bigger feast: the star-studded wrestling extravaganza in Greensboro, North Carolina, called "Starcade '83."

The battle at the Greensboro Coliseum pitted the two and only: Ric Flair and Harley Race met in a battle that would go down as one of the greatest grudge matches in the history of professional wrestling-dom.

To set the stage: Flair had lost the prestigious NWA belt to Race during the summer of 1983, and in the months that followed his sole goal had been to regain the title, *his* title. But despite the fact that he had enticed Race into the ring on several occasions, Flair had come up empty. On the other hand, Race had tired of hearing Flair's constant challenges and now resorted to a "Race-saving" tactic—one worthy of Machiavelli. He offered $25,000 to anyone who could sidetrack his persistent foe.

Ric Flair and Harley Race go at it (Source: Norman Kietzer)

No sooner had the bounty been placed on Flair's golden-tressed head than Cowboy Bob Orton and Dirty Dick Slater appeared at a match between Flair and Race and set upon Flair. They left him with an injured neck, and injured pride, and the two of them split the check for 25 grand.

Flair dropped out of sight for awhile after that—long enough to heal his wounds and his pride. Then he resurfaced with a new determination—to get back into the race and to get Race. Picking up some markers along the way, he repaid both Orton and Slater in kind for their earlier courtesies, then set his sights on the one and only thing that mattered—the only thing between him and *his* belt—Harley Race.

In a battle to end all the battles—and one that will be remembered by anyone who saw it—the two now met once again. But this wasn't just some local event. It was telecast wherever a signal would carry it.

Waged in a 15-foot steel cage without benefit of rules—no time limit, no stoppages even for injury, and with a definite winner guaranteed to emerge from the cage—the battle was epic. Both men used everything at their disposal, and then some. The bout combined brutal force and scientific wrestling, cheap shots and extravagant moves, old-time know-how and modern, crowd-pleasing performance.

Fighting Words

The line-up for a wrestling event is often referred to as the **card**, referring to the listing of matches. **Top of the card** refers to the main event or headliner. The **undercard** refers to all the other matches that are fought before and after the main event.

Here Race used the steel cage to cave in Flair's brow. There Flair used his forearm to drive Race back. And everywhere there was the headlock, the body shot, and the back flip. Finally, Ric, his face etched in blood, his hopes slowly draining away, brought up a forearm and from somewhere deep down in the inner recesses of his championship found the strength to drive Race to the canvas.

It was all over. Flair had done the all but impossible and yanked victory from the brow of defeat. Now the fans in the stands trumpeted his name and the wrestlers who had been on the undercard all rushed the ring to hail his triumph. Ric Flair had regained *his* belt and once again stood as the NWA king of the wrestling hill.

Hulk Hogan Versus the Iron Sheik

Through wrestling's long, colorful history, American rings have been besieged by hordes of foreign invaders—a veritable rogue's gallery that would do justice to central casting. Mr. Moto, El Mongo, Kendo Nagasaki, Baron Von Rasche, and hundreds of others sought to rival their fellows in villainy.

The Evil Foreigner Incarnate

But none of these villainous characters could hold a candle to the Iron Sheik, wrestling's version of the exorcist, who scared the living hell out of his opponents. And when he couldn't scare them, he beat them with his infamous Camel Clutch.

Wrestling in the name of the hated Ayatollah, the Sheik invaded America's wrestling rings to prove that "American's are weaklings" and to "show what pieces of garbage American wrestlers are." Those are *his* words. He culminated his campaign against America by beating Bob Backlund on December 26, 1983, to become only the ninth champion in WWF history.

Backlund, who had entered the ring that night with an injury, demanded a rematch. But when he was hurt in a subsequent bout, his tag-team partner Hulk Hogan took his place to prevent the Iron Sheik from taking the belt back to Iran.

Hulk Hogan to America's Defense

Announcing that he would take the Sheik on, Hogan said: "It would be a great crime if the Sheik took that belt out of the United States. It's got to stay right here in the good ol' U.S. of A." And even though the Sheik and his manager, Classie Freddie Blassie, protested, saying they had trained for Backlund, not the Hulkster, they agreed to one match, one time, before the Sheik returned to his native Iran forever.

And so, in January of 1984, in front of a jam-packed house at New York's Madison Square Garden, the two went at it to settle more than a territorial war—they fought for national pride as well. The crowd greeted Hogan with a rousing exhibition of "Hulkmania," while the Sheik responded, true to character, by jumping atop the turnbuckle and giving the audience an "Iranian salute": middle finger extended.

Without waiting for the opening bell, Hogan tore out of his corner and began pummeling the Sheik. No preliminaries, no Treaty of Geneva, thank you. Just a good old fashioned whuppin', American-style. For a brief second it appeared that the Sheik's reign would be a short one, as Hogan rained blow after blow on the Iranian's shaven head. But just as Hogan was about to apply the *coup de grace* by charging into the cornered Sheik, his opponent moved quickly out of the way and Hogan, unable to alter his charge, slammed headlong into the ringpost. He fell to the canvas like a stricken King Kong falling from the Empire State building.

Captain Lou's Corner

Unlike the usual case where wrestlers use made-up bios with all sorts of outrageous claims, the Iron Sheik really *was* an Iranian.

Dispatching the Dastardly Villain

The Sheik, seeing his moment, seized it. He went to work on the inert body of the Hulk, stepping over Hogan with his pointy yellow shoes to apply the dreaded Camel Clutch. An eerie silence fell over the crowd as Hogan, his face contorted in pain, tried mightily to resist the Sheik's submission hold. All to no avail.

What seemed like an eternity ticked away—10 ticks of the second hand of the big Madison Square Garden clock, then 20, 30, 40.... The Sheik continued to exert his pressure on Hogan. Finally, after an excruciating 52 seconds, Hogan managed to maneuver his arms underneath the Sheik's massive body. By degrees he began to lift himself and his tormentor up off the canvas. With an incredible show of brute strength his red, white, and blue corpuscles straining to the task, Hogan managed to stand erect, the Sheik still clinging to his back. Slowly he turned, and Hogan now backed the Sheik into a corner. Finally, with one giant burst of energy, Hogan rammed the Sheik's back into the turnbuckle and the Iranian fell to the mat with a thud.

As the dazed Sheik unsteadily made it to legs that were now strangers to him, he was met by a Hulk Hogan "Ax Bomber"—the Hulkster leaped high into the air and crashed his leg into the Sheik's upper torso. The Sheik fell to the canvas as if pole-axed, there to be covered by Hogan for a one-two-three pin count.

As the referee intoned "three," the more than 22,500 fans at the Garden erupted with a bellow, hailing their hero—and the new WWF champion. It had taken five minutes and 30 seconds, but Hulk Hogan had turned the tables on the Sheik and saved the belt from forever going back to Iran.

Ricky Steamboat Versus Ric Flair

It has been said that a real friend is someone who walks in when everybody else walks out. And so it was with Ricky Steamboat and Ric Flair, although you'd never have expected it to work out that way, judging from their first few meetings. Ricky Steamboat and Ric Flair had several encounters in the ring, the intensity of their skills matched only by the intensity of their dislike for each other.

Ricky Steamboat versus Ric Flair (Source: Norman Kietzer)

However, as the wrestling wheel turned, the two patched up their differences and became fast friends—so much so that after Flair had lost his NWA belt to Harley Race, his former adversary was there for him, consoling him and encouraging him to make a comeback. And, when Flair recaptured his belt, it was Steamboat who ran into the ring and placed the "10 pounds of gold" around his friend's waist. It was enough to bring tears to a grown man's eyes.

This could have been the beginning of a beautiful story—something akin to Claude Rains and Humphrey Bogart walking off into the mist at the end of the movie *Casablanca* with Rains muttering "This is the beginning of a beautiful friendship...." But while cinematic endings are one thing, in wrestling, friendships have to stand up to the challenge of competition in the ring.

Steamboat had gone into retirement, devoting his time and energy to his new gym in Charlotte, North Carolina. But his resolve to stay retired was somewhat less than cast in stone, and soon he was being pressured to return to the ring, not only by his fans but by promoter Jim Crockett. Crockett approached Steamboat in front of his home-town fans in the Greensboro (North Carolina) Coliseum with an open contract signed by Flair.

At first Steamboat stuck to his (retired) guns. But when told that the match would be for the NWA world championship, he relented. Afterward he was to credit Flair with his decision to sign on the dotted line: "It was a very hard decision," he said. "But the man who pushed me into it was none other than Rick Flair. He reminded me of what I had told him when *he* wanted to retire. And he was right! I may not be able to live with myself several years from now if I don't give myself the opportunity to wrestle for the world's belt today."

Before the bout the two greats came to center ring and exchanged handshakes. Then, in front of a packed house, the two put on a scientific exhibition of wrestling, the likes of which hadn't been seen in many a year. The fans were treated to perfectly executed holds, counter holds, submission holds, and takedowns for the full 60 minutes. First one combatant, then the other, attempted to get the upper hand. With time running out and neither man having had the advantage, Steamboat tried one last-ditch, figure-four leg lock on Flair. It looked like it might be the end of Flair's championship reign as he flopped around like a freshly caught fish. Then the bell rang, signifying the end of the bout and of Steamboat's hopes for the belt.

With that, Steamboat merely released his hold and went over to shake Flair's hand. Thus ended one of the finest wrestling matches ever between two straight shooters in recent wrestling history. And the beautiful friendship remained.

The Undertaker Versus Kane

It was one of the most outer-worldly match-ups in the history of wrestling. The Undertaker, one of those inhuman beings who sometimes haunt arenas (usually concocted in the fertile imagination of a promoter) had for years been claiming to hail from the Dark Side. Now he was one of the top stars of the WWF. Sometimes known as The Dead Guy, his matches usually carried some morbid stipulations, such as casket matches in which the winner had to put the loser in a casket and slam the lid on him.

The Undertaker's manager at the time was one Paul Bearer. However, as happens in many wrestling story lines, Bearer had turned on the Undertaker and taken up with a new wrestler named Kane. Kane, not incidental to our story, was the same size and shape as the Undertaker, and he wore a mask.

Bearer told anyone who would listen that his new discovery was, in fact, the Undertaker's younger brother. However, Bearer would continue, when the Undertaker was but a boy, he had set his own house on fire and in the ensuing inferno his mother and father had both perished. Not only that, little brother Kane had been believed to have perished in the same fire but instead had survived, although horribly disfigured (hence the mask). Now Kane wanted revenge on the boy-man who had ruined his face and his life.

To further roil the potboiler and make an ugly story even uglier, Bearer let it be known that the Undertaker and Kane were only half brothers. And that he, Bearer, was Kane's real father—the Undertaker's mother being, in Bearer's words, "nothing but a two-bit...."

With a story line like that, the only thing to be done was to match the two fighters to settle this extended family feud—in the most ghastly manner possible. A casket match was stipulated, and once the loser was inside the casket, it was to be set on fire.

The Undertaker and Kane got together to settle matters "once and for all" many times, but every time it looked as if the Undertaker was about to triumph, he'd resort to one of his trademark heinous tricks and get disqualified. The feud has never been settled, and for now the two seem to have united in a ghoulish twosome to take on a common enemy—Vince McMahon, the WWF promoter-turned-wrestler known as The Evil Owner.

Dennis Rodman Versus Karl Malone

It all started during the finals of the 1998 NBA playoffs between the Chicago Bulls and the Utah Jazz. Then it was a little grappling, pushing, and shoving—with an elbow or two thrown in for good measure. Just weeks later the two announced on Jay Leno's *Tonight Show* that they would get it on again at the *Bash at the Beach* event on pay-per-view, with Rodman (Rodzilla) teaming up with Hollywood Hogan and Malone (The Mailman) joined by his real-life buddy, Diamond Dallas Page.

The match was a natural. The colorful Rodman, who wears different colored dandruff with each new 'do, had already made a couple of guest appearances in WCW rings. But while Malone had been a lifelong wrestling fan and had always harbored a desire to join the "grunt 'n' groan" circuit, it was a first.

The actual match was held on July 12, 1998, and it had more than the anticipated action. Fifteen minutes into the bout, Hogan was working Page over when Malone came to his partner's aid. Then, in the best tag-team style, he "tagged off" to his partner, Page, who went after Hogan with a vengeance.

At this magic moment, Rodman (quite willing to indulge in dirty tricks) distracted the referee while The Disciple, a compatriot of Hogan's from the nWo, entered the ring and slammed Page to the mat.

The ref counted to three, signifying the end of the bout and giving the win to Hogan and Rodman, but The Mailman went postal. Re-entering the ring to settle matters, he administered a "diamond cutter" (Page's trademark move) on the dastardly Disciple, then attacked Hogan and Rodman in turn. Demanding that the ref declare *him* the victor and being denied, Malone turned on the hapless official as well, smashing him face-first into the canvas.

But matters remained unsettled, so Malone and Page entered the stands to do battle with the fans themselves, while Hogan and Rodman stood by, gloating.

Eddie Guerrero Versus Chavo Guerrero Jr.

It was the oldest story in the world: an elder takes one of his youngsters out behind the barn to "teach him a lesson." The elder in this case was Eddie, and the youngster was his nephew, Chavo. Just a few months before, Eddie had been seated ringside at a WCW bout when Chavo lost and decided then and there that Chavo was an embarrassment to the family name.

Determined to make Chavo into a "real man," even if it killed him, Eddie began psychologically tormenting his nephew. The taunts he threw in Chavo's direction were supposedly designed to motivate the younger Guerrero. The uncle forced his nephew to cheat and even made him wear a T-shirt that read "Eddie Guerrero is my favorite wrestler" on one side, and "Cheat to Win" on the other. Uncle Eddie even took to interfering in Chavo's matches to insure that he lost.

After weeks of humiliation, Chavo finally snapped and challenged his uncle. The match was set for the *Great American Bash* show on pay-per-view.

True to his newly-evinced mean streak, Eddie now declared that the loser would truly have to be humiliated, and stipulated that their match would be a "Loser Gets a Haircut" bout.

Eddie was to win the match—by cheating, of course—and gleefully prepared to shear his nephew's locks. But as he turned to Chavo, something in the younger man's eyes signaled a change in his character. No longer the docile youth in the Guerrero family, Chavo screamed that he would cut his own hair. Grabbing the clippers from his startled uncle's hand, he shaved a big bald patch on his own head, then turned on Eddie. With that, Eddie turned tail and ran—in fear for both his hair and his life.

Thus climaxed the most dysfunctional family scene since *Mommie Dearest,* and the stage was set for a family reunion that is sure not to be of the friendliest variety.

Jerry Lawler Versus Andy Kaufman

He was better known as Latka Gravas on the TV sitcom *Taxi*, but in the early 1980s Kaufman became known to wrestling fans at the Memphis Mid-South Coliseum as the World InterGender Wrestling Champion—a title as made-up as the championship belt he fashioned for himself.

But unlike his gibberish-spouting *Taxi* character or his dead-on impersonations of Elvis, this was no act. And the only laughter it generated was nervous laughter, especially among Kaufman's friends.

Kaufman was serious about his wrestling persona and even made a videotape in which he came off, a la his boyhood idol Buddy "Nature Boy" Rogers, as a baddie. He challenged all women to pin him for $1,000 and even offered to marry the woman who could beat him.

Kaufman sent his tape to several promoters, but only one took interest—Eddie Marlin of the Memphis Mid-South Coliseum. It was a decision that brought fans to the arena in record numbers—they all wanted to see Kaufman get beaten. But in the first four matches, no one came close to succeeding.

Then came Foxy—an oversized lady who outweighed Kaufman by at least 100 pounds. As the bell for their match rang, Kaufman was strutting around the ring in his thermal underwear, boasting about his earlier victories that evening. Foxy came roaring out of her corner and was all over the self-proclaimed InterGender Champion. Finally, after she had thrown him to the canvas and nearly pinned him, Kaufman prevailed. But the bout had been close enough to warrant a rematch.

This time around, Foxy had help—Jerry Lawler coached her. Still, Kaufman managed the win, and added insult to injury by rubbing her face into the mat. The fans went wild, and screamed for Lawler to enter the ring and help Foxy. When Lawler complied, Kaufman jumped off Foxy screaming, "Lawler, don't you touch me! I'm from Hollywood! I'll sue you for everything you've got...."

No one ever knew if this was all an act, but it was enough to ignite a feud with Lawler, fueled by Kaufman's media appearances taunting The King and mocking the Memphis fans. Lawler responded by threatening Kaufman, whom he now called "the Wimp," and warning "I'm gonna end your fantasy, Andy Kaufman, you're gonna get hurt."

The verbal gauntlet having been thrown, Kaufman picked it up and accepted the challenge to wrestle. But he never let anybody in on "the deal"—he never met with Lawler beforehand to discuss the course the bout should take. As Lawler put it: "I never could understand why...he would agree to that if he didn't think there would be some kind of meeting, something mutually agreed upon where he wouldn't get hurt."

Instead, Kaufman just showed up, and Lawler was left no option but to really wrestle. "I can't just let a little 150-pound comedian come in there and have a match with the Southern heavyweight champion and walk out unscathed. People would have thought *we* were a joke."

On April 5, 1982, the two faced each other in the ring. Kaufman began by ducking out of the ring every time Lawler got near enough to touch him, prompting Lawler to commandeer the ring microphone and mock him. Finally, Lawler let Kaufman near enough to try a headlock, but turned it into a surprise move and pile-drove Kaufman into the mat—not once, but twice. After the second, Kaufman was unconscious.

The comedian was taken by ambulance to the local hospital, where he spent the next 3 days in traction. But that was not the end of it. The media took after Lawler for his "barbarity." And Kaufman spent his time obsessing about the match.

Three months later the two met again, on the Letterman show, and Kaufman broke into a stream of obscenities. The King swatted the comedian out of his chair, and Kaufman responded by flinging Letterman's coffee into Lawler's face. The brouhaha sparked a deluge of calls from outraged viewers—outraged by Kaufman, that is. The whole deal made headlines across the country.

The two continued their rivalry in arenas across the country, with plots, plans, and double-crosses galore. But the confrontation between wrestling and comedy would forever blur the line between reality and pretense.

New Age Outlaws Versus Cactus Jack and Chainsaw Charlie

Chainsaw Charlie (in reality, Terry Funk) was engaged in a "falls count anywhere" match against Cactus Jack and they'd just wrestled themselves up a ramp and into a Dumpster when the New Age Outlaws (Bad Ass Billy Gunn and Road Dog Jesse James) appeared out of nowhere and clamped the Dumpster shut. They pushed it off the ramp and it fell, crashing onto the arena floor 10 feet below. Doctors came a-running and the arena fell silent, the only sound to be heard was Sunny, the valet, sobbing.

Fast-forward, post recuperation for both Chainsaw Charlie and Cactus Jack—they wanted revenge. So a Dumpster match was arranged, slated to be part of *Wrestlemania XIV*.

The bout was more of a brawl, with most of it taking place in the nether regions of the arena (Boston's Fleet Center), far from the eyes of the fans. TV cameras followed the action, however—and what action it was! Ultimately, Chainsaw Charlie commandeered a forklift to pick up the Outlaws and put them in the Dumpster. It appeared the aggrieved pair were victorious.

But victory was only apparent—turns out that the rules stipulated a specific Dumpster be used, not the one the Outlaws ended up in. So another trashing will have to be arranged.

The Least You Need To Know

➤ Even the best of the good guys can get trounced by a bad enough baddie—as Kevin Sullivan showed in his bouts with Dusty Rhodes.

➤ The "biggest" grudge match, at least in terms of the size of the opponents, was between Andre the Giant and Black Jack Mulligan.

➤ The rivalries of pro wrestling are a key feature that keeps the fans coming back week after week.

➤ The Kaufman-Lawler feud forever confused the distinction between real and pretense when wrestling confronted comedy.

Part 3
Modern Madness: Wrestling Today

As you learned in Part 2, Gorgeous George was one of the first and best showmen in professional wrestling. All of the gimmicks, the looks, and the flair used in modern wrestling to whip a wrestling audience into a frenzy is his legacy.

The allure of pro wrestling has been compared to the lure of soap operas. Wrestlers develop a loyal following. There are the good guys fans love and the bad guys fans love to hate. This part will introduce you to the most popular wrestlers in the ring today. You will also meet the managers and promoters, who make the matches happen.

Believe it or not, women have been wrestling for decades. Today, female managers, valets, and wrestlers are frequent sights in the ring. You'll meet the women of wrestling in Chapter 14.

Novelty acts add a lot to the promotion of pro wrestling, as you'll discover in Chapter 15. Find out what impact the media has on pro wrestling when you read Chapter 16. This is a power-packed part of your book, so buckle up and get ready for a fast ride.

Chapter 12

Holding the Leash on 300-Pound Pulverizers: Managers

> ### In This Chapter
>
> ➤ The basic tasks of the wrestling manager
>
> ➤ Running the hype and how it contributes to the gate
>
> ➤ Everybody wants to get into the act: Managers in the ring

What is a manager? Look it up in the dictionary and you'll find something like the following: "A person in charge of the training and performance of an athlete or team." Well, that only begins to tell you what we do.

First of all, let me clarify one thing: We are not managers in the traditional sense of the word. We do not train the wrestlers the way a traditional sports manager does. Truth be told, if they didn't already know how to train, wrestlers wouldn't have gotten to the point where we would be interested in representing them as managers. No, we're less manager-trainers than we are business managers. We make the matches, get our wrestlers what we consider their fair share of the gate, and keep them pumped up for the big bouts.

And we're part of a team effort. Most times our wrestlers' performances in the ring are dependent upon our performances outside of it. You've seen us at ringside jumping up and down like Rumplestiltskin, doing anything and everything we can to help our wrestler win—fair or foul.

And, without a doubt, we are—both male and female managers—the most colorful characters in all of professional wrestling. Therein lies our biggest asset: our ability to "hype" or "heat up" a match. So here's the insider info on wrestling's managers.

Bert's Corner

How important is a manager? Ask Strangler Lewis: "Billy [Sandow, his manager] is a wonder in my corner and I have come to depend on him entirely in my big matches. He can see what I cannot, and his presence back there is certainly a relief. When I lost the title I wanted to retire, but Billy insisted I could beat [Stanislaus] Zbyszko and further insisted I keep on training. I decided to take Sandow's advice and take care of myself, and thanks to Billy I am champion once again."

Captain Lou's Corner

One of the wordiest managers I ever knew was Wild Red Berry. Berry studied the dictionary and books like *Bartlett's Familiar Quotations* and would incorporate them into his hype. Once he described a wrestler as having "the sagacity of a chipmunk and the jaws of a lion." Another time he was issuing challenges in the name of his tag team, the Kangaroos, and called on all the "insidious mug wumps" that stood in their path.

Management 101

To illustrate what a manager does, and how he or she does it, let me tell you about my own career as manager, and maybe you'll begin to understand.

As a wrestler, I was an also-ran who also ran—away from the likes of Bruno Sammartino, Andre the Giant, and anyone else who looked like they could do me bodily harm. Granted, we sold out all the arenas where I pulled my feet-don't-fail-me-now act, but I was giving my career more than a few second thoughts nonetheless. It was at one of these magic moments of self-doubt that Bruno Sammartino said to me, "You're not a great wrestler, but you never shut up. You'd be a good manager."

Intrigued by Bruno's suggestion, I went to see Vince McMahon Sr. He agreed with Bruno's assessment, saying "You'd be a natural—you're a good b***s*****r." Great! But before I realized it, the words were out of my mouth: "What the heck *is* a manager?"

Vince's answer was simple, but to the point: "You do all the hype for your men." That was it. Well, ever since I was a little kid I've had a motor mouth. In fact, people used to rib me about it, saying I had a mouth so big I could play the tuba from both ends. And what better way to use it than as a manager, where I could walk into a room, voice first, and hype my wrestlers until my tongue got tired?!

Learning the Managerial Ropes

The first wrestler I ever managed was Oscar Ladue, back in 1969. The kid was a natural for me. He mumbled and couldn't put two words together, so I became his mouthpiece—much like what was done for Abdullah the Butcher in more recent times—if you remember, he never uttered a word and had his manager do the talking for him. Anyway, like a kind of dishonest ventriloquist, I represented Ladue as both a manager and a spokesman. And operating on the theory that you can get anywhere if you keep putting one word in front of another, I was able to maneuver him into the main event at the brand-new Madison Square Garden for its very first wrestling show against Bruno Sammartino—ironically, the man who first suggested I become a manager.

Manager Notes: Paul Bearer

The Undertaker is Paul Bearer's biggest draw in his stable of wrestlers, but he's not the only one. There's also the Undertaker's brother, Kane. And there are more. Paul Bearer (a great name for the Undertaker's manager, don't you think?) has a ghoulish face and a fat body. He goes a little too heavy on the eye makeup. Sure, it's part of the total gimmick, but let's get real here. Who's going to take Bearer seriously as a man from the Dark Side? Now the Undertaker, *he's* scary. And as comical as Paul Bearer may look, he's done an excellent job of hyping media attention for the Undertaker and Kane. He may look silly in his ringside garb, but he draws plenty of press attention, which is a big part of the manager's job.

I soon found out that if I didn't hype my wrestler well, and do well for him and for the promoter at the gate, then I would hear from Vince saying, "Well, you're not doing your job: Your guys aren't selling out, they're not drawing." So I'd up my hype to the high-octane level.

Let me tell you about one of those high-octane hypes that worked—too well, it turns out.

Captain Lou poses with the Headshrinkers, one of his WWF champion tag teams

Back in the 1970s I managed Ivan Koloff, who was scheduled to take on Bruno Sammartino at the Garden for the world title—or at least the WWF version of it. Figuring that if I put my finger in the ethnic melting pot and stirred I could build the necessary heat for Koloff, I went on TV to promote the bout. Now, this was back in the days before political correctness became our national virus, so you could say things you wouldn't dare say today.

Running the Hype

Anyone who knows me knows that I'm proud of my Italian heritage, proud of the fact that my father was born and educated there, and proud that I was born in Rome while he was studying medicine over there. However, my ethnic pride didn't stop me from using hype to build Ivan's match.

Manager Notes: Classy Freddie Blassie

After he retired as a wrestler, Blassie soon became one of the most hated managers in the WWF lineup, guiding some of the meanest baddies in the ring. He specialized in foreign-invader baddies: Spiros Arion, Victor Rivera, Killer Khan, Mr. Fuji, The Iron Sheik, to name just a few. In addition to these evil-doers from foreign lands, he had American ne'er-do-wells on his roster, too: Dick Murdoch, Jesse Ventura, Big John Studd, Stan Hansen, and Adrian Adonis were just a few of those. He's the guy who brought Hulk Hogan into the WWF for the first time, in 1979. He retired from wrestling in the mid 1980s. After that, his biggest claim to fame was when he released the song "Pencil Neck Geek"—a huge novelty hit, named for the term he called wrestling's fans.

I went on television where I played it for all I was worth. With tongue planted firmly in my safety-pinned cheek, I said "Bruno Sammartino's Italian. I *used* to be an Italian, but I changed my name to Captain Lou Albert. Let's face it, what have 'guineas' ever done? Here I decided to let it all hang out, as they say: "All they've ever done is drive garbage trucks. I mean, you take the garbage trucks in New York and you see an Italian driving and a Puerto Rican loading. At midday they switch off...."

Well, that tore it. The hue and cry went up from all quarters. The Young Lords, a Puerto Rican gang, threatened to kill me. My "gumbas" were only a little less incensed. But what the heck, it was only part of my job as manager—to hype the match. Or so I thought.

The night of the Madison Square Garden bout, I still didn't have a clue. I looked at the capacity house and thought "What a good manager am I." But Vince had other thoughts. "We're going to have trouble," he kept saying. Even Koloff sensed something and told me not to get too close to him.

They were both right. Almost as soon as Koloff pinned Sammartino to win the belt, someone threw a firecracker from the balcony and it went off with a resounding

Body Slam

Not all interviews go as planned. One time, when I was on TV being interviewed by Vince McMahon Jr., I stood there yammering away and smoking a cigar, spilling ashes all over myself. I didn't know my shirt was made of polyester. Suddenly, Vince Jr. looked at me in horror and yelled—I looked down and saw my shirt was on fire! Burned my back and part of my arm—but what the heck, it added to the hype!

BOOOOM! Vince hollered to me "Don't go into the ring!" but that was unnecessary: I had no intention of doing so, and reverted to my old shtick of running—fast!—straight out of the Garden. But not before everyone in the capacity crowd had thrown anything and everything they could lay hands on at me. There were flowerpots, beer cups, and all manner of other unidentifiable fly-bys. It was a wild scene, and my managerial hype had created it.

> ## Manager Notes: Ted DiBiase
>
> Ted DiBiase, after a Hall-of-Fame-quality career as a wrestler in his own right, has made a smooth transition into managerial duties. DiBiase, who hails from Omaha, Nebraska, has managed some famous names within the industry: Champions who gained their titles under his management include The Outsiders, Styxx, and the Steiners. His own achievements as a title holder span the period from 1976 through 1993—clearly he's a manager who knows how to wrestle and how to win. His impressive list of wrestlers include Nikolai Volkoff, Bam Bam Bigelow, Kama, Steve Austin, The Evil Undertaker, King Kong Bundy, IRS, Tatanka, Sid, and the 1-2-3 Kid.

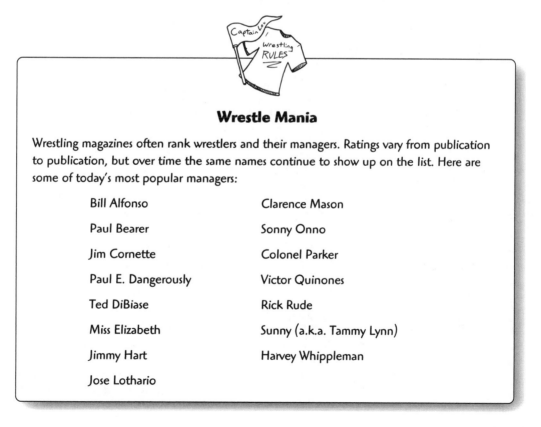

> ### Wrestle Mania
>
> Wrestling magazines often rank wrestlers and their managers. Ratings vary from publication to publication, but over time the same names continue to show up on the list. Here are some of today's most popular managers:
>
> | | |
> | --- | --- |
> | Bill Alfonso | Clarence Mason |
> | Paul Bearer | Sonny Onno |
> | Jim Cornette | Colonel Parker |
> | Paul E. Dangerously | Victor Quinones |
> | Ted DiBiase | Rick Rude |
> | Miss Elizabeth | Sunny (a.k.a. Tammy Lynn) |
> | Jimmy Hart | Harvey Whippleman |
> | Jose Lothario | |

I sought sanctuary in a nearby restaurant. As I ran in, the bartender yelled "Captain Lou, you'd better get out of here!" I saw a bunch of young guys, maybe 25 or so, staring menacingly in my direction. So I hollered, "Call the cops," and ran back out into the street to grab a cab. But as I got in, some of the young toughs started banging on the windows and the roof and rocking the cab. Heeding the driver's pleas to get out, I exited and raced back into the bar. The gang ultimately wrecked the joint, causing $27,000 worth of damage.

Interviews for Managerial Fun and Profit

I've also done interviews that were of a different style altogether—fun and funny. One of them was with my tag team, the Moon Dogs. They would come out and, on camera, eat raw meat—like the Samoans—and then they'd let out a howl. Then I'd say something to the announcer like, "Watch it! We have to keep an eye on these Moon Dogs. If they start picking up their legs you know what's happening—like when a dog lifts its leg? They'll do the same thing to you, so keep an eye on them!"

Another time, I showed up on the set with a goldfish. The gimmick was that I'd hold it over one of the Moon Dogs and say "Open up, Spot" and he'd howl. He'd usually get it into his mouth and then, when the camera went off, spit it out, but this time he accidentally swallowed it. He started screaming at me, totally out of character, and there went the gag.

Perpetual Prankster

You know me. I never met a joke I didn't like—especially one I could pull on the announcers, the audience, or the wrestlers, including my own. And George "The Animal" Steele was the perfect straight man for such jokes. The Animal was one of the weirdest wrestlers I have ever met, never mind managed. Sometimes I thought he would have been as much at home in a zoo as in the ring.

Bert's Corner

Conflicts seen around the ring between managers or between managers and wrestlers are often the setup for an upcoming grudge match that has not yet been announced.

Anyway, we were both on Vince Jr.'s TV show and I brought in a third person, introduced as Doctor Ziff or some such nonsense name. And then I added, "He's a psychiatrist and a gynecologist—you know, someone who works both ends." Anyway, the "doctor" (really an actor) sat The Animal down and George utters one of his multisyllabic grunts, drooling copiously. The doctor peers at his head and says, "It's a jungle in there." Then he decides that George needs shock treatments, and straps a metal helmet onto his head and hooks it up to some machine that looks like it came straight off the set of the movie *Frankenstein*. He throws a switch and all of a sudden George bolts upright in his chair and starts speaking in pear-shaped tones: "How now Brown Cow?" Of course, when the helmet came off, George reverted to

The Animal, mumbling intelligible gibberish, and I slam into the doctor: "You're nothing but a quack. You're no doctor...you're a veterinarian!"

But fans believe the hype—even hype like this. Later that same week I was at Kennedy Airport, about to board a plane for the next show. Suddenly this woman comes up and hugs and kisses me. She said, "Captain Lou, I want to thank you for sending George Steele to a gynecologist and curing him."

Making the Match

If the manager's first job is to hype the wrestlers, his second is to make the matches. By that I mean that the manager suggests to the promoter who might make up the best-drawing matches.

> ### Manager Notes: Jimmy Hart
>
> Jimmy Hart hails from Memphis, Tennessee, and has managed some great wrestlers. Among the wrestlers he's handled, you'll find such big names as Hulk Hogan, Kevin Sullivan, Randy Savage, Lex Luger, and The Giant. He's also handled Brutus Beefcake, The Faces of Fear, King Kong Bundy, Greg Valentine, Earthquake, Honky Tonk Man, The Hart Foundation, Money Inc., and Dino Bravo. Under Hart's direction, Hogan became the WCW World Champ. His Hart Foundation and Money Inc won the WWF tag-team championship. Greg Valentine climbed to the top of the WWF with Hart leading the way, as did the Honky Tonk Man. And the Giant won the WCW World Championship with Jimmy's help.

It's just like in boxing—which match will draw the most money? Would you put a Bruno Sammartino in against a Killer Kowalski? Yes. Would you put Bruno in against Charlie Brown? No. You're looking for something that will be very productive for your wrestler—something that suits his talent. Take, for instance, the Iron Sheik. You want him in against somebody like Sergeant Slaughter, so you've got the United States going up against Iran. That's a natural.

Pitting good versus bad is always a crowd pleaser, because fans want somebody to lose, but not the hero. So good guy versus good guy is a problem. Sometimes you can put a Killer Kowalski against another, maybe worse, villain and have a good outcome, but normally the classic pair-up is virtue over evil.

In Your Face

A wrestler—especially a babyface—has to remember that he's not just going up against the opponent listed on the card. He's probably going to have to take the baddie's manager into account too. Bad-guy wrestlers often work together with their managers to win any way they can, with the manager distracting the referee or trying to disable the good guy.

So you go to the promoter and suggest a possible match. I remember when my tag team, the Wild Samoans, came to me and suggested that I match Andre the Giant (one of my wrestlers) with a wrestler named Junkyard Dog. I brought the suggestion to Vince Sr. and it did well. Promoters *do* listen—if the manager has a record of coming up with good match-ups.

Of course, when suggesting matches, you're looking out for your guys. You cut the best deal for them that you can get. That's part of the job, too.

Ringside Antics

This brings us to the most obvious of all the manager's duties. These are the ones *everybody* knows about, the ones everybody sees: our antics at ringside.

As a group, managers are among the most colorful to be found in professional wrestling, and I say that with absolutely no humility. We're usually the wildest ones, patrolling the ring apron—often carrying our trademark props like walking canes, bullhorns, or even a 2×4—and doing our best to effect the outcome of the match. Doesn't matter how we do it: tripping up the opponent, or even coldcocking him if the action spills out of the ring.

We have other tricks too—including plain old distraction of either the opponent or the referee. Take Sunny, the former manager of Legion of Doom 2000. She resorted to gentler measures, like flirting with the opponents or the refs. And Marlena, who represents Golddust at ringside, has been known to drop the top of her dress at crucial times to reveal her feminine charms and completely sidetrack the opposite side.

Male managers don't have these options, of course. After all, what good would it do *me* if I flashed open my Hawaiian shirt. Maybe some referee would fall over in a fit of helpless laughter, but that's about all.

Manager Notes: Rick Rude

Rude is a man who is more than willing to take matters into his own hands, and is unafraid to use any means necessary. Since he's an ex-wrestler he's not afraid to crack a sweat during a match. His retirement from the ring was forced on him by a back injury, but the fires of battle still burn deep, and it shows. He's not afraid to wade into the thick of battle, as he did during the Hennig-Hart match-up in the *WCW Uncensored*.

Rick Rude, who never hesitates to prove himself worthy of his name, used a traditional method of distraction recently to help his wrestler, Curt "Mr. Perfect" Hennig. Dressed in his trademark suit, Rude jumped in and out of the ring to administer a beating to Hennig's opponent, Bret "Hit Man" Hart. He was so quick he was in and out before the referee could even catch a glimpse of him, despite all the screaming fans trying to alert the ref to the rule violations.

Wrestle Mania

One incident that Rude might like to forget is the time he grabbed Francine (a female manager). During a grudge match between Shane "The Franchise" Douglas and Pit Bull #1, Douglas was clearly on the winning end of the game. Other wrestlers decided to get into the mix, including Pit Bull #2, Bam Bam Bigelow, and Chris Candido. Rick Rude piled in himself, wielding a wall stud to clear a path straight to Francine, whom he essentially kidnapped. Such behavior is not common, but it does happen.

A Singular Case in Point

I remember one time I entered the ring to help my wrestler, Freddie Blassie. We were somewhere in Pennsylvania, where my charge was scheduled to wrestle Pedro Morales, then the WWF champion. As Morales stood center-ring, bathed in the applause of the crowd, Blassie came out in street clothes, his arm in a sling.

"I can't wrestle," he told announcer Vince McMahon Jr., "My arm's busted." Then he climbed into the ring to show Morales the note he had from his doctor. But as he did, I came up behind Morales and hit him with a shot over the head—with a chair. Then Blassie ripped off his sling and started pummeling Pedro with his "broken arm." Morales was finally rescued by Gorilla Monsoon and Chief Jay Strongbow, who carried him off to the dressing room, unconscious. When he revived he demanded that Blassie be made his top challenger for the WWF title, which was what we wanted all along.

You Win Some, You Lose Some

Sometimes, though, our tricks don't work. Take the time I managed the Wild Samoans, Afa and Sika. On the night they defended their tag-team title against Tony Atlas and Rocky Johnson, I decided that there was no such thing as too little help from the manager. So I brought a solid oak chair with me down to ringside. I hoped the fans would believe I'd brought it just so I could have the best seat in the house, but I had other plans—it was to be my secret weapon.

The match itself was wild—as anything that features the Samoans tends to be. Finally, all 300 pounds of Afa grabbed Tony Atlas in a full nelson. As they struggled, the referee somehow got in the way and was knocked on his keister. This was my chance! No referee in sight, so I climbed into the ring, chair in hand. As Atlas struggled to get out of the full nelson, I brought the carefully aimed chair down, right where his head was.

But at the last second he moved, and instead I hit Afa. He went down as if shot, and Tony pinned him. I felt like a total jerk.

Illegal Interference

Most managers find some way to interfere in the progress of a match. One of the most unusual methods I've seen was used by Marlena, who not only managed Golddust but was also his wife. She once smashed her purse into the face of her hubby's opponent, Brian Pillman. It's just another variation on the gimmick theme.

Call them illegal weapons if you want, but they are *all* gimmicks. They come in all sizes, shapes, and structures. They range from cola cans to ballpoint pens to knives, pieces of metal, and (my favorite) chairs. And they are often passed from manager to wrestler at crucial moments in the match.

Probably the best at passing gimmicks was Abdullah Farouk, better known as the Grand Wizard, but who was born Ernie Roth. He was a master at this trick of the trade. Usually your wrestler can maneuver his opponent over towards where you, the manager, are standing. It's not difficult for a wrestler to get his opponent where he wants him—whether it's a certain point in the ring or, better yet, on the ropes. Brute force works well. So does a baited lure. Experienced wrestlers have many ways of manipulating the position of their opponents so that the manager has a chance to do that voodoo he does so well. A manager and wrestler working together as a team can achieve really rewarding results—and wreak disaster on the opponent.

Maybe that's why you mostly see managers in the corners of the baddies, not the faces. Maybe the baddies need more help. Well, that's what we're there for. So when you see us wandering around, ringside, about to inflict all of wrestling's versions of the biblical plagues on our wrestler's opponent, watch us carefully. Somebody's got to!

Management's Best

Now, I'm good. But there are other good managers out there too. Otherwise, I'd have nobody to play off of. You've noticed the bios of some of the true greats scattered throughout this chapter. Here's the rundown on a few more:

Freddie Blassie, I have to admit, is a good manager. That is, if you like dirty tricks. During his days as a wrestler, he was known as a biter—during interviews he would always take out a file to sharpen his teeth. As a manager he's no less scary, in part because he's a little crazy. Even so, I have respect for Blassie. I have to—I've got to negotiate contracts with him, pitting my guys against his. But even when negotiating, I always keep my eye on his cane. You never know when he'll try to whack you with it.

And then there's Bobby "The Brain" Heenan. He calls himself the brain, but he has none. Let me tell you about something he pulled on me back in 1985. I'd just been picked as the WWF Manager of the Year, but Heenan wanted the title and there was nothing he wouldn't do to get it. So even after the fans' vote was in, he got other managers like Blassie, Jimmy Hart, and Johnny Valiant to give him their votes. Coulda worked—but Hillbilly Jim gave me his votes and that secured the award. Heenan was so furious that he hit me over the head with the trophy.

Johnny Valiant's a manager that I respect because of his wrestling reputation. But as a manager, he's a thief. He stole the tag-team title for Beefcake and Valentine, and he's a bully, too. And then there's Jimmy Hart, of the so-called Hart Foundation. He was once a great rock musician, but now he's a sneak. He sent his wrestlers, like Terry Funk, Jim Neidhart, and Bret Hart, out to ruin people in the ring.

The Least You Need to Know

➤ Managers are the most colorful characters in all of pro wrestling.

➤ The first job of the manager is to hype his or her wrestlers.

➤ Making the match is part of the job: A good match-up means great gate, and great profits for the wrestlers.

➤ A manager's job is never done: At ringside, the manager is right there in the middle of the action.

Chapter 13

Star Makers: Promoters

In his treatise *The Hustler's Handbook*, the great sports impresario Bill Veeck traced the genesis of the promoter. With tongue never far removed from his cheek, the impish Veeck wrote: "An eminent Professor of Egyptology recently deciphered the quaint markings and scrawlings on the walls of Syracuse, which depicted the stirring saga of one Tuttutantutt, a prehistoric promoter who was forced to beat a hasty exit from that normally hospitable city when half his bear-baiting team failed to show up. He did manage, it seems, to maintain his composure well enough to take the day's receipts with him, which resulted in the complete destruction of the arena by his irate customers. Tuttutantutt not only kept the receipts, he had his customers provide their own show." Now *that's* what I'd call a promoter!

If we didn't know Veeck—and his humorous spin on things—better, we could easily believe that his fanciful yarn documented the birth of the wrestling promoter.

From Carney to Cable Meister: The Evolution of the Promoter

To understand the origins of the wrestling promoter you must understand that they began as carney operators who ran athletic shows in the post–Civil War era. Back then,

Bert's Corner

The wrestling promoter's job is to make sure that every living, breathing human in the area where the show is being held knows: when the bout will take place, where it will be held, who will be performing, and that the fan's life will just not be worth living if he or she misses out on the event.

the operator would pitch his figurative tent in the town *du jour* and accept challenges from all local comers to try to take down one of his wrestlers. In the true spirit of the carney, these operators were not only skilled in setting up matches but also gifted in grifting every last available dollar from the local rubes' pockets—by any means possible.

Return with us now, dear reader, to about 1913. The wrestling great, Frank Gotch, has retired from the regular ring, taking his show on the road with the Sells-Floto Circus. Wrestling, once one of America's major sports, has fallen into disrepute with both the public and the press—largely because there was no one on the circuit to replace Gotch in the public's affection and because the slow, scientific bouts of that era were too slow paced to keep the fans interested. In addition, the press had learned of some of the behind-the-scenes manipulations that plagued the sport, and they became critical.

It was at this nadir of wrestling's fortunes that a promoter stepped forward to pump some new life into the dying sport. That promoter was Jack Curley, up to then better known in boxing circles for having co-promoted the Jess Willard-Jack Johnson heavyweight championship fight in Havana in 1915 with New York financier and Boston Red Sox owner Harry Frazee. Curley was ready to take on the proud—or not so proud—tradition of the carneys and shake money out of the rubes, but the rubes he had his eyes on were cynical New Yorkers.

Jack Curley, the Masked Marvel, and the 1915 Tournament

Curley's gambit was this: He staged an international wrestling tournament in the fall of 1915 to select a successor to Gotch. The tournament, held at the Manhattan Opera House, featured many of the top wrestlers of the day, including Alex Aberg, Dr. B. F. Roller, Charles Cutler, Wladek Sbyszko, Pierre le Colosse (billed as Pierre the Giant), Ivan Linow (The Russian Lion), Sula Hevonpaa (The Furious Finn), Demetrius Tofalos, and a newcomer who entered as Ed Lewis and came out as The Strangler.

There was no shortage of wrestlers for the event, but still everyone was quickly aware of one that wasn't entered. A hulking hooded man sat in the orchestra pit and shouted that "the best wrestler had been barred from competition." He was hurriedly ushered out, only to return again, night after night while the tournament went on. Naturally, the press picked up the story, courtesy of a tip planted by Curley. This brought the spectators into the act—just as Curley hoped it would—and they began demanding that the hooded man, who called himself the Masked Marvel, be allowed to participate.

Magnanimously, Curley bowed to public pressure and allowed the mysterious wrestler into the tournament. He won several preliminary bouts before finally being eliminated, and in so doing he brought Curley the publicity—and the gate—he needed to turn a pretty profit. Only later was the Masked Marvel revealed to be a railroad detective from Pennsylvania hired by Curley himself to perform. This was promoting at its best.

But the most important figure to emerge from the tournament wasn't the Masked Marvel. Instead, it was the newcomer, Ed "Strangler" Lewis. He ultimately became the new idol in all of wrestling-dom—replacing Gotch atop the pedestal. In addition, he became the most valuable commodity in professional wrestling over the next decade. And, in the process, he became the pivotal figure in the most important promotional team of early wrestling: a threesome consisting of Lewis, his manager Billy Sandow, and a promoter named Joseph "Toots" Mondt. The three were quickly dubbed "The Gold Dust Trio" by the press.

Captain Lou's Corner

Lots of wrestlers go on to become managers, like I did, but several have also gone into promotion. Former wrestlers who took on promotion duties include Toots Mondt, Joe Stecher, George Zaharias, Rudy Dusek, Ray Gunkle, Paul Boesche, Eddie Graham, Verne Gagne, and Cowboy Bill Watts.

Mondt Moves In

From a promotional standpoint, the most important member of the triumvirate was Mondt, a former wrestler from Greeley, Colorado, who still wore the cauliflower badge of his early career. A born con man and corrupt to his soul, in the fashion of the old-time carneys, Mondt was always looking for an angle, always scouting new ways to make a buck.

From the start, Mondt sensed the public's growing dissatisfaction with the long, boring scientific matches of the day. No one wanted to sit still for bouts that went five hours to end in a draw. Mondt's first innovation was to introduce time limits. But he didn't stop there. He introduced more spectacular moves into the ring and, perhaps

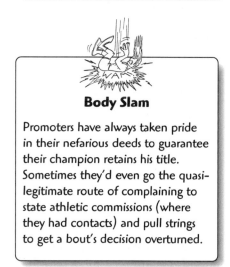

Body Slam

Promoters have always taken pride in their nefarious deeds to guarantee their champion retains his title. Sometimes they'd even go the quasi-legitimate route of complaining to state athletic commissions (where they had contacts) and pull strings to get a bout's decision overturned.

most important, he introduced the concept of the "packaged" show. Up to that time, wrestlers had barnstormed—they travelled around almost like an acting troupe, trying to get bookings for themselves wherever, and whenever, they could. They'd spend usually a day or two, at the most, in any one town. Promoters of the time were really little more than matchmakers. Mondt changed all that. Borrowing from the operating style of vaudeville, he moved the wrestlers around on a circuit, maintaining a stable of wrestlers, and every now and then bringing in new talent to keep his shows fresh.

Lewis was the linchpin of the stable. With him on board, it was easy for Mondt to tie up his stable of wrestlers with (mostly verbal) contracts, and to lean on other promoters to book matches against his men. It was in everybody's profit-making interests to cooperate with the Gold Dust Trio rather than to operate independently—particularly if they wanted the top-drawing Strangler Lewis to appear on their cards. In no time, Mondt and Co. controlled wrestling throughout most of the United States.

In Your Face

Promoter Toots Mondt, once an outstanding hooker himself, would discipline his wayward wrestlers by taking them into the ring and administering a beating. Jack Pfefer kept his charges in line by continually imposing high fines.

Throughout most of the 1920s, Lewis played tag with the heavyweight wrestling title. Whenever it was deemed good for business, Mondt would make sure he lost it—as he did to Stanislaus Zbyszko, Big Munn, and Gus Sonnenberg—but then he'd quickly win it back. This control over possession of the title, whether by Lewis or a hand-picked successor, was the most important asset in the Gold Dust Trio's portfolio—it kept them on top of the wrestling world.

But the wrestling world has always had all the intrigue of a Borgia family reunion, and Mondt fit that profile all too well. Within a few short years, he had deserted his partners to align himself with other promoters and set himself up in opposition to Lewis and Sandow. One of he new allies was a strange duck named Jack Pfefer.

Pfefer's Rise in the Promotional Ranks

Pfefer had come to the United States as a stagehand with a Russian ballet company, 25 cents in his pocket, and a willingness to compromise anything—including his morals—to make more. But even though he would pick up several of the hustles practiced by his fellow promoters he retained vestiges of Old World gentility, not to mention his strong Yiddish accent. He even autographed his photographs with an accent, signing them "Life is just a bowl of pickled herrings. You must taste it to like it."

Even though Mondt and Pfefer came from two different worlds, they had one thing in common: They both believed that they had a license to live off the fatheads of the land. And they treated wrestlers and wrestling fans accordingly.

This was the Depression era, and wrestling's fortunes had gone south once again—this time because even the most die-hard fans just didn't want to spend their hard-to-get cash on entertainment. Struggling to remain solvent, most promoters resorted to old carney-spawned hustles to cheat their wrestlers out of their due. They'd claim "higher-than-expected expenses" and "lower-than-anticipated attendance" and just about everything else to subtract everything they could from the wrestlers' purses. One wrestler of the time remembered a promoter deducting the costs of a maintenance worker who supposedly put in 168 hours of labor the week before the bout. That just happens to be the total number of hours in a week.

Pfefer was no more innocent than the rest of his fellow promoters. One time, Hans Steinke, a giant of a wrestler who was unhappy with his payoff, confronted Pfefer in the booking office and hung him up by his ankles out a 10th-story window over Times Square. Pfefer speedily found a mutually satisfactory way to resolve their differences. But more often than not, when it came to outsmarting wrestlers, Pfefer came out the winner. When Herb Freeman lost a match against Jim Londos in Madison Square Garden and went to Pfefer for his payoff, Pfefer slid the check over, face down, for Freeman to endorse and paid out $1,500 in cash. What Freeman didn't know was that the purse check read $2,000.

Body Slam

Promoters were traditionally a shady lot. One of their favorite tricks to pull on the fans was to book their star attraction into two or three towns on the same night, wait to see which had the biggest advance ticket sale, send the star to that arena, and send substitutes to the ones that had smaller crowds, claiming the star was injured.

Wrestle Mania

Promoters were always looking for ways to draw the fans. Back in the early 1920s, Stanislaus Zbyszko was the champion, but according to Lou Thesz, he was "totally lacking in color. Business got so bad that there was no choice but to make Ed 'Strangler' Lewis champion again. Zbyszko was a proud man, but he was a businessman, too, and agreed something had to be done. So on March 22, 1922, Zbyszko dropped the title back to Lewis. It was a good decision, because the switch signaled the start of a two-year run that was the Gold Dust Trio's most lucrative period."

Dissension in the Ranks

The Mondt/Pfefer alliance in the 1920s was short-lived—as were most promotional alliances of the time. Promoters jumped into and out of such pair-ups at the drop of the proverbial fedora, often taking their wrestlers with them. It got so that by the mid 1930s, in the words of *Ring* magazine's Nat Loubet, "champions grew on bushes."

In January of 1934, tired of the internecine warfare going on among the professional groups, the New York State Athletic Commission called in several promoters, among them Toots Mondt and Jack Curley, as well as several wrestlers, including Jim Londos and Dick Shikat, to investigate charges of "secret agreements" and "title juggling." After all the testimony was heard, the Commission could say only that "We have heard all the testimony. We have sent it out to be translated into English. When that is done, we will consider it."

Meanwhile, Jack Pfefer started what the papers called "The Tattletale Wars." Pfefer told the press that Londos's win against Shikat for the title had been predetermined, and that both Jim Browning and Ed Don George, two other title claimants, were in reality managed by the same promoter, Paul Bowser of Boston.

In Your Face

According to the November 1948 issue of *Ring* magazine, promoter Rudy Dusek was fond of making his wrestlers toe the line by sheer force: "When a grappler in the Rudy Dusek troupe fails to show to the best of his ability, the boss takes him on soon after and teaches the fellow a lesson. After Rudy gets finished with him, he is ready to exert every effort to please rather than experience another match with the Boss."

The situation would get worse before it got better as the promoters sniped at one another rather than attend to their dwindling audience. This was a shortsightedness that would cost them. Dearly. The outpouring of fans, which had climbed to as many as 22,000 at Madison Square Garden in 1930 and 35,000 at Chicago's Wrigley Field in 1934, had by the end of the decade turned into a mere trickle. Some promoters, like Jack Curley, simply threw in the towel. And Madison Square Garden, once one of wrestling's great showcases, went "dark" in 1937, slamming its doors on wrestling events.

Promoters tried everything they could think of to regain their audience. This was the era when scientific wrestling finally gave up the ghost, and the likes of the Omaha Riot Squad, the four Dusek Brothers, led the way to the new style of "rasslin'"—pure exhibitions featuring plenty of rough stuff. And the freaks were introduced: midgets, hillbillies, hairy wrestlers, and other such oddities. Not to mention mud wrestling and Jell-O wrestling, as promoters threw in every attraction they could think of to save the failing sport.

The Way It Worked

Herman Hickman, writing for the February 6, 1954 issue of *The Saturday Evening Post*, pulled back the curtain a bit to let readers in on how the promoters of the day worked. Writing about the Jack Curley office in New York in the 1930s, he noted that "the job of booking wrestlers in 20 or 30 cities all over the United States each night of the week is a complex operation." In that era, the Curley office was actually run by Toots Mondt, Jack Pfefer, and Ed White (who managed Jim Londos). The office sent instructions out to wrestlers across the country, setting the match-ups and dictating the outcome of the week's bouts.

Hickman notes: "All the wrestlers had code names. For instance, Jim Londos was Chris, Rudy Dusek was Mitch, George Zaharias was Subway, I was Cannonball. In those days the Postal Telegraph Company was still in existence, in addition to Western Union. The New York office would send out the instructions on one wire service and have them confirmed on the other. This is a sample message: 'Cannonball moon Subway around 35 confirm.' It meant that I was to lose—look up to the moon—to George Zaharias in about 35 minutes."

Wrestle Mania

One promoter who did everything he could to stay in business during the 1930s was Chicago's Fred Kohler. Every week he'd take on the persona of a wrestler known as "Freddie King" and would be thrown in against the strongest opposition available at the old Rainbow Arena. Sometimes he won, but mostly he lost. One day someone asked him why he bothered to wrestle at all. "I have to," he answered, "otherwise Fred Kohler, the promoter, would go broke.

World War II and the Post-war Years: Promoters Regroup

The dearth of talent during World War II was more than matched by the public's total apathy as professional wrestling began to look like one more casualty of war. And after the end of the hostilities, things looked little better. Fans, by now weaned off professional wrestling, found other forms of entertainment to spend their newfound money and leisure time on.

But promoters still had a few tricks up their sleeves. One of the more enterprising promoters during this dance-with-death period was Jack Pfefer. He put on entire cards with wrestlers no one had ever heard of. A show bill for a typical Pfefer post-war card read: "For the heavyweight championship of the world, Dave Levin vs. 'Zuma,' the Man from Mars; Tarzan Lord Pincerton vs. The Mighty Titan; Hopalong Rokko, The Flying Saucer vs. the Volga Boatman; and Pancho Romero, Mexican Champion vs. The Red Devil."

Bert's Corner

One way to keep the fans coming was to keep them satisfied—and promoters wanted to make sure to part those fans from every dime they could pry loose. By the mid 1930s most matches were held as two-out-of-three falls, with the wrestlers returning to their dressing rooms in between each fall. The claim was that this let the wrestlers rest, but the real reason was to give fans time to visit the concession stand without missing any of the action.

With his list of no-names, Pfefer was famous for building up wrestling's large ethnic audiences. If he thought he could appeal to a community's Polish constituency, he'd change the wrestler's name to something Polish, create a phony bio, and advertise him as such. One time, according to Joe Jares, Pfefer gave one of his "Polish" wrestlers a real jawbreaker of a name, something that sounded like Lavakowski. Calling another promoter in New England to sell his "new sensation," Pfefer announced "Next veek have I got for ya a great, a real vinner, a Polack." The promoter on the other end of the line, biting, asked Pfefer how to spell the wrestler's name so he could include it in the advertising for the show. Pfefer started: "L-a-v..." paused, then tried again, "L-a-v-..." Finally he said, "Oh, to hell with it—don't book him!"

But in the end it wasn't Pfefer who came up with one of the greatest ethnic draws in the history of professional wrestling. That honor goes instead to his former partner, Toots Mondt. Mondt was to bring out the wrestler he would claim had done more for legs than Betty Grable—Antonino Rocca.

Rocca would be the start of a long line of stars who would appeal to specific ethnic communities—a line that included Bruno Sammartino, Victor Rivera, Migel Perez, and Pedro Morales. And he would become, along with Gorgeous George on the West Coast, one of the two great wrestling stars of the 1950s. Together, Rocca and George ushered in the so-called Golden Age of Wrestling, made all the more golden by the newfangled medium of television.

And, just as important, Rocca's entrance onto the New York wrestling scene would signal the formation of a new promotional alliance that would reshape the world of wrestling: Mondt, with Rocca in tow, now joined forces with another promoter who had the contacts and contracts with TV—Vince McMahon Sr.

Capital Wrestling and the WWWF

Mondt and McMahon formed Capital Wrestling and opened up Madison Square Garden—which had been without wrestling since the 1937 bout between Dick Shikat and Danno O. Mahoney. And they went looking for their champion.

They found him in Buddy Rogers, whom Mondt stole from his old partner, Pfefer—much as Mondt had persuaded Rocca to skip out on *his* original promoter, Morris Siegel in Houston. But Pfefer was not one to take such treachery lying down, so he retaliated by printing up fliers labelling Rogers a "fake" and hired legions of poster plasterers to put them up everywhere Rogers was booked.

Wrestle Mania

One of the biggest promotional circuits during the 1960s and 1970s was the American Wrestling Alliance (AWA), headed by Verne Gagne, its champion. The regional territory was a breakaway from the NWA and extended from Minneapolis throughout the Midwest, including Milwaukee, Chicago, Indianapolis, Omaha, and Denver. It stretched to include Hawaii and parts of Japan.

Now, Rogers had been the National Wrestling Alliance (NWA) champion, having won that title from Pat O'Connor in 1961. He was later to lose it to the NWA's perennial champion, Lou Thesz, in 1963. But the fact that he lost the NWA crown made no nevermind to Mondt and McMahon as they set up shop in opposition to the then-most-powerful promotional combine in America. They changed the name of their promotional outfit from Capital Wrestling to the World Wide Wrestling Federation (WWWF), and immediately named Rogers as *their* outfit's champion.

With Rogers in their stable, Mondt and McMahon now maneuvered another star, Bruno Sammartino, into a title match against Rogers for the WWWF championship. Sammartino's reputation had been previously made on having been able to body slam the 600-pound Haystacks Calhoun, and he had no trouble against Rogers. Having been severely injured in a recent match, Rogers had to be literally carried into the ring. And he was pinned in 18 seconds. Flat.

Citing Rogers's injury, Sammartino—a very proud man—refused to take the championship. So Mondt and McMahon staged a championship rematch, this time in Madison Square Garden where, in front of a capacity house, Sammartino repeated his conquest of Rogers. This time it took a little longer—48 seconds.

For the rest of the decade and on into the 1970s, the WWWF rode the broad back of Bruno Sammartino—and those of his successors: Ivan Koloff, Pedro Morales, and Stan Stasiak—to the top of the wrestling heap. Now, having captured the field, they were ready to move on to bigger things.

A Match Made in Heaven: Vince McMahon Jr. and Television

By the end of the 1970s, Mondt was gone. So, too, was the first *W* in WWWF. The newly named WWF set its sights on new territory under the leadership of Vince Sr.'s hand-picked successor, Vince Jr.

Wrestle Mania

Vince says his favorite promotion would be *Wrestlemania III*, with Andre the Giant against Hulk Hogan in the main event. "We had 93,000 in the Pontiac Silverdome—more than the Pope had the next month.... Hulk was in his glory days, and Andre...was finishing up *The Princess Bride*. He had severe back problems, but I went over to where they were filming and pleaded with him. I asked him to wrestle one more time for my father, who had just passed away...since Andre was one of my dad's favorites."

In the old days, most promoters recognized that they had to work together, sometimes lending their stars for use in another's territory, and at the very least exchanging information on who was drawing what kinds of crowds. Even when they were stabbing one another in the back, there was at least a facade of professional cooperation. And one of the most universally honored of professional courtesies was respecting one another's territory. Vince Jr. would change all that, and in so doing he would change the face of professional wrestling.

Unbound by any agreements, gentlemen's or otherwise, and not part of any old-boy's network, Vince Jr. determined to make the WWF a national firm, one worthy of the name World Wrestling Federation. To do so he employed TV production values and utilized the existing stable of WWF stars. Among them was a newcomer named Terry Bollea, whose *nom de* mat, Hulk Hogan, was concocted from two of the biggest TV hits of the period: *Hogan's Heroes* and *The Hulk*. Hogan would prove to be one of wrestling's all-time great draws. But at this early period, Vince Jr. was just beginning: He'd tape his shows and ship them to stations all over the country.

In Your Face

In years past, promoters would relegate their rowdy wrestlers to the bottom of the card—or even blackball them in a territory. Today's promoters often punish wrestlers that are deemed "bad to the bone" by withholding bookings.

Buying time on local TV stations—even if it meant elbowing local promoters out of the way by outbidding them for the time they once controlled—McMahon soon blanketed the country with his wrestlers' bouts, gaining a monopoly on visibility. Fans were now watching the WWF shows on their local stations rather than attending the matches put on in arenas by the regional promoters.

Had the other promoters banded together, perhaps they could have stopped Vince Jr.'s onslaught. But the three most powerful promoters of the time—Verne Gagne of Minnesota and the AWA; Cowboy Bill Watts; and Jim

Crockett of North Carolina and the NWA—never saw what was coming at them. That gave Vince Jr. the opening he needed.

With Vince Jr. blitzing the airways with his shows, soon one promoter after another bit the dust. Within less than five years, the old system of 20 or so regional territories had gone the way of the dinosaurs. By the end of Vince's onslaught they had been reduced to maybe five, with only one—Jim Crockett's NWA—considered to be anything near viable.

Then, in 1985, McMahon made wrestling history once again by promoting the sport's first true extravaganza, *Wrestlemania*. With celebrities like Liberace, Mr. T, Muhammad Ali, Cyndi Lauper, and Billy Martin in attendance, and with wrestlers like Hulk Hogan, Wonderful Paul Orndorff, Rowdy Roddy Piper, Wendi Richter, Fabulous Moolah, and yours truly, Captain Lou Albano, his superstar event cemented McMahon's claim to being wrestling's all-time greatest promoter.

Wrestling in the Post-*Wrestlemania* Era

By 1988, Vince Jr.'s electronic onslaught with the WWF had also gained the attention of Madison Avenue, which began courting it, in the words of *Adweek,* "because of its numbers." With a heavy penetration of the teenage and 21- to 34-year-old audience, advertisers like Nike, Faberge, Procter and Gamble, M&M candy, and the National Dairy Association had come on board, advertising their wares. And the WWF had begun marketing its wrestling souvenirs through catalogs. Its net worth at this time was estimated by *Forbes* magazine to have reached $100 million.

Late in that same year, Ted Turner purchased the remains of Crockett's old outfit, the NWA, and a new battle was on—a battle of anything-you-can-do-I-can-do-better, which continues today.

In one corner you have the WWF, led by Vince McMahon Jr., who prided himself on having his finger on the pulse of the marketplace. And he did—alone among promoters, he sensed that the audience for wrestling had changed, radically, and he had the wit to change with it. In the other corner you have World Championship Wrestling (WCW), overseen by media genius Ted Turner, with all his Time-Warner money and the help of his imaginative head of operations, Eric Bischoff. Together the two competitors have taken pro wrestling to dizzying heights.

Bert's Corner

Fans often fail to realize that Eric Bischoff is World Championship Wrestling's promoter. They know him only as just one of the New World Order boys.

Eric Bischoff of the WCW: A Challenge to the McMahon Monopoly

So today there are two major federations: the WWF and the WCW. And there are two major promoters: Vince McMahon Jr. and Eric Bischoff. Vince Jr. was well-known in wrestling circles long before taking the active role he plays today, having been highly visible as an announcer. Bischoff is a true newcomer, and much less is known about him. That hasn't stopped him from successfully taking the WCW from a distant also-ran to the WWF to it's direct rival in a nose-to-nose battle. His achievements include raiding name talent from the competition—he got Hulk (now Hollywood) Hogan, Randy Savage, Kevin Nash (known in his WWF days as Diesel), and Scott Hall (who wrestled in the WWF as Razor Ramon). And he invented the so-called "civil war" within his own organization, with half of his stable battling an organization of rebels known as the New World Order (the nWo)—thus giving the WCW a wildly successful ongoing plot line.

Bischoff himself has taken on the role of spokesman for the nWo. And although he is thought of by most of the fans as simply the nWo's promoter, he really still runs the whole WCW shebang.

McMahon, of course, is hardly likely to take a backseat to anyone, especially Bischoff. In response to the success of Bischoff's nWo plot line, McMahon has morphed from the WWF announcer into a WWF baddie: a promoter who's carrying on a feud with some of his own wrestlers.

Captain Lou's Corner

If professional wrestling is more than just alive and well but actually burgeoning, that's a tribute not to just McMahon and Bischoff but also to the independent promoters (Indies) who keep the sport alive on the local level: Ed Vetrano, Pete Pecora, Blaine DeSantis, Afa Anoai, Jim Kitner, Tony Rumble, Harry Geiger, Ken Patera, Windy City Championship Wrestling, and many others.

Wrestle Mania

Eric Bischoff has carried his act into the ring, agreeing to a match against wrestler-turned-WCW-commentator Larry Zbyszko, with Bret Hart as the special referee. Before the bout Bischoff did what he does best—he talked a lot. But once the match got under way, Zbyszko was well in control. Bret Hart had to cut the match short to forestall Bischoff's ultimate destruction—though the fallen promoter claimed he was only lulling Zbyszko into a trap.

Now that both promoters have become major players in the ring as well, Bischoff recently challenged McMahon to a match on, what else? A WCW pay-per-view telecast. Since Vince Jr. is extremely savvy about such things, the last thing he'd want to do is encourage his WWF fans to cross over and patronize the WCW. Quite naturally, then, he didn't show up to answer Bischoff's challenge. Equally natural, Bischoff simply declared himself the winner of the nonmatch. (While McMahon wouldn't answer the challenge issued by Bischoff for pay-per-view, he *did* plant an item on the Internet stating he'd be glad to take Bischoff on anytime—in a parking lot with no cameras or spectators allowed.)

The Least You Need to Know

➤ Promoters are the natural descendants of the old carney operators.

➤ Old-time wrestling promoters each controlled his own territory.

➤ Many promoters, like Toots Mondt and Jack Pfefer, are as colorful as the personalities they book to wrestle.

➤ The face of wrestling changed radically when Vince McMahon Jr. took over the WWF from his father.

➤ There are two "majors" today: the WWF and the WCW.

Chapter 14

Sexy, Serious, and Supreme in Their Roles

Once on the *David Letterman Show,* I uttered the immortal words, "Women are good only for having babies and cleaning house." Little did I realize at the time that I was in a spot you wouldn't give a leopard. Thousands of angry women called the CBS network switchboard to protest my comments. And hundreds more picketed the studio demanding I take back my words. And I won't even *begin* to tell you how mad my wife, Geri, was.

While I can't promise I learned my lesson, I will say this: women wrestlers have been in the sport for a long time now. They helped keep it alive during the lean years of the Depression, and without them in today's pro wrestling, it would be a whole lot uglier to watch. In this chapter you'll learn about the pulchritudinous pro wrestling professionals of the female persuasion.

Girls Just Want to Have Fun

After *Wrestlemania I,* when Cyndi Lauper's wrestler, Wendi Richter, beat my hand-picked champion, the great Fabulous Moolah, I apologized for my remark, telling Cyndi: "Women are at least as good as men…if not, in most cases, better." Well, I'd really known that all along, you see—but I waited until after the bout to say it (remember, it's a manager's job to hype a bout). Anyway, the point to the story is this: when it comes to wrestling, women have *always* been as good as men, if not better!

Wrestle Mania

Vince McMahon Sr. said, "Most girls will tell you they'll keep going as long as the body holds out, but...as soon as they meet the right fella, they get out." Lots of the time, Mr. Right is a fellow wrestler—marriages made in center ring include Penny Banner and Johnny Weaver, Joyce Fowler and George Becker, and June Byers and Sammy Menacker. More recently Randy Savage and Elizabeth, Goldust and Marlena, Sunny and Chris Candido, and Marc Mero and Sable have been partners both in the ring and out.

Women have been a part of wrestling since "back in the Greek era of super sports," according to the February 1953 issue of *Ring* magazine. Of course, that was just a little bit before my time.

More recently, women were always a part of the old carney "At Shows" that traveled the country in the early 20th century. And some, like Cora Livingstone, also wrestled on the theatrical circuit in the old days of vaudeville. And most of the time, these early women of the ring wrestled against men who challenged them from the audience.

Captain Lou's Corner

Wrestling's version of the Dallas Cowboy Cheerleaders is found in the Nitro Girls who perform on *Monday Nite Nitro* to spice up the lulls in the action and make sure the male viewers stay awake through the whole show.

Bertha Rapp

Perhaps the first woman to gain any measure of fame by challenging males was Bertha Rapp, a teacher of calisthenics at a Cincinnati school. She made history of sorts by challenging her fellow passengers aboard the White Star liner *Adriatic* back in 1911.

While not small in size, Ms. Rapp was no Big Bertha either. She stood all of 5'9" and weighed in at 150 pounds. Her two challengers weighed in at 149 and 185 pounds respectively (if not respectfully). The first one she pinned in eight minutes. The second she battled to a 30 minute draw, proving that the so-called weaker sex could more than hold its own in a wrestling bout.

Mildred Burke

Jump ahead to two decades later, to the mid 1930s, and you'll find Mildred Burke, the first great woman wrestler, started in much the same way as Bertha: She challenged any and all males to wrestle her. When the young Mildred Bliss of Kansas City first decided to try her hand at the sport, she called the promoter in her area and asked if he would book her.

Mildred Burke—first female pro wrestler—in a publicity pose (Source: Norman Kietzer)

"Sure, I'll let you wrestle," came the reply, "but I don't know who you're going to wrestle. If you can find somebody to wrestle you, it's all right with me."

There being no other women on the wrestling landscape at the time, Mildred Bliss, soon to become Mildred Burke, wrote the sports editor of her local paper, and issued her challenge to any man within 20 pounds of her weight to "beat" her for the then-princely sum of 25 hard-earned Depression dollars.

As Burke, Mildred wrestled almost 200 men. She says: "The only time I was defeated it wasn't because I was pinned…I got knocked out. I was wrestling a collegiate wrestler in Omaha and I picked him up to body slam him. When I did, he doubled up his knee between us and when I fell it knocked all the air out of me."

Having proved that women were not just men's equals but, in 199 cases out of 200, their superiors, Burke (and her manager, Billy Wolfe) now sought to display her talents against other women. However, there were no other female wrestlers on the circuit at the time, so they took their act to the carnivals, challenging all comers. During their

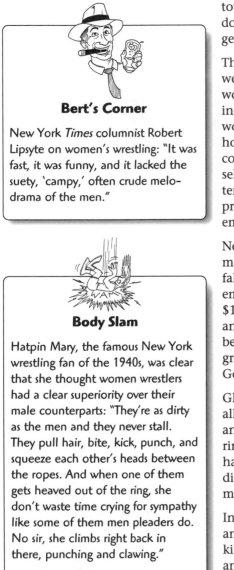

Bert's Corner

New York *Times* columnist Robert Lipsyte on women's wrestling: "It was fast, it was funny, and it lacked the suety, 'campy,' often crude melodrama of the men."

Body Slam

Hatpin Mary, the famous New York wrestling fan of the 1940s, was clear that she thought women wrestlers had a clear superiority over their male counterparts: "They're as dirty as the men and they never stall. They pull hair, bite, kick, punch, and squeeze each other's heads between the ropes. And when one of them gets heaved out of the ring, she don't waste time crying for sympathy like some of them men pleaders do. No sir, she climbs right back in there, punching and clawing."

tour they chanced to meet another woman who was also doing the challenge-all-males shtick. The two decided to get it on in the first woman versus woman bout.

The next question was, where to stage the match? They went to a Birmingham, Alabama, promoter to see if he would put it on. "Oh, good heavens—girls?" he asked incredulously. "That would really kill the town. They wouldn't be able to do anything but pull hair!" Finally, however, he relented—only to be rewarded with a completely sold-out house. In fact, he had nothing but sellouts wherever he booked them throughout his territory—a fact that did not go unnoticed by other promoters who had been staging all-men cards to mostly empty seats.

News of the capacity-house draw for women's wrestling matches began to circulate, and soon promoters were falling all over themselves to book women into their empty arenas. With the women wrestlers making up to $100 a match, and promoters putting out calls for any and all to wrestle, the ranks of women wrestlers soon began to fill. This was the era of such female wrestling greats as Gladys "Kill 'Em" Gillam, Rose Evans, Wilma Gordon, Mae Weston, and many, many others.

Gladys Gillem was probably the most colorful of them all. She was, by turns, a wrestler, a circus lion tamer, and an alligator wrestler. Called a hellcat in the wrestling ring and a daredevil in the circus ring, Gladys had a habit, recalls Mildred Burke, of landing on her head. She did it so often that Burke remembers "her head was just mushy back there—you could just push in on it."

In one bout, Burke had sent Gillem through the ropes and onto the concrete floor head first. "My God, I've killed her!" thought Burke. But Gladys got right back up and charged into the ring, swinging.

The Opposition Gets Organized

But there were those who believed that women in the ring was something like a crime against nature. One of those who opposed their entry into the sport was all-time wrestling great Lou Thesz, who thought that their whole act was just a ploy to titillate the men in the audience.

Thesz was not alone in his opinion. Other traditionalists who agreed with him included the Michigan State Athletic Commissioner, who asked, "Would you like to see your *sister* wrestling?" And then there was the Roman Catholic bishop of Saskatoon, who preached that women's wrestling "fed the lower and baser appetites of those who watch." Even *Ring* magazine, which ran a monthly wrestling column, sermonized on the topic: "The *Ring* does not recognize matches between members of the fair sex as a sport."

But there seemed to be more than enough would-be female wrestlers out there who believed, with Noel Coward, that "certain women should be struck regularly, like gongs." As Betty Niccoli, an early wrestler, put it, "Men shouldn't be the only ones allowed to get hurt." So many women traded in their rolling pins for mat pins. Those wonder women who filled the ranks of women's wrestling to overflowing included June Byers, who succeeded Mildred Burke as women's champion, Nell Stewart, Elvira Snodgrass, Mars Bennett, Cot Cotson, Lilly Bitter and the one that would dominate women's wrestling for the next three decades: Fabulous Moolah.

The Fabulous Career of Fabulous Moolah

Fabulous Moolah started life as Lillian Ellison, the 12th of 13 children and the only girl in the carload. As a young girl of nine, she fell in love with the sport of professional wrestling after watching a match in her native Columbia, South Carolina. From that time onward wrestling was her calling.

Lillian began her professional career as a wrestler for Mildred Burke's manager and husband, Billy Wolfe, in Kansas City in October of 1949. In her first bout, she pinned a wrestler named Cecilia Blevens in 15 minutes flat. Looking for bigger and better conquests, she came east to seek out wrestling promoter Jack Pfefer. "Vhy do you vant to wrestle?" he asked her. "For the moolah," she replied with all the straightforwardness of youth. And so, Moolah she became.

Before her wrestling career truly took off she served as Slave Girl Moolah, valeting first for Buddy Rogers and later for the Elephant Boy, a bushy-haired warrior who posed as an Indian mahatma of tremendous wealth. He'd enter the ring with Slave Girl Moolah trailing in his wake. She would be dressed in an eye-catching sarong rather than the more traditional (and less revealing) sari. Her major function in life seemed to be the constant folding and refolding of the Elephant Boy's robe.

However, Lillian had bigger ambitions than to be a mere robe carrier, and she soon let it be known that she intended to perform in the ring—and *not* as a slave girl. So Slave Girl Moolah became the Fabulous Moolah and made her debut in Boston in 1954. Within two years she had taken the title "Women's Champion," defeating 13 other women in a Baltimore tournament, among whose number was the then-reigning champion, June Byers.

For the longest time, the Fabulous one dominated women's wrestling, both as its champion and as its foremost villain. She had a bag of dirty tricks that even *I* envied; she was sneaky and, like me, would do anything to win—and to rake in the moolah.

The Fabulous Moolah
(Source: Norman Kietzer)

Her three-decade reign included becoming the first woman wrestler to win a match at that bastion of male supremacy, Madison Square Garden, in June of 1972, and lasted into the 1980s when she finally lost her belt to Wendi Richter at *Wrestlemania I*. I was her manager at the time, and I think she blamed the loss on me.

Wrestle Mania

At the WWF's *Summer Slam*, Sable and Edge took on Ms. Jacqueline and Marc Mero in a mixed tag-team bout. Sable went at both Mero and Jacky right from the start, tossing Jacky around the ring and giving Mero a flying flip from the top rope. While Mero lay on the mat, Edge took Sable by the ankles and spun her a couple of times before dropping her on Mero for the pin. It was a triumph for Sable and Edge, and a throwback to the days of yore when women met men in mixed matches.

The Fabulous Moolah pins Vicki Page (Source: Norman Kietzer)

A Temporary Lapse—Women's Wrestling Fades in the 1970s

Moolah's success in the ring inspired others to try their hands at wrestling. Some of the comely newcomers included Penny Banner, Maria Laverne, Marie Vagnone, and Viviane Vachone.

But sometime during the 30 years that Moolah ruled the women's roost, the bloom came off the rose of women's wrestling. Once a fan favorite, women's participation in the sport became first an afterthought, and then a nonthought.

No telling just exactly why women's wrestling faded in the 1970s. It had begun as a way to fill the empty Depression era arenas and blossomed during the war years when male wrestlers were thin on the ground. And it had a good run in the first post-war decade, during the first third of Moolah's heyday. But interest in women's bouts seemed to wither away just as male wrestling was beginning to fill the houses again. Maybe it was because a new crop of male superstars had begun to fill the talent pipelines and the arenas. Whatever the reason, women's wrestling began to fade from public consciousness.

It looked dire in the mid 1970s, but the situation was only temporary. At about this time, there was a change in the wrestling roles for women, one that had its earliest roots as long ago as the late 1940s, when Gorgeous George traded in his male valet for a shapely female model. After that, the number of women who began their careers as valets—like Moolah during her Slave Girl period—increased exponentially. At the same time, female managers were exploding on the scene.

Madame Manager

The women of today's pro wrestling are magnificent and numerous. We're not talking about the women who compete for titles, though there are still a few, but rather we're talking about the ones who manage male wrestlers. Their presence, as managers or valets, is always welcomed by fans. After all, the mere fact that a wrestler comes into the ring with a beautiful woman is enough to draw a good deal of crowd attention.

Captain Lou's Corner

In one memorable mixed bout of the 1930s (1937 to be exact), Billy Wolfe, who was Mildred Burke's manager and husband, defeated Clara Mortensen via disqualification in Atlanta, Georgia.

But women valets and managers are not just part of the wrestling scenery—they're an important part of the sport itself. There's Elizabeth, or Liz. She looks like the girl next door, only way better. And then there's the ever-skimpily-clad Francine. Not to mention the foxy Marlena. These women have a black belt in beauty.

The ladies of the ring are as tough as they are beautiful. Here's a list of the best known female managers/valets in pro wrestling today:

Soft Curves and Hard Shoulders

Miss Alexandra	Jacquelyn	Debra McMichael
Beulah	Kimberly	Miss Patricia
Chyna	Kimona	Peaches
Cloudy*	Kitten	Sable
Destiny	Lun	Sherri
Elizabeth	Madusa	Sunny
Missy Hyatt	Marlena	Woman

But is she a he?

And more than that—oh, how they can act up! Many have the temper of a belligerent hornet, and they've been known to use that temper to get what they want. It's not unheard of for one of them to grab the referee and try to intimidate him. Or they can go the other route, and try distracting him with their feminine wiles. That's one of

Sunny's favored gambits: The current manager of Legion of Doom 2000 will happily resort to measures like flirting with the referee—or the opponents—if that's what it takes to help her wrestlers win.

Marlena has a different style. She's Golddust's manager, and she sits around the ring in a director's chair, smoking a big cigar and wearing a gold outfit that looks like she just threw it on—and damned near missed. She's been known to go into action as well. Like any manager—no matter what sex—her job is to make sure her wrestlers win by whatever means is at her disposal.

Chyna's a tough one—she's done some serious damage to opponents of her wrestlers. And Jacquelyn, the manager of the Harlem Heat, has the temperament of the most terrible of Turks. Just ask Disco—she picked him up, inverted him, and slammed him to the mat. This lady doesn't *lose* her temper—she always knows *exactly* where it is.

Bert's Corner

In the late 1950s, *Reader's Digest* ran the story of a 70-plus lady who always claimed to dislike wrestling. She watched it every night, however, because she professed she couldn't sleep. One night a burglar climbed into the house, tripped, and fell. Like a shot, this little granny took him down and called for help. When congratulated for her actions, she replied: "I just took him with my step-over toe hold."

The Least You Need to Know

➤ Women have been part of professional wrestling almost as long as men, first appearing in the carnival shows.

➤ The first woman wrestler was Mildred Burke, who pioneered women's wrestling by challenging any male who dared to take her on.

➤ Women wrestling women, which was introduced as a novelty in the 1930s to fill empty houses, became a standard part of wrestling during the 1940s and 1950s.

➤ By the 1950s, women's role in wrestling had changed, and the once-popular women's circuit had slowly begun to disappear.

➤ Today's pro wrestling features women in the ring, but now as valets and managers.

Chapter 15

Novelty Acts—This Ain't No Circus Sideshow

> **In This Chapter:**
>
> ➤ In the cage: Caged matches
>
> ➤ Barbed-wire matches
>
> ➤ Pint-sized but pugnacious: Midget wrestlers
>
> ➤ Crossover dreams: Athletes from other sports join the fray
>
> ➤ A smorgasbord of wild rituals

Regular wrestling matches pull large audiences, but novelty acts push the already great ratings way off the charts. And the variety of novelty acts out there in the ring is amazing. There's everything from bouts between midgets like the Mexican Minis, to putting familiar wrestlers in cages—like when Hollywood Hogan fought it out with Macho Man Savage.

And there's lots of changes that can be rung on that cage theme, while we're on the subject. Terry Funk's famous for his barbed-wire matches, where the ring ropes are replaced by barbed wire. All in all, there are as many novelty situations as there are imaginative promoters to think them up. This chapter will tell you about some of the ones that have caught the fans' attention over the years.

Wrestling and Novelty Acts—A Match Made in Promoter's Heaven

It's doubtful that anybody could pinpoint the exact date when all the "wonderful nonsense" of novelty acts first started. But it may well be back in 1877. That's when

Emil Regnier, proprietor of a New York beer parlor, borrowed an idea that goes all the way back to the Middle Ages: He staged wrestling bouts that pitted Greco-Roman wrestlers against bears.

Bear Brawls

The bear most likely "did not understand the fun of the thing," as the New York *Times* reported. It apparently didn't want to be thrown, "but exhibited no desire to throw his opponent." Still, the spectators *did* understand, and the spectacle soon took off in popularity, spreading to other venues and drawing sizeable audiences where ever it was performed. Regnier even sent the show on the road, touring the United States, but eventually the bears lost patience with the game. One grabbed its human opponent and squeezed him until he collapsed. He later died of internal injuries.

With that, the charm of bear wrestling lost some of its luster. It had a brief revival years later, when a pack of bears (named Lena, Ginger, Gorgeous Gus, Terrible Ted, and Not-So-Gentle-Ben) took to prowling the rings, mostly on the Southern circuit. And not so long ago, Terrible Ted went up against Baron von Raschke and Bobby Heenan in Detroit's Olympia Stadium. The bear was supposed to be muzzled, but his trainer took off the restraint in the middle of the bout, forcing his two human heel opponents to flee the ring. Much to the delight of 10,000 fans.

Captain Lou's Corner

Fred Kohler, wrestling in the 1930s under the name of Fred King, remembers touring the Midwest with a 700-pound bear. He found it something of a challenge. As he told writer Joe Jares: "It kept outthinking me. I finally won a match with it in Dubuque, Iowa, and turned to wrestling more orthodox opponents."

Bert's Corner

Back in the days when many wrestlers were still trying to keep some credibility for their sport, novelty acts weren't always welcomed by the athletes of the ring. Lou Thesz, for example, refused to appear on cards that featured "midgets, wrestling bears, or any sort of carnival act."

Crossover Competitions

Such acts were, however, more the exception than the rule. The standard form for a novelty act was usually a little more mundane—a wrestler pitted against a boxer, fighting for supremacy between the two popular sports. The first such competition pitted William Muldoon against heavyweight champion John L. Sullivan in Sullivan's hometown of Gloucester, Massachusetts in 1887. But when Muldoon slammed the local favorite to the mat, the fans stopped the show.

Depression Era Diversions

The Depression's depressing effect on all forms of entertainment pushed wrestling into desperate straits, and that was the true beginning of an explosion of novelty acts as promoters tried everything they could think of to bring the fans back into the arenas. Masked men, hairy men, hillbillies, midgets, giants, and all manner of sideshow grotesqueries were brought into the act.

One of the more famous acts of the period was Man Mountain Dean—probably the first of the successful hillbilly characters. He brought forth a whole crowd of hairy men, like Farmer Burns, Farmer Marlin, Hillbilly Spunky, and The Scufflin' Hillbillies. There were enough of them to hold a moonshiner's convention. The ultimate expression of the theme was a hairy hillbilly, "Whiskers" Savage—he became the biggest draw in the Houston area.

Wrestle Mania

"Whiskers" Savage claimed to hail from Boone County, Kentucky. He'd parade around town barefoot and dragging a couple of "hound dawgs" behind him. On the night of the bout he'd arrive at the arena early, tie the "dawgs" to a telephone pole, and sit on the curb waiting for the crowd. In the ring, he'd park a chicken on the turnbuckle before getting down to "scufflin'." The fans so loved his act that before long the rings were filled to overflowing with Okie characters.

Bigger Is Best—for Pulling in the Fans

My favorite of this whole clan of hillbilly characters was the legendary Haystacks Calhoun. He was a 600-pound mountain of a man. His wife, Mary, was an impressive 400 pounds herself. Family squabbles in *that* household could get pretty interesting.

He was not just a hillbilly—he personified another category of novelty wrestler, too. You can call them the dreadnaught class—oversized behemoths like Happy Humphrey (620 pounds), Martin Levy (over 700 pounds), and the McGuire Twins (727 pounds) apiece.

Add height to weight and you get another novelty act: the giants. Andre the Giant is perhaps the best known—7-foot, 4-inches and weighing in at somewhere between 490 and 520 pounds. And if you've got giants, you've got to go with the other end of the spectrum too: midget wrestlers soon became all the rage, too.

Size Doesn't Count

The public has always had a strange fascination with midgets, dating back to P.T. Barnum's Tom Thumb—the most famous performer of the 19th century. And vaudeville had the Singer Midgets—a troupe of pint-sized acrobats from Germany. So it was no surprise that wrestling would want to get them into the act, too.

Suddenly midgets were tumbling into the wrestling rings all across America—Sky Low Low, Fuzzy Cupid, Little Beaver, Little Brutus, Pee Wee James, Lord Littlebrook, Billy the Kid (a cowboy), and Gentleman Jim Corbett. They were acrobatic and fun to watch.

Grotesqueries and Gargoyles

Some wrestlers get their uglies from masks or paint, but some come by it naturally. And in the years just after the Second World War, uglies were all the rage. They were usually called "angels" just to be perverse—The Swedish Angel, the Polish Angel…a whole United Nations of angels started popping up in American wrestling rings. And they made wonderful villains.

Maurice Tillet is the man who started this whole vogue. His facial features were distorted by some glandular dysfunction, and he had been a circus strongman in England where he was billed as a "ferocious monstrosity, not a human being." He wrestled as the French Angel, and fearsome features aside, he was a lovely man.

Captain Lou's Corner

My favorite midget wrestler was Sky Low Low. He was a committed pool player—no easy trick when you stand only as tall as the table itself. Once, when we were all staying in a Detroit hotel, some guy came over to him at the table, rubbed his head, and said "Hiya Shorty." *Not* a midget's favorite form of address. So he hauls off and belts the guy where he could reach best—right in the *cojones.*

Novelties of Today

In the early years of wrestling, all you really needed was a performer who looked a little different from the norm to come up with a novelty act. These days they *all* look pretty weird, so promoters had to find other ways to tittilate the crowd. Never slouches when it comes to building the heat for the shows, they soon introduced whole new angles into the wrestling game. From cages to crossover competitions, wrestling's never been at a loss for new ideas to spice up the competition.

Caged Competitors

What do you get when you put two wrestlers in a locked cage that stands 15 feet tall, and tell them to fight at will, with no rules? One heck of a sellout crowd, that's what. It might seem inhumane—and if the wrestlers were roosters or dogs, the bout would be illegal. But in pro wrestling, this is one scenario that's sure to get the fans heated. Maybe it's got something to do with history. You know, Roman gladiators fighting to the death in the Coliseum. Well, today's gladiators of the squared circle stop short of death, but they pull out all the stops in their efforts to subdue their competitors.

Cage matches can be brutal. It's not at all unusual for the wrestlers to get slammed up against the walls and the rough edges and burrs in the wire can inflict nasty wounds, especially on the face. Not to mention that the wrestlers are just as likely to use the wire as a weapon, shoving their opponent's head into it for truly bloody effect.

Violent cage matches have a passionate following. Here are a few of the more notorious ones of past years.

WCW Uncensored

Hollywood Hogan and Macho Man Randy Savage did battle in a cage at *WCW Uncensored*. It was a no-holds-barred match of epic proportions, fought inside a steel cage that surrounded the ring.

Hogan and Savage exchanged furious blows, and neither one was above using the cage wire against his opponent. It wasn't long before both men were bleeding profusely. At first, Hollywood Hogan looked like he was going to emerge the victor of the match—he got hold of Macho Man by the back of the neck and slammed his face into the wire again and again until it looked like Savage was a goner. But Macho Man isn't called Macho for nothing—he broke free and staged a comeback. And when the cage was unlocked, the two wrestlers brought their fight out of the ring entirely.

Their freedom from the cage, however, was short lived. And Savage was intent on getting his revenge for his earlier beating. Appalled at the sight of one of their own losing ground to the beating Macho Man was administering, Hollywood's fellow members of the New World Order (nWo) rushed the cage. Things began to look pretty bleak for Macho Man at this point—he was beginning to look a lot like mincemeat.

In Your Face

Lazy or unimaginative promoters can sometimes fall into bad habits, like overworking a gimmick. Cage matches, for example, have been overdone at times—promoters will sometimes use them even when they have no real justification in any storyline.

Bert's Corner

The Depression has been over for a long time now, but promoters still find a reason to include novelty acts—usually as the opening match of the card. It's a good way to get the crowd warmed up.

Just when things looked bad enough for Savage, the situation took a turn for the worse: A dark figure descended from the ceiling. It was Sting, coming to lend a hand to the nWo gang. He landed right in the middle of the action, carrying his baseball bat. Bloodied but unbowed, Savage grabbed the bat and belted Sting, knocking him right out of the action. Seeing his chance, the Macho Man made his escape from the cage, leaving Hogan and his nWo buddies standing in awe.

WWF Summer Slam

ManKind—a.k.a. Mickey Foley—was matched against Hunter Hearst Helmsley in a cage match of epic proportions during the *Summer Slam*. But what started out as a typical cage match soon turned into something more—lots more.

Foley's idol was Superfly Snuka, he of the acrobatic leaps off the ring ropes. As a kid, Foley would jump off roofs to imitate the Superfly's famous flying leaps during cage matches. He once even hitchhiked hundreds of miles to see the great Superfly perform, and he worked overtime to perfect his imitation of all of his hero's famous moves. This would turn out to be a crucial skill.

The masked ManKind faced off with Helmsley inside the 15-foot cage, warily keeping an eye of Helmsley's manager, the fearsome Chyna who was lurking right outside. The match seemed lackluster—ManKind just didn't seem to have his heart into the action. Helmsley tried to bring the battle to a pitch, but he was powerfully overmatched, and ManKind fought him off with relative ease.

It seemed like the match was a foregone conclusion, and that there were no surprises in store. ManKind eventually brought Helmsley down, rendering him unconscious, and everyone thought the match was over. But everyone was wrong.

Suddenly, ManKind climbed out of the cage, swarming up to the top, where he posed, victorious, for the crowd. His lifelong emulation of Superfly Snuka was clear—he even held out his hands in the same symbolic gesture that the Superfly made famous.

Wrestle Mania

One of the reasons why cage matches first came into vogue was that wrestlers started taking advantage of a technicality in the (admittedly very few) rules: You can't lose the belt on a disqualification. And the easiest way to get disqualified was to be counted out of the ring. To keep wrestlers from slipping under the ropes, promoters started putting cages around the ring. Once inside, the combatants had to stay there until the match had a winner.

From his precarious perch high atop the cage, ManKind jumped down to land on the comatose Helmsley. The crowd roared, egging him on, and ManKind climbed once again to the top of the cage. Once there, he ripped off his mask and threw it into the ring. In that gesture, and at that moment, ManKind was no more: He traded his freakish image for a new one—Dude Love. The rest, as they say, is wrestling history.

When Worlds Collide

When Worlds Collide was a cage match that combined American and Mexican wrestlers, and it generated a lot of heat among the fans when it occurred. Konnan el Barbaro was pitted against Perro Aguaya in the cage, and both were determined to emerge the victor. As is so typical in cage matches, both wrestlers turned bloody quickly—I can tell you that the fencing causes more than enough cuts to keep the claret flowing.

At one point it looked like Konnan was a sure thing to win. He'd brought Aguayo down, and things looked pretty hopeless for the feisty Mexican. But Aguayo didn't give up, even though Konnan had rammed him into the cage often enough to turn his face to mush. Aguayo's heart and stamina ruled the cage that night: He turned the tables on Konnan and earned his great victory—and the respect of fans of all nationalities.

A Cage With an Attitude

Any cage match is a dangerous situation, but when you replace the chain-link with barbed wire, you've moved into a whole new world of potential hurt. Just ask Genichiro Tenryu and Atsushi Onita—they've still got the scars to show for their battle. When Onita and Tenryu got it on in Japan, they fought in a barbed-wire cage that had the electrifying added attraction of high voltage. Talk about extreme!

Tenryu and Onita squared off in the cage, each sizing up the other and looking for an advantage. The atmosphere was tense, and the fans, who'd flocked to the match in hopes of literally seeing sparks fly, were wild with anticipation. The fans got what they came for: Onita found his opening and threw Tenryu into the wire—and sparks really *did* fly. But Tenryu was tough, and never gave up. In what must be one of wrestling's wildest matches ever, Tenryu eventually got the better of Onita, and emerged from that cage the victor.

Sticking It to Them: More Barbed-Wire Matches

You don't need high voltage to make a match dangerous. Just plain ol' barbed wire of the unelectrified variety is more than enough danger for most wrestlers. It's a guarantee that one or both of the contenders is going to walk away with some serious injuries. Which is why they pull in such big crowds.

Sabu Sacks Funk

Terry Funk is the undisputed master of the barbed-wire match. He seems to spend more time in the cage than outside of it. And you'd think that, with all his experience, he'd soon run out of challengers. But that's

Captain Lou's Corner

In a barbed wire match, the most devastating move is to whip your opponent's face into the wire. You can tell barbed-wire match veterans just by taking a good look at all the scars on their faces.

211

not reckoning with Sabu, who faced him in a bid for the Eastern Championship Wrestling (ECW) belt and proved to be more than Funk could handle.

From the very start of the match, Sabu took control and wrestled like a man possessed. Since it was a title bout, no one was surprised by Sabu's aggressive intensity, but it still seemed unlikely that he could succeed at beating Funk, the king of the barbed-wire match, at his own game.

Well, Funk pulled out all the stops to defend his title, and prepared to bash a chair over Sabu's head. While Funk was playing with chairs and looking for ways to put Sabu down for the count, he managed to get his head entangled in the barbed wire. At the same time, Sabu's manager, Bill Alfonzo, got into the act. His interference infuriated Funk, who pulled Alfonzo into the ring, right over the barbed-wire ring ropes. Ouch!

In retaliation to Sabu's constant and effective attacks, Funk finally managed to get a grip on his opponent and lift him high into the air. The fans were wild, anticipating the next move: a slam of some kind was bound to follow, everybody thought. What really happened was far worse, and had every man in the audience cringing in their seats: Instead of running Sabu into the wire as per normal, Funk crashed his hapless opponent down, crotch first, on the waiting barbed wire.

That one hard encounter with the wire wasn't enough for Sabu—he went looking for more. Intending to take his revenge, he mounted the top strand of wire and prepared to jump on Funk. But, maybe because of the pain from his recent confrontation with the wire, Sabu badly misjudged his move, slicing his arm wide open in the process. If the fans had come to the bout looking for blood, they certainly got their money's worth. But even with the injury, Sabu was man enough to put Funk down and take his title belt away from him.

A Texas Tornado: Table Fights

People who don't follow wrestling might think that a Texas Tornado is a mixed drink. It's not, but maybe it should be. No, the Texas Tornado was a wrestling match that took place in Japan. And for this match, tables were a weapon of choice, and used for good effect.

The legendary Terry Funk was in this match, too, teamed up with the Gladiator and ManKind (before his metamorphosis into Dude Love). The three of them faced off against Wing Kanemura, Masato Tanaka, and Atsushi Onita.

At the very start of the match, Funk took a table slammed square in the face. Meanwhile, the Gladiator began to educate his peers in the arts of power bombing and table breaking. But tables weren't the only weapons available to the enterprising wrestler in this match—a baseball bat wrapped in barbed wire was the object of desire for all the wrestlers in the ring, and ultimately ended up in Funk's possession.

As if the bat wasn't advantage enough, Funk heated up the action with a little help from manager Victor Quinones, who set fire to a branding iron and passed it off to Funk. With all this going for him, Funk should have walked off with victory for his side. Instead, he made a major misjudgment when he attempted a backward moonsault on Onita. Just before contact, the Japanese wrestler moved out of harm's way. Funk hit the floor head first with a BOOM that resounded throughout the arena and knocked him senseless. When Kanemura pinned the Gladiator the match was over, but Funk didn't know where he was or why he was in Tokyo. An ambulance carried Funk to a hospital where a CAT scan showed that Funk was suffering from a concussion. It took several days for Funk to recover from his injury—and the loss of the match.

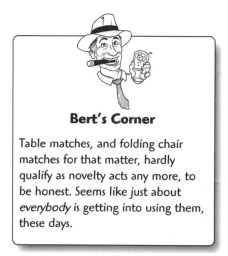

Bert's Corner

Table matches, and folding chair matches for that matter, hardly qualify as novelty acts any more, to be honest. Seems like just about *everybody* is getting into using them, these days.

Modern Midget Marvels

Midget wrestling always pulls a big crowd, even today. Due to their diminutive size (most stand from 40 to 50 inches tall and weigh between 70 and 100 pounds), these compact wrestlers can pull off moves that fans fall in love with. For example, they often go flying across the ring when their larger counterparts would barely be trundling across the floor. They are renowned for their stunning skills, speed, and agility.

The best modern example of such wrestlers may be the Mexican Minis (midgets are called minis in Mexico). Look for Espectritio, Piratito Morgan, Mascarita Sagrada, and Octagoncito if you want to see the Mexican Minis in action. These guys don't stand tall, but they ride high on energy and respect when in the wrestling ring.

But as popular as the Mexican Minis are today, they are following a path cut years ago by other famous miniature wrestlers. Here are some of the little legends of the past:

Baby Face Maren	Mighty Fritz
Fuzzy Cupid	Pancho, The Bull
Gorgeous Jimmy Little	Pee Wee James
Little Beaver	Sky Lou Lou
Marvelous Miltie	Tom Thumb
Mighty Atom	

Crashing the Gate: Crossover Wrestlers

How often do athletes from one sport cross over into another? It happens from time to time and has been happening more in recent years. Wrestling attracts a fair amount of crossover traffic—dating back to the early days when collegiate stars of the gridiron flocked to the sport. More recently, many NFL football players have tried their hands in the wrestling ring. Some of them try to make a career out of wrestling; and others simply make special appearances.

Dennis Rodman, the colorful star of the Chicago Bulls, partnered up with Hollywood Hogan to take on Lex Luger and the Giant. There would be no slam dunking here; when Rodman came to the ring he was wearing a nWo shirt and bandanna. He even had on sunglasses, like Hogan did. Just before the match, Randy "Macho Man" Savage whispered words of advice into Rodman's ear. When the bell rang all the wrestlers were ready to rumble.

Luger was working Hogan over pretty good at first, but Hollywood turned the tables and Luger lost control. At one point, Rodman rolled out of the ring in search of sanctuary. The Giant took a turn on Rodman while Luger got Hogan in the famous Torture Rack. Hollywood could not work his way loose and submitted to the Rack. Rodman made a fair showing in the ring, but he should probably stick to shooting baskets instead of attempting to be a Giant killer.

It goes without saying that if the nWo can have Rodman, the WWF can have Iron Mike Tyson. As a boxer, Tyson is currently out of business for his illegal behavior. Wrestling offered Tyson a place to vent his frustrations and to stay in shape.

When Tyson affiliated with the WWF, it was in the role of an enforcer. According to Tyson, the WWF wasn't paying him enough to make a fist. Stone Cold Steve Austin, bad boy of the WWF, had his own opinions regarding Iron Mike's role, and didn't think particularly highly of this new member of the wrestling stable. Austin broke into an interview between Tyson and Vince McMahon to make his opinion clear. A pushing match between Stone Cold and Iron Mike ensued, but nothing came of it.

Many press conferences and interviews later, Tyson joined the D-Generation X in a surprise meeting in the ring. Will Tyson do any serious wrestling? It's doubtful. Most believe he is using his new wrestling gig as a way to make some money while he is barred from boxing and to rebuild his public image. Just having Tyson on hand at a match is enough to qualify the match as a big draw and novelty match. But it's highly unlikely that we'll be seeing Tyson get it on in a serious match with the best pro wrestlers anytime soon.

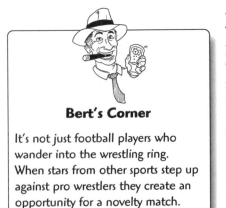

Bert's Corner

It's not just football players who wander into the wrestling ring. When stars from other sports step up against pro wrestlers they create an opportunity for a novelty match.

Newer Novelties

It should be clear by now: Novelty acts are good for business. For that reason, promoters and managers like them, as do the wrestlers. The more bizarre the matches become, the more money they make.

Novelty matches range from ladder matches to matches where valets are put up for prizes. There have been matches where the losing wrestler was forced to cut his hair or to retire from the profession. There was even a match between Golddust and Brian Pillman in which the loser would have to wear a dress to each following match until he finally won. What follows is a brief look at some of the more famous recent novelty matches to catch the attention of the fans.

The Ladder of Success

The ECW created the ladder match—a match that fans would be sure to love. It started by hanging a title belt high above the ring on a cable. Then a ladder was placed in the ring. Once the scene was set, three wrestlers entered into the ring. They were Lance Diamond, Ace Darling, and Reckless Youth.

As you might imagine, the object of the match was to retrieve the belt. With three pro wrestlers in the same ring, going for the same belt, with only one ladder, things were sure to be exciting. After an engaging battle, Reckless Youth made himself King of the Hill and retrieved the title belt for his collection.

In other ladder matches, a title belt is placed on top of the ladder and two wrestlers compete for it. A ladder has two sides, but generally only one side that is meant to be climbed. When two big wrestlers go up a ladder together, one on each side, and meet at the top, anything can happen. The object of the match is to gain possession of the belt and carry it to the mat for a victory. There are variations of ladder matches, but they are all exciting—and they can be dangerous.

Battle Royale

A Battle Royale is a big match that involves a lot of wrestlers—sometimes as many as 30 wrestlers will join in the fight. The idea behind a Battle Royale is to have a new wrestler enter the ring every three minutes. All of the wrestlers are battling each other, with the intent of only one winner. If a wrestler gets tossed over the top rope, he is disqualified. The match continues until only one wrestler is left in the ring.

Of all the champions of Battle Royales, Andre the Giant was the best. He never lost a Battle Royale match.

Wrestle Mania

During a Brass Knux Match, brass knuckles are placed on top of a pole in a neutral corner of the ring. It is up to the competing wrestlers to gain possession of them. The first wrestler to acquire them gets to use them. (Sometimes chains are substituted for brass knuckles.) In any case, the wrestler gaining access to the weapon has a decided advantage. Putting brass knuckles in the hand of a shooter can result in some serious damage for an opponent.

Three's a Crowd

Sometimes three wrestlers are placed in the ring—and only one of them gets to leave.More accurately, the first man to win a pinfall is the winner of the match. In a recent *WCW Uncensored* match, Raven, Chris Benoit, and Diamond Dallas Page (DDP) were the players in the game. Page's title was on the line. It was one of the rare occasions when Raven actually competed without the help of his crows, err—flock.

The match was wild and woolly. Diamond Dallas Page was shoved into a sign behind the audience. This happened not once, but twice. With Page immobilized, Raven and Benoit reentered the ring and went for the belt. Shortly afterwards, an injured Page was seen pulling himself along the runway, trying to get back into the ring. It was a long and painful match, but Diamond Dallas Page finally won, and thus retained his belt.

Novelty matches are limited only by the willingness of wrestlers and the imaginations of promoters and managers. Fans love these special matches. As long as this is the case, you can count on seeing more of them.

The Least You Need to Know:

➤ Cage matches, in which wrestlers fight in a cage, often result in cuts due to the burrs on the wire.

➤ Terry Funk is one of the kings of barbed-wire matches.

➤ In Japan, barbed-wire cage matches frequently have the wire electrified.

➤ The Mexican Minis are the most popular midget wrestlers in America.

➤ Wrestlers from other sports sometimes step into the wrestling ring for novelty matches.

➤ Novelty matches pull larger draws and bigger money than traditional matches do.

Chapter 16

From Saturday Morning to Pay-Per-View: Wrestling in the Media

In This Chapter

➤ From bullhorns to the boob tube

➤ How wrestling developed on the small screen

➤ Cable changes the face of wrestling

➤ Storylines and casts of characters

➤ Major wrestling broadcasts on cable and PPV

Does the media have any impact on the success of professional wrestling? Absolutely! Just like all the other major sports, wrestling owes its widespread popularity today to the successful use of television coverage of events—especially to Vince McMahon Jr.'s visionary exploitation of the new resources of cable networks and pay-per-view access. These days, *all* sports—basketball, baseball, football, you name it—rely on media coverage far beyond the obvious broadcasting of games or matches, and pro wrestling is no exception.

In this chapter you'll learn all about how modern pro wrestling developed in tandem with the evolution of television, from its early beginnings to the era of cable and pay-per-view.

Bullhorns and Strong Lungs

Before the advent of mass media, old-time promoters, and the carneys before them relied on putting up posters, staging gimmicks, and otherwise calling press attention to themselves in order to heat up the local spectators and get them to come to the

matches. Show representatives travelled from town to town to drum up business. Today's promoters have the same job to do, but they've got very different ways to do it.

Can you imagine Vince McMahon Jr. pitching a tent on the city hall steps and staging a confrontation with the police just to get the crowd to come out and see Sting and Hollywood Hogan do battle at Madison Square Garden? He'd do it if he had to, but these days, who has to?

In the end, the promoter's job is to keep the fans interested and flocking to the arena to hand over their money for tickets. Generating public interest was, and still is, the name of the game. Television didn't change that game, it just changed the rules of how to play. And Vince McMahon Sr. knew that right from the start, when the TV first became a common household appliance.

Wrestling on TV

Back in television's infancy, the most interesting thing on the newfangled box in the nation's living rooms was the test pattern (my favorite was the one with the Indian's head in the center). What little programming there was consisted of "how to" shows and inexpensively produced game shows, usually with children for panelists. And there were afternoon kiddie shows. All in all, comedian Fred Allen got it right when he called the television of the day "a device that permits people who haven't anything to do to watch people who can't do anything."

Slowly, the powers-that-be started looking for other programming. Soon TV sets, complete with that optional bubble that magnified the screen, were filled with wall-to-wall wrestling shows.

In New York, you got *Wrestling from Sunnyside Garden*, with Arnold "Golden Boy" Skaaland, Thomas Marin, and Abe Jacobs. From St. Louis, there was *Wrestling at the Chase*. Cincinnati gave us the Crosley Broadcasting System's studio wrestling. And all over the country, in cities like Washington, Portland, Pittsburgh, Los Angeles, and all points north, east, south, and west, wrestling shows came beaming our way from arenas, hotels, and studios.

Every night of the week, you could find wrestling on the tube. There were so many wrestling shows that by the end of 1947 *TV Guide* had even set up a department to compile match results for the growing army of wrestling fans.

Wrestling's Early TV Stars

By the end of the 1940s, wrestlers like Gorgeous George, Baron Michel Leone, Johnny Valentine, the Zebra Kid, Ricki Starr, and Antonino Rocca had become household names—all because of their exposure on the tube. So too had the announcers, like Dennis James from New York, Ray Morgan from Washington, Dick Lane from Los Angeles, Paul Boesch from Houston, and Slammin' Sammy Menaker from Boston.

WWF Wrestling Telecasts

Monday Nights:

➤ 9-10pm   *RAW is WAR*

➤ 10-11pm   *Warzone*

Major WWF pay-per-view events:

➤ February: *Royal Rumble* (winner faces champion at *Wrestlemania*)

➤ March: *Wrestlemania*

➤ June: *King of the Ring*

➤ August: *Summer Slam*

➤ November: *Survivors Series*

And just as wrestlers had developed their shtick for the TV audiences, so too did the announcers. Dick Lane was famous for his "Whoa, Nellie!" a catchphrase later adopted by football announcer Keith Jackson. Dennis James used sound effects to accompany the action, and Guy LeBow donned an air-raid warden's helmet when the action heated up. Paul Boesch, noted for his interviewing technique, once conducted an interview with tag-team partners Ivan Kalmikoff and Karol Krauser while wearing a gas mask to ward off the overpowering smell of garlic they gave off as a result of their latest meal.

It was wonderful fun in the days of unsophisticated television, and the shows drew in millions of new TV viewers. It helped popularize the new medium so much that Gorgeous George was labeled "Mr. Television" in part for his contribution to fueling the sale of sets to new viewers.

But, just as suddenly as it appeared, wrestling all but disappeared from the small screen, as television placed its bets on horse operas instead of wrestlings' soap operas. So Hopalong Cassidy and Roy Rogers replaced Gorgeous George and Antonino Rocca, and wrestling sank slowly into the west, not to rise again for another three-plus decades.

The Evolution of Television

To understand the "second coming" of wrestling on TV, you must first understand the changes in the television industry over those three-plus decades. For the resurgence of TV wrestling in the 1980s was two parts telecasting innovation, one part human innovator.

Wrestle Mania

Wrestling shows today not only promote future arena events, but also promote future episodes of the studio-produced televised show as well, such as the PPV special events featuring Kane's confrontation with The Undertaker in late October, 1998. Viewers will rarely see a wrestling show that is more than 50% actual wrestling. The bulk of the show is dedicated to interviews and vignettes establishing storylines and generating audience involvement in the great events to come.

In 1948, approximately the same time as wrestling's first "Golden Age" on TV, antennas began to be erected on mountain tops or other high points as a service to households in geographically remote areas where over-the-air TV signal reception was poor. Homes were wired and connected to these towers with cable—hence the term "cable TV." Though, back then, it was more frequently referred to as CATV, for Community Antenna Television. By 1950, 70 cable systems served the small towns of the nation.

By the late 1950s, cable operators began to change the nature of these towers' roles in transmitting local broadcasting signals—they began to provide cable subscribers with new programming. By the 1970s, cable operators had pioneered in satellite communications technology. One of the first services to use the satellite was a local television station in Atlanta, which came to be known as the first "Superstation"—WTBS—the rock on which Turner Broadcasting would be built.

Not incidentally, by the mid 1970s the use of videotape, long a staple in the entertainment portion of TV, began to be used regularly in the world of TV sports because it made taped events look "live."

Put these technological advances together and add one more element—the acquisition of the WWF by Vince McMahon Jr., and you have the makings of the current wrestling explosion on TV.

The McMahon Magic: Cable Wrestling Comes of Age

Using cable television and videotape as his two weapons, Vince Jr. began an all-out assault on the established baronial structure of wrestling promotions, invading other promoters' territories by buying up air time and running his videotaped "live" shows in hundreds of cities simultaneously. This blitzkreig generated interest in the WWF product, and stimulated interest in its touring shows. This brought interested—avid, even—advertisers to Vince's shows.

Captain Lou's Corner

The legendary Lou Thesz had this to say about TV wrestling phenomenon Hulk Hogan: "On marketing I would give him a 9 or a 10. On wrestling, a 1 or a 0. I had a grandmother who could do a better leglock."

The McMahon Machine Powers Onward

One of the most important beachheads McMahon secured in his scorched-earth campaign to dominate wrestling was the acquisition, in July of 1984, of air time on Superstation WTBS, long a TV stronghold of Jim Crockett's NWA. In the face of thousands of complaints from NWA loyalists, McMahon was quoted in the Atlanta *Constitution* as saying "We'll show these complainers the difference between a major league and a minor league production, given time."

Over the next two years, McMahon made television and wrestling an "item." For the first time in 30-plus years, wrestling returned to network TV in 1985, with the WWF's *Saturday Night Live's Main Event*, in the *Saturday Night Live* time slot. Then, in what was to be the beginning of the connection between wrestling and rock 'n' roll, the WWF telecast *The War to Settle the Score* live on MTV. And finally, the WWF pioneered pay-per-view wrestling with its first card in 1985.

WCW Telecasts

➤ Monday Nights: 8-11pm *Monday Nite Nitro*
➤ Tursday Nights: 8-11pm *Thunder*
➤ Syndicated shows: *WCW Worldwide/WCW Saturday Night*

Major WCW pay-per-view events:

➤ January: *nWo Souled Out*
➤ February: *Superbrawl*
➤ May: *Slamboree*
➤ June: *Great American Bash*
➤ July: *Bash at the Beach*
➤ August: *Road Wild; Clash of the Champions*
➤ October: *Halloween Havoc*
➤ December: *Starcade*

Enter Turner, Stage Left

Just as McMahon was on the cusp of making the WWF the only show in television town, his overly ambitious plans to monopolize both wrestling and television ran into serious problems—his reach had far exceeded the depths of his pockets. In short, he was short of cash, and was forced to sell back his WTBS time slot to Ted Turner for a reported $1 million.

So now there were two wrestling superpowers: McMahon's WWF, and Turner's WCW. And their head-to-head battles for audience share would fuel the increasing popularity of wrestling as each upped the ante with better product, better production, and better promotion.

The Boob Tube Today

Monday night, once thought to be the exclusive province of *Monday Night Football*, has now become wrestling's night. The WWF and WCW go all out, telecasting their shows to millions of wrestling fans. Their combined cable ratings now equal 50% of those scored by *Monday Night Football*.

Wrestling's Modern Metamorphosis

But the wheel has turned. Unlike the first time around, when television used wrestling to provide cheap original programming, today it's wrestling that uses TV—presenting what Hollywood Hogan calls the "three hour show," with less than 50% of the program devoted to actual wrestling. The rest of the time is dedicated to interviews that establish the storylines for future bouts, infomercials for upcoming events like PPV shows, and promotions of future shows on the cable channel.

Wrestle Mania

Getting Jay Leno involved in a WCW pay-per-view event was an idea that came up after Hollywood Hogan appeared on the *Tonight Show*. His segment of the show did extremely well in the ratings, so the *Tonight Show* executives started calling the WCW exploring ways to get Leno in on the wrestling action. WCW promoter Eric Bischoff came up with a storyline that had him and Hogan taking over Leno's set, leading to a score-settling ring-challenge. Leno's take on the wrestling scene? "It's no different from going to Disneyland," he said.

Monday night's telecasts have not only changed the landscape of wrestling, but wrestling itself. The production values have been upgraded, as the shows take advantage of improved technology and special effects. The storylines have been vastly improved over the old-fashioned "heels versus faces" by accommodating all sorts of characters and plots. And the overall product is more appealing, especially to kids who appreciate the addition of Star Wars technology and identify with the wrestlers as adult comic-book characters.

The Impact of the Cable Innovation

No longer are fans given the traditional "squash" matches that used to be good enough. These old-style matches pitted a name wrestler against a no-name—even no-nickname and no-gimmick—who would get "squashed" in less time than it took to introduce him. Instead, every week, big name wrestlers face other big name wrestlers on BIG televised matches.

And promoters could no longer get away with the repetitiveness of the bouts of yesteryear. They found themselves in the position of the old borscht-belt comedian who could go from club to club using the same old jokes for years, but who ruined his career with a single appearance on a national TV show because now everybody knew all his routines. Similarly, in the years B.C. (before cable, that is), promoters could work the same angles and outcomes every night as their wrestlers traveled from arena to arena. Now, once a match appears on *RAW is WAR* or *Monday Nite Nitro* it's seen by millions. A new angle has to be worked out every week or the show will go stale.

The Storyline's the Thing

Eric Bischoff, president of World Championship Wrestling, calls it "The soap storyline." He's talking about the soap opera-like cliffhanger at the end of every telecast. In days of old, "bookers"—the people responsible for coming up with the storylines—only had to worry about arena shows. Now they have to concern themselves with the unexpected at the end of a televised show. Things like a wrestler who has been missing in action for weeks suddenly returning; or somebody suddenly losing his temper and punching out a rival; or an unanticipated event that starts a feud. Most shows end in planned chaos, with the announcer intoning "We're out of time, but we'll keep the cameras rolling, so tune in next week and make sure you don't miss a thing."

Even people who *don't* follow wrestling have heard of the two big televised broadcasts: the WWF's *RAW is WAR* on USA network, and the WCW's *Monday Nitro* on TNT. These two shows are broadcast head-to-head, and they're only the two best-known of all the TV coverage on wrestling that's out there. And there's more than just the matches themselves on TV. There are talk shows too. And commercials are everywhere, hyping arena matches, televised bouts, and pay-per-view events. It all means big bucks for wrestling.

Monday nights are the big nights for wrestling, but the WCW has some heavy coverage on Thursdays too, broadcast to anywhere there's a cable hookup. These shows are wrestling events in themselves, of course, but you can think of them also as advertising—they set up the storylines for upcoming pay-per-view matches, hyping the action to come. These days, after all, arenas are just not the major cash cows that televised events have become.

Wrestling always used to make a good living for the people involved in the sport, from promoters to wrestlers. But these days "a good living" for a popular wrestler means something very different from the $100 purses of old take-on-all-challengers bouts of wrestling's earliest days. Even sellout houses in big arenas don't generate the kind of income that commercial spots can bring.

Bert's Corner

Some of wrestling's greatest early announcers include Dennis James, Ray Morgan, Chris Schenkel, and Steve Allen. More recently, there are Vince McMahon Jr., Jim Ross, Tony Schiavone, Gordon Solie, Lord Alfred Hayes, Gene Okerlund, Jesse "The Body" Ventura, Gorilla Monsoon, and Bobby Heenan.

Besides, when you watch a televised match, you may see crowds of fans cheering their heroes or booing their favorite villains, but don't be fooled. Lots of times, most of that crowd didn't even pay for their tickets. When a match is going to be televised, the people running the show want viewers to see a full house. Free tickets will be handed out if that's what it takes to fill every seat around the ring.

But the money must be coming in from somewhere, right? Right. And where it's coming from is endorsements, pay-per-view events, and commercials. There are still some big-money matches at major arenas, but these are only a small part of wrestling's income—and even they depend on television to hype the matches and get the fans to turn out in droves.

The Announcers

With television being so important to the sport, the announcers who call the action have, for the most part, become highly visible—they're not just background noise anymore. Many of them are wrestlers themselves—some retired, some still active in the ring. And they have a lot more to do than just report the action—it's not unusual for an announcer to liven up a slow match by joining in the fray with a little verbal abuse. And they hype future matches, as well as setting up new possible plot lines by egging on grudge matches.

The Wrestlers

Wrestlers are there in the ring to do battle, of course, but they're also always thinking ahead to the next match. And they're not about to let an opportunity to hype the next bout slip away just because they're busy with the current opponent.

How do they do it? Well, suppose Hollywood Hogan is wrestling Lex Luger, and Sting slides under the ropes to get in on the action unofficially. The action between Sting and the other wrestlers can lay down a blueprint for a future match.

And of course, they brag all the time—both inside and around the ring. They're constantly issuing warnings, ultimatums, and challenges to other wrestlers. It's all part of the show.

The Managers

I don't have to tell you that I think managers are pretty important in all this, do I? It's our job to use everything we can to hype our charges and get people interested in upcoming matches. And we're not above going to extremes to heat up the fans. That's why you'll see us mixing it up in the ring, if that's what it takes to get the fans to go wild.

The Audience

The TV camera even makes the fans in the audience part of the action. You'll see it panning the crowd all the time, singling out hand-held signs and other such. Lots of times the crowd action is completely genuine, but that's not necessarily the case. Sometimes, members of the audience are planted with signs that suit the needs of the wrestlers, the promoters, or even the advertisers. And the camera catches it all.

Captain Lou's Corner

Lots of wrestlers have made the crossover to the silver screen: Mike Mazurski, Hulk Hogan, Dusty Rhodes, Roddy Piper, Mil Mascaras, El Santo, and your's truly (I was in *Wiseguys*). Other's have put in cameo appearances: Toro Tanaka played Oddjob in *Goldfinger*, and Lenny Montana played Lucca Brazzi in *The Godfather*.

The Networks

You've got wrestlers against wrestlers and tag teams against tag teams, but those are not the only ones that go head-to-head in today's pro wrestling. Maybe the biggest grudge match out there is the one between Vince McMahon Jr. and Ted Turner, and that match is fought network-against-network: TNN and USA battling it out for the lion's share of Monday night's ratings. After all, commercial spots on TV are priced according to the ratings, and the winner in the ratings war gets the biggest advertising dollars.

All in all, television is essential to today's professional wrestling. It provides the outlet for hype, it gives a place where storylines can be developed, and above all else it makes wrestling available to millions more fans than could ever fit into the biggest arenas. In short, it's the driving force behind the power and the money in the industry. It's what brought in the huge audiences, and what made superstars of today's real-life action-figures of the ring. But it's not the only form of the media that plays a role in wrestling's present-day success.

The Least You Need to Know

➤ Media coverage of Gorgeous George helped create modern pro wrestling.

➤ Cable and PPV were instrumental to the growth of pro wrestling.

➤ Talk shows are often used to hype upcoming wrestling matches.

➤ Television is the most effective media for pro wrestling.

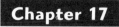

Chapter 17

All the Better to See You With: Fans and Arenas

In This Chapter

➤ Live matches versus pay-per-view: What's the difference?

➤ A list of the top wrestling arenas

➤ How to prepare for a trip to the arena

➤ What to expect when you get there

Professional wrestling works on many different levels—as an athletic exhibition, as a multimedia event, as a soap opera—and fans have always been a major part of the equation. Wrestling as an audience-participation event is a very important aspect of the whole experience—so the fans at a wrestling show are as important as the event itself.

It's always been this way, since time immemorial. But as times have changed, so too have the audiences. In this chapter you'll learn about the role played by wrestling's fans and how that role has changed over the years. You'll learn about the rituals of arena attendance, and about fan-wrestler interaction—all the elements that come together to make a live show an event to remember.

Wrestling Fan-dom Over the Years

Back in the old-old days, sports were once called "leisure activities." And the fans took them in leisurely, content just to be passive attendants at an event. Those were the days when boxing bouts lasted the better part of 20 rounds; when baseball was dominated by pitchers and single-run games were the rule; when action on a football field meant 3 yard gains—with no such thing as forward passing; and when wrestling matches went on forever, with little or no movement as the combatants strained and pushed against each other in the ring.

Those days changed radically sometime in the 1920s, when both society and sports speeded up. Baseball introduced the livelier ball, boxing began the shortened bout, football brought in the forward pass, and wrestling set time limits. And with these livelier sports came livelier crowds, no longer sitting passively in the stands but leaping up to exhort their heroes on to victory in rah-rah college fashion.

And with the end of World War II, the wheel of change turned once more as sports became a national obsession. And spectators at sporting events became the nationally obsessed.

Wrestling was no exception to all this change. But its fans were the most obsessed of all. Much of that fan involvement had to do with the fact that those in attendance believed, whole-heartedly, in what was taking place in front of them—the harsh violence of a wrestling match was viewed with complete credulity. And the audience quickly became part of the show.

Living in the Land of Creative Reality

In arena after arena—places too big for an insane asylum and too weird for anything else—wrestling's true believers became caught up in the spirit of the moment. At the Montreal Forum, when the loser of the main event refused to unmask as he was supposed to, the fans rioted. They tore up the seats, broke the windows, and stormed the box office. At the Olympic Auditorium in L.A., the crowd exploded when Gorgeous George threw Jim "The Black Panther" Mitchell out of the ring and kept him out by kicking him in the face every time he tried to crawl back in. And at Madison Square Garden, fans intent on seeing justice done erupted in rage after a defeated Dr. Jerry Graham slugged his opponent, Antonino Rocca, as Rocca was acknowledging the cheers of his loyal following.

Bert's Corner

The wildness of wrestling's early fans has toned down some today, but precautions still need to be taken to protect the stars. Entrance aisles for most big shows are purposefully made wide enough so that wrestlers can't be touched or hassled by overzealous fans.

Maniacal Mob Scenes

Wrestlers have had to fight their way back through phalanxes of angry fans intent on righting the wrongs they thought they'd just viewed in the ring. Reb Russell remembers one night in Bluefield, West Virginia, after he defeated a local in what he himself called "a very unsportsmanlike manner." The crowd came at him "like a wall of human flesh" and he had to "fight like a man possessed" just to reach the safety of the dressing room.

Every wrestler worth his trunks learned the art of survival back in those days—having had to learn it under fire, in a riot or two. As one said: "If you don't have the experience, you can get killed."

Vengeful Vigilantes

The mob scene, and what one wrestler called "the silent heat"—that devastating quiet before the storm that presages an eruption from a vicious crowd—were only one threat to the safety of a post-war wrestler. Of equal concern were the self-appointed vigilantes acting alone—the obsessed who took it upon themselves to right some perceived wrong out of misguided notions of vengeance.

I was there the night in Boston when a crazed fan jumped into the ring and assaulted Black Jack Mulligan with a carpet knife, opening up his leg. It took 187 stitches to put Jack back together again. And I was in the ring with Bruno Sammartino in Washington, doing my usual feet-don't-fail-me-now trick by fleeing up the aisle when some nitwit reached out with a knife and caught me across the arm. I ran back to the locker room bleeding like a stuck pig where my friend Pedro Morales put a tourniquet on to stop the bleeding. (With my luck, is it any surprise that the towel he used for the tourniquet was filthy, infected my wound, and nearly killed me?)

These are just a few examples of fanatic fans taking justice into their own hands. Freddie Blassie looked down mid-bout to find a knife stuck in his calf. He handled that just fine: he went back to the dressing room and poured iodine on the wound. Art Neilson wasn't so lucky. Stabbed in the side at a Chattanooga arena, he ended up undergoing 2 hours of surgery. Stabbings were common: Billy Edwards in Waco, Texas; George Lenihan in New Haven, Connecticut; and Pedro Zapata in Florence, Alabama, all found themselves at the pointy end of a knife. And let's not forget Dan Hodge. He was stabbed in the back and arm while wrestling in Oklahoma City's Municipal Auditorium—his assailant was his own father.

Captain Lou's Corner

Watching wrestling on TV has its advantages of convenience, but to me it's like eating a ham sandwich with the waxed paper still on it...It just doesn't have the taste and flavor of the real thing. Getting caught up in the audience response is a big part of the whole experience.

Early Interactive Participation

Not all the assailants used knives. Weapons of choice ranged from whiskey bottles to lighted cigarettes, paper clips shot from rubber bands to fingernails, hatpins, and bare fists. And wrestlers weren't always content to stay on the receiving end of their mistreatment.

Sportswriter Joe Jares's father, who wrestled under the name "The Mormon Mauler," was hit by a lighted book of matches, thrown by an angry female fan as he made his way to the dressing room. He wouldn't hit a lady—but that didn't stop him from making a few pithy observations about her ancestry. Suddenly a belligerant man stepped between them, shouting "That's my wife!" The Mauler slugged him, offering the advice "Teach her better manners!"

A Sign of the Times?

I don't know what possessed the fans—especially the ladies—to join in the fray so viciously. It could have been the times that bred them. This was, after all, the era of the McCarthy red scare and backyard bomb shelters. Emotions tended to run a little high back then.

Or maybe it was just because the small arenas of the day were so crammed with howling fans that the hysteria of the moment took over. I do know that some of the small towns I wrestled in had arenas so bad that they'd have to have major improvements just to qualify as slums.

In Your Face

Tickets for wrestling shows usually sell out faster than those for rock concerts. Gene Okerlund recalls a recent show in Minneapolis where the 18,000 tickets sold out in less than 90 minutes.

But then again, some of those old arenas were great—like Madison Square Garden; the old Boston Garden; Washington's Uline arena; the Mosque in Richmond, Virginia; and Sunnyside Gardens in New York.

So I guess you can't blame fan frenzies on the arenas themselves. After all, there's the guy who got so upset watching a televised bout in which his idol, Verne Gagne, got the bejabbers beaten out of him. This fan got so involved that he took out his .38 caliber pistol and shot out the screen. Like many fans, he was just caught up in the whole wrestling mystique—a true believer.

Taking Control of the Audience Urge to Participate

By the 1980s and 1990s, wrestling in particular and society in general had changed again. A more "in your face" attitude came into vogue, youth became the obsession of consumers and advertisers, and the worlds of entertainment and sports began to cater to what can best be described as the MTV world of instant gratification.

Wrestling addressed this change in audience expectations by coming up with more confrontational themes, more complex character development, and enough salaciousness to intrigue any dozen special prosecutors. With these changes, wrestling actively encouraged audience identification with the characters, storylines, and—of course—any tie-in merchandise they could come up with.

Wrestlemania Brings the Audiences into the Fold

It all began at *Wrestlemania I* at Madison Square Garden. On March 31, 1985, 23,000 wrestling-crazed fans identified with Hulk Hogan and Mr. T as together they took on Rowdy Roddy Piper and Paul Orndorff. The Hulk played the crowd like a maestro—in wrestling terminology, he was "building heat." The crowd connected with his every move and inflection—they roared when he pumped his biceps, and when he shouted, they shouted their "amens."

That was the defining moment of the new world of audience involvement in wrestling. Like the cult movie phenomenon of the time, *The Rocky Horror Picture Show*, wrestling invited its audiences to share in the experience unfolding before them. And they responded by throwing themselves into the moment, voice-first, with all the enthusiasm they had.

Add to this the "greening" of the audiences, as the crowds attending the events were made up of younger and younger fans. Now the wrestlers weren't seen as sports legends any more—they were more like real-life action figures. And all the old questions of "real" or "fake" no longer mattered. The performance was everything. With Star Wars laser shows, smoke machines, and theme music marking the wrestlers' entrances, you've got an overall event the new young audiences could not only identify with, but really get *into*.

Fans on Camera: The Proliferation of Signs

Vocal participation is one thing—but this is the video generation, and for lots of younger fans an event isn't real unless it's on TV—including their own attendance at an event. So fan-made signs at sporting events have become a major means of participation.

Wrestle Mania

Wrestling today is a huge audience draw. It's so big that it can command the largest arena in every city—usually the facilities that normally house the local hockey and/or basketball teams. Only a few cities—Dallas, Philadelphia, and Memphis—have arenas that specialize in wrestling alone. These are cities that have a long, long history of regular wrestling events.

Now signs have always been a problem area at sporting events. They were long banned from arenas and stadiums because they blocked other fans' views of the action. But then the New York Mets franchise changed all that. Fans began toting in signs, placards, even bedsheets proclaiming their loyalty to their "amazin'" team. Across town, the New York Yankees still continued their policy of confiscating signs whenever fans brought them into the stadium—until the Mets' attendance figures began to surpass their own. Signs suddenly came into their own, first in baseball—then every-where in sports.

Wrestling was slow to pick up on this shift—the major federations continued to ban them from the arenas. Partly because of the old concern that they'd block the view, but partly because of fears that the opinions expressed would be objectionable on TV—and TV was the heart and soul of the new wrestling.

Enter the ECW

It took the ECW to change all that. Extreme Championship Wrestling, staging its matches in a former Bingo hall in South Philadelphia, was an upstart challenger to the two major federations, the WWF and the WCW. It was looking for ways to set itself apart from its major-league competitors, so it wrote into its storyline a fellow named "Sign Guy." This character always sat in the same spot, around the third row, so he was easily caught by the TV cameras. And he had a sign for every occasion—each one wackier than the one that went before.

Back in the Monday night ratings battles between the WWF and the WCW, this phenomenon was duly noted. Signs started popping up everywhere—on both *RAW is WAR* and *Nitro*. At first they seemed planted by the federations themselves—and they probably were. But that changed quickly as fans started bringing their own. Now they're everywhere.

Sensational Signage

The signs originally planted by the federations were all pretty tame, and maybe you could call them a little uninspired. They praised the good guys. They insulted the baddies. Audience signs can be much more creative. Kevin Nash recalls a particularly effective sign—if that's what you'd call it. The article in question was a huge set of fingers, obviously lovingly crafted by their proud owner, who wrapped them around the Nitro Girls from his seat of safety back in the audience. It was a unique take on the more ubiquitous sponge hands—favorite digit extended to the skies—that lots of other fans have settled for.

Tools, Gimmicks, and GeeGaws

The ECW has tried to introduce other elements of audience participation that have had less success crossing over to the more mainstream federations. Working off of their "extreme" image, they've attempted to further fan interaction with the wrestlers by encouraging the audience to bring in weapons to pass along to their wrestler of choice to help him in his struggles when he tumbles out of the ring—everything from frying pans to rolling pins.

But Nothing Beats Tradition— Noise Rules

All innovations aside, the main way audiences get into the act is the good old fashioned way: vocally. They cheer, they boo, they shout words your mama wouldn't approve of at Eric Bischoff, the b-a-a-a-d boss of the WCW, when he enters the ring.

Perhaps the best example of a cheer-inspiring wrestling hero is Bill Goldberg. When Goldberg enters the ring, his fans react with the intensity that Frank Sinatra kicked off two generations ago— except Goldberg's fans don't swoon, they shout. They're there in full regalia, wearing Goldberg T-shirts, some even with shaven heads in imitation of their idol. When he makes his entrance they're on their feet, and the chant begins: Gold-berg, Gold-berg, GOLD-berg, GOOOOLLLLDBEERRRRG! He is the ultimate in fan connection.

Goldberg himself, trying to explain the phenomenon, came up with this: "People love to see violence; it's just our way of throwing Christians to the lions." Commedian Steve Allen, a one-time wrestling announcer, had a different take on the situation. He says, "Be comfortable in the knowledge that we prefer our mayhem to be make-believe."

Whatever the case, today's fan enjoys wrestling for what it is: entertainment of the highest order. And now they're a full-fledged part of it.

In Your Face

For a while, an enterprising fan set up a small stand outside the ECW arena from which he sold potential weapons for fans to give their favorite wrestlers—much like the stands selling ladies underwear that are set up outside Vegas casinos when Tom Jones is headlining.

Bert's Corner

Fans often request seats near the entrance and exit aisle, hoping that they'll get a high-five from their favorite heroes. Most of the time, security arrangements are such that they have to settle for just a little eye contact

Wrestling Venues

Pro-wrestling arenas come in all sizes, shapes, and qualities. Sometimes the facilities are bare-bones basic, other arenas are as luxurious as wrestling's idea of the Taj Mahal. And while the wrestling industry makes a major effort to get their shows out to the fans, no matter where they live, you can bet that the big shows will go where there are facilities that can handle all the hoopla. Still, big stars will still perform in small venues—after all, the fans, wherever they happen to live, are what made the pro wrestling business the multimillion dollar industry it is today.

The true hard-core fans know in their bones that there's nothing on TV that can come close to seeing a live match, and they'll make the effort to catch the action in the arenas whenever they can. Extreme fans are like the Deadheads—they'll travel with the wrestling circuit and visit arenas all over the country. But most people can't just drop their jobs or school to follow their favorite wrestlers around like groupies, so they have to settle for second best: pay-per-view events on television.

Is It Live or Is It Pay-Per-View?

True enough, no live event can beat pay-per-view for convenience. You get a guaranteed great view, the best seat in the house, no parking or traffic problems, and you can tape it so you can see it whenever you want, as often as you want. But television—no matter how good the camera work, sound, and editing—can never really capture the atmosphere of a live match. There's just a thrill that comes with watching the event at ringside that PPV can't duplicate.

And then there's the rush that comes from being part of the crowd—no PPV broadcast has ever found a way to duplicate that. Thousands of screaming, booing, cheering fans all around, bright lights, and the smell of the ring—nope, you won't get that on pay-per-view.

Watch Out for That Flying Wrestler

You just can't get the flavor of a live match when you're watching from your living-room sofa. There's no sense of *immediacy*. For the true wrestling fan, that just can't be beat. However, keep in mind that sometimes things can, and do, get out of hand.

Captain Lou's Corner

The audiences at wrestling events can get pretty wild, but there's really little to worry about if you're sitting back beyond the first few rows nearest to the ring. It's just a case of using your common sense when choosing your seating.

Timid people need not apply to the ticket offices of the arenas.

Still, despite the occasional tossed chair or flying wrestler, the risk of injury during a live match is almost nonexistent. Both the performers and the arena owners take safety precautions—after all, who wants to wipe out a hall full of fans? And besides, it's only the seats right up at ringside that are in harm's way: Even the biggest of brawlers can't throw an opponent too much farther than the first few rows. If you're nervous about some unexpected action landing up close and personal, you can just sit a few rows back—the seats will be cheaper anyway, most likely. Of course, you lose out on the chance to touch a wrestler as he flies by, and you probably won't catch any of the souvenirs that might be tossed from the ring.

Great Arenas Make a Difference

Any hardcore wrestling fan will tell you that *every* live match is a good match. But there's good and there's *grrr-eat*, and the difference has a lot to do with the arena you see it in. If you're stuck sitting for 3 hours on a metal folding chair, you just aren't going to have as much enjoyment as if the match were held in a fancy stadium with cushioned theater seats. And having to crane your neck to look around the Panama hat of the guy in front of you cuts down your visibility tremendously—it's much better to go to a stadium with raised seating platforms. After all, you want to see the ring, not the back of some fan's neck.

Then there's the size factor. Most of the time, big arenas are best—they've usually got more to offer the fans, and they're usually profitable enough to invest in some creature comforts for the fans. But smaller venues have one major plus: They offer fans the chance to come into close contact with their favorite stars.

Casino-style matches, held in gambling meccas like Las Vegas, give you a party atmosphere—maybe the most comfortable way to go. And the bigger arenas can put on light shows like you see on pay-per-view, while the smaller ones just don't have the facilities to do so. But all this is secondary—wrestling fans don't go to the arena to compare decorating styles, they go to see the wrestling stars themselves. That's it—end of story. If the only place to see the show is the local high-school gym, that's where they'll be.

The hardcore fans who follow their stars around the wrestling circuit will sooner or later develop a list of favorite venues. So will the wrestlers themselves, and the managers. But the reasons that the fans like an arena will have little in common with the reasons the wrestlers come up with. Wrestlers know that the arena they're booked into can have a real effect on the strategy of their match. The size of the ring affects the style of the match. A small ring favors the classic brawler who specializes in up-close work, for example, while the larger ring is great for the more athletic wrestlers who leap from the ring ropes.

Not to mention the location effect. Ric Flair loves booking into North Carolina—he's the hometown favorite there, and the crowd will turn out in droves to cheer him on.

Our Favorite Arenas

After some serious head scratching, we've come up with a list of our favorite arenas, past and present. The list is not inclusive of all good wrestling venues, but it's a start. They're all sure bets for giving a good live-match experience for the fans, as well as offering up what wrestlers and managers would agree to be key facilities to stage a great battle. Here are our favorites:

➤ Boston Garden (Boston, Mass.)

➤ Madison Square Garden (New York, N.Y.) It's hard to beat MSG as a premier place to view an event. The facility is located at 4 Pennsylvania Plaza, at the corner of 34th Street and 7th Avenue, over Pennsylvania Station. It seats 19,763 people and was opened in 1968. If you wish to call the stadium, the phone number is (212)-465-6741.

➤ Uline Arena (Washington, D.C.)

➤ Market Street Arena (Philadelphia, Pa.)

➤ Lamosque (Richmond, Va.)

➤ Pittsburgh Civic Center (Pittsburgh, Pa.)

➤ Sunnyside (San Francisco, Ca.)

➤ Marigold Arena (Pittsburgh, Pa.)

➤ St. Nicks Parkway Arena (San Francisco, Ca.)

➤ Olympic Auditorium (Los Angeles, Ca.)

➤ Mid-South Coliseum (Memphis, Tenn.) Mid-South Coliseum is located at 996 Early Maxwell Street, Memphis, Tenn. This facility can accommodate 11,667 patrons, and the phone number is (901)-274-3982.

➤ ECW Arena (Philadelphia, Pa.)

➤ Reunion Arena (Dallas, Tex.) If you happen to be in the Dallas area, check out the Reunion Arena. It opened in 1980 at a cost of $27 million and is situated on 6.2 acres. There is parking for 6,400 vehicles, and this stadium has some of the finest safety features available.

Beyond this list, there are lots of other places—large and small—that book wrestling. And professional wrestling is such a phenomenon now that new venues are opening up every day, it seems. Pro wrestling comes to cities across the country, so chances are you'll get to see your favorite wrestlers at an arena near you.

How do you find out where the wrestlers are? Most matches are publicized well in advance. If you watch wrestling on television, you'll see promotional spots for upcoming matches. Fans who have access to the Internet can check Web sites for information on live matches in their areas.

A Night to Remember

Getting ready for a night at a live wrestling match doesn't take much planning—you've got the will, the way, and the tickets, so who needs anything more? But like anything else, your experience is what you make of it. And there's lots of things that fans have found to add some extra excitement, enjoyment, and even comfort.

One big thing is that wrestling is now very kid-friendly—and the kids love it right back. If you're taking your kids along, you really want to do a little advance work—the events are intense and kids do sometimes need a little preparation for the noise, the lights, and all that action. Beyond that, here are a few tips to improve your ringside experience:

➤ **A lot of facilities have restrictions on what attendees may and may not bring to a match.** For example, you may not be allowed to bring a camera or camcorder to a match. Check with the individual facility to find out what you are allowed to bring into the ring area. If you can bring a camera, do so. Always bring a few ink pens and some paper, on the chance that you might be able to get an autograph or two.

➤ **If the seating in the ring area is not padded, bring a stadium cushion with you.** Hard chairs, metal or wooden, can get uncomfortable during a long event. Most arenas will not prohibit the use of personal cushions, but you should check local regulations on anything you plan to bring into the seating area.

➤ **If your seats aren't right up close to ringside, bring along a pair of wide-angle binoculars.** You don't want to miss any of the action if you're stuck way up in the back of the hall.

➤ **Find out if bringing food is allowed.** Matches can last for hours, so you might think it's a good idea. But this is often against house rules—they're hoping to make a lot of money at their concession stands, so they don't want you bringing your own. Check the rules before you decide to haul along a beer cooler and picnic basket.

Body Slam

If you have questions about what you can and cannot bring to a match, call the ticket office and ask. Don't wait until you get to the event to find out that your camera will not be allowed inside.

Body Slam

Some overzealous fans have been known to attack pro wrestlers that they identify as enemies of their favorite stars. If you are going to approach a pro for an autograph or even just a quick touch, make your intentions known and keep an eye open for enraged fans.

➤ **About those kids…Call ahead and see what facilities, if any, are available for you and your baby.** Fans who bring small children to wrestling events have to make arrangements for everything from feeding, to napping, to changing diapers, if the kids are *really* little. Don't sit too close to the ring if you have really young children. It's rare that anything goes wrong at a match, but the first few rows of seats is not an ideal place for extremely young children. Parents of infants and even toddlers should respect the needs of other fans. Not everyone is tolerant of crying children. If you have very young children, you might consider arranging for a babysitter for the night. (Hey, you deserve a break now and then anyway.)

➤ **Check your judgmental tendencies at the stadium door.** Some of your fellow fans are really into their favorite wrestlers. Guys will paint messages to their stars on their bodies, or they'll bring along signs proclaiming their loyalty (or their undying hatred) of one or another of the featured wrestlers. Be prepared for this type of behavior. The fans are, for the most part, harmless, but they can be outrageous—this *is* after all, wrestling...outrageous is the name of the game.

➤ **If you are not out for a close encounter, buy tickets for seats that are a few rows back.** Wrestlers often roll out of the ring and perform close to the safety barriers. This drives some fans over the edge with excitement—but while its one thing to see a fan squashed under a misplaced brawler, it's another thing to *be* the fan under the monster. Unless you want to take a chance on getting that kind of up-close-and-personal, find a seat further back.

When You're Ready to Rumble

Okay, you've gotten to the arena, found your seat, and you're ready for the show. Let's hope you're ready for anything—'cause anything *can* happen. But that doesn't mean you have anything to worry about. Remember, these are pros you're watching perform. They've trained long and hard to make the violence you see *look* real, but they're just as concerned about safety as you are. Even the spectacular effects you see on TV—like flames shooting out of the audience area—are all carefully, and professionally, staged.

When the wrestlers move their fight into the audience area, they rarely come across the safety barriers. Even when they do, the moves are most often planned for a crowd-pleasing contact, rather than a rowdy bout that has gotten out of hand. As rough as real wrestling matches are, it's extremely rare for anyone in the audience to be at risk. The only really risky times are when wrestlers get carried away, or miss their timing when they're out in the audience area.

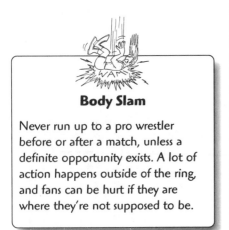

Body Slam

Never run up to a pro wrestler before or after a match, unless a definite opportunity exists. A lot of action happens outside of the ring, and fans can be hurt if they are where they're not supposed to be.

Matches are typically confined to the ring and the area immediately adjacent to the it. Sometimes wrestlers take their action up runways through the seating area, but the fans are separated from the wrestlers by barriers. Some memorable battles have been fought all the way to the concession stands, but you can be sure that the action was carefully planned, every step, grunt, body slam, and kick of the way.

The only thing that gets really scary is when young kids are in the arena—they can move like greased lightning if parents aren't on the ball to keep them in their seats. If you're bringing along the whole family, find seats in the middle of the crowd—away from the barriers. You don't want your young ones running out into the middle of a full-scale, tag-team melee.

Fans who've watched televised events know that the unexpected often happens. Two wrestlers scheduled for a match might suddenly be joined by a multitude of other wrestlers who aren't on the card. If Kane or The Undertaker decides to make an un-scheduled entrance, the lights can suddenly go off. They're both big on burning a coffin in the ring—it's a regular part of their show.

Sometimes large trash containers are rolled off ramps and inflatable dolls or real wrestlers can be dumped into the show area. Chainsaw Charlie might rev up his tree-cutting tool. Raven and his flock may decide to disrupt an ongoing match. There is almost no limit to what might happen. Keep in mind that most of the action is planned, at least to some extent, so safety is not a big concern.

Mostly, what you'll see will be intense wrestling and some of the most spectacular acrobatic moves imaginable, performed by extremely talented, highly trained athletes. These men and women know what they're doing, and they're doing it for the sake of the show. I'm not saying that wrestling is like a Sunday walk in the park—this is *wrestling*, after all, and the name of the game is action. But it's professionally done, by some of the finest athletes in sports today.

So get up off your sofa and find a seat around the ring if you want to experience all the elements of pro wrestling! Until you attend a live house match, you have not seen pro wrestling at it's best. Get into the mix and experience one of the most exciting events you are likely to ever see.

The Least You Need to Know

➤ Pay-per-view showings don't deliver the same spice as live house matches do.

➤ The risk of personal injury at live events is almost nonexistent.

➤ Madison Square Garden and the Reunion Arena are top-notch facilities to see a match in.

➤ Call ahead to see what you are and are not allowed to bring to a live match.

➤ Seriously consider leaving very small children with a sitter when you go to a live match.

Part 4

All the Right Moves: Inner (and Outer) Workings of the Ring

Pro wrestling might be compared to an act of magic: What you see is not always what you get.

The athletic ability of the ring warriors is indisputable. Pro wrestlers are in tremendous physical condition, and they work very hard for their money. But let's get real—what human could really absorb a full body slam move and get up? No one can. Part of the fun of watching wrestling is figuring out which parts are real and which parts are staged.

This part begins with a tour of schools that teach athletes how to become proficient professional wrestlers. Then it goes on to explain all the right moves for winning a pro-wrestling match. After that we take an insider's look at the true magic of pro wrestling: the stunts, moves, and illusions. We take on tag teams in Chapter 21. Then, Chapter 22 takes you all the way behind the scenes, behind the locker-room doors, in fact.

Come on, roll up your sleves and enter the ring of Part 4 with us.

Chapter 18

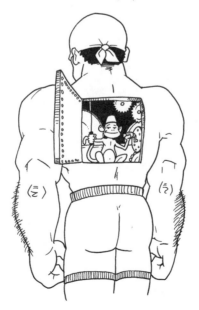

School of Hard Knocks

In This Chapter

➤ Breaking into wrestling—the wrestling schools

➤ Choosing a good wrestling school

➤ Requirements for enrollment

➤ Surviving day-to-day training

➤ From student to pro: Breaking into pro wrestling

You've heard the old saying about gaining life experience: "I learned it in the school of hard knocks." For most people that's just a figure of speech—but for pro wrestlers, it's literally true. Like any other field, professional wrestling's future depends upon it's continual influx of talent. Especially now that it has exploded into the fastest growing field in all of sports entertainment. As Pretty Boy Larry Sharpe, owner of the school "The Monster Factory" puts it: "Wrestling needs all the monsters we can get."

Over the years, wrestling has conscripted its recruits from other fields of athletics—football, amateur wrestling, even weight lifting. Those who have crossed over to join its ranks include former football players like Bronko Nagurski, Leo Nominelli, Alex Karras, and—yes—Bill Goldberg. Former amateur wrestlers include Verne Gagne, Danny Hodge, Terry Funk, and Ric Flair. Ken Patera came in from a former career as a weight lifter. But wrestling still needs many, many more wide-bodies to fill its ever expanding ranks.

Captain Lou's Corner

Breaking into wrestling is hard. Sometimes it's not what you know, it's who you know. I had help when I was breaking in, and over the years I've helped others—like when I recommended Terry Bollea (the Hulk), Jack Armstrong, and Junkyard Dog. And I listen to the recommendations of school operators, like Afa of the Wild Samoan School. So make yourself known to those who can help you.

So, what does it take to become a professional wrestler? And where and how does one enlist? This chapter will look into the schools where champions are made, and the training regimen you must go through to become the next Bill Goldberg.

Training in the Early Days

Back in the days of old, pro wrestling reached out and took anyone and everyone it could find to fill its talent pool—willing plowboys, farmers, rodeo riders, anyone at all. Most hailed from the Midwest and came from European stock—men like Iowan Frank Gotch; "Strangler" Lewis, from the back roads of Wisconsin; and Lou Thesz from the ethnic neighborhood athletic clubs of St. Louis.

Wherever they came from, most of these early pro wrestlers were skilled in the disciplines of Greco-Roman wrestling. Some, like Dr. B. F. Roller, were even amateur champions. And all received their schooling in pro wrestling's world through on-the-job training—learning while earning, if you will.

The College Football Connection

By the third decade of the twentieth century, promoters began scouring the landscape for athletes and, naturally, turned to the gridiron for their recruits. The first was Wayne "Big" Munn of Nebraska. In short order he was joined in the ranks by Gus Sonnenberg of Dartmouth, Jumpin' Joe Savoldi of Notre Dame, Jim McMillan of Illinois, and Herman Hickman of Tennessee.

From Gridiron to Wrestling Ring: Herman Hickman

For those too young to remember, Herman Hickman was one of the greatest linemen in the history of Southern football, playing at my own alma mater, the University of Tennessee. He even played for my old coach—General Bob Neyland. The New York *Sun* described him as being able "to demolish one side of an enemy line single-handedly" with "Samson-like strength...surprisingly nimble for his weight."

After graduation in 1931, Hickman turned to wrestling—his mentors were Toots Mondt and Rudy Dusek who, as Herman put it, "taught me how to 'work,' how to put on a performance...They showed me how to take a fall without getting hurt, how to go with a wristlock without getting a dislocated shoulder, how to slam an opponent without injuring him."

"You know," Herman told me, "that was back in the early 1930s, and it ain't changed much since!"

Amateur Wrestlers, Weight Lifters, Boxers: Everybody's Welcome

Another pool of talent were the collegiate amateur wrestlers. Verne Gagne won four Big Ten wrestling championships at the University of Minnesota before joining the world of pro wrestling. Jack Brisco won the NCAA wrestling title in the 191-pound class when he wrestled for Oklahoma State. Bob Backlund captured the NCAA Division II title at North Dakota State, and Allen "Bad News" Coage won a bronze medal in judo at the 1976 Olympics.

Weightlifter Ken Patera, who represented the United States at the 1972 Olympic games, crossed over to wrestling too. So did a few boxers, like Arnold Skaaland. After Skaaland temporarily paralyzed his left arm, his trainer asked: "Do you have any dramatic talents? Why not try wrestling?" Similarly, Freddie Blassie was boxing in a Golden Gloves tournament at the age of 16 when he was spotted by Jack Dempsey. "You've got a punch like a Missouri Mule," said Dempsey. "Only your arms are too short—the pro's will murder you. You like to wrestle...so wrestle!"

Body Slam

Check out any wrestling school you're considering for their credentials. Find out who their trainers are, their history and experience. And get a list of graduates. Make sure to do this *before* you write that check for tuition.

Captain Lou's Story

My experience was a lot like Blassie's and Skaaland's. After I had gotten out of the service I went to Willie Gilzenberg, who handled "Two Ton" Tony Galento and Red Cochrane, and I told him I wanted to be a boxer. Gilzenberg said I was too short, and suggested I try wrestling as a career move.

Not incidentally, Gilzenberg was also part of the World Wrestling Federation. He arranged for me to train, one-on-one, with Soldier Barry and Arnold Skaaland. That's how *I* got into wrestling.

Lots of others were "discovered" from outside the world of wrestling, too. Take Terry Bollea. You know him better as the Hulkster, or Hollywood Hogan. He was playing bass guitar with a Tampa-based rock band when Jack Brisco (who ran wrestling shows in the area) discovered him. And Bill Goldberg was on the injured reserve list of the Atlanta Falcons while he recovered from a painful pelvic injury. He happened to be hanging out in an Atlanta sports bar, standing next to Diamond Dallas Page. Page suggested he try his hand at wrestling. The list goes on and on.

And there are the "legacies"—wrestlers born to the black and blue, like Kerry and Kevin Von Erich, sons of the fabled Fritz Von Erich. And Bret Hart, whose father was the all-time great, Stu Hart. Not to mention Dustin Rhodes, formerly Golddust, son of the legendary Dusty Rhodes.

Do You Got What It Takes?

Getting "discovered" is one way to get into wrestling, but most of todays wrestlers—and yesterday's, for that matter—came to the sport through the wrestling school. And there's no better way to go, really, than to pass through the portals of what can be called "Cauliflower State University."

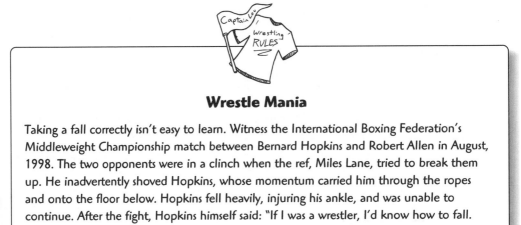

Wrestle Mania

Taking a fall correctly isn't easy to learn. Witness the International Boxing Federation's Middleweight Championship match between Bernard Hopkins and Robert Allen in August, 1998. The two opponents were in a clinch when the ref, Miles Lane, tried to break them up. He inadvertently shoved Hopkins, whose momentum carried him through the ropes and onto the floor below. Hopkins fell heavily, injuring his ankle, and was unable to continue. After the fight, Hopkins himself said: "If I was a wrestler, I'd know how to fall. But I'm a boxer, so I don't."

So you wannabe a wrestler? Well, let me tell you, it ain't for wimps. You've got to have athletic ability, some skills, and above all else you've got to be in good shape.

Not that you have to be built like a brick skyscraper. But you *do* have to be in reasonably good condition. Otherwise, the school might turn you down. After all, they don't want someone who'll get into their rowing machines and sink them.

Several schools will give you a look-see—a session of rope work, calisthenics, and workouts—to find out if you're in good enough shape to take on their intensive program. They want to know if you can handle their "hard time"—if you've got the ability and agility to see it through without jeopardizing yourself or your health.

So, if you're really, *really* serious about pursuing a career in professional wrestling, and if you're in good shape, you'll want to contact a wrestling school. That's the first step on the ladder to becoming a professional wrestler.

Here's a list of some of the current wrestling schools. It's by no means exhaustive, so don't think your options are limited to the ones listed here. And keep in mind that wrestling schools come and go—as do the trainers that teach at them. This list is not an endorsement of any particular schools—it's just a convenient place for you to start your search.

Wrestling Schools That Rule

Roland Alexander Superstars Training
3833 Peralta, Suite B
Freemont, CA 94536

School of Hard Knocks
3265 North E Street
San Bernardino, CA 92405

Institute of Professional Wrestling
10 Stemmers Run Road
Essex, MD 21221

Mike Shaw Wrestling School
PO Box 200
Skandia, MI 49885

Killer Kowalski Wrestling School
PO Box 67
Reading, MA 01867

Skullkrusher's Wrestling School
PO Box 6188
Gulf Breeze, FL 32561

Ivan Koloff Wrestling School
PO Box 23360
Charlotte, NC 28227

Slammer's Wrestling Gym
PO Box 1602
Studio City, CA 91614

Main Event Pro Wrestling Camp
10235 Spartan Dr., Suite D
Cincinnati, OH 45215

Spoiler's Wrestling Academy
3615 W. Waters, Box 110
Tampa, FL 33614

Walenko Wrestling School
2122 W. Vina de Mar Blvd.
St. Petersburg Beach, FL 33706

Superstars Pro Wrestling Camp
21063 Cabot Blvd, Suite 1
Hayward, CA 94545

The Monster Factory
PO Box 345
Westville, NJ 08093

Wild Samoan Pro Wrestling Center
719 Jordan Parkway
Whitehall, PA 18052

Check around, do your homework, and find out about school facilities, trainers on staff, and lists of graduates. In other words, check their credentials. Above all else, look for a school that fits both your budget and your schedule.

Choosing Your School

Once you've checked a school's credentials, check your schedule. Many would-be wrestlers have day jobs or come from faraway places. Many wrestling schools, like the Monster Factory, have a four-day-a-week, four-month course for regular students. But if you're a weekend warrior—if your schedule only lets you train on weekends—your program will take 8 months.

Bert's Corner

Bob Goldberg never went the route of a formal wrestling school course, but that doesn't mean he didn't get training. He just trained outside the field of wrestling until he realized where he really wanted to go in his career: "I did my homework. I studied martial arts. But I had an idea to portray a character that people would like."

And you need to consider your budget. The normal price range for most wrestling schools like the ones on our list runs from $3,000 to $5,000 for intensive training. Some offer a free first session before you go under contract. Many will finance your tuition for a few months, interest free. And some have a basic charge, with additional set charges per session.

Here's a basic list of the questions to ask while you're checking out your school options:

➤ **How long has this outfit been in operation?** A long-established school will have graduates you can check out, so you can get an idea of how good their program is. New operations are always risky—there's no track record for you to check.

➤ **Who owns the school?** Fred No-Name from the local YMCA probably doesn't have the expertise you're looking for. It's kind of like the blind leading the blind, since he probably doesn't know any more than you already do.

➤ **Does the owner do the training personally, or does the school hire employees as trainers?** Many ex-wrestlers run training schools, and they've got years of personal experience to pass on to you. That's what you want—not just some big guy who's never been inside an arena past the general seating.

➤ **What level of experience do the trainers have?** The guy who runs a local weight-training course is fine to a point, but he's not going to know the tricks of the trade. You need to get in shape, yes—but to make it as a pro you need lots more than that.

➤ **What kind of contract do you have to sign?** Is there any escape clause that will let you pull out of the school with at least a partial refund if you think your training is below par?

➤ **Who are some of the pro wrestlers who have attended the school?** What are they doing now? It's always a good sign if some of the school's graduates have gone on to greatness.

➤ **Will the school assist you with promotional matters, such as demo tapes?** They're at least as important as the physical conditioning you need to get into shape. You want to pick a school that offers the *total* package—one where you will learn everything from interview techniques to developing a gimmick.

➤ **Will the school help you relocate?** If you're really committed to breaking into wrestling, you may be willing to move on your own dime, but since some schools help you find employment and lodging in their area it doesn't hurt to ask.

School Days, School Days, Dear Old Golden Rule Days

So, you've taken the big step and signed with one of the wrestling schools. Be prepared—it's no walk in the park. As The Monster Factory's Larry Sharpe says, "You've got to have what it takes to cut the mustard."

And you'll be trying to cut the mustard from Day One. Before you even enter the ring you'll be subjected to a rigorous set of calisthenics to ensure that you're not only fit, but limber. Fifty push-ups, BOOM! BOOM! BOOM! Fifty more. Another fifty. Limbering up exercises until you feel you can't do anymore and your body's numb, and then there'll be more exercises, weight training, and more preparation. All before you enter the ring. After all, any wrestling school worth its salt wants to make sure you're physically fit to survive what lays ahead of you.

Just like Marine boot camp, there'll be times when you doubt you'll make it. And almost half of those who enroll don't. You might as well shake hands with the guy standing next to you on that first day, because only one of you is (according to the odds) gonna make it all the way.

Body Slam

Wrestling school is *tough*. Champion weightlifter Paul Anderson tried it and quit—because it was too hard. But if you make it past the preliminary exercise sessions, hang in there—there's a good chance you'll make it.

Making Your Moves

Once past the preliminary exercises, it'll be time for your first inside-the-ring instruction. This isn't going to be mano-a-mano—this will be instruction in the finer points of wrestling, like the holds. You'll learn the armlock, the suplex, the body slam—et cetera, et cetera, et cetera. And you'll learn the most important element in any wrestler's kit bag of tricks—how to fall.

Taking the Fall

You'll learn how to hit the mat (or your opponent) with your back, your buttocks, your hands. You'll learn to curl in your shoulders when you hit the ground. And you'll be taught these with painstaking care, over and over and over again, rehearsing them to a fare-thee-well. Remember the Chinese gymnast in the recent Goodwill Games who was paralyzed for life when she dismounted from the horse incorrectly—in wrestling and in any other sport, you can't practice falling too many times. It's your most basic stock-in-trade.

Tugboat Tayler, owner and instructor at the Tugboat Tayler School of Professional Wrestling in Houston, Texas, teaches his students that there are five rules of wrestling:

1. Your opponent is in fact your partner.

2. When you hit the ropes, hit all three at once or fly over.

3. Make noise.

4. When you fall, slap the mat to reduce impact on your back.

5. Use the headlock as a time to rest.

You can add one more rule, even if you never go to Tugboat's school: Don't try these moves at home without proper training.

Inside the Squared Circle

Now you're ready to really get into some ring action, to try out all those moves and falls you've been practicing on your lonesome. Here's the time when the instructors will separate those who are candidates for the front of the Wheaties box from those who belong on the sides of milk cartons. He'll teach you the margin for safety for each hold and fall, how to look like you're mauling your opponent instead of just gingerly lacing him. And how to take good care of your opponent—remembering that you're only as good as your opponent wants you to look.

But all this is only for starters, like an NFL player learning his playbook and attending a few practice sessions against his own teammates. You've still got a long way to go— learning how to perform those moves with a verve and application that appeals to the crowd, how to be the "total package."

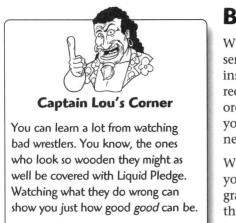

Captain Lou's Corner

You can learn a lot from watching bad wrestlers. You know, the ones who look so wooden they might as well be covered with Liquid Pledge. Watching what they do wrong can show you just how good *good* can be.

Beyond the Basics

While there are usually no official "chalk talks," no seminars, no classroom discussions and so forth, your instructor will give you personalized lessons and even recommend that you watch certain wrestlers on TV in order to pick up pointers from those who've gone before you. Call it post-graduate work, if you will, but it's necessary if you want to make it in the profession.

When you're ready to "graduate," most schools will help you develop a demo tape wrestling against a fellow graduate-to-be. This will be about 3 minutes long, since that's usually all that the major organizations have time to review.

Moving On Up, to the Big Time

Don't expect a placement service, by the way. But what you can expect is that your instructor is wired into the major organizations and can recommend the students he judges to be good enough to go on in the sport. For instance, the WWF's Jim Cornette is in regular contact with wrestling school instructors and checks with them to get recommendations of likely prospects—sort of like the scouting process used by major league teams. He asks about the real talent, the wannabe's that have well-conceived moves and pleasing personalities.

And I've got my own sources, too. Like Afa of the Wild Samoan School. He'll tout me a graduate who has something special, and his recommendation will give that candidate a start up the ladder to a pro wrestling gig.

Graduates that aren't picked right off the proverbial vine—don't get a gig right out of wrestling school—shouldn't despair. If they're really serious about a career in pro wrestling, they can break into the profession by apprenticing, so to speak, at the small shows that have sprung up all over the country. Many of these are staged by instructors, who can place their students in them.

The Captain Lou Career Route

I started in those small shows myself—my first one after training (with Soldier Barry) was in a little, local church show. Then, as now, scouts from the major federations frequently attended these small shows, and I was fortunate enough to be spotted by someone from the old WWWF.

Starting Small

My first bouts for the WWWF were as a prelim boy—wrestling in preliminary bouts instead of major matches. But I had made it into the big time, sort of. My pro debut for the WWWF was in Montreal, back in 1953, against Bob Lazaro. Soon I was offered a spot on TV in Washington—against Antonino Rocca. On TV! I told my friends and between us we figured that a spot like that could be worth hundreds—maybe thousands—of dollars. So I hitched up with one of the other wrestlers on the card and paid my share of $10 trans (transportation money) and $5 for food. After all, what was a $15 outlay against all the money I figured to make now that I'd hit it big in wrestling?

Reality Strikes

When we arrived at Uline Arena, I asked Rocca's manager what I was supposed to do. In his heavily flavored Russian accent he said that Rocca would do "dis" and Rocca would do "dat" and then Rocca would do it all over again. I was very green back then, so I asked "When do *I* get to do 'dis' and 'dat?'" His answer: "When you get back to the locker room!"

So I went out and Rocca whaled the bejabbers out of me. After he used his patented foot moves and basically used me as grist for his own mill, I was almost glad when he finally ended it all with a drop kick.

I finally made my way back to the dressing room and Phil Zacko, who was paying off the wrestlers after the show. He shoved two tens and a five in my direction. "What's this?" I said, laughing—visions of hundreds, even thousands dancing in my head. "That's what you get! Move along, punk!" was his response. *That* was my introduction to pro wrestling.

Times They Are A-Changing

That was then. This is now. The stakes today are much, much different. If you're thinking of going into the profession and have the backing and experience of a good school, the pay-off can be rich, indeed.

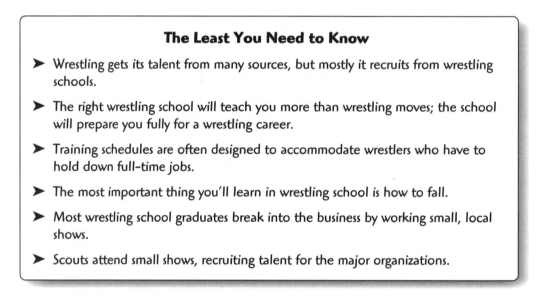

The Least You Need to Know

➤ Wrestling gets its talent from many sources, but mostly it recruits from wrestling schools.

➤ The right wrestling school will teach you more than wrestling moves; the school will prepare you fully for a wrestling career.

➤ Training schedules are often designed to accommodate wrestlers who have to hold down full-time jobs.

➤ The most important thing you'll learn in wrestling school is how to fall.

➤ Most wrestling school graduates break into the business by working small, local shows.

➤ Scouts attend small shows, recruiting talent for the major organizations.

Fist →

Head →

How to smash - Fig. 1

Chapter 19

Bone Crushers and Back-breakers: All the Right Moves

In This Chapter

➤ Classic wrestling holds

➤ Modern moves and techniques

➤ The favorite moves of top wrestlers

When he first came into baseball, the great sports promoter Bill Veeck saw the game as more than just a game—he saw it as entertainment. So he gussied up the staid old game with bat days, exploding scoreboards, and even a midget—all in the name of "entertainment."

Wrestling was no different. For generations it plodded along, with matches that went on interminably. Old timers like George Hackenschmidt, yearned for those good old days—reminiscing about the past on a 1950s radio show, the fabled "Russian Lion" regaled the listening audience with tales of his four-hour draw with the Terrible Turk, and of how certain holds were held for as long as fifty minutes. He sighed and said "Ah, that was *real* wrestling.

What Hackenschmidt was talking about were the matches of the first couple of decades of the 20th century—legitimate scientific matches, called "shoots," in which a true hammerlock could break a guy's arm and a step-over toehold could do the same to an ankle. When wrestling was gussied up, as Veeck had done with baseball, new and more crowd-pleasing holds were added to the repertoire of the classic ones. And this chapter will tell you about all of them, from those dating back to Greco-Roman style wrestling to the modern ones in use today.

The Four Basic Wrestling Holds

Back in 1948, an article in *Ring* magazine listed "the most effective holds in the history of wrestling. These were "'Strangler' Lewis's headlock, Joe Stetcher's body scissors, Frank Gotch's toehold, and Jim Browning's flying scissors."

That was it! Four plain vanilla holds, all of which dated back to the beginnings of the sport—and even before! Four. No more.

But something happened to professional wrestling on its way to television: new holds and moves that went beyond the stalk-your-opponent-to-his-knees variety. Now there were flashy moves, like Jim Londos' "Airplane Spin," Junpin' Joe Savoldi's "Drop Kick," and Gus Sonnenberg's "Flying Tackle." And there'd be more to come.

In this chapter you'll learn the moves of the pros. But before we take you through the recently-developed holds and moves, lets run through the classic holds, the ones that are a part and parcel of every wrestler's repertoire.

A Quick Caveat

While modern wrestling is highly acrobatic, classic wrestling depends on effective submission holds and pins. But before we talk about them in detail, two notes. First of all, many of these holds, such as the picket-four and figure-four leglock, go by several different names. Secondly, you must keep in mind that these moves are very, very dangerous. The wrestlers you see on TV are trained athletes and professionals who've taken many years to master them, with long, intensive training. DO NOT—I repeat DO NOT—try them at home, or you're asking for a quick trip to the hospital. Great wrestlers usually have one or two holds they're experts at, but it's not unusual for a wrestler to have one favorite hold to finish a match with.

Wrestle Mania

Some early wrestlers had so much confidence in their holds that they offered bounties for anyone who could break them. For example, Nanjo Singh perfected his impressive cobra hold. Singh had so much confidence that he put up $1,000 for anyone who could escape its grip. Nanjo's boast was met with a vengeance by Jim Londos. In fact, Londos not only beat the cobra hold, he tossed Nanjo from the ring in the process. The cobra hold was extremely effective—but it wasn't unbeatable.

Who were the men and what where their cherished holds? Let's find out.

Six-time World Heavyweight Champion Lou Thesz had plenty of tools in his war chest, but his favorite was his crotch hold-and-spin. Antonio Rocca, whose exploits you read about in Chapter 7, was noted for his use of the barefoot flying kick. Then there was the Indian death lock that Don Eagle liked to use. Primo Carnera used his bulky body effectively with a massive body slam. Mike Mazurki made his figure-four scissors lock a piece of wrestling history. The Canadian avalanche was a trademark of Whipper Billy Watson. All of these men and their moves have charted a piece a modern wrestling.

Dick Raines was building a fire one day and, as he broke kindling over his knee, realized that a similar action would work in the ring—thus inspiring the backbreaker. The half nelson and the flying body scissors were used extensively by Hollander Henry Piers. The flying head scissors was Frankie Taylor's move of choice. Body slams and dropkicks were the painful ways that Marshall Lewis dealt with his opponents. Ken Ackles's abdominal stretch was barred in many states, due to the injuries he caused with it.

Captain Lou's Corner

The flying scissors might have been done best by Ferenc Szikszay and Bert Ruby. But Jim Browning made the move famous, and most fans feel he perfected the move like no one else. Jack Terry liked to use the Japanese sleeper, which involved putting his palm on his opponent's carotid artery to reduce blood flow and render his opponent unconscious.

Kaiman Kudo borrowed from jiu jitsu to create his arm strangle. Verne Gagne had a rolling leg split that he liked to use. The creation of no less than 40 wrestling holds is credited to Frank Sexton, but his favorite was the giant swing. Buddy Rogers, an unforgettable figure, used a pile driver to stop his competitors. Ben Morgan and Jim Austeri both favored knee backbreaker. Jarque of Spain preferred a bouncing backbreaker.

Classic Submission Holds

There are two main types of holds: pins and submission holds. In a pin, a wrestler is put down so that his (or her) shoulders touch the mat. But some holds are so effective that although they don't constitute an actual pin, the wrestler in the hold has no chance of extricating himself. Here are some of the classic submission holds:

Abdominal Stretch: Standing to the side of your opponent, you hook one of his legs (you hook his left leg with your right, or his right leg with your left). At the same time, you've wrapped one of your arms in front of his body and pull his upper arm up behind your head.

Achilles Tendon Hold: With your opponent on his back, you grab his leg so that his foot is wedged in your armpit. You slide that arm under your opponent's knee, then lean back while applying a leg scissorlock.

Bert's Corner

Lex Luger's famous "Human Torture Rack" was a really effective variation on on the backbreaker theme. He lifted his opponent up onto his shoulders, facing upward. Luger then hooks an arm around the neck and the other around the legs—and presses downward on each side, forcing his opponent's back to bend against his neck.

Ankle Lock: Again, your opponent is on his back. Grab his leg, twisting the ankle, then go to the mat and apply a scissor lock to his leg.

Armbar: Take the opponent's arm with one hand at the wrist, the other gripping behind the elbow, then hold it fully extended. Applying pressure in opposite directions at the wrist and elbow, lock the joint so that it can't be bent.

Backbreaker: Once your opponent has been forced to the mat face down, you place both your knees on his back. Put one arm around his neck, the other around one or both of his legs. Lean back until you are lying on your back—your opponent is lifted in the air. Pull back on his neck and legs, forcing him to bend backwards.

Bear Hug: Like it sounds—facing your opponent, you wrap your arms around his body and squeeze. This move is used most effectively by the BIG wrestlers like Andre the Giant.

Boston Crab: This can be set up in two different ways.

1. With the opponent on his back, grap both his legs. Holding them, you step over his body, turning him onto his stomach. Then lean back to apply pressure.

2. With the opponent on his stomach, grab his legs and pull backward.

Camel Clutch: This is the Steiner Recliner, used by Scott Steiner. With your opponent face down on the mat, sit on his back and slide your arms under his legs. Apply a chinlock (see below), and then pull back.

Chinlock: With your opponent either sitting or lying on his stomach and you standing or kneeling above, link your hands under his chin and pull back.

Choke hold: Grab the opponent by the throat with one or both hands.

Claw Hold: This comes in two versions.

1. Abdominal (made famous by the von Erichs): grab the opponent's stomach muscles with your fingers and dig in.

2. Head: Grip your opponent's face in your hand and dig in.

Cloverleaf Leglock: With your opponent on his back you lock his legs into a figure four (see below) with his arms, and place his straight leg under his armpit. Step over him, rolling him onto his stomach (like for a Boston Crab), then lean back.

Crossface: Wrap one arm across your opponent's face and pull back. This is not a submission hold itself, but is usually applied in conjunction with one. Bob Backlund is known for his "crossface chickenwing" submission hold.

Crucifix Kneebar: Your opponent is down on his back. You apply a standing scissor lock around his leg and, holding the leg, fall to the mat just to his side, landing at a 90 degree angle to his body.

Figure-Four Leglock: While your opponent is on his back you grab one leg and bend it sideways across the other and behind one of your own—this forms a figure "4" of your opponent's legs. Holding his straight leg, you fall backwards to the mat, securing his bent leg in place by placing your free leg on top of the ankle.

Front Face Lock: Standing face to face with your opponent, you grab his head and tuck it under your arm. Locking his head in place by squeezing it against your side, you reach across your chest, around his head, and grab his face, squeezing it.

Full Nelson: Standing behind your opponent, place both your arms under his and lock your hands behind the back of his neck. Apply pressure by pressing down on the neck.

Half Crab: This can be set up in one of two ways.

1. With opponent on his back, grab one of his legs and step over his body, turning him on his stomach. Pull back, thereby applying pressure to his back.

2. If he's on his stomach, grab one of his legs and pull backward, again applying pressure to his back.

Body Slam

A full nelson can be a very dangerous hold. Apply too much pressure and you can break your opponent's neck.

Hammerlock: Hard to say who invented this one—probably some schoolyard bully. Grab one of your opponent's arms and pull it behind his back—continuing to pull while applying pressure to the elbow.

Head Lock: Stand to your opponent's side, facing in the same direction he's facing. Wrap your arm around his head and apply pressure, increasing the force of it by using both arms.

Head Vise: Place a hand on either side of your opponent's head and squeeze.

Indian Deathlock: With your opponent on his back, cross his legs as if he were sitting "Indian style." Then place your knee on his shins and apply pressure on his knees.

Neck Twist: Your opponent is sitting and you're standing behind him. Push down on one side of his head while gripping his jaw and pulling upward.

Nerve Hold: While restraining your opponent in an armbar (see above), apply a nerve pinch at the neck.

Sleeper Hold: Rowdy Roddy Piper perfected this move. Place one arm across your opponent's throat and the other up against the side of his head, then lock your hands.

This cuts off the supply of blood to your opponent's head and will render him unconscious. Complete the move by stepping one leg across your opponent's body to hold it down, while pulling upward on the head. Once the hold is completely applied, slowly tighten your grip at the side of your opponent's head.

Spinning Cobra Clutch: Apply a step-over toe hold (see below) and turn your opponent over onto his stomach. Then apply a cross face hold (see above).

Step-over Toe Hold: Your opponent is on his back, and you're facing him, holding one of his legs. If you've grabbed the right leg, you step around with your own right leg so that you've wrapped *his* around your left leg. You then apply pressure to the knee and leg you're holding. This is usually a set up for the figure four leglock (above), or you can spin your opponent around for submission.

Stump Puller: Stand behind a sitting opponent. Straddle his neck, grabbing one of his legs. Pull up on the leg, stretching his hamstring while compressing his neck.

Surfboard: With your opponent on his stomach, stand on the back of his knees/thighs and lock his ankles behind your legs. Grab both his arms from behind and lean backward, until you're sitting down. This pulls your opponent up onto his knees. From this position you can apply a chinlock (above), and this would be called a **Surfboard Chinlock**.

Wristlock: While your opponent is lying on his back you lay across his body. With one hand, grab the arm nearest to his head, then increase the pressure by reaching through his bent arm to grab hold with your other hand, pulling upward to put pressure on the elbow and wrist.

A Plethora of Pins

Pins are the classic way of winning a wrestling match—as you'll remember from the discussion of the rules in Chapter 5. Here are a few of the more common ones:

Back Slide: This move requires that you get back to back to your opponent and hook both of his arms with yours. Drop down to your knees, leaning forward. This drags your opponent up over your back, from which position you can force him to slide over your head to the mat, where you pin his shoulders. Once he's pinned down, you brace your legs to keep him there long enough to get that all-important 1-2-3 count.

Cradle: With your opponent on his stomach, you set him up for a camel clutch (see submission holds, above) by putting his arms over your legs. Stand, while simultaneously pushing his head down. You end the move on your knees with your opponent's shoulders pinned to the mat and trapped under your legs.

Roll Up: There are two versions of this one.

1. In the "Bridging Double Leg Pickup" version, your opponent is on his back. You grab both his legs and do a forward flip, landing on your feet.

2. In the "School Boy" version, you kneel down behind your opponent, reach through his legs with one arm, grabbing hold of one leg. Lean in the opposite direction of the leg you've grabbed, pulling your opponent across your body so that he lands on his back, ready for pinning.

Sunset Flip: Jump over your opponent, grabbing him at the waist on your way down and rolling over his back so that he ends up sitting on the mat. Now, pull him down onto his back, grab his legs, and use them to pin his arms flat.

Victory Roll: Jump up to sit on your opponent's shoulders, facing the same way he is. Roll forward, reaching down to grab his legs and hook them over his shoulders, in effect "cradling" him. This pins his shoulders to the mat.

Suplex: Standing behind your opponent, take each of his hands into your opposite hand (that is, hold his left hand in your right, his right hand in your left) so that his arms are crossed in front of his body. Pull backward until you've got him on his back on the mat for the pin.

Captain Lou's Corner

The Suplex is a very popular hold, and has been throughout pro wrestling's history. Used alone or in combination with other moves, it's one of wrestling's most versatile holds.

Acrobats and Aerialists

Today, many wrestling moves aren't holds at all. Instead, they're a blend of acrobatics and striking blows. Here's a sampling of some of the moves most popular with the fans:

Airplane Spin: Lift your opponent up by the shoulders. Start spinning around to make him dizzy, then drop him to the mat with a thud.

Airplane Spin Toss: This variation requires that you lift your opponent up over your shoulder (this is called an "inverted shoulder rack"). Spin around a few times and then toss him into the air. Gravity takes care of the rest.

Apron Dive: Run down the ring apron and jump onto your opponent, who's on the floor. Cactus Jack is known for his variation on this one, called the "Hipbuster Apron Dive Elbow Drop."

Arm Breaker: With the opponent in an armlock, step forward and drive his arm across your knees. Antonio Inoki uses a variation in which he applied an arm- or wristlock so that he holds his opponent's arm over his shoulder. Then he wrenches the arm in an attempt to hyper-extend the elbow.

Arm Drag: Ricky Steamboat uses this one, which is also known as the **Arm Whip.** Hook one of your opponent's arms and fall to the mat, pulling him down with you.

Arm Wringer: This one's also called the **Spinning Wristlock**. Grab your opponent's arm by the wrist, twist it over his head, and spin him.

Atomic Drop: Stand behind and slightly to your opponent's side. Grab his midsection with one arm and hook one of his legs with the other. Lift him over your shoulder, so he's parallel to the mat. Kneel slightly, dropping him tailbone-first onto your knee.

Back Drop: As your opponent charges toward you, bend forward. When he reaches your position, grab him, stand erect, and lift him up and over so his own momentum carries him to land on the mat, back first. This is commonly used to counter attacks where the opponent is bent over, say for a piledriver or a powerbomb (see below).

Bert's Corner

The modern move called the "back-breaker" may have the same name as the submission hold (see above), but it's a very different move. In this version, you ift your opponent up, then drop him across your knee, back first.

Back Fist: This is a standard martial arts blow—you hit your opponent with the back of your fisted hand.

Back Rake: Scratch down your opponent's back with your fingernails. This move is largely outdated, but Hollywood Hogan is still known to use it.

Bell Clap: Commonly used to break a bear hug, you clasp your hands or forearms around the opponent's head, knocking him off balance.

Body Press: Jump at your opponent, hitting him at an angle and knocking him to the mat.

Boot Scrape: This is a spinning move used famously by Eddie Guerrero. Your opponent is on his back and you put your foot in his face. As you lean forward to put more weight on that foot, you spin around.

Brainbuster: Lift your opponent so that you're chest-to-chest. Now hook both of his legs so they're up off the ground. Release one leg and with the arm you've just freed, tuck his head under your armpit. From their, fall backward, driving his trapped head into the mat behind you.

Bulldog: Holding your opponent in a headlock, run forward, then drive him down to the mat onto his face.

Chokeslam: Grab your opponent around the throat with one hand, pick him up, and then throw him down onto the mat on his back. 98-pound weaklings need not apply for this one.

Chop: Another blow taken from the martial arts—it looks just like it sounds.

Clothesline: Stick your arm out, hitting your opponent in the front of his neck with it.

Corkscrew: This term describes any move that begins with you spinning around. Hector Garza is well known for a move called the "Corkscrew Plancha Dive."

DDT: With a front facelock on your opponent, fall straight down or back, driving his head into the mat.

Double Axhandle Smash: Lock both of your hands together, then use them to strike your opponent.

Drop Kick: Jump in the air and kick out with both feet at your opponent. This attack can be focused on your opponent's head, chest, stomach, back, or legs.

Drop Toe Hold: Drop down to the mat, placing one foot in front of your opponents leg (or legs) and hooking your other leg behind him, thus tripping him and bringing him down.

Elbow Drop: This is a simple fall onto your opponent—you just make sure you land on him elbow-first.

Elbow Smash: With your back to your opponent, drive backward with your elbow to hit him in the head.

Face Driver: While standing, get your opponent's head into a scissor hold, then drop down and drive him face-first into the mat.

Fist Drop: When your opponent is down, drop onto him fist-first. Ted DiBiase and Hawk (of the Road Warriors) use this one.

Flap Jack: Lift your opponent up into the air as if you're setting up for a back drop (above), but once you've got his body parallel to the mat, instead of tossing him over, push him straight up into the air. This way, he'll land on his face and chest when he hits the mat.

More Classic Holds

It's amazing how simple some of the most effective holds are. Simple moves are still enough to get the job done, but they don't produce the flash that fans want from modern wrestling.

➤ **Double Arm Lock.** A double arm lock is a simple wrestling hold. Basically, a wrestler wraps both arms around an opponent's back and interlocks the hands. It's common for the attacker to pull the opponent's head close to his body, possibly under the armpit. This hold is rarely effective as a submission hold, but it can set up a wrestler for a fall.

➤ **Toe Hold.** A toe hold can become a submission hold. With a toe hold, one wrestler places pressure on his competitor's foot. Applied properly, it's very painful and difficult to break.

➤ **Crab Hold.** The crab hold is an extremely effective submission hold. In fact, it's one of the most devastating holds in the ring. The wrestler sits on the back of his opponent, grabs both of his legs, and bends them backwards. It is nearly impossible to get free from a crab hold if the wrestler on top is large enough to maintain it.

➤ **Figure-Four.** A figure-four leg lock is another effective submission hold. A wrestler gets an opponent to the mat and then ties up his legs, with his hands laced between them. An attacking wrestler lifts the opponent's legs to pin the opponent's shoulders.

➤ **Grapevine.** An inside grapevine is used when the opponent is on his hands and knees. The attacker wraps a leg inside an opponent's thigh and over the back of his calf. This move can be used for a flip in an effort to gain a pin. The risk is that an opponent with superior strength might spin and roll to put the aggressor on the mat.

➤ **Half Nelson.** With the half nelson, the attacking wrestler has an arm under the armpit of his opponent and a hand clasped on the opponent's neck. The half nelson is applied while the opponent has his other hand secured behind his back with pressure applied from the attacking wrestler. This move can be used on a wrestler who is standing or prone on the mat.

A half nelson can be used on its own, but isn't very powerful without additional restraint. One effective combination is the hammerlock and half nelson.

Another variation is to use the half nelson with the top scissors hold. The opponent is on the mat with the other wrestler's legs applying pressure on his legs and applying the half nelson. Any half nelson hold can be a submission hold.

➤ **Leg Split.** The leg split is pretty simple: The opponent is on the mat, and the aggressive wrestler kneels on one of his legs while lifting the other leg to uncomfortable proportions. This, too, is a submission hold that works when applied by a large, strong wrestler.

➤ **Leg Holds.** There are several leg holds. The leg and arm Lock is accomplished by applying pressure with both an arm and a leg to the arm of an opponent lying on the canvas.

A better submission hold is the combination hammerlock and leg hold. In this move, an opponent is almost standing on his head. The aggressive wrestler puts one leg in a bad bend while bringing the opponent's arm to his back. The pressure can be intense, and submission is likely.

An arm and leg hold is a standing hold that is used to bring an opponent to the mat. The aggressive wrestler uses both an arm and a leg to lock up an opponent, in an attempt to put the opponent to the mat.

➤ **Front Chancery.** A front chancery is a standing hold used to set up other moves. In a front chancery, the opponent's head is locked under the armpit of the aggressive wrestler.

Wrestlers may also combine the chancery and a bar arm hold. Both moves are standing moves and are not considered submission holds.

Other old-time holds include the flying mare, a reverse wrist and arm lock, a double wrist lock and head scissors, and a plain double wrist lock.

Modern wrestlers have designed new and powerful moves based on these simple yet effective holds. Let's examine them next.

Modern Moves

Pro wrestling has become more acrobatic and flashy in an attempt to keep audiences on the edges of their seats. In addition to chair bashing, chain slinging, and the use of chain saws, modern wrestlers have modified proven holds to suit their styles. They have also developed a lot of eye-opening moves of their own. Let's look at all the right wrestling moves.

➤ **Octopus On Your Back.** The octopus is a variation of the abdominal stretch. The aggressive wrestler stands to one side of his opponent, grapevines the opponent's leg, bends the opponent's body, and hooks a leg over the opponent's head. In the process, the aggressive wrestler wraps his arms around the opponent's chest. When the move is fully executed, the aggressive wrestler is off the mat completely, clinging to the back of the opponent.

➤ **Giant Swing.** The giant swing is a newer edition of the airplane swing. It starts out like a Boston crab. Once an aggressive wrestler has an opponent's legs, the opponent is swung around and around. It's a *very* disorienting move.

➤ **Backbreakers.** Backbreakers are a common move in modern matches. They are done over the knee of an aggressive wrestler. There are several variations. The hanging backbreaker, for instance, is set up with a basic pile driver positioning. We'll explain the pile driver later in the chapter.

Wrestle Mania

Backbreakers are a favorite show-stopping move with many wrestlers. Jesse Ventura called the move a body breaker and an inverted body vice. There is also the tilt-a-whirl back-breaker, a favorite move of Demolition Crush.

➤ **Gator Buster.** Have you ever watched anyone wrestle an alligator? Well, pro wrestling has adopted the concept with a hold known as the gator buster. The aggressive wrestler comes up from behind his opponent, places both hands around the opponent's head, and grabs on tight. Then the aggressive wrestler pulls the head of the opponent backwards, so that the opponent is looking skyward. At this point, the aggressive wrestler falls backwards to drop the opponent on his head.

➤ **Your Basic Clothesline.** This move was taken from pro football. It is simply a matter of extending an arm at throat level for an opponent to run into. Anyone who follows pro wrestling is sure to see the clothesline from time to time.

Body Slam

Wrestlers have to use their stunt skills to pull off the pile driver without injury; if they attempted a pile driver for real, they could kill their opponents. Given painful moves like the pile driver, is it any wonder that most serious pro-wrestling injuries are neck related?

➤ **Pile Driver.** The pile driver is very popular, perhaps because it's so dangerous. The opponent is picked up with his head down and his feet skyward. The aggressive wrestler drives the opponent into the mat, head first.

➤ **Power Bomb.** Take a pile driver, add a touch of the suplex, and mix in a hanging backbreaker, and you've got a power bomb. This dangerous move can be lethal, and has resulted in many recent injuries. Because it is so damaging, most wrestlers frown upon the use of the power bomb.

➤ **Sleeper.** A sleeper hold, sometimes called a Weaver lock after its creator, Johnny Weaver, can put the lights out on anyone caught in it. Pressure applied to the neck and head results in the opponent seeing stars and then total darkness.

Wrestle Mania

Dusty Rhodes used to apply the sleeper hold on the Four Horsemen.

Over the years, there have been variations of the sleeper, such as the dragon sleeper, which has an aggressive wrestler clasping his hands behind an opponent's back and squeezing.

➤ **Slingshot.** The slingshot requires the use of the ring ropes. A wrestler grips the ropes, leans back, and flies into the ring, landing on his opponent. Some fans call it a splash and other call it a swan dive. Most people think of the move as a slingshot.

➤ **Stump Puller.** The stump puller isn't pretty, but it's effective. A wrestler gets an opponent into a sitting position and climbs onto his shoulders. Then he grabs his opponent's legs and pulls upward. The pressure on the legs, combined with the weight of the wrestler sitting in the neck area can result in a quick submission ruling.

Winning Moves

Professional wrestlers utilize many moves and holds throughout their careers. During their time in the ring, wrestlers gain confidence in moves and holds that are guaranteed winners. The following list shows some of today's top wrestlers and the finishing moves and holds that they use time and time again:

Wrestler	Move/Hold
Ole Anderson	Standing Armbar
Tony Atlas	Bear Hug
Stone Cold Steve Austin	Stone Cold Stunner
Bob Backlund	Atomic Drop
Chris Benoit	Head Butt
Ultimo Dragon	Stepover Armbar
Ric Flair	Figure Four
Jimmy Garvin	Neck Breaker
Glacier	Cryonic Kick
Billy Graham	Bear Hug
Owen Hart	Dropkick
Curt Hennig	Dropkick
Hollywood Hogan	Leg Drop
Disco Inferno	Standing Bulldog
Ahmed Johnson	Power Bomb
Ivan Koloff	Bear Hug
Killer Kowalski	Claw
Jerry Lawler	Fist Drop
Lex Luger	Horizontal Backbreaker
Wahoo McDaniel	Tomahawk Chop
Shawn Michaels	Pile Driver
Kevin Nash	Power Bomb

continues

265

continued

Wrestler	Move/Hold
Diamond Dallas Page	Diamond Cutter
Dusty Rhodes	Elbow Drop
Antonio Rocca	Backbreaker
Buddy Rogers	Figure Four
Bruno Sammartino	Bear Hug
Iron Sheik	Camel Clutch
Sting	Boston Crab Grapevine
Booker T	Leg Drop

While the wrestlers above have been noted for their signature holds, they may well develop other moves as they continue in the ring. Wrestlers often add to their arsenal as they grow in the business. You can bet that all pro wrestlers have more than one or two winning moves—all the better to defeat their opponents.

Michael Benson is well known in the wrestling industry. He's an editor of wrestling magazines and a man who has his finger on the pulse of the sport. When asked to name the five most popular holds/moves in modern wrestling, here is what he said:

1. **The figure-four leg lock.** According to Benson, Ric Flair has used this hold with the most effectiveness in modern wrestling.
2. **The sharpshooter.** Bret Hart uses it to thrill fans, and Sting uses the same hold, but calls it the scorpion deathlock.
3. **The sleeper.**
4. **The torture rack.** Used by Lex Luger.
5. **The claw.** Made famous by Killer Kowalski. Benson feels that this move should be ranked as #5 even though it is rarely seen in modern wrestling.

Ask any fan to name his or her five favorite holds or moves and you might see a very different list. Every fan has his or her own opinion of what the best moves and holds are.

The best hold or move is one that *works*—and thrills a wrestling audience. Pro wrestlers experiment to combine effectiveness with crowd-pleasing potential, and no doubt the great moves and holds of the ring will continue to excite viewers and win title belts.

The Least You Need to Know

➤ Classical wrestling relies on submission holds, which are still used in modern wrestling.

➤ Modern wrestling has become much more acrobatic than earlier wrestling.

➤ Classic holds include the toe hold, the crab hold, and the half nelson, among others.

➤ Modern wrestling moves include backbreakers, slingshots, and sleepers.

➤ Some modern moves, such as power bombs and pile drivers, are too dangerous to use in the ring. These moves are often faked as stunts.

Chapter 20

Masters of Illusion

In This Chapter

➤ Arm antics and powerless punches

➤ Flying fakes and frauds

➤ Pulling your leg: Effective high kicks

➤ Snap, crackle, pop—the sound of pain

➤ Taking a fall

People who watch professional wrestling for the first time are often stunned by the action in the ring. 300-pound men go flying through the air; small wrestlers slam their hulking opponents to the mat; sumo-sized wrestlers launch themselves off the ropes and belly-flop onto their hapless opponents.

Most mortals couldn't take that abuse, so how do pro wrestlers not only *survive* such attacks, but *keep wrestling?* Hmm…maybe there's more going on than meets the eye. In this chapter you'll learn not just *what's* going on in the ring, but *how* they do it.

The Show Does Go On

As we explained in Chapter 4, the wrestling industry is laced with real-action and fantasy stunts. Die-hard fans are convinced that every move in the ring is real; skeptics claim none of it's real. Both are wrong. Wrestling is a hybrid of illusion and reality.

Experienced professional wrestlers put on terrific shows. If you don't think they really get hurt, look up their medical records. Some public injuries may be staged and embellished, but others are real. Most injuries that occur in the ring are accidental, but some

wrestlers, known as *shooters,* come to the ring with bad intentions of causing real pain. When the action is supplied by true professionals, fans can never be sure what is and isn't real.

Not all pro wrestlers have the skills to make their moves convincing. Watch a few matches and you'll see plenty of action that's as staged as a high-school play. Some matches are almost laughable. But, everyone has to learn their trade, and a lot of wrestlers learn theirs in front of the cameras, which aren't too forgiving of mistakes, missed moves, and poor acting. If you concentrate on the pros, you'll see far fewer mistakes and a lot of hard-hitting, realistic wrestling.

Getting to the top in pro wrestling is far from easy. Even if some of the matches are staged, pro wrestlers do a lot of training, from weight lifting to sophisticated gymnastics. Men and women in the ring have to be in terrific physical condition. Done properly, the special effects of pro wrestling are almost impossible to expose. There are, however, some signs to look for in order to see when the moves are full contact and when they are pulled up to lessen the blow. That's what we're about to explore.

Blows and Blunders

Wrestling is supposed to be a sport of tactical moves and holds. It's not boxing and it's not supposed to look like a street fight. However, pro wrestling does frequently resemble a rumble in an alley. So how can a person take repeated blows to the head from a huge competitor and keep coming back for more? Because most of the punching makes relatively little impact.

The *illusion* requires that fans see and hear the contact— but it's rarely as forceful as the audience believes it is. Sometimes the pull up of a punch can be seen, but many good, experienced wrestlers perform flawlessly in their deception of the audience.

Closed fists are not used too often in the wrestling ring. Why? Knuckles are bony and hard. If you're hit with a fist, there's not a lot of noise, but there could be a lot of pain. Instead of fists, wrestlers tend to use their forearms. The thick flesh makes a slapping sound when it hits, and the flesh softens the blow for both wrestlers.

If you look closely, you'll notice that wrestlers normally hit with the wide portion of their arms. The narrow, outside edge of the arm has bone close to the surface, while the wide section is better padded, enabling wrestlers to put a lot of motion into an attack, make a lot of noise, and do little damage.

When a closed fist is used, the punch is pulled up just before impact. Contact is made, sometimes, but with little power behind the punch. Some wrestlers don't perform this move convincingly. A close inspection of fist punching will sometimes reveal that no contact is really made. The difficulty of faking a fist punch makes the move less desirable than slaps, chops, and forearm attacks.

Slapping is easy. An open-hand slap makes a lot of noise and only stings. The slap can turn a wrestler's skin red, adding to the excitement of a match. Chops work in a similar fashion. If you keep your eye on a chop right to the end, you may see the edge of the hand being turned at the last moment, to result in a slap. It looks like a chop, sounds like a slap, and adds intensity for the audience's benefit.

How bad does it hurt when a wrestler has his head rammed into a turnbuckle? Not much. The padding on the turnbuckles is very thick; it cushions blows extremely well. It's one of the softest places in the ring. Flexibility and padding make the turnbuckles a safe place to put on a big show. But sometimes the padding slips and part of the turnbuckle is exposed. If a wrestler hits an exposed turnbuckle, real damage can be done.

Captain Lou's Corner

To make the action look real, wrestlers have to be highly trained and highly skilled. And while it's obvious that watching a pro is one way to pick up pointers, a less obvious but equally valuable learning tool is watching the *bad* wrestlers. You can get an idea of what *not* to do that way.

Wrestle Mania

In a recent match, a wrestler with long hair was on the mat. His opponent grabbed him by his hair with both hands. The downed wrestler reached up and locked his hands with those of his opponent. Then, the long-haired wrestler was lifted, apparently by his hair, and whirled around in the ring.

If this move had been real-real, the pain would have been excruciating. What was the secret? The wrestler with the hair had his hands locked over the wrists of the other wrestler. It looked as though he was struggling to get free, but he was probably supporting his weight and being swung around by his arms, rather than his hair. It was a clean, good-looking stunt—a sure sign of experienced pro wrestlers.

It's a Bird! It's a Plane! No, It's a 350-Pound Flying Wrestler!

There was a time when the ropes existed to keep wrestlers in the ring. Now, the ropes are a part of a skilled wrestler's arsenal. The ropes are used for bouncing, throat drops, and most often as a jumping-off spot for aerial acrobatics suitable for a carnival.

One wrestler recently managed three complete rotations of his balled-up body between the time he left the top rope and the time he landed—splat!—on his challenger, who was flat on the mat at the time. Lying on the mat and seeing some bruiser crashing down on you isn't pretty, but pro wrestlers see it often. How can big men jump on each other from great heights without crushing internal organs and breaking bones? Very carefully.

There are a number of techniques for accomplishing successful jumps. One is the near-miss. This is a landing that is executed to look like a direct hit but in fact is not. The flying wrestler has landed extremely close to the opponent, without hitting his body.

Another way is to make landings look real but feel (relatively) painless is to land flesh-to-flesh. The jumping wrestler's knees, elbows, and other hard and pointy parts don't lead the way in a flying fall. Instead, the wrestlers go belly to belly. When doing this, most of the power of the jump is absorbed by the jumping wrestler as his hands and knees hit the canvas.

Body Slam

Boxing rings do not contain springs. This makes it more difficult for wrestlers who perform in boxing rings to execute crowd-pleasing falls and bounces off the rings. There's no bounce, and the fall is going to hurt—a lot.

A lot of wrestling rings have springs under them, which make it easier for falls to look more devastating. Seeing a wrestler bounce off the canvas is impressive—it looks like the wrestler must have hit really hard to bounce so high. In reality, the spring aids in the illusion, and it helps to absorb the impact.

Flying wrestlers have to be accurate, or someone will get hurt. A good example of a stunt gone bad occurred during a match between Wladek "Killer" Kowalski and Yukon Eric in 1954. Kowalski came off the ropes in a flying leap. When he landed with his famed knee drop, he got more than he bargained for. Kowalski's knee made contact with Yukon Eric's ear and ripped it off. This was no theatrical performance; it was real. Serious injuries can, and sometimes do, occur when wrestlers become airborne.

Getting a Leg Up

I've said it before: Of all the action in the ring, leg work is likely to be the most real. Legs are a good target for wrestlers. Many submission holds involve the restraint of a person's leg or legs. Wrestlers use their legs as weapons, and their legs are used against them to force them to forfeit a match. When you see a wrestler who has his legs bent backwards, you can assume it is real. There are no tricks for leg bending.

The physiology of the legs makes them a great target for impressive moves and crippling holds. For example, the thigh has a lot of meat around the bone, making it a good contact point for a leg drop. The flesh acts as padding and protects both wrestlers. Another way to make impressive leg drops without doing much damage is to land with the back of the knee on the contact spot. The knee can bend moments before impact to lessen the blow to the wrestler being attacked.

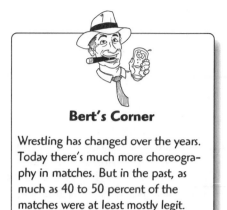

Bert's Corner

Wrestling has changed over the years. Today there's much more choreography in matches. But in the past, as much as 40 to 50 percent of the matches were at least mostly legit.

Knee drops can be painful if not executed properly. Having a 300-pound wrestler land on your stomach with an extended knee would be devastating. And the wrestler under attack is not the only one in danger. A wrestler making a knee drop has to be careful; knees can be hurt easily and are extremely painful. The key is to execute a near miss—just like a fist punch.

Turning Up the Volume

The use of sound to amplify a fight dates back to ancient times. Martial artists grunt, yell, or scream as they make their moves. For wrestling fans, hearing, as well as seeing, is believing. Don't believe it? Watch a televised match with the sound turned down. You'll *see* the action, but the match won't have nearly the impact it would if the sound was cranked up.

Wrestlers and their managers and promoters are all well aware of the importance that sound has on a match. The sound of pain is the big pull for a match. The more it *sounds* like it hurt, the more it must have. So wrestlers have had to come up with ways to make matches sound painful.

In Your Face

Wrestlers try to hit the mat with their feet to make a lot of noise. They land on their feet, tuck their chins, and try to catch blows from the other wrestler with their shoulders and backs.

The ring itself is a good starting point for sound effects. If you take a wrestling ring, put springs under it, create a hollow cavity for sound to echo from, and put big men in it to bounce off the mat, you've got sound and visuals. A big wrestler hitting the mat makes a lot of noise. The wrestler bounces for visual effect, and the sound of the impact is monstrous.

Slapping, in its many forms, is another way to get a lot of sound out of a match. Open slaps make a lot of noise. So do meaty forearms hitting flesh. Flat, full contact makes the most noise.

What else do wrestlers do for sound effects? They sometimes hit one another with metal chairs. The sound and visual effects are thrilling. And, it should be said, the chairs are real.

Screaming and grunting are a natural. Wrestlers cry out in mock pain. They screech and holler as they make and miss their moves, such as when they catapult from the top ring rope and miss their target, ending up with a face full of mat. Growls and muttering add to the excitement. So, of course, do the insults that wrestlers hurl at each other throughout the match.

Kicking Is a Habit

Kicking, which is unheard of in classical wrestling, is common in pro wrestling. Looking at the heavy ring boots worn by most wrestlers, any spectator would agree that a full-contact kick would be, uh, detrimental to one's health. Certainly, the wrestlers pack enough power in their lower bodies to do extreme damage with their boots. So, how do they kick so hard without hurting anyone? Simple!

There are a few different kick moves in pro wrestling:

Captain Lou's Corner

You usually kick with the inside of your foot, the instep of the foot. Sometimes the toe of the foot is used. Kicking today is much tamer than it used to be. In the older days, guys would get mad and kick hard and real.

➤ **The near miss.** You'll see plenty of these when inexperienced wrestlers take to the mat. And I mean *see* them, if the newcomer is not skilled at making his moves look real. Near-miss kicks aren't particularly impressive, so they're the least effective in terms of crowd appeal.

➤ **Contact, but controlled.** Some kicks actually connect with the opponent's body, but a skilled wrestler does this in such a way that there's little risk and pain. Knowledgeable wrestlers use the inside, arch portion of their boots to kick with. Kicking with the inside of the foot—and taking the power out of the kick at the last second—is very effective. It looks real because it *is*, except that the pain is not as great as the audience imagines.

➤ **Contact, but careful placement.** The third technique is to kick, but to kick in safe locations. For example, kicking someone in the kneecap could easily result in a painful and crippling injury. But, kicking the knee from the side won't do much damage when the wrestlers execute the stunt together. Kicks to the thighs, biceps, gut, or shoulders, if properly placed, are also acceptable.

As long as the wrestlers involved are fully trained, experienced, and working in tandem, a lot of kicking can go on without serious injury. But a single flying kick to the throat that's improperly executed could spell disaster.

Slamming and Jamming, Again

A whole lot of slamming and jamming goes on during a pro-wrestling match. The wrestlers are put in awkward positions and abused in ways that would cripple or kill lesser humans. If all the moves were real, even the biggest, toughest wrestlers couldn't hold up under the pain and destruction.

Not to worry—there is a mixture of real and staged work going on during the more colorful slams and jams. For example, a wrestler who *really* suffered a pile driver (see Chapter 19) probably wouldn't survive. His neck would likely be broken, or at least badly jammed. Luckily, pile drivers are *staged* stunts.

As are some of the other impressive moves that you see happen in almost every match. Fans are awed when they see smaller wrestlers hoist up heavyweights and throw them around a ring. But watch closely—you'll probably see that the two wrestlers are working together to sell the stunt. The big wrestler will push off from the mat, helping the smaller one get the momentum he needs to execute the stunt. Successfully putting this kind of move over on the fans takes real skill, timing, and a fine sense of balance.

Body slams are a big part of practically every wrestling match. Pro wrestlers, for the most part, have trained in the proper ways to fall without injury—that's one of the first things they learned in training school. Think of them as stunt men. They tuck their chins, roll their shoulders, and prepare their bodies for as soft a landing as possible. Don't think that the fall doesn't sting a bit, but don't buy into all of the mock pain and suffering, either. A true professional learns how to master the moves and turn them into an art form—you never guess that he's taken the sting out of his fall, and you really buy into his agonized groans.

There *is* magic in pro wrestling, and it's what keeps the fans coming back for more, week after week. Even when fans know that the illusions are there, many of them love to figure out what is real and what is staged—for these fans, figuring out what's going on *behind* the staged show is what watching wrestling is all about. It can be hard to separate the reality from the scripted moves. Most fans, however, simply settle back and enjoy watching their favorite, and their hated, wrestlers meet in the middle of the mat. For the duration of the action, they willingly suspend their sense of disbelief.

Which is probably the best way to go, when you think about it. Accept pro wrestling for what it is—the most action-packed entertainment form available today—and enjoy it. If you ever feel cheated because it's not all real, you're just not getting into the spirit of the show. Think about the hard work good wrestlers put in to give you the most bang for your buck. Their efforts are strenuous, dangerous, and complex—they are true athletes, even if some (even most) of the stunts and outcomes are staged. Good wrestlers deserve full credit for all they do to entertain their many fans.

The Least You Need to Know

➤ Wrestling isn't all special effects—it's skill and athleticism mixed in with real show-biz savvy.

➤ The best wrestlers use skillful showmanship to put their acts over to the audience.

➤ Just like with movie stuntmen, wrestlers run the risk of serious injury even when performing well-rehearsed moves.

➤ The hooplah and showmanship of wrestling isn't the problem, it's the point— fans don't care about "is it fake" but about the whole event experience.

Chapter 21

Double Your Pleasure, Double Your Pain: Tag Teams

> ## In This Chapter
>
> ➤ How tag-team matches are different from one-on-one bouts
>
> ➤ What makes a good tag-team player?
>
> ➤ The art of distraction in tag-team matches
>
> ➤ Famous tag teams

Wrestling matches are generally fought one-on-one. But when tag teams enter the ring, there are at least four people prepared to do battle.

While most matches in the squared ring are solo matches, tag-team duos are always in demand. There is room for both types of matches on the wrestling circuit, and fans like their variety. In fact, their over-the-top theatrics and action make them one of wrestling's most popular features. In this chapter, we'll show you what tag-team wrestling is all about.

A Brief History of Tag Teams

The very first tag team match was held in San Francisco sometime in 1901, but it didn't make much of an impact at the time. Wrestling fans usually date the effective beginning of the tag team to three decades later—1937 or 1938, in Houston. That's when a new style of wrestling match—called variously "Texas Tornado" or "Australian" tag team matches began.

The guy who usually gets credited for this innovation was Houston promoter Morris Siegel—well, really, his nephew. The story goes that the Siegel nephew was sitting in the john when he was struck by an inspiration—if you can have one-on-one wrestling, why not two-on-two? He shared this bolt from the blue with his uncle, and the rest is wrestling history.

An Idea Whose Time Had Come

It didn't take long for the concept to spread far beyond Houston—especially since this was the era when promoters were trying *anything* to get Depression-depressed fans back into the arenas. And it got expanded—if two were good, why not more? Eventually the "Battle Royale" came into being, where as many as 20 wrestlers would all pile into the ring and the one left standing in the end would be the winner.

Tag Teams Come Into Their Own

The innovation that really turned tag-teams into a keeper of an idea for wrestling was a simple one: Have one wrestler inside the ropes, and one outside, at all times. Initially, they were also restricted by being tethered to a turnbuckle, but that particular detail has long disappeared from the scene.

Wrestle Mania

Tag team matches were often used as the novelty act to open a show, and midgets were often used in them for comic relief. A famous duo, the Bushwackers, were the prototype for this kind of act. These New Zealanders were funny looking, dressed alike, and began a match by licking each other's head for luck. They looked harmless, but they got their start as the Sheepherders—a hardcore blood and guts tandem that worked with barbed wire and other foreign objects.

The entire concept of tag team wrestling changed in the 1950s when Vince McMahon Sr. came up with the idea of teaming two solo headliners—Antonino Rocca and Miguel Perez—to capture the fancy of Latino fans. From that point onward, tag team matches were no longer thought of as novelty acts but became a major part of every wrestling show.

Mix and Match Magic

Coming up with just the right mix for a successful tag team isn't easy. I should know, I've managed enough of them in my time. You have to look for the right combination of sizes, strength, and wrestling styles. And you have to make sure that they have drawing power as a pair. Most of all, the wrestlers have to be able to operate smoothly, as a single unit.

One of the best tag teams of the early TV era was known as The Fabulous Kangaroos—Al Costello and Roy Heffernan. They were both very proficient single wrestlers, but their ability to work together made them *great* as a team.

One-Plus-One Can Be Better Than Two

The synergy of a well put together tag team can make all the difference in the world. Look at me, for example. I was never a particularly talented single wrestler. But when I got paired up with Tony Altimore in The Sicilians, we became much more popular. Well—with most people, anyway.

Vince McMahon Sr. was the one who matched us up, and the one to give us our name. It was supposed to be a play off the TV series *The Untouchables*, which was very popular at the time. And we played our roles for all we were worth—dressing in black tux jackets, fedoras, the whole nine yards. On our first TV interview, we both held up our black-gloved hands to the camera and shouted "MAFIA!"

Not a good idea. When we went back to our hotel after the interview we were met by a very special welcoming committee—which included "Tough" Tony Accardo, the head of the Chicago "family." Not one to travel alone, he was escorted by five or six of his enforcers.

After ascertaining that we were both Italian (a lucky thing, that), Accardo proceeded to lay a few home truths out for us: "Well, my boy…there is no such thing as the Mafia. We're businessmen." And so forth. He then strongly advised us never to wear black gloves anymore, and never, ever, *ever* to use the word Mafia again. Having got a good look at Accardo's companions, we were more than happy to comply.

But that little unpleasantness aside, we had a great run as a team—one of the many popular combos of the 1950s and 1960s. That seemed to be the way of it in the wrestling world back then: take two wrestlers who weren't particulary talented on their own and put them together—bingo! instant popularity with the crowds.

Captain Lou's Corner

I look for a certain indefinable "something" in my teams, and I must be finding it because I've had 19 world championship teams. My first was The Mongols, then there were Tarzan Tyler and Luke Graham, King Curtis and Baron Sciluna, The Lumberjacks, the two Black Jacks (Lanza and Mulligan), The Moondogs, The British Bulldogs, The Headshrinkers, The Wild Samoans, and on, and on, and on….

The Celebrity Effect

As tag teams grew in popularity, a new gimmick was added to the mix: celebrity guest team members. Mr. T—then riding the wave of his popularity on the hit TV series *The A Team* was one of the first. His pairing with Hulk Hogan against Rowdy Roddy Piper and Paul "Mr. Wonderful" Orndorff was a big hit at the first *Wrestlemania*.

Hogan's celebrity pairings didn't stop there, of course. Much more recently, he partnered up with the bad boy of basketball, Chicago Bull Dennis Rodman, to take on Diamond Dallas Page and his own celebrity playmate, Karl Malone of the Utah Jazz.

Hitching Tag Team Wagons to Pop Culture Helps, Too

Wrestlers take their inspiration for persona from the pop culture at large all the time— so why not tag teams? The Road Warriors (also known as the Legion of Doom), were for the better part of the 1980s the biggest and baddest tag team on the planet. They drew their inspiration from the Mad Max series of movies. And the Fabulous Freebirds, out of Atlanta, Georgia, took their name from the ultimate encore rock tune by Lynard Skynard.

Wrestle Mania

The Steiner Brothers (Rick and Scott), both out of the University of Michigan's wrestling program, are a great example of tag-teamwork at its best. They've wrestled for the WCW, the WWF, and briefly for the ECW. Now they're back in the WCW, but this time they've split up. Scott has turned evil, and now goes by the name "Big Daddy Pump." Rick has stayed the same simple soul he always was, and wonders why his brother has turned on him.

Together Forever? Not

What was once joined together can always be put asunder, of course. Especially if it's good for the storyline. The most famous tag-team split up was the one that occurred between Bruno Sammartino and Cowboy Bill Watts, back in 1965. Pitted against Smasher Sloan and The Golden Terror, Sammartino was downed by the dastardly duo and reaching desperately toward his partner for help—but Watts inexplicably pulled back out of Bruno's reach, leaving his partner to get the whey beaten out of him by the two baddies. When the bout finally ended, Watts came out to center ring, where Bruno was still lying prone—and *kicked* him.

Of course, the grudge matches between Watts and Sammartino that came out of this whole incident were legendary, and in the end Watts got his comeuppance. At their last meeting, Sammartino mutilated Watts' cowboy regalia and kicked his former partner into submission, roaring: "We'll see who does the kicking and gets away with it."

The Latest Trend—Gangs and Outlaws

The standard tag teams that began as novelties and grew to be major attractions in their own right are no longer as prevalent as they were in the 1970s and 1980s. The big trend today is for storylines featuring gangs. Now the promoters are emphasizing larger groups, like the nWo and the Nations of Domination. As someone who has worked with tag teams—as wrestler and as manager—for much of my career, I think that's just a shame.

Singles or Doubles?

Today, some wrestlers specialize in tag-team wrestling. Others play in both single and tag-team matches. It can be difficult for wrestlers who made their names as part of a tag-team duo to break out as solo wrestlers; it's sort of like an actor becoming typecast in a single role.

There is no rule that says a wrestler must choose between tag-team events and solo events. Logically, however, it is often best for the wrestlers and their teams if they concentrate their efforts on team play. Moving back and forth from solo to tag matches can be confusing.

And one-on-one wrestling and tag-team matches require markedly different skills and techniques. Let's look at the differences between one-on-one and tag-team matches more closely.

The Need for Speed

Speed is one of the most important elements of a successful tag team. A wrestler has to move fast to get from one side of the ring to the other for a tag with a partner. If a wrestler isn't fast enough, his opponent will prevent him from making a tag. When this happens, the match turns into more of a solo bout.

Granted, in modern wrestling, tagging up is not considered a necessity for a partner to enter the ring. But, by the rules, a tag must be made. It is, however, one of those rules that is made to be winked at.

There's another reason why speed is essential in a tag-team match. Fast wrestlers can evade big wrestlers. They can use the ropes to launch flying attacks, and can roll with the punches (so to speak) more easily than less agile wrestlers.

Captain Lou's Corner

Quick tagging is about the most important part of winning a tag-team match. Speed is essential.

Team Players

Tag-team players must also be able to anticipate the moves and needs of their partners. Learning to time moves, jumps, and tackles is important; the wrestlers on a team must also know how to pace themselves so that they stay fresh in the ring. Tag team players must know when to make a tag, and when to relieve a partner for a rest.

Until a team has worked together during numerous matches, the rough edges show during a bout. But, wrestlers who do battle regularly with the same team partners fare much better. This is why some wrestlers settle into tag-team matches and don't go solo.

Breaking All the Rules

Another feature of many tag team matches is their grand tradition of flamboyant rule breaking. It's easier to flaunt the rules in a tag-team match—while the ref is monitoring one dueling duo, the other wrestlers in the ring have a huge chance to cheat. The referee is outnumbered, and simply cannot see everything that's going on.

Wrestlers know this and take advantage of the opportunities afforded by it. Good tag wrestlers know that distracting a referee can be crucial in deciding a match.

If a tag team has a manager or valet to help them, their distracting deeds will grow. Wrestlers who do not have ringside help have to devise their own strategies for getting a referee to look the other way. (This is another reason why wrestlers who work together regularly tend to be more successful. They have the time and experience needed to pull off major masquerades.)

Distractions work best when a third party can be counted on to make a ruckus that a referee will turn to face. In this way, both members of the tag team are free to damage their opponents. (It was said earlier that fast wrestlers are an asset to a tag team. Distractions are another reason why: It takes a fast wrestler to jump into the ring, do his damage, and return to the other side of the ropes before an official spots the illegal activity.)

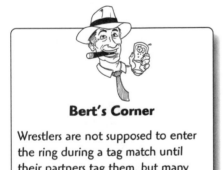

Bert's Corner

Wrestlers are not supposed to enter the ring during a tag match until their partners tag them, but many wrestlers jump into the ring early. It's considered a necessity when wrestling the villains of the sport.

Consider this example: One wrestler is nearly pinned by another. The referee is watching closely and ready to count. The partner of the wrestler on the mat is also watching, waiting for a tag or a decision to rush into the ring for a save. He doesn't notice the manager of the opposing team coming up from behind him with a metal chair. All of a sudden, the ruthless manager whacks the wrestler's knee with the edge of the chair. The waiting wrestler falls from the apron writhing in pain. Meanwhile, the ref has not seen anything, so the manager's team is not penalized.

As the manager slips back around the ring, the wrestler on the mat squirms loose and looks to tag his partner. But his partner is not there to tag, thanks to the cheating manager. Worn out, the wrestler loses the match. He might well have won, had it not been for the devious manager.

There are other sneaky moves that can lead to tag-team victory. Someone may attack a wrestler who is outside the ring. A valet might distract a referee to allow a wrestler from outside the ring to come inside and inflict damage on an opponent. For example, while one wrestler is held in submission on the mat, a valet may distract the referee while another wrestler leaps off the top rope and crushes the man on the mat.

Another popular (and illegal) tactic is for other wrestlers to join in the game. If other wrestlers decide to enter the ring to save their friends, a large number of bustling bodies can be found within the ropes at any given time. During a tag-team match, there can easily be as many as five men in the ring.

With the poor enforcement of ring rules, tag matches have become more of a gang riot than a wrestling match. There are some wrestlers who play it straight, but their observance of the rules often results in lost matches. It's a shame, but it seems that cheating during a tag match is not only acceptable, but necessary.

Matching Up the Maniacs

The best tag-team players are matched closely to their partners. Good managers have an ability to put together teams that compliment each other. Their wrestling skills, their size, their speed, and their experience are all factored into a decision of making them partners in the ring. There can be times when specific wrestlers are brought together as a team for promotional purposes, but the teams that continually finish in the victory circle are carefully created.

Members of a tag team have to be willing to work in conjunction with one another. Neither wrestler can afford to showboat. It is, after all, a team effort. Some wrestlers are not willing to share the glory during a tag match. (Think of it as the basketball hero in high school who would not pass the ball to teammates.) Unless members of a tag team are willing, and able, to work together, the team will suffer.

Managers who are serious about building durable tag teams will invest a lot of time and money in the evaluation process. Wrestlers will be tested in practice matches. Sometimes the wrestlers will perform together a few times in real matches to see if they have any chemistry.

Captain Lou's Corner

Good tag-team managers film tag matches of opponents and watch them for weaknesses that can be attacked in future matches. A lot of time goes into getting to know potential opponents and putting an effective team together to beat them.

The process of creating an excellent wrestling team can take a lot of time. It can also be quite frustrating. Just because two wrestlers are excellent in their sport during solo bouts doesn't mean that they will perform perfectly as a part of a tag team.

Winning Teams

Before we talk about one of the current winning tag teams, let's take a quick look at a tag-team heading act from the recent past.

Raising Cane

March 1985 found a fearsome foursome in the wrestling ring, and they weren't all welcomed by the 22,000 fans who crowded the arena to watch the show. The Iron Sheik and Nikolai "The Russian Bear" Volkoff were getting abuse from the audience. Barry Windham and Mike Rotundo stood on the other side of the ring, ready to defend their WWF title belt. It was sure to be a fierce fight; given the political climate of the times, American fans held great distaste for the Russian and the Iranian.

The match started early, as Windham and Rotundo were exchanging last-minute glances and high-fives. The Russian Bear made his move before the bell ever rang, attacking both opponents simultaneously. Rotundo sent the Sheik flying to the mat. After a tag off, Windham used his extreme agility to leapfrog and nearly pin the Sheik. During one scuffle, Rotundo pulled the Bear's arm out of its socket. Crowd reaction was enthusiastic. It looked like the Americans would retain their belt without a doubt—but looks can be deceiving.

Up until a certain point, the match had been played mostly by the rules. As the Bear and the Sheik sensed a losing battle, though, tactics changed. The big turning point came as Rotundo got Volkoff in a submission hold that looked like it would get the job done. Thinking fast, the Sheik grabbed a cane from Fred Blassie and leapt into the ring. Windham saw the Sheik's bad intentions and entered the ring to cut him off. It was like two bighorn rams rushing each other on a mountaintop.

As the Sheik met Windham in the ring, Blassie's cane became the star of the match. The Sheik raised the cane and crashed it down over Windham's head. Splinters of wood from the cane flew into the first few rows. Windham collapsed to the mat. During all of this, the referee was concentrating on the other activity in the ring and missed the cane trick. The Sheik jumped on Windham and pinned him for a full count. In a matter of illegal moments, the Sheik had stolen the title from the Americans.

Captain Lou's Corner

I've had 18 or 19 World Tag Team Champions. I'm the leader of that. I had 23 champions all together."

It wasn't pretty. It wasn't fair. It wasn't appreciated by the crowd, but it was effective. By raising cane, the Sheik captured a championship title. This type of cheating is still prevalent in modern wrestling matches.

On the Road Again

Hawk and Animal, the Road Warriors, have never been known for their gentlemen-like tactics in the ring. Their preference for dirty tactics and win-at-all-cost ways have made them successful, but they don't fight fairly.

Many years ago, the Road Warriors faced Stan Lane and Steve Keirn (otherwise known as the Fabulous Ones) in a classic match of good versus evil. The odds might have been reasonably even—except for the third player on the Warrior's team. This, of course, was unofficial, illegal, and wrong, but it was effective.

It started fast, with the Warriors ganging up on Lane and throwing him from the ring. Keirn faced both Hawk and Animal, using karate skills to keep them at bay as Lane recovered. It didn't take much for the tag-team match to turn into a four-man brawl.

In all the excitement, Paul Ellering, the Road Warriors' manager, bashed Keirn over the head with a chair. The referee didn't see this, and when Hawk covered the motionless body of Keirn for a pin, the referee awarded the match to the Warriors. This allowed the Road Warriors to maintain possession of their AWA title belt.

The Least You Need to Know

➤ Once a novelty act, tag teams became so popular that they became major attractions in their own right.

➤ The methods used in tag-team wrestling differ from those used in solo matches.

➤ Good managers spend a lot of time in matching the right wrestlers to create a tag team.

➤ Speed is considered one of the most important qualities for a tag-team wrestler to possess.

➤ People outside the ropes, like managers and valets, often influence the outcome of tag matches.

➤ The art of distraction is the most important tool for a tag-team wrestler.

Chapter 22

Behind the Locker-Room Door

In This Chapter

➤ How wrestlers get ready in the ready room

➤ Pre-bout preparation

➤ The real fights behind the scenes

➤ The lighter side of the locker room

What really goes on in the locker rooms where pro wrestlers congregate? Millions of fans see their favorite wrestlers on TV, but they don't see inside the dressing rooms. But locker-room action can be plenty wilder than anything that goes on in the ring—some very real fights happen behind the scenes. And in addition to the fights, promoters cut deals in locker rooms and news people bombard the wrestlers with hard questions the fans never hear. Some wrestlers get on their soapboxes and lecture the other pros. Strategies are made—and so are stars.

Some locker-room talk is hostile, but most of it is friendly, funny, and basically normal. The wrestlers gripe about all the expected things, especially their accommodations. And this is where they'll brag among themselves about their latest accomplishments or trade ideas on the best places to eat in the area. They talk about women, sports, hobbies, families, and how much money they make. Sure, there's competition, but it's not all about wrestling.

It can get very crowded in a locker room. There are managers, wrestlers, promoters, photographers, journalists, valets, and others who breathe the moist, dirty air and sidestep the wet towels on the floor. The behind-the-scenes antics of the players are integral to the complexion of pro wrestling. So step right up, and we'll swing open the doors to the locker room just before a major event.

The Dressing Room

You can pretty much guess the obvious reasons for the locker room—or dressing room or *ready room*—it's called all those things. The name doesn't much matter, and it doesn't tell the whole story anyway. A lot more than changing into costume goes on behind those locker room doors.

Fighting Words

The locker room is sometimes called a **ready room,** because that's where the wrestlers prepare themselves before a match.

In Your Face

Fans can usually get autographs *after* the show. The best place to wait, however, is by the exit door. Don't hang out around the locker room door—it gets pretty congested there after a bout.

What's called the locker room—singular—is almost always really a suite of rooms. Along with the main changing area there's usually a few offices mixed in, where high rollers have a place to cut their deals, relax, and take on the media. Accommodations are usually pretty basic, too. You won't see wrestlers soaking in saunas or hot tubs, smoking cigars, and drinking their favorite cocktails while waiting for their curtain call. These places are like locker rooms throughout the sporting world: hot, wet, cramped, and smelly. There are, of course, some exceptions to this general rule—and believe me, when you get an arena with above par accommodations, wrestlers really appreciate the change.

Separate Accommodations

People in the wrestling industry prefer to have one ready room for the good-guy wrestlers (the faces), and a separate place for the villains (heels) to get ready in. The main reason for separate rooms is to maintain the mythology of the wrestling match. You don't want the public to see the faces hanging out and sharing restaurant tips with their sworn enemies. It just ruins the whole effect of their carefully established feud. But that's just what usually happens—long-established opponents often are good buddies behind the scenes. You just don't want to let the public see it when it happens.

Since in the ready room there's no public audience, the wrestlers and managers can let down the show for awhile. They don't have to live up to their fans' cherished images of them. So good guys can turn bad, and bad guys can even be (gasp) nice.

Roll Call

It may not be a public area, but that doesn't change the fact that the pro wrestling locker room can fill up quickly, especially before and after major matches. Exactly who can be found in a locker room? The list can get long, so let's see who's who, and why they are allowed into the inner sanctum.

Ladies and Gentlemen, the Star of the Show!

Of course, the star wrestlers will get ready for the match in the locker room. But there are always more wrestlers than the actual card calls for. In addition to the wrestlers who are scheduled to perform, some standby wrestlers are almost always in attendance as well. There's too much riding on every major match to take a chance on running the show without emergency replacements. If a scheduled wrestler is injured or fails to show up, one of these standbys is available to fill in at a moment's notice.

And then there's always the possibility that wrestlers who aren't on the official schedule might be planning a little "unofficial" participation—such as rushing from the dressing room into the ring to save a scheduled wrestler, one of their buddies, when he gets into trouble. This type of save is pretty commonplace, and it's almost always planned in advance.

The locker room might also house a few ambitious hopefuls waiting for a break, or those with only a few matches under their belts who are looking for a shot at a bigger payday. By being in the dressing room, ready to rumble, the wrestlers waiting to climb the ladder might be called on to fill in on short notice. If they do well, they're likely to get work in future matches.

Attendants to His Majesty...

Then, of course, there are the managers. We naturally gravitate to the locker rooms where our players are hanging out. We have to—it's our job to keep our men pumped up and ready, and to work out any details about the match that haven't yet been settled. It's all part of the job.

A lot of people don't see wrestling managers as much more than sidekick showmen who occasionally pop into the ring to help their wrestlers by clobbering the opponent with a chair when the ref isn't looking. And we certainly do a lot of that. But while wrestling managers may not have the same tactical duties as their counterparts in the boxing arena, that doesn't mean we don't have *anything* useful to contribute. Good managers pay close attention to their wrestlers' needs. Successful managers, and I'm speaking for myself here, know that there's more to managing a champion than running around the ring during a match.

Promoters come around dressing rooms to cut deals and to schedule events—they're the guys who get the offices in the locker room area. They also make suggestions, or demands, for how a match is to turn out. Managers talk to promoters in the locker rooms to get bookings for their wrestlers, to

Captain Lou's Corner

The "No Admittance" sign on the locker room door means exactly that. NO ADMITTANCE. Don't try to insinuate yourself into the dressing room unless someone has asked you to come in. It's our sanctuary, and it's fiercely protected.

suggest match ideas, and so forth. A lot of business is done in the confines of musty locker rooms.

Valets are regulars in and around the ready rooms, too. Their close association with wrestlers keeps them where the action is. They also pull in photographers for photo opportunities. Male wrestlers and female valets in the same dressing room? Sure. Come on, they're all adults, and it's strictly business.

Mixed Media

Photographers are a constant in and around pro-wrestling locker rooms. Most professional wrestlers are happy to pose for pictures before and after their matches. After all, the pictures are going to find their way into wrestling magazines and other media, and hey—that's good for a guy's career! Without photographers, pro wrestlers would have a much tougher time getting fan acknowledgement. And all those wrestling magazines would be a lot skimpier on the illustrations front.

Journalists, like photographers, roam around dressing rooms in search of juicy interviews with pro wrestlers, managers, promoters, and valets. While you won't find many major news journalists hanging around hoping to write about the average match, there'll always be one or two for a truly major event, and entertainment reporters are always on the scene.

Finally, there's the catch-all crowd: friends and invited guests of the wrestlers. These could be just about anybody from celebrities, to business associates, to lady friends—anybody who's got an interest in seeing behind the scenes.

Bert's Corner

One common topic of conversation in the locker room is what to do after the wrestling days are done. One wrestler who found life after the ring was Abdullah the Butcher. This obese villain was known for his bloodbath matches. Once retired, he opened "Abdullah the Butcher's House of Ribs and Chinese Food" in Atlanta, Georgia.

Making Matches

Like I said, locker room business is about more than changing into costume. Managers and promoters do a lot of business in the locker rooms. There are probably more deals made in the dressing rooms than in any office. In addition to making new deals, the managers and promoters structure matches that are already made. New gimmicks are added at the last minute, moves are discussed, and changes in who wins and loses can be made in the dressing room prior to a match. Wrestling is a very fluid sport, and good promoters and managers will always tailor an event to suit the needs and desires of the fans—because pleasing the crowd is what it's all about.

It takes a lot of planning to stage a successful match, and that means that the wrestlers, managers, and promoters all together just before show time can be more than a little beneficial. A lot of what goes on in the ring is staged, as you well know by now, and it's in the locker room where the plans for the match are hatched, the details are worked out, and the instructions are handed down.

This is especially true for the average, bread-and-butter wrestlers. Big-name stars may know for weeks in advance how a match is expected to play out. They might even practice moves during training sessions to prepare for a major match. But for your average match, the wrestlers are generally not in on the storyline in advance. They're usually going to have to improvise at the match itself—so the locker room confab about how to do the job is extremely helpful. A little planning can substantially reduce the risk of injury.

Finally, the locker room is one of those places where managers may try to recruit new wrestlers—or even steal away some other manager's star. When that happens, the action in the locker room can turn very real.

My Mascara, Please

Do you think wrestling personalities like Sting and Elizabeth share makeup in the dressing room? Hey, Sting's stuff is good. He can put on one heck of a performance and his opponents often run before his makeup does. Obviously, there's some dressing going on in the dressing room. And, face painting is a part of the preparation for some wrestlers.

The personal hygiene routines wrestlers go through in preparation for the match involves much more than slapping on the greasepaint. Muscle men often shave their chest hair, and slather oil on their skin to make their bodies shine. Some wrestlers tape their wrists, ankles, or fingers—although the tape work isn't usually as important for wrestling as it is for boxing. Some wrestlers who wear complex, eye-catching outfits need a surprising amount of time to slip on, strap in, and zip up.

Some prep work doesn't have anything to do with clothes, oil, or makeup. For some wrestlers, the pre-match preparation is more mental than physical. Concentration is key to any truly great athletic performance, and that's as true for wrestling as it is in any other sport. Different strokes for different folks—every wrestler has his or her own way to get into the "zone." Some wrestlers get there by punching lockers. Others get it by hitting themselves. Sitting and meditating may sound a little too Zen for these big bruisers, but lots of wrestlers go the quiet, contemplative route when preparing in the minutes before a match. Others talk with their managers, who are only too happy to help pump their wrestlers up. Pre-bout preparation can be as unique as the wrestlers themselves, but the dressing room is where most of it goes on.

Wrestle Mania

George "The Animal" Steel had an interesting dressing room ritual. He would fill his mouth with Chicklets and chew them to turn his tongue green. He also had sharp fangs for teeth and he would chew apart the turnbuckle padding. Between the fangs and the green tongue, The Animal got a lot of camera attention in the ring.

Every Punch Counts

Wrestlers sometimes get it on for real in the locker room. There are shooters in the ring who wrestle for real, but the scuffles in the dressing room can be much more dangerous. This is due, in part, to the conditions in the ready room. Hard floors, sharp edges, and no excuses abound in the locker room. Some of the most destructive injuries, not to mention some deaths, like when promoter Jose Gonzales stabbed Bruiser Brody to death, have happened in the dressing room—a place where most wrestlers aren't prepared for an attack.

Granted, most arguments don't get beyond shoving matches, but sometimes the violence is serious. Certain topics tend to spark more fights than others and, as you might imagine, at the top of the list is women. Whether a valet, a manager, a girl-friend, a wife, or an ex-wife, women are frequent contributors to disagreements between wrestlers.

Another common reason for locker-room bouts is the status of certain wrestlers. A pushed wrestler, one who is being spotlighted and moved up the list towards championships, might be challenged by a wrestler who is not pushed but feels he should be. This type of confrontation can't take place in the ring, because big money is at stake, so the wrestlers sometimes try to prove themselves in the privacy of the dressing room. If this happens, the standby wrestlers are likely to be rooting for someone to get hurt, so they can get in the ring. Pro wrestling may be more entertainment than true sport, but it's a rough business any way you cut it.

Only the wrestlers with the biggest names and public profiles can get away with being disruptive in a big way while in the locker room. Lesser wrestlers will find themselves replaced quickly if they get too rowdy. This helps to keep altercations to a minimum, but the action in the dressing room can be pretty intense.

Clowns to the Left, Jokers to the Right

It's not all fighting in the dressing room. Sometimes the wrestlers loosen up and play practical jokes, but this can also lead to a fight.

Jake would always have a snake rented for his match, and of course he'd bring it to the locker room. One time, some other wrestlers brought in a machete and whacked the snake out in the bag. When Jake came in, the snake was gone. It probably cost about $5,000 to replace it.

Then there was the time S.T. Jones had a run-in with a remote-controlled car and got hurt. Jones was in the bathroom, minding his own business. Some midget wrestlers had brought a remote-controlled car into the dressing room. They also had some M-80 fireworks. The midgets put three M-80s in the car and ran the car from about 20 feet away from the stall. Jones saw the car come under the door and tried to stand up. The M-80s went off and blew a hole in his leg. Jones was ready to kill somebody. (Nowadays, Jones runs a restaurant in the Bronx.)

Dressing rooms are a sanctuary for wrestlers and other members of the industry. The locker room is also a place to relieve stress and to keep things cool between wrestlers. Sometimes there are fights, but most of the activity in a dressing room is fun-filled or purely business. The ready room is much more than just a place to dress.

Captain Lou's Corner

All kinds of crazy stuff can go on in the dressing room. Wrestlers may hide their foes' (and friends') outfits. When the clock is ticking down to ring time and you can't find your tights, you have a problem. There are also wrestlers who like to shoot behind-the-scenes photos that no wrestler would want to see in print. Threats of blackmail might be made to change the outcome of a match, but it's all in good fun.

The Least You Need to Know

➤ The industry prefers to have separate locker rooms for faces and heels.

➤ You'll find a lot more than wrestlers in the locker room. Managers, valets, promoters, and media reps all congregate in the locker room.

➤ Many big pro-wrestling deals are set up in the locker room.

➤ Real fights sometimes break out in the locker room.

➤ Practical jokes and tricks are often played out in the locker room.

Part 5

Beyond the Squared Circle: Wrestling Extras

The world of wrestling is vast; there's much more to the industry than the action in the ring. There are entire peripheral industries related to, but not exactly part of, the wrestling you watch on Monday nights. For example, there's a whole world of media dedicated to providing you with all the latest and greatest information on your favorite stars. From newsprint to radio to the World Wide Web, information and excitement is ready and waiting for you. Chapter 23 gives you all you need to know to keep yourself up to date and in constant touch with the world of wrestling.

And there's gold in them thar' wrestlers, even for people who don't own a TV network. That gold is to be found in collectibles. Wrestling has spawned a lively market in everything from autographs to action figures, clothing to comic books. Whether you just like having memorabilia of your favorite stars around or you're into collecting as an investment, you'll want to check out Chapter 24. It's full of tips on what's collectible, where to find it, and how to turn it into cash.

Come on, roll up your sleeves and enter the ring of Part 4 with us.

Chapter 23

The Press: Tracking the Wild Warriors of the Roped Jungle

In This Chapter

➤ Rockum-sockum radio shows

➤ Magazines of mayhem

➤ Newsletters by snail mail

➤ Siphoning off the cyber sheets

➤ Digests and other sources of information

From the time when news was exclusively delivered in print to today when it comes in a variety of formats, wrestling coverge by the media has undergone a radical change. Time was, you had to follow the news through small columns in the paper or maybe pick up a radio broadcast if you were lucky enough to live near a station that covered the sport.

These days, however, keeping track of pro wrestlers is pretty easy. If you have access to the Internet and World Wide Web, you can follow all of your favorite wrestlers day by day or minute by minute. Magazines devoted to pro wrestling are plentiful. And while there are very few newspapers that are willing to provide regular space for the coverage of wrestling news and matches, there are plenty of radio stations and newsletters out there that are more than willing to pick up the slack.

In Chapter 16 you learned about the role of television and other media as purveyors of wrestling matches themselves. But that's not the only role the media plays. In these pages you'll learn a bit about the history of wrestling coverage. But more importantly you'll learn about all the print and internet sources available to you, so you can tap into all the information out there and follow the shows, stars, and events on your own.

Keeping a Finger on Wrestling's Pulse

Staying in touch with what's going on in the world of pro wrestling has probably never been easier. The Internet, not to mention homepages and other Web sites, and chat rooms by the score, have opened up an almost unbelievable opportunity for wrestling fans. There are official sites of all the major promotions to visit, and countless personal sites dedicated to wrestling. Beyond the World Wide Web there are also some talk shows on television that keep fans up to date on pro wrestlers. When you put together all the wrestling-oriented media, you'll quickly see that you could make just staying on top of the news of the industry into a full time job.

Captain Lou's Corner

One of the best looks at wrestling in the good ol' days is the no-holds-barred book by Lou Thesz. Called *Hooker: An Authentic Wrestler's Adventures Inside the Bizarre World of Pro Wrestling*, it's available for $25.00, postpaid, directly from the author. Write Lou Thesz at P. O. Box 7467, Granby Street, Norfolk, VA 23504.

The Relationship Between the Press and Wrestling: A Brief History

Once upon a time, back before the Great Flood, wrestling was big news and dominated the sports pages of the newspapers. Of course, back then there were far fewer forms of entertainment available, so wrestling had a lot less competition.

All of that changed in 1910, when the press got word that Frank Gotch beat George Hackenschmidt by means most foul—suddenly reporters found themselves outraged that all in wrestling wasn't quite as it appeared to be. Wrestling and the press were no longer cozy buddies, and press coverage of wrestling was of the "oddity" variety. Only Strangler Lewis and Jim Londos got serious coverage.

Wrestling languished in the darkness of anonymity for the next 4 decades, and on the rare occasion when it *was* mentioned, it was only to provide a columnist the opportunity to write some cynical, snide reference to it as performance rather than sport.

Exposure!

Nobody had more fun putting professional wrestling down than Dan Parker, the well-respected sports editor of the New York *Daily Mirror* who wrote in the 1930s. Week after week he would not only predict the winner of the upcoming bout, but even toss in the particular hold that would end the match and give the exact time of the winning pin. So much for wrestling's credibility as a competitive sport.

The wrestlers decided to throw him a curve ball, so to speak. The occasion was one of the famous Jim Londos/Ray Steele matches, a series that lit up wrestling's skies in that era. The *Mirror* had carried Parker's column predicting that Londos would win with his famous Airplain Spin in 50 minutes. Well, 1 out of 3 ain't bad: Londos did, indeed, win—but he did it with a series of flying tackles and took 57 minutes and 30 seconds. Parker's omniscience was struck a cruel blow.

The next day, Parker's column was bordered in black and headlined: "An Apology To The Public." He wrote that he was deeply humiliated about having been off on the time and for getting the winning hold wrong. This, after all, was wrestling—there was no excuse for such an error.

Well, Parker's columns were nationally syndicated. His exposure of wrestling's non-competitive nature was so widespread that *nobody* could fool himself into believing the action was real-real anymore, and gates dropped off to nothing almost overnight.

Bi-coastal Condescension

While many reporters took to sneering at wrestling's staginess, there were exceptions to the rule. *Time* magazine ran a profile on the Dusek brothers in 1935 and local papers still hyped the performers at local shows. But the major-city papers continued to put pro wrestling down with condescension and snobbery.

New York *Herald Tribune* columnist Red Smith, for example, lamented that "Rassling has degenerated as entertainment since the dear, dead days of Londos and Lewis…" And he later critiqued a performance by Gorgeous George with the trenchant "It's difficult to do justice to Gorgeous George's act, this side the libel laws." A colleague over at the *Times* wrote from the drama desk: "Gorgeous George. Phooey!"

Wrestling didn't get much respect from the West coast press, either. Writers out there weighed in with equally stinging appraisals of what they called "the rasslin' dodge." Jim Murray of the L.A. *Times* wrote: "The World Wrestling Federation matches are all faked…."

The true believers, the hard-core wrestling fans, just ignored such coverage. But wrestling promoters needed more than the hard-core: For them, press coverage was a depressant—it depressed their psyches, and it depressed their receipts at the gate. Small wonder, then, that they began eschewing the mainstream press and turning to friendlier venues.

Bert's Corner

As Frank Deford, writing for *Sports Illustrated* has put it: "I believe that professional wrestling is clean. Everything else is fixed."

Slick Pages for Slick Wrestlers

The first alternative media outlet was the boxing bible, *Ring* magazine. Its very first issue, published in February of 1922, was devoted to "boxing, wrestling, and billiards." It's editor, Nat Fleischer, devoted an entire section of the magazine to wrestling throughout the lean years of the 1930s, 1940s, and 1950s.

The combination of boxing and wrestling was picked up on in the late 1950s by Stanley Weston, formerly *Ring*'s wrestling section editor, who now published his own magazine: *Boxing Illustrated-Wrestling Revue*. By 1961, the two subjects had gone their separate ways, and *Wrestling Revue* became the first publication totally dedicated to the sport.

With *Wrestling Revue*'s first issue, wrestling had finally come up with its own voice, and its first real alternative to the mainstream press. This was the beginning of print media expressly devoted to wrestling. Within a few short years, this one publication was joined by a burgeoning field of fanzines. And wrestling promoters turned to the noncritical coverage provided by these publications to put out their gospel to the fans through interviews and exclusives.

From Hooliganism to Heroes, the Changing Face of Fanzine Coverage

Early wrestling magazines like *Wrestling Review, Wrestling Monthly,* and *The Wrestler* fell all over themselves to report on the latest happenings in the ring—like when Freddie Blassie begot blood from the brow of Rikidozan in his famous match in Japan. They all ran screaming cover stories with headlines like "Bloodbath of the Year!" "A Saga Written in Blood!" and "Where There's Blood, There's Blassie!"

Wrestle Mania

Wrestling magazines in their early days based their marketing on the perceived bloodiness of the sport—they learned early on that the gorier the cover, the better their sales. So they loved the Terry Funk battle with Harley Race—it meant more gory covers, as did any bout featuring the "blood thirsty" Taro Myaki. And so it went, up through the 1970s.

But with the explosion of wrestling as an entertainment phenomenon in the 1980s, a whole *new* dimension was added. Wrestling was now all over the tube, and heroes galore were emerging overnight. Wrestling was suddenly coming out of the sports closet and was on the cusp of becoming socially acceptable. The magazines responded by toning down their bloody, exploitative covers and moving into coverage of the stars, rather than the events.

And even the mainstream press started covering wrestling again. This time around, however, the stories treated wrestling as an event, not a sport, and focused on the celebrities that suddenly began appearing at ringside.

A New Generation Updates Wrestling's Image

While the tone and content of wrestling's media coverage changed, another revolution was in the wind. A whole new generation of writers and reporters had sprung up—one whose opinions of the sport weren't colored by old-time attitudes and prejudices. Most of these new writers knew wrestling from TV, expected it to be entertainment instead of competition, and reported on it accordingly.

Ira Berkow in Chicago, Bert Sugar (my co-author) in Washington, Warner Wolf of Washington and New York—these are just a few of this new breed of wrestling reporters. Wolf, an announcer, remembers growing up in D.C. in the late 1940s "when wrestling was the *only* regular sporting event on television." He watched all the greats: Antonino Rocca, Gorgeous George, and Slave Girl Moolah.

Chet Coppock, "The Voice of Chicago," is another of the new breed. He recalls the old Jack Brickhouse broadcasts from Marigold Arena: "To [me as] an 8 year old boy, Hans Schmidt was more frightening than learning the multiplication tables…And to me, Verne Gagne was the Eisenhower administration in tights." He learned early on the allure of these larger-than-life heroes.

The upshot of this change in orientation among reporters was that the press was no longer obsessively concerned with exposing the "fakery" of wrestling. The focus was on wrestling as a part of popular culture.

Tuning In to the World of Wrestling

Today, in sharp contrast to the past, professional wrestling is covered by a wide variety of media. There are specialized magazines, Internet sites, newsletters, radio shows, and even a few major city newspapers have returned to the fold to provide coverage. Read on for a broad sampling of the options available to you, the fan, in your quest to follow your favorite stars, shows, events, and extravaganzas.

Rasslin' on the Radio

Hollywood Hogan likes to play air guitar as he approaches the ring—no surprise, since he used to play for a rock band. You can see this in a televised match, or out there in the arena, but it's just the sort of detail you miss out on if you get your match coverage only on the radio. But then again, sometimes you can't get to the live show and a TV's not available. Radio programming is there to fill in the gap, and there are more than a dozen radio stations that dedicate regular air time to the coverage of

Body Slam

Radio venues are hard to keep current. A fan will buy a license and hold forth on the air for a time, then fade into the woodwork at renewal time. So any listings for radio shows can only be provisional.

wrestling. The odds are good that you can find at least a few radios that regularly broadcast wrestling matches, no matter where you live. Here's a sampling of what's out there in some parts of the country:

➤ If you live in the Atlanta, Georgia, area, you can tune into radio station 1010 AM on Sunday afternoons to catch the *Wrestling Insider* show.

➤ Fans in the Baltimore, Maryland, area should listen to *Pro Wrestling 11* from 5:00 to 7:30 p.m. on Saturdays on WLG 1360 AM.

➤ Florida gives wrestling fans *The Wrestling Insiders* on Saturdays from 10 a.m. to noon. Check out WAMT 1060 AM for this show.

➤ Folks in Knoxville, Tennessee, have access to *Pro Wrestling Insider*. This show runs from 12:30 to 1:30 p.m. on Saturday afternoons on WQBB 1040 AM.

➤ *The Rowdy Roddy Piper Show* on KXYX 1010 AM is out there for people in Portland, Oregon. The show runs from noon to 1:00 p.m.

➤ Washington, D.C., is home to the *Main Event*. This radio spot runs from 11:00 p.m. to midnight on WTEM 570 AM, generally on Saturdays.

➤ Residents of Rhode Island have *Pro Wrestling* and *Pro Boxing Digest* to tune into. The station is AM 1320 WARA and the time is from 3:00 p.m. to 5:00 p.m. on Saturdays.

➤ People in and around Detroit, Michigan, can listen to *Pro Wrestling Ringside* on Thursday nights from 9:00 p.m. to 10:00 p.m. on WCAR 1090 AM.

Wrestling fans in New York, New Jersey, and Philadelphia have a wide choice of radio programs on which they can keep track of their wresting heroes and villains. There are at least five radio stations that blast the airwaves with wrestling facts, figures, and news in the Jersey area. The following is a list of them:

WGBB 1240 AM, Sunday 1–3 p.m., John Arezzi

WRUN 1150 AM, Sunday 6–8 p.m., *Let's Talk Wrestling*

WNWR 1540 AM, Sunday 6–7 p.m., *Wrestling Radio*

90.5 FM, Saturday at 1 p.m., Hofstra University Radio

Off the Rack: Magazines

There are entire racks of magazines devoted exclusively to professional wrestling, and it seems like a new one sprouts up on the stands every time you look. Most of the publications are dedicated to news and pictures of wrestlers, managers, valets, promoters, and other key players involved in the wrestling industry.

The magazines carry some advertising, but most of them are dedicated heavily to pro wrestling. What advertising there is tends to be focused on peripherals to the industry: collectibles, training schools, and so forth. It takes only a stroll through a newstand to see how prolific wrestling magazines have become—publishers haven't been slow to catch on to the huge interest out there among the fans for *any* kind of news about their favorite stars of the ring. Here are a few to start with, but keep your eyes open for the new ones appearing all the time.

Magazines Published by Wrestling Organizations

➤ *WWF Magazine* is the official magazine of the WWF. If you buy it at a newsstand, it costs $3.99. As you might imagine, the publication is centered on the wrestlers of the WWF. This one's a true high-quality read.

➤ *RAW* is put out as a subsidiary of the *RAW is WAR* television production. It's published monthly, with a newsstand price of $3.99 and an annual subscription price of $24.00. For a subscription to this or *WWF Magazine*, write to Titan Sports, PO Box 394, Mt. Morris, IL 61054-0394.

➤ *WCW Magazine*, the official magazine of Turner's WCW, is published monthly, sells for $3.95 an issue in the newsstands, and has an annual subscription price of $20.00. Write *WCW Magazine* c/o Colin Bowman, 1 CNN Center, Box 105366, Atlanta, GA 30348-5366.

Magazines Published by Starlog Group

➤ *Ringside Wrestling* is published 10 times a year. Newsstand price is $3.99. George Napolitano, *Ringside*'s editor, is one of the best writers currently associated with pro wrestling, so you can count on the real deal, presented in style.

Captain Lou's Corner

Everybody most likely has a favorite magazine, and I'm no different. I look for in-depth coverage, great writing, and plenty of photographs. And I give high marks to publications that keep their readers informed about what's going on behind the scenes, in the offices of the station and arena owners, promoters, and managers.

Bert's Corner

Of the Starlog Group publications, the only title available by subscription is *Wrestling All Stars Heroes and Villains*. Write to Starlog Group, 475 Park Avenue South, New York, NY 10016.

➤ Some fans just can't live without a plethora of color photos and pull-out pinups. If that's your bag, *Superstar Wrestlers* is definitely going to be your cup of tea (or scotch or vodka). Published quarterly, it'll run you $4.99 at the newsstand. With Michael Benson as managing editor and George Napolitano (see the *Ringside Wrestling* entry, above) as editor, this magazine delivers plenty of punch.

➤ *Wrestling All Stars Heroes and Villains* is another high-quality magazine that's well worth checking out. It's published 10 times a year. Single-issue price is $3.99.

➤ If you're keeping your finger on the pulse of pro wrestling, don't overlook *TV Wrestlers*. It's published six times a year, with a cover price of $4.99. It's a little heavier on the color photos than text, but it's a great source for up-to-the-minute news of your favorite televised shows and stars.

➤ Whether your preference is for wrestling's beauties or its beasts, there are specialized magazines just for you. *The Beauties of Wrestling* and *Bad Ass Dudes* are both published twice annually, with a cover price of $4.99.

Magazines Published by London Publishing Company

➤ *Inside Wrestling* provides fewer color photos than most other wrestling publications, but there's real meat on this magazine's bones. It sells on the newsstand for $3.50. An annual subscription (13 issues) will set you back $29.20.

➤ *The Wrestler* is another publication that comes out 13 times a year. This monthly magazine carries a cover price of $2.50. For a 13-issue subscription you'll have to shell out $29.20. This is one to get for the sake of the text—they don't do much with color photos, but they do run good black-and-whites. It's definitely worth a look.

➤ *Pro Wrestling Illustrated* also comes out 13 times a year, with a cover price of $2.50 and an annual subscription price of $34.70.

➤ *Wrestle America, Wrestling Analyst,* and *Wrestling Superstars* all come out six times a year. For each of these, a single issue will run you $3.95, and a year's subscription goes for $20.14.

Captain Lou's Corner

For a subscription, mail to London Publishing Company, PO Box 2021, Department #9, Marion, OH 43302. There are some combination subscription offers: order *The Wrestler* and *Inside Wrestling* for a year and you'll pay $54.75; add *Pro Wrestling Illustrated* and you'll be shelling out $81.50; and if you go with the *Wrestle America* and *Wrestling Superstars* combo you'll pay $37.95.

The Snail Mail Express: Newsletters

If you're one of that shrinking minority that hasn't yet entered the age of the personal computer, you're at a distinct disadvantage. Without online access you're missing out on the latest gold mine of information. You can fill the gaps in your knowledge of what's going on in the industry by subscribing to traditional newsletters (most of them have an online counterpart, these days). Check out some or all of the following:

Figure Four Newsletter, C/O Youth Wrestling Federation, Box 426, Woodinville, WA 98072

Mat Marketplace, P. O. Box 2371, Jamaica Plain, MA 02130

On The Mat, 124 Maple Street, Newport, VT 05855-1418

Piledriver, Glenhuntly, VIC 3163, Australia

Pro Wrestling Monthly, 5678 Speedwell Ave., Morris Plains, NJ 07950

Pro Wrestling Torch Weekly, P.O. Box 201844, Minneapolis, MN 55420

Pro-Wrestling Update, 19 Oakland Road, Mumbles, Swansea, Wales SA3 4AQ, UK

Western Ringside Report, P. O. Box 31004, St. Johns Postal Outlet, Port Moody, BC V3H2CO, Canada

The Wrestling Chatterbox, 23-44 33rd Dr., Astoria, NY 11102-3252

Wrestling Down Under, P. O. Box 988, Bayswater, VIC 3153, Australia

Wrestling Lariat, P. O. Box 612, Marmora, NJ 08223

Wrestling Observer, P. O. Box 1228, Campbell, CA 95009

Wrestling Perspective, Box 351, Lyndon Center, VT 05850-0351

Wrestling Then & Now, P. O. Box 640471, Flushing, NY 11364

Wizards of the Web

Online access opens up a whole new world for professional wrestling fans. If you're fortunate enough to have access to the Web, you've probably already discovered just what typing a well-chosen keyword will get you. There's plenty of wrestling news and data available, in all sorts of formats. Many Web sites are updated daily or weekly to keep up with the latest matches, grudges, and gossip. In preparing this section we did an extensive search of the Net. What follows are some of our preferred sites that you might like to visit.

➤ One of the most complete and freshest sites we found is called MiCasa98 (**http://www.micasawrestling.com/**). You can find info on WCW and WWF events here. Categories include the latest news, the WCW arena, WWF attitude, archives, a PPV live section, MiCasa TV, and a voting booth.

➤ One of the most popular Web sites for wrestling news is Scoops Magazine. Log onto **http://www.scoopscentral.com/** and you will get a full dose of what's going on in the pro wrestling industry.

➤ Solie's Vintage Wrestling at **http://members.aol.com/Solie/**, is another premier Internet site for news on pro wrestling. This site offers a What's New category, a newsletter, features on the sport, links, and more. We especially like the history section of this site, where you can find the win-loss records of wrestlers, chat transcripts, and so forth. The site is well worth a good look.

➤ The Wrestling Review (TWR) is another good source of information for wrestling fans. You can log onto TWR at **http://www.members.aol.com/jeffr95340/wrestlingreview.html**. There are a number of pages associated with this site, so give it a spin.

➤ The motto of Online Onslaught is, "Wrestling News, Analysis, and Commentary with Attitude." A trip to **http://www.homepages.udayton.edu/~scaiarij/oo/oo.htm** will reveal yet another quality news site for wrestling fans. Onslaught options include the following: Daily News, Weekly Wrap, Interactive, Archives, Calendar, Local News, Independents, Fantasy, and Links.

➤ Ray's Wrestling Review, located at **http://www.onrampinc.net/~rhagen/wrest.html**, is another worthy wrestling site. So is The Bagpipe Report (TBR). You can find TBR at **http://www.twc-online.com/TBR/.index.html**.

➤ Fans who like newsletters should enjoy The Torture Rack. You can subscribe to it by e-mailing mickalobe@hotmail.com. The Web page for this newsletter can be found at **http://www.angelfire.com/va/rack/index.html**.

➤ The Shooting Star Press, at **http://www.geocities.com/Hollywood/Set/7920/**, is another good place to go for wrestling news and analysis.

If that's not enough, here are a few more to check out:

➤ The Bagpipe Report: **http://www.twc-online.com/TBR**

➤ The Cauliflower Alley Club: **http://www.geocities.com/colosseum/field 9099/cac-page.htm**

➤ Oh My God Wrestling (a multimedia site): **http://www.ohmygod.simplenet.com/**

➤ Professional Wrestling Online Museum: **http://www.wrestlingmuseum.com/**

➤ Whoo! Wrestling: **http://www.whoowrestling.com/**

➤ Wrestlemaniacs: **http://www.wrestlmaniacs.com/**

➤ 1Wrestling: **http://www.1wrestling.com/**

Finally, there are the official federation Web sites:

➤ **http://www.wwf.com**

➤ **http://www.wcwwrestling.com**

➤ **http://www.ecwwrestling.com**

Wrestle Mania

New Web sites spring up all the time, so use the large search engines, like Yahoo! or Excite, and type in keywords like "wrestling" or the name of your favorite wrestler. You'll find thousands of "hits"—directions to individual Web pages that are dedicated to wrestling. And most of those pages will hyperlink you to even more pages. You can spend hours—days even—just cruising from one site to the next to dig up all you could ever want to know about the insider's world of wrestling.

Hotlines and Digests

Magazines and Web sites are probably the most-used forms of keeping track of pro wrestling and wrestlers. Newsletters and radio stations do a great job of filling in whatever gaps the first two leave in your information base. If you *still* can't get enough, never fear—wrestling digests and wrestling hotlines are out there just for fans like you.

The Dandy Digests

Two of the many wrestling digests out there are particularly good:

➤ *Pro Wrestling Illustrated* (PWI) is heavy into facts and statistics. The 1998 edition carries the 10 biggest stories of the previous year, a date-by-date overview of all of 1997's wrestling events, PWI weekly honors, vital statistics on wrestlers (height, weight, birthdays, and so forth), the top 500 wrestlers, title histories of active and inactive wrestlers, 100 years of wrestling highlights, wrestling obituaries, the greatest wrestling crowds, historic wrestling bouts that were not on pay-per-view, who's in and who's out, and pay-per-view listings and results. Believe us when we say that PWI is worth much more than it's cover price of $4.95. This is one source of wrestling data that can't be beat—it's a champion.

➤ *The Wrestler,* published quarterly, is thick with stories about performers, managers, and valets. It doesn't carry the statistical histories found in PWI, but the feature stories are abundant and full of juicy details. It makes up for the lack of statistical data by featuring interviews with all the major players in the industry today. Reading *The Wrestler Digest* is a true treat. Get a copy and enjoy it. You'll learn a lot, and it'll only put a $3.50 hole in your wallet.

These and other wrestling digests are only available on the newsstands.

Information, Puh-leeze

Fans who want instant information can let their fingers do the walking straight to the telephone keypad to tap into the wrestling grapevine. Hotlines for the determined fans include:

➤ **The Pro Wrestling Illustrated Hotline.** It can be reached at (900)-884-4PWI. Callers get news on behind-the-scenes activities, upcoming events, current results, title changes and transactions, PPV reports, the wrestler of the week, and exclusive scouting reports. The call costs $1.99 a minute.

➤ **The ECW's hardcore hotline.** This one is an official source of ECW information. The phone number is (900)-446-4329, and the cost is $1.99 per minute. Information made available includes ECW match results, ECW hot news, and details of upcoming ECW matches.

➤ **The Wrestling Ringside Hotline.** George Napolitano and Black Jack Brown can be found here, providing generous helpings of insider information. Like all the others, this one's going to cost you—$2.00 per minute—but the information is current, and it's the real lowdown on the industry. The phone number is (900)-680-SLAM.

Considering the wide array of sources for news on pro wrestling, there's no excuse for not keeping tabs on the winners, the losers, the movers, the shakers, the events, and all the players within the wrestling industry. Use the source or sources of your choice, but please, take advantage of all the news and data available to you on your favorite sport. It's all there waiting for you.

The Least You Need to Know

➤ The press has not been overly friendly to pro wrestling through much of its history.

➤ Many radio stations feature wrestling shows.

➤ Magazines are an essential source of information for wrestling fans.

➤ The Internet and World Wide Web provide fast, abundant information unlike any other source.

➤ Periodical digests are chock full of terrific wrestling stories, statistics, and interviews.

➤ Pay-by-the-minute phone lines are a source of instant information on the pro wrestling industry.

Chapter 24

Cash Cows and How You Can Cash In

In This Chapter

➤ Who buys wrestling collectibles?

➤ Where to find collectibles on the World Wide Web

➤ Mail-order companies to try

➤ Buying at wrestling events

Just as Star Trek has its Trekkies, pro wrestling has its own form of fans (or maybe fanatics is a better word). Die-hard wrestling fans will spend good money on almost anything that has to do with their sport. Some people get to the point where their interest in wrestling collectibles becomes an obsession. And there is no shortage of products for loyal fans to collect.

You can be sure that the wrestling industry is more than happy to accommodate the desires of fans. And in addition to products generated by the wrestling industry itself, wrestlers can pull in some truly serious cash by endorsing products. For example, Macho Man Randy Savage pulls in a hefty fee for promoting the sale of Slim Jims. But for the fans, it's the cash cow known as collectibles that has the real cachet. In this chapter you'll learn about the how, where, and how much of collecting wrestling memorabilia.

Wrestling Collectibles

What makes a fan want to collect memorabilia associated with professional wrestling? Right off the top, a big part of the attraction has to do with loyalty to their favorite wrestler. If you're a die-hard Hogan fan, you're going to want all the merchandise that's been spun off of his image (or images, as the Hulkster and as Hollywood).

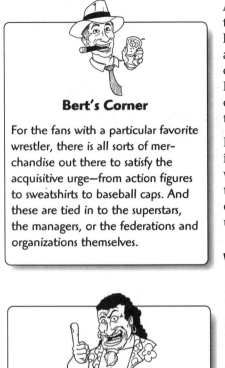

Bert's Corner

For the fans with a particular favorite wrestler, there is all sorts of merchandise out there to satisfy the acquisitive urge—from action figures to sweatshirts to baseball caps. And these are tied in to the superstars, the managers, or the federations and organizations themselves.

Captain Lou's Corner

For those who are into the more conventional form of video, there are countless tapes on the market, released by the major federations. And for the particularly strong of heart, you can get CDs of your favorite grappler crooning—including Freddie Blassie's hit single "Pencil Neck Geek."

Another draw is the love of the sport. And there are those far-thinking souls that collect memorabilia in hopes that 20 or 30 years down the line they'll be worth a lot of money. It's true that some collectibles do increase in value—sometimes to astronomical amounts. However, money usually isn't the primary reason for collectors buying wrestling materials. A fan's passion for the sport is the most likely reason for purchases.

Every collector is unique—whether his or her obsession is wrestling memorabilia or postage stamps. Some will get actively into trading, going to swap meets or trading online. Whether the actual collection is kept on display or hidden away in a fireproof safe, the collector's urge is the same in all of them.

What's Out There

So what's a collectible? There's the standards of course: T-shirts, action figures, that sort of thing. But there's more, much more. For example, there are several great video games out for the Sega, Sony, and Nintendo systems: "WWF Warzone," for example, and "WCW vs. The World." Playing on the popularity of the outlaw gangs, you can pick up the "WCW vs. nWo" for your Nintendo, and "WCW Revenge"—which has great graphics and plenty of wrestling characters to control.

Surfing for Souvenirs

So, say you're interested in starting—or adding to—your wrestling memorabilia. One good place to check out is the Internet—there are plenty of places where you can surf for souvenirs. When we went online, we found more Web sites that discussed and/or offered wrestling collectibles than we could possibly visit in a single online stint. Check out our results:

➤ Would you like a long listing of Hasbro WWF wrestling toys? Check out **http://www.personal.umich.edu/~dbtaub/wwffigs.htm**. This site gives you an extensive listing of wrestling toys offered from the mid 1980s to the mid 1990s.

➤ The Wrestling Warehouse offers photos, videotapes, buttons, masks, programs, and autographed photos for sale. Check it out at **http://www.apprisebbs.com/collectable/wrestling_wh/**. (If you don't have Web access, you can contact the Wrestling Warehouse at P. O. Box 951, Humble, TX 77347.)

➤ We enjoyed browsing the wrestling figures available at **http://www. grandstandcol.com/wrest.htm**. This site offers wrestling figures from Hasbro with prices as low as $5. (Andre the Giant, however, carries a gigantic price of $42.) Most of the figures range from $5 to $12.

Wrestle Mania

The wrestling market has grown exponentially, along with wrestling's popularity. In May of 1998, for example, the WCW put Bill Goldberg's T-shirts on sale in the arenas. 60,000 were sold in the first two months, for a total of $1.4 million. Stone Cold Steve Austin's T's sell just as briskly, and then there are the Hollywood Hogan shirts, shirts for the nWo, and every other popular star out there.

➤ Collectors who are into photos should check out **http://www.escape.ca/ ~abdcards/w_photo.htm**. This site offers a wide selection of 8 × 10 photos. Prices are currently listed at $3.75 each with discounts on multiple purchases. You can get pictures of Mariana, Shawn Michaels, Golddust, the British Bulldog, Sable, The Undertaker, Sunny, and many more from this site.

➤ JB's Wrestling World, found at **http://www.members.aol.com/jcblanks/wwf/ justoys.html**, offers a wide selection of wrestling toys. Their Bend-Ums toys currently cost as little as $7. This site is well worth your time if you are into wrestling collectibles.

➤ Backyard Sports sells T-shirts, caps, posters, pennants, standees, pins, belt buckles, and action figures. It also claims to offer more than 50 styles of pro-wrestling shirts. The store has a Web site at **http://www.backyardsport.qpg.com/**. However, you can't make purchases from the site. Instead, write to Backyard Sports, at 655 Washington Street, Eden, NC 27288, call (336)-627-9192, or e-mail them at nWo2sweet@webtv.net.

➤ If you don't mind buying second-hand goods, check out the Collector's Connection at **http://www.efn.org/~jabrams/wrestler.htm**. You'll find many collectible wrestling figures priced from less than $5 to about $14. In addition to the action figures, we found the site offering posters for $5.25 and they even had a WWF board game for sale.

➤ Another source of 8 × 10 photos of wrestling's greatest stars can be found at **http://www.espn.simplenet.com/wrestling/**. This site sells pictures for $6 apiece, and it has a good selection to choose from. Austin, Sable, and many other major players of pro wrestling can be captured in a photo from this site.

➤ A huge variety of wrestling figures can be found at Plastic Dreams at **http://members.aol.com/plasticdrm/wrestler.htm**. We were really impressed with the long list of figures offered for sale at this site. Prices run from under $15 to over $200. Of all the Web sites we visited, this one had one of the best selections of wrestling figures we could find.

Captain Lou's Corner

Some fans specialize in collecting items relating to a specific wrestler, like Hulk Hogan or Stone Cold Steve Austin. Others just want everything they can get their hands on. One big favorite is Austin's 3:16 T-shirt. What does 3:16 mean? "It means I just whupped your a**," says Stone Cold himself.

➤ Ringside Collectibles, at **http://www.wrestlingfigures.com/JakksFigures**, offers a large variety of wrestling collectibles. One collectible that really caught our attention on this site was the Vince McMahon Ringside Microphone. It's priced at $14 and supposedly actually amplifies a user's voice. Many of the figures on this site are priced as low as $10.

When we checked out the WWF Managers Series at Ringside Collectibles, we were surprised to find two-figure sets priced as low as $15. A full eight-pack of managers, which includes Paul Bearer, Mankind, Clarence Mason, Crush, Marc Mero, Sable, Bob Backlund, and Sultan, goes for only $58. Anyone interested in wrestling figures should visit Ringside Collectibles online.

➤ If you want to see a magnificent selection of collectibles, go to the Action Figures and Collectible Toys (AFACT) site at **http://www.kpgroup.com/wrestlers/wrestlers.html**. This large Web site really impressed us. We were especially impressed with the series collection of Jimmy "Superfly" Snuka and Andre the Giant. The figures stand seven inches tall and come with a biography card—all for only $20.

Another eye-catcher from AFACT is their Talking Undertaker figure. This movable figure stands 14 inches tall and has intricate tattoos on its arms. The talking figure also intones The Undertaker's favorite phrases: "Face your worst nightmare" and "Rest in peace." This collectible is priced at $40. AFACT also offers a WWF Super Slam Wrestling Ring that comes with a Bend-Em figure of Paul Bearer. The set comes with bungee ropes, carrying case with handle, and storage compartment at a cost of only $25.

➤ This list wouldn't be complete if we didn't list the official site of the WWF at **http://www.wwfshopzone.com/cgi-bin/wwfshopzone/1405657546/Catalog/10046**. The site offers official WWF merchandise. You can buy an 18-month wrestling calendar for $12, a Dude Love bandanna for $10, a Sultry Sable Pillow for $36, or an Undertaker bandanna for $8. (We don't know why a bandanna from The Undertaker is less than one from Dude Love, but it is.) A foam championship belt costs $16. In addition, the WWF site offers a large variety of goods that range from caps to shirts to pillows and pictures.

In Your Face

Don't just sit there waiting for memorabilia to drop into your lap. If you're interested, consider running a Web page, or a more conventional print ad, and let the world out there know what you're looking for.

Mail-Order Madness

While the Internet has opened up an entirely new world for pro wrestling fans, you can still purchase collectibles the old fashioned way, through traditional mail-order companies. Let's look at some of the collectibles profiled through the medium of the printed catalog.

➤ Figures Inc. (P. O. Box 19482, Johnston, Rhode Island 02919) offers trading cards, action figures, replicas of championship belts, caps and slammers, video games, and other collectibles. A catalog is available for $2.

➤ You can also order the WWF Legends series of The Original Superstars. The figures are available at Toys 'Я' Us and include Classy Freddie Blassie, Jimmy "Superfly" Snuka, Andre the Giant, and yours truly, Captain Lou Albano.

As you can see, the Internet offers a much broader range of suppliers and products. It's definitely your best bet for finding a variety of wrestling collectibles.

On-Site Buying Opportunities

Let's not forget the obvious: You can also buy an incredible array of collectibles at wrestling events like autograph signings, matches, or press conferences. I remember a time when a fan came up and offered me $500 for the shirt off my back. Well $500 sounded good, but $750 sounded even better, and how was the fan to know if that wasn't my all-time favorite piece of clothing! It must have sounded like a deal to the fan—I got paid on the spot. So if you're looking for that one-of-a-kind item, don't be shy—you never know when your favorite wrestler, manager, or valet might be willing to part with some trinket or other. (But don't even *think* about asking for my safety pin!)

Freebies for the First Rows

One thing that happens all the time at wrestling matches is that stuff gets thrown out of the ring. No, I don't mean a wrestler or two, although that's been known to happen—I mean stuff like a bandanna, or a glove. If you're lucky enough to be in the right seat at the right time, you've got yourself a collectible. But even if you don't personally catch the brass ring, so to speak, you can certainly hustle yourself on over to the lucky guy who caught it and try making a deal right then and there. No guarantees, but it's worth a shot, right?

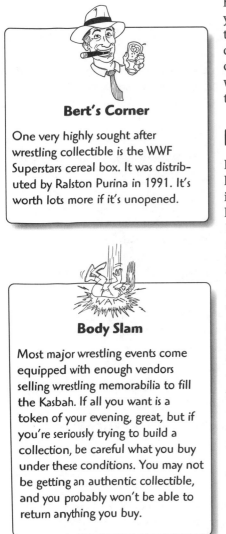

Bert's Corner

One very highly sought after wrestling collectible is the WWF Superstars cereal box. It was distributed by Ralston Purina in 1991. It's worth lots more if it's unopened.

Body Slam

Most major wrestling events come equipped with enough vendors selling wrestling memorabilia to fill the Kasbah. If all you want is a token of your evening, great, but if you're seriously trying to build a collection, be careful what you buy under these conditions. You may not be getting an authentic collectible, and you probably won't be able to return anything you buy.

Dealing for Dollars

Like I said earlier, some fans purchase collectibles with a long-term goal in mind—they're buying collectibles as investments. If that's what you're into, you're going to have to be more careful than the average fan who just buys for the fun of it. Scope out the collectibles situation, and don't sink your money into anything but the best—the merchandise most likely to increase in value. This may mean that you have to go to dozens of shows, flea markets, swap meets, and other sources to find just what you're looking for. This kind of collecting requires a great deal of focus—if you're hunting down that last item in a series of action figures, you don't want to get sidetracked by something else that comes along.

Whether you are a profit-motivated investor, a serious collector, or a standard-issue, dyed-in-the-wool fan who just enjoys owning wrestling collectibles, you should consider all of your buying options. Look in magazines, newsletters, and industry journals for advertisements. Don't expect to find great bargains at these sources, but you may find what you're looking for. The Internet is an excellent place to scout for collectibles, too. And if you want to turn up some rock-bottom deals that may produce quick profits, pay close attention to flea markets, swap meets, and local classified ads.

It's just like any other kind of collecting—you've just got to keep your eyes peeled. Some of the best deals on wrestling collectibles come from the least likely sources. For example, you may come across some old wrestling figures at a yard sale. If you know the collectibles market and spot a good piece, you can probably buy it at a very reasonable price. So don't limit your looking to advertisements. Get out there and beat the bushes. Consider running your own ads offering to buy wrestling-related items. Many sellers are willing to sell at below-market prices, and you might profit from the purchase. If money is not your motivation, running your own ads can fill out your collection more quickly than cruising yard sales. Be creative in your quest for collectibles.

The Least You Need to Know

➤ The Internet and World Wide Web is one of the best sources for wrestling collectibles.

➤ Wrestling magazines don't offer much advertising for wrestling collectibles.

➤ Be careful of what you purchase at wrestling matches and events.

➤ Flea markets, yard sales, and swap meets can be good sources of collectibles.

➤ Don't hesitate to run your own ads to find collectibles needed for your collection.

Who's Who in Pro Wrestling

Here's a list of some of the major names in wrestling, from yesterday's stars to today's. It's not complete, of course—stats for some major figures weren't available and so their entries weren't included.

Name	Height (in ft. & in.)	Weight (in lbs.)
Abdullah the Butcher	6-1	360
Adams, Chris	6-1	228
Sheik Adnan al-Kaissie	5-10	245
Adonis, Adrian	5-11	312
Afa Anoia	6-1	304
Anderson, Arn	6-0	249
Anderson, Ole	6-1	256
Andre the Giant	7-5	520
Animal	6-5	310
Atlas, Tony	6-2	247
Austin, Steve	6-2	241
AX	6-2	303
Backlund, Bob	6-1	234
Badd, Johnny B.	6-0	235
Beefcake, Brutus	6-4	273
Benoit, Chris	5-10	218
Blanchard, Tully	5-10	235
Bockwinkel, Nick	6-1	245

continues

continued

Name	Height (in ft. & in.)	Weight (in lbs.)
Booker T	5-11	250
Bravo, Dino	6-1	256
Bundy, King Kong	6-4	446
Carnera, Primo	6-6	263
Condrey, Dennis	6-0	256
DiBiase, Ted	6-3	247
Douglas, Shane	6-0	223
Dundee, Bill	5-7	214
Eaton, Bobby	6-0	233
Flair, Ric	6-1	243
Fuji, Mr.	5-11	265
Funk, Dory, Jr.	6-2	250
Funk, Terry	6-1	247
Gagne, Verne	5-11	215
Garea, Tony	Unknown	240
Garvin, Jim	5-10	231
Garvin, Ron	6-2	231
George, Mike	6-2	265
Gibson, Robert	5-11	225
Gilbert, Eddie	5-10	222
Gordy, Terry	6-4	275
Gorgeous George	5-9	210
Gotch, Frank	6-0	205
Graham, Bill "Superstar"	6-3	265
Hall, Scott	6-8	287
Hart, Bret	5-11	235
Hart, Owen	5-10	227
Hawk	6-3	277
Hayes, Michael P.S.	6-1	255
Hogan, Hollywood/Hulk	6-8	275
Honky Tonk Man	6-1	255
Iron Sheik	6-0	262
Irwin, Wild Bill	6-1	250
Jannetty, Marty	5-11	230
Jarrett, Jeff	5-10	230
Johnson, Rocky	6-2	244

Name	Height (in ft. & in.)	Weight (in lbs.)
Keirn, Steve	6-0	235
Kiniski, Gene	6-5	285
Koloff, Ivan	5-11	249
Koloff, Nikita	6-2	275
Kowalski, Walter "Killer"	6-7	275
Ladd, Ernie	6-9	315
Lawler, Jerry	6-0	234
Luger, Lex	6-5	265
McDaniel, Wahoo	5-11	280
McGraw, Herman E. Bugsy	6-3	280
Madril, Al	6-1	231
Martel, Rick	6-0	236
Martel, Sherri	5-7	132
Miceli, Madusa	5-9	150
Michaels, Shawn	6-0	230
Mil Mascaras	5-11	245
Mills, Tiny	6-3	258
Mr. Wrestling 11	6-0	247
Mongolian Stomper	6-2	239
Monsoon, Gorilla	6-7	401
Moondog Spot	6-2	298
Morales, Pedro	5-11	240
Morton, Rick	5-11	228
Mulligan, Blackjack	6-7	310
Muraco, Don	6-4	274
Murdoch, Dick	6-4	280
Nash, Kevin	7-0	356
Negro, Ciclon	6-3	260
Neidhart, Jim "The Anvil"	6-1	275
Orndorff, Paul	5-11	252
Orton, Cowboy Bob, Jr.	6-1	245
Page, Diamond Dallas	6-5	260
Patera, Ken	6-1	256
Piper, Rowdy Roddy	6-2	231
Race, Harley	6-1	268
Raven	6-1	235

continues

continued

Name	Height (in ft. & in.)	Weight (in lbs.)
Regal, Steve	6-0	205
Rhodes, Dustin	6-5	254
Rhodes, Dusty	6-1	302
Rich, Tommy	6-0	248
Richter, Wendi	5-8	142
Robert, Yvon	6-1	210
Roberts, Jake "The Snake"	6-5	246
Rocca, Antonio	6-0	226
Rogers, Buddy	6-0	227
Roop, Bob	6-1	270
Rose, Buddy	6-0	312
Rotunda, Mike	6-2	245
Rougeau, Jacques, Jr.	6-2	232
Rude, Rick	6-4	246
Sags, Jerry	6-3	290
Saito, Masa	5-11	247
Sammartino, Bruno	5-10	265
Santana, Ricky	5-10	235
Santana, Tito	6-1	245
Savage, Randy "Macho Man"	6-2	237
Shults, David "Dr. D"	6-5	270
Sierra, David	6-1	246
Sika	6-2	320
Slater, Dick	6-1	235
Slaughter, Sergeant	6-3	310
Smash	6-1	282
Smith, Davey Boy	5-9	245
Snow, Al	6-1	237
Snuka, Jimmy "Superfly"	6-0	250
Starr, Ron	5-11	235
Steamboat, Rick	6-1	238
Steele, George "The Animal"	6-2	280
Steiner, Rick	5-11	248
Steiner, Scott	6-1	235
Stevens, Ray "The Crippler"	6-1	248

Name	Height (in ft. & in.)	Weight (in lbs.)
Sting	6-2	260
Strongbow, Chief Jay	6-6	325
Studd, Big John	6-7	364
Sullivan, Kevin	5-10	252
Sweetan, Bob	6-0	272
Szabo, Sandor	6-1	225
Taylor, Terry	6-2	225
Thesz, Lou	6-1	225
Thornton, Les	5-9	238
Torres, Enrique Miguel	5-11	230
The Ultimate Warrior	6-4	280
The Undertaker	6-9	328
Vader, Big Van	6-5	450
Valentine, Greg "The Hammer"	6-0	243
Valiant, Jimmy	6-3	251
Valiant, Johnny	6-4	250
Ventura, Jesse "The Body"	6-3	280
Vicious, Sid	6-8	318
Volkoff, Nikolai	6-7	280
Von Erich, David	6-4	247
Von Erich, Kerry	6-2	260
Von Raschke, Baron	6-2	271
Watts, Bill	6-3	278
Williams, Steve "Dr. Death"	6-1	265
Windham, Barry	6-5	263
Yamamoto, Tojo	5-7	230
Yokozuna	6-4	340
Zbyszko, Larry	5-11	248

Rasslin' Resources

Books

An exhaustive list of books on wrestling and wrestlers would be impossibly long. So I've listed here some of the books that I can personally recommend. Remember, this is just the tip of the iceberg—once you've made it through these books, there's a whole lot more waiting for you!

Fans of the WWF should get their hands on *All About WWF Superstars*, written by Larry Humber and published by Checkerboard Press, Inc.

If you are a Hogan fan, check out *All About Hulk Hogan*, written by Larry Humber and published by Checkerboard Press, Inc.

Kings of the Ring, written by Joe Bosko and published by Parachute Press.

Inside Pro Wrestling, written by Champ Thomas and published by USA Books.

Ritual Drama in American Popular Culture: The Case of Professional Wrestling, written by Michael Ball and published by Popular Technology.

If you are a fan of The Undertaker, check out Edward Ricciuti's book, *Undertaker*, published by Blackbirch Press, Inc.

Tag-team fans will enjoy Larry Humber's book, *All About WWF Tag Teams*, published by Checkerboard Press, Inc.

Pro-Wrestling Finishing Holds, written by Judo LeBell and published by Pro-Action Publishing.

Fans of Macho Man Randy Savage should enjoy *Macho Man Randy Savage*, written by Edward Ricciuti and published by Blackbirch Press, Inc.

Want more info on pro wrestling? Read *Pro Wrestling's True Facts*, written by Tom Burke and published by D. Pettiglio.

Web Sites

Official Wrestling Federation Sites

http://www.ecwwrestling.com

http://www.wcwwrestling.com

http://www.wwf.com

Official Wrestlers' Web Pages

Andre the Giant:
www.albany.net/-hit/puroresu/hallfame/andre/

Steve Austin:
www.steveaustin.com
www.geocities.com/Hollywood/Hills/8266/austin.html
www.sob.web-page.net/
www.geocities.com/Colosseum/4049/
www.angelfire.com/az/secr/index.html
www.geocities.com/Colosseum/Track/4113/menu.htm
www.geocities.com/Colosseum/Arena/1993

Chyna:
bunburry.simplenet.com/tmpll.htm

Ric Flair:
flair.angband.org/
www.geocities.com/Colosseum/Field/2399/fliehr.html

Dory Funk, Jr.:
www.dory-funk.com

Terry Funk:
www.doublecrossranch.com

Bill Goldberg:
www.members.tripod.com/-GreatGoldbert/index.html
www.amigonet.org/goldbert.htm
members.aol.com/toothpick/index.html

Eddie Guerrero:
www.eddysucks.com/

Bret Hart:
www.wcwwrestling.com/indiv/hart
hitman.tierranet.com

Owen Hart:
www.geocities.com/Colosseum/Track/4113/menuowen.htm

Curt Hennig:
www.geocities.com/Colosseum/7692/index.html

Chris Jericho:
www.chrisjericho.com
members.tripod.com/-dxrules75

Kane:
www.angelfire.com/ca/wwfkane/entrance.html

Lodi:
www.geocities.com/TimesSquare/Battlefield/hss9

Rocky Maivia:
www.geocities.com/Colosseum/Bench/4770

Kevin Nash:
www.geocities.com/Colosseum/Track/4113/nashmenu.htm

Nitro Girls:
www.wcwwrestling.com/nitrogirls/

Raven:
www.geocities.com/Colosseum/Sideline/8034
www.rlh.simplenet.com
www.members.tripod.com/~RAVEN_316

Sable:
www.wwfsable.com/
hardcore.simplenet.com/sable/sable.htm

Sting:
www.geocities.com/Colosseum/5242
www.angelfire.com/ca2/wolfpack333

Sunny:
www.crosswind.net/kingston/-sunnycity/main/sunnycity.htm
www.geocities.com/SiliconValley/Way/7550/sunny.html

Ultimate Warrior:
www.ultimatewarrior.com

The Undertaker:
members.aol.com/Tigger1985/DarkerSide.html
www.geocities.com/Colosseum/Track/4113/takermen.htm
www.geocities.com/Hollywood/8982
www.angelfire.com/de/soulreeper/

Rob Van Dam:
www.robvandam.com

Wrestling Collectibles on the Web

General merchandise Web sites

Backyard Sports:
www.backyardsport.qpg.com/

Collector's Connection:
www.enf.org/jabrams/wrestler.htm

Ringside Collectibles (features action figures):
www.wrestlingfigures.com/JakksFigures

WWF (merchandise only):
www.wwfshopzone.com/cgi-bin/wwfshopzone/1405657546/Catalog/10046

Wrestling Warehouse:
www.apprisebbs.com/collectable/wrestling-wh/

Photos only
www.wwescape.ca/abcards/w-photo.htm
www.espn.simplenet.com/wrestling/

Toys
www.personal.umich.edu/dbtaub/wwfigs.htm
www.grandstandcol.com/wrest.htm
www.members.aol.com/jcblanks/wwf/justoys.html
www.members.aol.com/plasticdrm/wrestler.htm
www.kpgroup.com/wrestlers/wrestlers.html

Addresses of the Major Federations

WWF
P.O. Box 744
Mt. Morris, IL 61054

WCW
P.O. Box 60063
Tampa, FL 33660

ECW
P.O. Box 791
Hartsdale, NY 10580

Where to Write for Stars' Autographs

WWF (c/o your favorite star)
1241 East Main St.
Stamford, CT 06902

WCW (c/o your favorite star)
1 CNN Center
Box 105366
Atlanta, GA 30348

ECW (c/o your favorite star)
P.O. Box 791
Hartsdale, NY 10580

Fighting-Words Glossary

Angle   A technique used by promoters and managers to create a feud or a grudge match. It may involve only one match or continue over several matches.

At Show   Short for "athletic show." A regular feature of carnivals in the 19th century that showcased athletic prowess.

Babyface   See **Face**.

Battle Royale   An awesome match that involves 30 or more wrestlers who enter the ring one at a time every three minutes. It's every man for himself, and anyone thrown over the top rope is eliminated. The last wrestler in the ring wins the match.

Blading   In the old days, wrestlers would hide blades on their bodies and cut themselves during a match to create a dramatic gush of blood; this practice was called blading. It is now an illegal practice.

Blow Up   To become weary or depleted of energy. Some wrestlers blow up on the entry ramp.

Booker   The person in charge of planning a match. Promoters hire bookers to create just the right combination of talent, angles, and finishes for an exciting match.

Brass Knux Match   A match in which brass knuckles are placed on top of a corner pole in the ring. The first wrestler to get to them can use them.

Bump   A fall or a hit which literally knocks the victim out of the ring; usually the high point of a match. Wrestlers, referees, managers, valets, and other participants can all suffer from bumps in the ring.

Cage Match   A match in which the ring is surrounded by a metal cage to keep competitors in and interference out. The cage can be climbed or rigged with an electrical current to keep the wrestlers off.

Card   A list of wrestling matches occurring at a specific place and time.

Carney   Term used to refer both to carnivals and to carnival operators and employees.

Countout   If a wrestler is knocked out of the ring, he has 10 seconds to get back in without help. The opponent must back off in a neutral corner. If he interferes in any way, the count starts over. This practice is worked into matches to allow wrestlers some breathing time. If both men are out of the ring for a 10 count, the match is over. This is called "double disqualification via countout" because "the ref called for the bell."

Cycle   Steroids are prescribed in cycles, so the building up or shrinking down of muscles as a result of the drug is called a cycle.

Disqualification   Losing a match for breaking the rules or leaving the ring, rather than by being pinned or forced into submission.

Do the Job   Getting pinned in the ring. It's a thankless job but someone has to do it.

DQ   See **Disqualification.**

Draw   A wrestler's public image, carefully created by promotion and performance, which is awesome enough to bring fans into the ring.

Dud   An extremely dull or boring match.

Exposing the Business   Giving away wrestling secrets, either on purpose or accidentally.

Face   A hero or good guy, also known as a Babyface. Faces can be very unpopular because they always follow the rules and are promoted as wimpy goody-goodies.

Fall   The referee's three-count as a wrestler's shoulders are pinned to the mat.

Falls-Count-Anywhere Match   To win a match you have to pin your opponent for a three count. In a falls-count-anywhere match, the pin can occur anywhere in the arena, even in the aisles.

Feud   Matches that are scheduled between wrestlers who annoy each other, usually the good guys versus the bad guys.

Finish   The final moves that signal who will win or lose as the match draws to a close.

First Blood Match   A match in which the first man to **juice** is the loser but both wrestlers juice before the match is over. A very controversial practice in modern pro wrestling.

Getting Heat   The role of the bad guy to get the crowd to boo or react with hostility to him. An enthusiastic cheer or boo means the match is successfully **getting heat**.

Getting Over   Connecting with the crowd by making the fans accept and react to your wrestling persona.

Gimmick   A prop used as a wrestler's trademark and also often as a weapon.

Greco-Roman Wrestling   An old form of wrestling, developed in France in the 1860s. This type of wrestling requires a wrestler to throw an opponent so that both shoulders touch the mat simultaneously. Tripping and holds below the waist are not allowed.

Green   An unseasoned wrestler who makes mistakes early in his career.

Hair versus Hair Match   In these matches the loser gets his head shaved as a humiliating punishment (but often escapes before he can be touched). A popular variation is the Mask versus Mask match, in which the loser must reveal his face.

Ham 'n' Egger   A professional opponent—one who hasn't yet made it to a high level of fan-recognition, so he (or she) is cast as the loser in bouts. Also known as a **jobber**.

Handicap Match   A match that is booked two-on-one or three-on-one in order to introduce a vicious new heel. He takes on two or three undersized **jobbers** who get completely destroyed.

Hardway juice   Blood drawn during a match without the use of blading.

Heat   The audience's excitement and anticipation of a match.

Heel   A bad guy who doesn't follow established rules; the opposite of a **face**.

Hook   Illegal tricks, moves, or gimmicks used to win a bout underhandedly.

Hooker   A wrestler who employs **hooks** to take out a challenger.

Hot Tag   A tag-team strategy often used in matches between heels and faces. The heels pulverize the smallest face, angering his partner, who is unable to get into the ring until he is tagged. The ref is distracted from the action by the gyrations outside the ring. Then, beaten nearly unconscious, the lesser face leaps across the ring to tag his partner. The partner proceeds to clean house in a triumphant victory.

House   The spectators at a match, usually made up mostly of **marks**.

Job   A wrestler's defeat in a planned match. A **clean job** means to beat a wrestler with a legal submission. Sometimes a job can be described by the way it was performed, such as a rope job, tights job.

Jobber   A wrestler who loses on purpose to make other wrestlers look good. New wrestlers just breaking into the business almost always spend some time as jobbers until they build a fan following.

Juice   Blood drawn during a match when **blading** is used.

Kayfabe   A private language used in wrestling, originated by carneys. Like "pig Latin," it allows people who use it to speak in public about secrets or tricks of the trade without worrying that anyone who overhears them will understand what's being said.

Kill   When the fans lose enthusiasm for a wrestler, the **heat** dies down. Wrestlers who do a lot of **jobs** suffer from this loss of drawing power. Also, if matches constantly have endings that are unclear in who won or lost, people will not be drawn to matches and the industry loses money.

331

Ladder Match   A specialty match in which the championship belt is placed at the top of a ladder and the wrestlers have to compete to climb up and grab it in order to win.

Legit   The real thing. A match is legit if there are no tricks involved. When **shooters** wrestle, the action is legit.

Loaded   Everyday items that have supposedly been altered for use as weapons in the ring; for example, a loaded tennis racket that could fell a 350-pound man or a loaded briefcase used to smash in an opponent's face. The alteration is often signalled by making the item oversized.

Lumberjack Match   A match designed to finalize a feud that fails to come to a conclusion due to frequent double disqualifications via **countout**. The ring is surrounded by neutral wrestlers who are instructed to throw anyone who comes out of the ring back in again.

Mark   A fan who believes everything he sees in the ring is real.

No Disqualification Match   A match in which the winner must pin his opponent or make him submit by any means possible (even cheating is allowed).

Nontitle Match   A match in which a champion wrestler can lose without affecting his future prospects.

Paper   Free tickets given to fans for a match; usually done to fill an arena before a television taping.

Pin   Forcing an opponent's shoulders to the mat and holding them there for a 3-count by the referee. Matches are won by pinning the opponent.

Pinfall   A fall that results in a pin.

Pop   The sudden rush of enthusiasm as a popular wrestler enters the ring or when a dramatic move is made.

Post   Slamming into the **ringpost**.

Potato   A head injury caused either by a direct hit or a crash. Usually results in a black eye, so **jobbers** have to be careful not to potato the main **face** accidentally.

Potato Shot   A blow that causes a **potato**.

Ref Bump   A planned strategy that eliminates the ref by knocking him out when he accidentally gets in the way. While the ref is unconscious, all kinds of hijinks could happen in the ring without being regulated.

Ringboy   A punk.

Ringrats   Wrestling groupies, who often come as families.

Ringpost   Another word for **turnbuckle**.

Run-in   What happens when wrestlers, managers, or others who are not part of a match jump in to join the fight.

Save   A run-in to stop any action that erupts between foes after a match is over.

Scaffold Match   A match that takes place on various contraptions up in the air and in which wrestlers have to climb, fight, and sometimes fall to their doom.

Scientific Wrestling   Old-style wrestling done as a sport, rather than purely for entertainment. Scientific matches are those that are based on the legit use of standard holds and moves, and are conducted strictly according to Greco-Roman rules. They involve no flamboyant tricks or gimmicks.

Screw-job   A match fought outside of the rules of wrestling.

Sell   To convince the crowd of the superiority of an opponent. A **jobber** does this by reacting to moves with the proper enthusiasm and pain. A wrestler can have big problems if his opponent does not sell for him when he is supposed to.

Shoot   A legitimate fight.

Shooter   A wrestler who is skilled at making matches seem legit even if they are not. Originally meant a wrestler who only wrestled on the "up and up." The word derives from the phrase "straight-shooter."

Shooting Match   A clean match, legit. Also can be used to refer to a match that is fought without overt gimmicks or showy tricks.

Squared Circle   Another term for the wrestling (or boxing) ring.

Squash Match   A match between a superstar and a **jobber**. The jobber is completely dominated by the star.

Stiff   Hitting hard even when the match is **worked**. **Jobbers** do not expect to be hurt much and they hate it when they are stiffed.

Strap   A championship belt.

Strap Match   A match in which the opponents are strapped, chained, or roped together; usually evolves into a **juice** match.

Stretch   A type of shoot in which one wrestler dominates rather than injures another wrestler.

Texas Death Match   A match with no rules; however, the booking might include some previously agreed-upon rules such as what **gimmicks** are allowed. For example, both wrestlers may be allowed to wear cowboy boots but the **heel**'s boot might be **loaded**. The match goes until one wrestler is unable to continue.

Turn   To change from a bad guy into a good guy or vice versa. **Angles** are often set up by turns.

Turnbuckle   The padded posts that are set at the four corners of a wrestling ring, to which the ropes are attached.

Work Any practice that is not legit. A match or an injury can be worked in order to give a wrestler some time off.

Work Rate An approximate ratio of good wrestling to rest holds in a match or in a wrestler's overall performance.

Index

M

X-Y-Z